NEW YORK UNIVERSITY

STUDIES IN NEAR EASTERN CIVILIZATION

NUMBER 7

General Editors
R. Bayly Winder
✠Richard Ettinghausen

ALSO IN THIS SERIES

maktel 248-249

NEW YORK UNIVERSITY STUDIES IN NEAR EASTERN CIVILIZATION

The participation of the New York University Press in the University's new commitment to Near Eastern Studies—building on a tradition of well over a century—will provide Americans and others with new opportunities for understanding the Near East. Concerned with those various peoples of the Near East who, throughout the centuries, have dramatically shaped many of mankind's most fundamental concepts and who have always had high importance in practical affairs, this series, New York University Studies in Near Eastern Civilization, seeks to publish important works in this vital area. The purview will be broad, open to varied approaches and historical periods. It will, however, be particularly receptive to work in two areas that reflect the University and that may have received insufficient attention elsewhere. These are literature and art. Furthermore, taking a stand that may be more utilitarian than that of other publications, the series will welcome both translations of important Near Eastern literature of imagination, and of significant scholarly works written in Near Eastern languages. In this way, a larger audience, unacquainted with these languages, will be able to deepen its knowledge of the cultural achievements of Near Eastern peoples.

✠ Richard Ettinghausen
R. Bayly Winder
General Editors

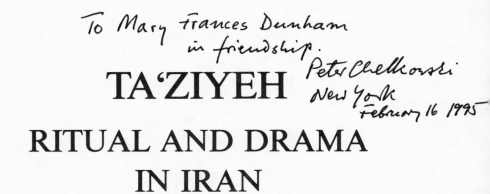

TA'ZIYEH

RITUAL AND DRAMA
IN IRAN

Edited by

PETER J. CHELKOWSKI

Published by
New York University Press
and
Soroush Press

Library of Congress Cataloging in Publication Data
Main entry under title:

Ta'ziyeh, ritual and drama in Iran.

    Proceedings of an international symposium
on Ta'ziyeh held in Aug. 1976 at the Shiraz Festival
of Arts, Shiraz, Iran.
    Includes bibliographical references.
    1. Ta'ziyeh—Congresses.   2. Shiites—Iran—
Congresses.   I. Chelkowski, Peter J.
PK6422.T3   891'.55'22   78-20543
ISBN 0-8147-1375-0

Manufactured in the United States of America

Foreword

It would be commonplace to say that tradition, both good and bad, is being swept away by the onslaught of technology and modernism. We need not concern ourselves here with the reasons except to inquire: is this because of a hatred for the impoverished conditions of yesteryear's living, or because of an eagerness to embrace new Western ways, or because of an inherent weakness of the traditions themselves—or possibly a combination of the three? What is definite is that the third world, with the exception of miraculous Japan (these monks that brew modern electronics) and to a certain extent India, is giving up its traditions.

I am certain that if students of anthropology had turned to Ta'ziyeh forty-eight years ago when it was banned by the Iranian Government for sociopolitical reasons, a major share of the Iranian National Theatre today would be plays (with or without religious subject-matter) directly derived from Ta'ziyeh: but much to our regret, this was not the case. Ta'ziyeh had almost been isolated in certain distant villages when individual Iranian scholars such as Bahram Baizai (1965), Mayel Baktash and myself (1971) began to turn their attention to it.

In the autumn of 1959 a Ta'ziyeh fragment was included in Parviz

Sayyad's Iranian collection which went on stage at the 25 Shahrivar state-owned theatre of Tehran. In September 1967, the Ta'ziyeh of Hurr was performed in the Shiraz Festival of Arts; and the same festival in 1976 witnessed, thanks to the efforts of Peter Chelkowski, an impassioned lover of Iranian religious drama, the lively sessions of the International Symposium on Ta'ziyeh whose proceedings make up the present volume. One result of the symposium was the creation of the Institute for Traditional Performance and Ritual in Tehran. This has been sending scholars on long exploratory trips into the field and has started a library on the traditional performances in Asia, Africa, and Latin America. It has also launched a publishing program whose fruits to date include the present volume and a collection of Ta'ziyeh pieces *(Jong-e Shahadat,* Vol. 1, Tehran: Soroush Press, 1976) some films, and a museum whose founders hope to make it one of the best of its kind.

May I take this opportunity to thank sincerely all those individuals, both inside and outside Iran, who are engaged in discovering the unique traditions of *Shabihkhani* and keeping them alive if possible.

Farrokh Gaffary, Director
Institute for Traditional Performance and Ritual
Tehran

NOTES ON CONTRIBUTORS

Metin And is Professor of Dramatic Arts at Ankara University and the Aegian University in Izmir. He has been the publisher of a political and cultural journal, a Rockefeller Foundation Grant Researcher, and has traveled widely for research and lectures in the Middle Eastern countries, in India, Japan, Europe and the Soviet Union. Professor And has written more than one thousand articles for various national and international periodicals, and has written twenty-five books—some in English and French, most in Turkish—on theatre, dance and folklore. One of his recent publications in English is entitled *Turkish Dancing* (Ankara, 1977).

William O. Beeman, currently Assistant Professor of Anthropology at Brown University in Providence, Rhode Island, has been conducting research in Iran at regular intervals since 1967. He is the author of a number of articles relating to Iranian languages and communication, and a forthcoming book: *Semantics and Style in Iranian Interaction.*

Mayel Baktash is Associate Professor at the College of Dramatic Arts in Tehran. He is also a film critic, and has written numerous articles on theatre and film for serious scholarly journals.

Jean Calmard studied oriental languages at L'Ecole Nationale des Langues Orientales in Paris and at the University of Tehran. Dr. Calmard is currently a researcher at the Centre National de la Recherche Scientifique in Paris; he also teaches Iranian Islamic History at the Sorbonne. He has published articles on Iranian history, geographical history, Shi'ism, Ta'ziyeh patronage, etc. Professor Calmard's Ph.D. thesis, under the title *Culte de l'Iman Husayn, Etude sur la commémoration du Drame de Kerbêlâ dans l'Iran pré-safavide,* will be published shortly.

Peter J. Chelkowski is Professor of Persian and Iranian Studies, Director of the Hagop Kevorkian Center for Near Eastern Studies, and Chairman of the Department of Near Eastern Languages and Literatures at New York University. He is a graduate of the Jagiellonian University of Cracow, the University of London, and the University of Tehran. His publications include *Iran: Continuity and Variety* (New York, 1971); The *Scholar and the Saint* (ed) (New York, 1975); *Studies in Art and Literature of the Near East* (ed) (Salt Lake City and New York, 1974); and *Mirror of the Invisible World: Tales from the Khamseh of Nizami* (New York, 1975).

L. P. Elwell-Sutton is at present Professor of Persian in the University of Edinburgh, where he has headed the Department of Persian since 1952. He first went to Iran in 1935, and has since then paid regular visits varying in length from four years to ten days. His publications range from language teaching manuals *(Colloquial Persian,* 1941; *Elementary Persian Grammar,* 1963) through studies of contemporary history and affairs *(Modern Iran,* 1941; *Guide to Iranian Area Study,* 1952; *Persian Oil,* 1955) to literary analysis *(The Persian Metres,* 1976) and works on folklore *(The Wonderful Sea-Horse and Other Persian Tales,* 1950; *Persian Proverbs,* 1954; *The Horoscope of Asadullah Mirza,* 1977).

Zahra Eqbal (Namdar) is a poet who studied at Tehran University and the Sorbonne. She has been engaged in the study of the elegiac genres in Persian literature and is the editor of the A. Chodzko collection of Ta'ziyeh plays being published by the Institute for Traditional Performance and Ritual in Tehran.

Enrico Fulchignoni is a physician, diplomat, playwright and scholar. For twenty-five years, he was the Director of the Artistic and Literary Section of UNESCO in Paris. He is also Professor of the History of the Italian Theatre at the Sorbonne. Professor Fulchignoni was the national collaborator with *Corriere Della Sera, Tempo* and other literary and theatrical journals in Italy, France and Germany. He is the author of: *La Civilisation de L'Image; L'Image à l'Ere Cosmique; Le Nō Japonais* and *Le Théâtre Kammerny.*

William L. Hanaway, Jr. is Associate Professor of Persian Language and Literature at the University of Pennsylvania. His interests in Persian literature are many-sided, but his research has focused mainly on the Persian epic, and on the popular literature of the past and present. He has published a general assessment of the study of Persian literature in L. Binder, ed., *The Study of the Middle East,* and articles on Persian popular literature in the *NYU Round Table* series and in *The Review of National Literatures.* Among his translations is *Love and War: Adventures from the Firuz Shah Nama,* an abridged translation of pre-Safavid popular romance.

Sadeq Humayuni holds an L.L.B. in Judiciary Law and is presently a judge with the Department of Justice in Shiraz, Iran. He has written extensively on Persian ritual and folklore. Some of his major works, all in Persian, are: *The Folklore of Sarvestan, One Thousand and Four Hundred Folkloric Songs, Ta'ziyeh and Ta'ziyeh-Khvani,* and a monograph, "Husseiniyye-ye Mushir."

Syed Husain Ali Jaffri is connected with the governing bodies of Dr. Zakir Husain College, Delhi College and the Rao Tula Ram College of The Delhi

University in India. He teaches Islamic History, Journalism, and Social Work. He has been Vice President of the All India Shia Conference, and is at present Chairman of Shia Auqaf and a member of the Waqf Board. He leads a number of Anjumans of "Ta'ziyeh dari" and has delivered many lectures on various aspects of Islam and the tragedy of Kerbela. For the past three years, he has been the Honorary Secretary of the Indo-Iranian Society.

Muhammad Ja'far Mahjub is an author, scholar and translator. He is a Professor at Tehran University and has written books on Persian grammar, literature and history. Among his publications we may mention *Bar Guzīdih-yi Shams-i Tabrīzī; Khaṭrāt-i Khānih-yi Murdigān; Dīvān-i Qāāni-yi Shīrāzi; Dīvān-i Surūsh-i Isfahānī (Shams al-Shu'arā);* Professor Mahjub has more than twenty books to his credit.

Parviz Mamnoun is the founder and chairman of the Theatre Department at Tehran University. He is a graduate of the University of Vienna and his doctoral dissertation *Ta'zija Schi'itisch—Persisches Passionsspiel* (Vienna, 1967), will be published shortly in English. He has written numerous articles in Persian and German, and has also translated several Western plays into Persian. He is presently working on the first encyclopedia of drama in the Persian language.

Michel M. Mazzaoui is Associate Professor of Iranian Studies in the Department of History of the University of Utah. He is a graduate of the American University of Beirut and earned his Ph.D. at Princeton University. He was also a Fulbright scholar in Iran. He has taught Islamic and Persian studies at the Universities of Indiana, McGill, Princeton and the American University of Beirut. In addition to many articles on Islamic civilization, his major publications are: *The Origins of the Safavids: Shi'ism, Sufism and the Ghulat; Social and Cultural Selections from Contemporary Persian.*

Samuel R. Peterson is Assistant Professor of Islamic Art at the Arizona State University where he directed an Islamic Arts festival. Previously, he has been a Visiting Lecturer of Islamic Art at the American University in Cairo. He has also spent three years in Istanbul at Roberts College and two years in Iran as a Fulbright Grantee. Among his other fellowships were the Erwin Panofsky Memorial Fellowship at New York University and an American Research in Egypt Fellowship. He is now a Ph.D. candidate at the Institute of Fine Arts of New York University. Mr. Peterson is, at present, a guest curator at the Phoenix Art Museum. In press: Articles in *Artibus Asiae,* and the memorial volumes of the *VIIth International Congress of Iranian Art.*

Annemarie Schimmel—Dr. Phil. (Berlin), Dr. sc. rel. (Marburg), D. Litt. h.c., University of Sind, D. Litt. h.c., Quaid-i Azym University of Islamabad. She is Professor of Indo-Muslim Culture at Harvard University, and the author of numerous books, particularly *Mystical Dimensions of Islam, Islamic Calligraphy* and *Gabriel's Wing: A Study into the Religious Ideas of Sir Muhammad Iqbal.* Her most recent work is *The Triumphal Sun: A Study of Maulana Jalaluddin Rumi's Work.*

Anayatullah Shahidi holds a doctorate in philosophy from Tehran University and has done research in philosophy, logic and theology. He is currently with the Iran Center for Anthropology and is studying Ta'ziyeh manuscripts in the Majlis Library.

Andrzej Wirth is Professor of Theatre and Comparative Literature at the City University of New York Graduate School and founder and Chairman of the American P.E.N. Committee on Dramatic Forms, a body for the promotion of the new American theatre. He worked with Brecht's Berliner Ensemble, has written the first structuralistic study of Brecht; two volumes of drama criticism; a standard work on Polish modern drama in German, and edited works of many contemporary Eastern European authors. Invited to the U.S. by Princeton University in 1966 after achieving an international reputation as a Brecht expert and drama critic in his native Poland, he has since taught at the Universities of Massachusetts, Stanford, Harvard and New York.

Ehsan Yarshater is the Hagop Kevorkian Professor of Iranian Studies and Director of the Center for Iranian Studies at Columbia University. He holds a degree of D.Litt. from the University of Tehran, and a Ph.D. in Iranian Philology from the University of London. Among his many published works may be mentioned: Avicenna's *Persian Translation of the Theorems and Remarks; Persian Poetry in the 15th Century; A Grammar of Southern Tati Dialects;* and *Iran Faces the Seventies* (ed.). Professor Yarshater has been the founding editor of a number of major publications in the Iranian field, among which are: *Persian Texts Series,* 1954–; *Journal of Persian Language and Literature,* 1957; *Persian Heritage* Series, 1963–; *Bibliothèque des Oeuvres Classiques Persanes,* 1966–. *Persian Studies Series,* 1971–; and the *Encyclopaedia Persica,* 1975–. He is also the editor of the *Cambridge History of Iran,* vol. III.

CREDITS

Ms. Leyly Matin-Daftary, for the dust cover

Mr. Jay R. Crook for translation from Persian into English of Chapters by:
M. Baktash, M. J. Mahjub, P. Mamnoun, and Z. Eqbal (Namdar)

Mr. John K. Newton for translation from Persian into English of Chapters
by: A. Shahidi and S. Humayuni

Contents

Introduction

> If the success of a drama is to be measured by the effects which it produces upon the people for whom it is composed, or upon the audiences before whom it is represented, no play has ever surpassed the tragedy known in the Mussulman world as that of Hasan and Husain.
>
> Sir Lewis Pelly
> *The Miracle Play of Hasan and Husain*
> (London, 1879) I, Preface

For almost two hundred years the foreigners who happened to live in, or pass through Iran have been fascinated with an extraordinary dramatic form popularly known as Ta'ziyeh (also spelled Ta'zieh, Ta'zie, Tazieh, or Tazia), or *Shabih* (called The Tragedy of Hasan and Husain in the quotation above.) This fascination actually goes back to the sixteenth century when the European visitors and residents of Persia started to write detailed accounts of the steadily growing pageantry of the annual Muharram commemoration of the Kerbela tragedy. Hussein (also spelled Husain, Hosein, Hossein, or Husayn), the grandson of the Prophet Muhammad, and a group of his relatives and supporters, were killed in a bloody massacre on the plain of Kerbela, in the month of Muharram in A.D. 680. To the Shi'ites, this has remained a martyrdom of the greatest magnitude and a sacred redemptive act. In the beginning of the sixteenth century, Shi'a Islam was established as the state religion in Persia by the Safavid Kings: the annual observance of Hussein's sacrifice, from which the Ta'ziyeh theatre evolved, received the royal patronage.

From the middle of the nineteenth century attempts were made to study the Ta'ziyeh phenomenon, the only indigenous drama in the world of Islam. However, despite the interest in this theatrical form by people such as Count de Gobineau or Matthew Arnold, Ta'ziyeh remained almost totally unknown to Western specialists in drama and theatre. After World War II, those who wanted to save the theatre from the steady encroachment on its territory by film and television, turned to Asia for the rescue of theatre by adapting Asian forms, overlooking Iran in their quest. Ta'ziyeh, even in its own country, Iran, has been neglected during the twentieth century and misconstrued by many as an unworthy ritual and a crude spectacle.

In order to remedy this situation and at the same time to save Ta'ziyeh from oblivion, an international symposium on Ta'ziyeh was organized by the Shiraz Festive of Arts in the summer of 1976 under the direction of Farrokh Gaffary. Taking into consideration the complexity of the subject, not only theatre people such as directors, producers, critics and drama specialists, but also anthropologists, musicologists, historians, sociologists, and art historians from many countries assembled there from August 20 to 25 for an exchange of views and information.

This book is the product of the labors of that conference, of which I had the honor to be the chairman. In addition to papers read and discussed, the best Ta'ziyeh troupes from various localities performed for ten days at the Husseiniyeh Mushir and in the small village of Kaftarak near Shiraz. There was also an exhibit of Ta'ziyeh-related materials, such as drawings and photographs of *takiyeh* (playhouses), costumes, props, scripts, films of Muharram observances and Ta'ziyeh performances, and various objects customarily carried in the Muharram parades. There were also oil paintings of scenes of the Kerbela tragedy used as backdrops for traveling one-man shows.

At the end of the symposium, all the participants realized that there should be an organization which would attend to the preservation of the indigenous performing arts of Iran. Subsequently, the Institute for Traditional Performance and Ritual was formed.

The papers included in this publication trace the development of a simple mourning Muharram ceremony to full-scale drama and theatre. Some chapters search for pre-Islamic roots of Ta'ziyeh, while others compare Ta'ziyeh with the medieval European Passion plays or describe the observance of Hussein's Passion in Iran's neighboring countries, Turkey, and the Indo-Pakistani sub-continent.

These papers were presented in Persian, English and French. This book, an English edition of the proceedings, includes two papers in French: there will subsequently be a Persian edition. The chapters differ greatly in quality and approach; however, they have all been included—unabridged, but edited to a certain extent.

Credit is due to Mr. Jay R. Crook for the translation from Persian into English of Chapters 8, 11, 12, and 15, and to Mr. John K. Newton for the similar translation of Chapters 2 and 5. Mrs. Elizabeth R. Dalgliesh took great pains in helping me with the editing of this book and I thank her for it. Thanks go also to Mr. Peter Zirnis for his help with transliterations.

Peter J. Chelkowski

Illustrations for "The Ta'ziyeh and Related Arts" by S. R. Peterson

Transliteration Note

This work is intended for a wider audience than the small circle of Iranologists and other Near Eastern specialists. Therefore, the editor took the liberty of eliminating as many transliteration marks as possible, trying however, to bring out the phonetic English equivalent of the Persian and Arabic words. Nevertheless, the full transliteration, according to the *International Journal of Middle East Studies,* is retained in the footnotes for bibliographical references. The transliteration of metrical terms follows the usage of L. P. Elwell-Sutton's *The Persian Metres.* The transliteration in the French chapters follows the customary French usage. Since modern Turkish is written in the Latin alphabet, the Turkish spelling is retained in the chapter on "The Muharram Observances in Anatolian Turkey."

TA'ZIYEH

RITUAL AND DRAMA
IN IRAN

1

Ta'ziyeh:
Indigenous Avant-Garde Theatre of Iran

PETER J. CHELKOWSKI

This title is deliberately controversial.[1] But it is, perhaps, the most accurate description of the only indigenous drama engendered by the world of Islam. The Ta'ziyeh of Iran is ritual theatre and derives its form and its content from deep-rooted religious traditions. But although it is Islamic in appearance, it is strongly Persian, drawing vital inspiration from its special political and cultural heritage. Its genius is that it combines immediacy and flexibility with universality. Uniting rural folk art with urban, royal entertainment, it admits no barriers between the archetype and the human, the wealthy and the poor, the sophisticated and the simple, the spectator and the actor. Each participates with and enriches the other.

The nucleus of the Ta'ziyeh is the heroic martyrdom of Hussein, the grandson of the prophet Muhammad. After the death of the Prophet (11 A.H./A.D. 632) the still young Muslim community was faced with the problem of providing new leadership. Almost immediately the community found itself divided into two bitterly opposed factions, those who espoused the ancient Arabic tradition of succession by election and those who desired succession by inheritance, through blood-relationship to the Prophet. The former are known as Sunnites; the latter as Shi'ites.

1

Three successive caliphs were elected; they had been companions to the Prophet. Then Ali, the cousin and son-in-law of Muhammad and the leader of the Shi'ite partisans was recognized as the legitimate caliph. To Shi'ites, Ali, "the Hand of God," is so exalted that it is said: "Muhammad is a city of learning, Ali is its Gate." But Ali was assassinated and later his elder son, Hassan, was poisoned and the Sunnite governor of Syria took over the caliphate and moved its capital to Damascus. Ali's younger son, Hussein, however, persisted in championing the cause of the House of Ali and was asked by a Shi'ite group in Kufa, a city near today's Baghdad, to join them as their head.

Hussein accepted and set out from Mecca with his family and an entourage of about seventy followers. But on the plain of Kerbela they were caught in an ambush set by the Sunnite caliph, Yazid. Though defeat was certain, Hussein refused to pay homage to him. Surrounded by a great enemy force, Hussein and his company existed without water for ten days in the burning desert of Kerbela. Finally Hussein, the adults and some male children of his family and his companions were cut to bits by the arrows and swords of Yazid's army; his women and remaining children were taken as captives to Yazid in Damascus. The renowned historian Abu Reyhan al-Biruni states; "... then fire was set to their camp and the bodies were trampled by the hoofs of the horses; nobody in the history of the human kind has seen such atrocities." [2]

The siege began on the first day of the Muslim month of Muharram and came to its bloody end on the tenth day, called Ashura. It was in the 61st year of the Muslim calendar which corresponds to A.D. 680. Soon after, the battlefield and tombs at Kerbela became a place of sacred pilgrimage for Shi'ites throughout the Islamic Empire.

The word *ta'ziyeh* literally means expressions of sympathy, mourning and consolation. As a dramatic form it has its origins in the Muharram processions commemorating Hussein's martyrdom and throughout its evolution the representation of the siege and carnage at Kerbela has remained its centerpoint. Ta'ziyeh has never lost its religious implications. Because early Shi'ites viewed Hussein's death as a sacred redemptive act, the performance of the Muharram ceremonies was believed to be an aid to salvation; later they also believed that participation, both by actors and spectators, in the Ta'ziyeh dramas would gain them Hussein's intercession on the day of the Last Judgment.

Perhaps because of their tradition of hereditary kingship and strong nationalism, the people of the Iranian plateau were particularly hospitable to the Shi'ite form of Islam. According to Persian legend, the daughter of the last Persian king of the Sasanid dynasty was taken captive during the Muslim invasion and married to Hussein. From the beginning, the annual Muharram mourning ceremonies were observed with great pageantry and emotion. Veneration of deceased heroes had long been an important part of

2

Persian culture; the theme of redemption through sacrifice found parallels in such pre-Islamic legends as the death of Siyavush and in the ancient Mesopotamian ritual of Adonis-Tamuz. By the tenth century A.D. impressive Muharram processions were well established. The reliable historian, Ibn al-Athir, tells of great numbers of participants, with black painted faces and disheveled hair circling round and round the city of Baghdad, beating their chests and moaning the mourning songs at the festival of Muharram. It was at the time when the Persian Buyid dynasty ruled from Baghdad.

In the first years of the sixteenth century, when under the Safavid dynasty Persia, which had always been a strong cultural power, again became a political power, Shi'ite Islam was established as the state religion and was used to unify the country, especially against the aggressive Ottomans and Uzbeks who were adherents of Sunnite Islam. The Muharram observances received royal encouragement; commemoration of Hussein's martyrdom became a patriotic as well as religious act. Many accounts of the processions, written mostly by European envoys, missionaries, merchants and travelers, tell of characters dressed in colorful costumes marching, or mounted on horses and camels, depicting the events leading up to the final tragedy at Kerbela. Living tableaux of butchered martyrs stained with blood, their bodies showing simulated amputations, were moved along on wheeled platforms. Mock battles were mimed by hundreds of uniformed mourners armed with bows, swords, and other weapons. The entire pageant was accompanied by funeral music and spectators, lined up along its path, beat their breasts and shouted "Hussein, O Hussein, the King of the Martyrs" as it passed by.

Certain similarities between the Muharram processions and the European medieval theatre of the Stations of the Cross was obvious. An important difference is, however, that during the Muharram ceremonies the spectators remained stationary while the tableaux moved and in the theatre of the Stations the tableaux were stationary while the viewer-penitents moved. The Muharram processions are, perhaps, more similar to the Passion Week celebrations which can still be seen in such Christian countries as Guatemala.

At the same time as the Muharram ceremonies were flourishing and developing under the Safavid rule, a second important and popular form of religious expression came into being. This was the dramatic narration of the life, deeds, suffering and death of Shi'ite martyrs. Virtually always connected, though sometimes only slightly, with the Kerbela ambush, these stories were taken from a book called *Rowzatu'l Shuhada* or *The Garden of Martyrs,* written in Persian and widely circulated among Shi'ites from the early sixteenth century onward.[3] Unlike the Muharram processions, the *rowzeh-khani*—garden recitations—were stationary, the narrator usually seated on a raised pulpit, his audience gathered in a semicircle beneath his feet. Soon, readings from *The Garden of Martyrs* began to serve only as a framework and a springboard for the professional narrators who improvised creatively on the suffering and deeds of the many Shi'ite heroes. Through choice of episodes and modulation of his voice, the narrator was able to excite and manipulate the emotions of his audience, to produce in them a unity of feeling of great intensity.

For about two hundred and fifty years the Muharram processions and the narrative recitations existed side by side, each becoming more complex and at the same time more refined and theatrical. Then in the middle of the eighteenth century they fused. A new dramatic form was born, Ta'ziyeh-Khani or, as it is more familiarly called, simply Ta'ziyeh. Interestingly, from the beginning, the antagonists recited their parts, while the protagonists sang theirs. The main theme was still the siege of Kerbela, but the focus was on individual heroes around whom separate plays were written. Martyrs who predated and postdated Kerbela were added to the repertoire.

Ta'ziyeh serves as an excellent illustration of the concept that the roots of drama are in funeral songs and commemoration of deceased heroes, and also that, in the development of the theatrical art, the text is one of the last elements to be added.

It is significant to remember that, in the entire Muslim world, Persia was the only country to nourish drama. This can perhaps be attributed to Persia's continuous attachment—in spite of religious prohibitions—to figural representation. Persia is justly famous for painting, sculpture, and the other visual arts. Nevertheless it must be noted that, although the Perisan literary heritage extends back over 2,500 years and is renowned for its carefully structured national and romantic epics, its only true drama is the Muslim inspired Ta'ziyeh, which took well over a millennium to develop. That this should be so, especially in view of Persia's close cultural and geographical ties with Greece and India, both of which had extraordinarily rich theatrical traditions, remains a puzzle. Indeed, no Greek amphitheatres have yet been discovered on the eastern bank of the Euphrates.

As a compromise between the moving procession and the stationary recitation, Ta'ziyeh was at first staged at street intersections and squares. Soon, however, it moved into the courtyards of caravan serais, bazaars, and private houses. By the nineteenth century, the nascent dramas were performed in arena theatres called takiyeh, built, usually by the well-to-do and the upper classes, as a religious and public service. Some takiyeh could seat thousands of spectators, but most were for a few hundred people. Simpler ones were prevalent in the small towns and villages. Many takiyeh were temporary structures erected especially for the Muharram observances. Even the British and Russian legations were drawn into the competition of arranging the most splendid takiyeh for the annual Muharram celebrations in Tehran.

In the beginning, Ta'ziyeh consisted of a few loosely connected episodes with long elegiac monologues followed by some dialogue. Hardly any

4

action was connected directly with these quite primitive recited and sung parts. In fact, the actors read their lines from scripts about two inches wide and about eight inches long which they held in their palms. This tradition continued and is practiced even today. It is perhaps at least in part an expression of the Muslim proscription against representation of living things; the script serves as a barrier to any suggestion that the actor actually becomes the person he portrays. In this respect it bears some similarity to the use of masks in the Greek theatre. The spectacle of the pageant rather than the text was most important. Nevertheless, within a century, this art form produced a corpus of several hundred lengthy dramas.

The design of the *takiyeh* preserved and enhanced the dramatic interplay between actors and spectators which was characteristic of the traditional Muharram rites. The main action took place on a stark, curtainless raised platform in the center of the building. Surrounding it was a narrow circular band of space used by the performers for sub-plots and to indicate journeys, passage of time, and change of scene. At the periphery of this space, extending into the audience-filled pit, small secondary stages were often erected. Scenes of special significance were acted upon them and sometimes players from these auxiliary stages would engage in dialogue or action with those on the central stage.

In addition, there were usually two or more corridors through the seating area, running from the central platform to the outer wall of the *takiyeh.* These provided access for message bearers, armies, and processions including horses, camels and vehicles. Skirmishes and duels often took place behind the audience in unwalled *takiyehs;* sometimes actors in their fervor literally plunged through the audience to gain the central stage. The *takiyeh* was indeed a model of the plain of Kerbela; it was a tradition that actors in plays about the Kerbela massacre never left the central playing area as a symbol of the martyrs encirclement by the enemy. It would probably not be going too far to say also that the *takiyeh* was a kind of Shi'ite omphalos.

The following synopsis of the Ta'ziyeh play from the Northern provinces, called *The Marriage of Qasem,* which was usually played between the fifth and the tenth day of Muharram as an introduction to the culminating martyrdom of Hussein, illustrates the dynamic interaction of audience and actor that took place in the Persian *takiyeh.*

Qasem is a son of Hussein's elder brother, Hassan, who was poisoned shortly after his father, Ali, was assassinated. It was Hassan's will that Qasem be married to Fatemeh, the daughter of Hussein. Both Qasem and Fatemeh are among the besieged at Kerbela. They are still in their teens, but Hussein, realizing that their deaths are imminent, desires to fulfill his promise to his brother and orders their wedding.

While Ali Akbar, the elder son of Hussein, is singlehandedly fighting off the attackers' army (the fight is not staged, but is referred to) both actors and spectators make preparations for the wedding on the central stage and in the area surrounding it. Finally they bring in the colorfully beribboned nuptial tent and lead the bride and bridegroom through one of the pit corridors to it. Festive wedding music accompanies their march. Cookies are joyfully passed among the audience. Then suddenly, from behind the audience, the horse of Ali Akbar appears. It is riderless. At this sign of Ali Akbar's death, everyone in the *takiyeh* freezes into position. Qasem leaves the main stage and rushes into the battlefield behind the audience. Almost immediately he returns, leading the procession that carries the body of Ali Akbar, raised high on shields, to the central stage. As it is the custom of Muslim countries for the entire community to participate in the last rites of the dead, the whole audience rises to its feet and weeps. Since it is also customary during the funeral processions that everyone should strive to help carry the coffin, those of the audience who cannot push close enough stretch their hands in symbolic gestures.

Finally, the body is laid on the main stage opposite the nuptial tent. On one side of the stage, funeral rites are performed with interludes of mournful music. The spectators dishevel their hair and beat their breasts. On the other side of the stage, the wedding ceremony continues accompanied by jubilant music. There is a cacophony of sound, the audience turning from side to side changing from weeping to laughter.

When the marriage rites are concluded and Qasem is preparing to consummate the marriage, he is called to the battlefield. First he attacks the young sons of the besieging generals who, at the sight of the gallant son of Hassan, flee in a comical manner. Then at last he must fight the whole army and is slain.

The most famous and influential of the nineteenth century Ta'ziyeh theatres was the Takiyeh Dowlat, or Royal Arena Theatre in Tehran, (construction started 1304 A.H.). Under the patronage of Naser al-Din Shah, who ruled Persia from 1848 to 1896, Ta'ziyeh reached the peak of its development. According to many travelers, its dazzling splendor and its intensity of dramatic action overshadowed even the opera of the western capitals. The American envoy, Samuel Benjamin, who attended the Muharram celebrations, left this vivid description of the Takiyeh Dowlat.

I was invited to attend on the fifth day of the Ta'ziyeh. We arrived at the Takiyeh toward noon. On alighting from the carriage I was surprised to see an immense circular building as large as the amphitheatre of Verona, solidly constructed of brick. Farrashes, or liveried footmen, cleared the way before us. Thrashing their staves right and left, they opened a way through the crowd that packed the great portal; and entering a dark, vaulted vestibule I groped, or rather was impelled by the throng, towards a staircase crowded with servants whose masters had already arrived. Like all stairs in Persia, these were adapted to the stride of giants.

A succession of springs upward finally landed me on the first gallery, which led around the building. A few steps in the twilight and then an embroidered curtain was raised and I entered the box of the Zahir-e Dowleh (Shah's son). It was in two parts, the first higher than the other; stepping into the front and lower division, I was invited to recline at the left of my host upon a superbly embroidered cushion of velvet—the seat of honor is at the left hand in Persia. The walls of the loggia were of plain brick, but they were hung with cashmere shawls of price, and the choicest of rugs enriched the floor. A number of Persian gentlemen of lower rank occupied the back part of the apartment by invitation.

On looking over the vast arena a sight met my gaze which was indeed extraordinary. The interior of the building is nearly two hundred feet in diameter and some eighty feet high. A domed frame of timbers, firmly spliced and braced with iron, springs from the walls, giving support to the awning that protects the interior from the sunlight and the rain. From the centre of the dome a large chandelier was suspended, furnished with four electric burners—a recent innovation. A more oriental form of illuminating the building was seen in the prodigious number of lustres and candlesticks, all of glass and protected from the air by glass shades open on the top and variously colored; they were concentrated against the wall in immense glittering clusters. Estimating from those attached on one box, I judged that there were upwards of five thousand candles in these lustres. . . .

In the centre of the arena was a circular stage of masonry, raised three feet and approached by two stairways. On one side of the building a pulpit of white marble was attached to the wall. . . . But I soon discovered that all the architectural details of this remarkable building were secondary to the extraordinary spectacle offered by the assembled multitude. The entire arena with the exception of a narrow passage around the stage, was absolutely packed with women, thousands on thousands. At a rough estimate it seemed to me that quite four thousand women were seated there cross-legged on the earthen floor, which was made slightly sloping in order to enable those in the rear to see over the heads of those before them. . . .

Refreshments were served in our box repeatedly, and cigars for myself. . . . But after the performance began, all smoking and refreshments were banned as indications of frivolity inconsistent with the tragical events of the dramas. . . .[4]

Ta'ziyeh, like other Muharram commemorations, was a communal event. Each individual contributed according to his means and ability. The men brought their most precious objects—crystal, lamps, mirrors, china, and tapestry—to decorate the walls of the *takiyeh*. Even the most humble objects were accepted as they were given or lent with religious devotion. Athletes

7

from the gymnasium eagerly donated their strength and agility to put up the *takiyeh*. The women provided refreshments; the children of the aristocracy served water, a symbol of the Kerbela martyrs' thirst, and sweetmeats to all spectators, rich and poor alike. Although the wealthy had their own gorgeously adorned loges, in accordance with the Muslim spirit of brotherhood, the poor could sit in them if there was space. The purpose of Ta'ziyeh remained true to its essence; participation was an aid to salvation, for the suffering and death of the martyrs of Kerbela were instruments of redemption for all believers.

Good actors were paid very well by their patrons and also received favors and bonuses from the audience. Their costumes and props were rich. At Takiyeh Dowlat many came from the royal treasuries. It is recorded that the Shah lent his own coach to carry Timur and later, a new royal automobile was used for King Solomon. Ta'ziyeh productions were lavish extravaganzas.

The texts of the Ta'ziyeh dramas were at first very simple with concentration on universal truths rather than on the dramatic power to be achieved through the skillful use of exposition, challenge and complication. Gradually, however, during the course of the nineteenth century, they became more developed and refined as literature. They also became more secular in content as the "high" court tradition, resplendent in its external aspects, began to filter down to the rural areas and the folk tradition, more organic and more natural, based on folk art, folk stories, and popular religion, and ingrained with social connotation, percolated up.

Digressions or *Guriz* were introduced to extend the scope of the Ta'ziyeh and to add variety and secular detail. These were based on episodes from Biblical or Koranic stories, and from national legend and tradition. Spectators were led to identify their own sufferings with those of these lesser heroes. For women especially, they served as a wound-healing agent, for the point was always made that all suffering was slight when compared to that of the victims of Kerbela.

Despite criticism by the majority of the religious authorities who considered it sacrilegious for mortal men to portray any holy personage, Ta'ziyeh became more and more beloved by the people. Performances, no longer restricted to the first ten days of the month of Muharram, lasted until the end of the following month of Safar. Plays commemorating the birthday of a saint or a prophet provided an excuse to extend the dramas to other months. Eventually, popular demand induced troupes to perform Ta'ziyeh throughout the year as an act of thanksgiving, celebrating such occasions as the happy conclusion of a journey, the recovery of health after sickness, or the return from a pilgrimage.

At the end of the nineteenth century, Ta'ziyeh was on the verge of giving birth to an Iranian secular theatre. But owing to fundamental social and political changes of the twentieth century, it lost its patrons. Ta'ziyeh

8

then became a commercial enterprise, centered not in the cities which at that time were given to imitating Western art forms, but rather in the rural areas. Troupes fought for the most lucrative places to perform and were often forced to lease them from the provincial governors. Actors collected contributions from the audience, usually interrupting the play in the middle of the most crucial episode. Rivalry among Ta'ziyeh troupes led to theft of manuscripts and shifting of actors from one troupe to another. Dissident political groups began using theatrical gatherings to further their own goals and subsequently the government imposed restrictions on the performances.

Although many critics have written that this retreat to the provinces had a swift and deleterious effect upon Ta'ziyeh as an art form, a strong case can be made to show that, to the contrary, it purified and preserved it. The Persian village tradition with its sources in popular religion is more simple, organic, and theatrical than the urban tradition. Its imagination is more closely attached to the essentials of life; it is less abstract and intellectual, less wedded to the spectacular effect. In the provincial setting, there is far greater potential for coherence and empathy between actor and audience.

In fact, it may be said that the twentieth century rural Ta'ziyeh is the unconscious avant-garde of the "poor theatre." It totally engages the participation of the audience and it has extraordinary dynamic flexibility. There are no barriers of time and space. For instance, Napoleon Bonaparte can appear on the stage along with Hussein, the Virgin Mary, Alexander the Great, and the Queen of Sheba. The text is not fixed; episodes from one play can be interpolated in another to suit the mood of the actors, the audience, and the weather. The producer is omnipresent, regulating the movements of actors, musicians and audience. He remains constantly on stage, giving the actors their cues, helping children and inexperienced actors, and handling props.

Costumes are contemporary, as they always have been in Ta'ziyeh and other visual arts. In the past strict division into symbolic colors was observed, e.g., green and white for protagonists and red for antagonists. Today, if no appropriate costume is at hand, any that differs from the usual dress of the audience is acceptable. But, when possible, costumes conform to certain symbolic conventions. Warriors wear British officers' jackets instead of coats of mail. Abbas, the standard-bearer of Hussein's troops, wears a long white Arabic shirt, embellished by a military jacket, Wellington boots, and a helmet. Bad characters often wear sun glasses, learned people wear reading glasses. The eminence of a character is signified by a walking stick. In the Western theatre, the use of everyday dress for historical characters has been practiced for some time as a shock device, but in Ta'ziyeh it had been traditional.

Props are casual, but often have symbolic meaning. Gabriel may carry an umbrella to indicate he has descended from heaven. Automobile hub-caps used as shields have been seen by the writer. A bowl of water signifies the Euphrates river. Classical Persian musical modes form the basis of the interludes, but themes from currently popular songs and marches are often incorporated. The company makes use of whatever space happens to be available for its stage. None of these practices ever proves distracting to the absorbed audience and actors. On the contrary, they give each Ta'ziyeh performance special freshness and immediacy.

After the decline of high court patronage there remain at the present time two strong Ta'ziyeh traditions. The first is in the hands of professional troupes; its practices form the basis of this discussion. It is active through-out the year both in towns and villages. The repertoire includes Shi'ite stories with the Kerbela tragedy as its core and the plays based on digressions. Usually the backbone of the troupe is a family for whom Ta'ziyeh has been a hereditary occupation. The actors are trained from childhood.

The second is the non-professional Muharram village tradition. This Ta'ziyeh is usually organized on or around the day of Ashura by an ex-professional or semi-professional Ta'ziyeh actor who brings together a group of villagers to perform, most commonly, the martyrdom of Hussein. This is an act of communal piety and has very little artistic value; its aim is to provide an archetype framework into which the spectators can pour their own hopes and sufferings. It arouses their deepest emotions and permits them to express these physically and publicly. It is a primitive ceremony with frenzied shouting and chest-beating. The performance is not only primitive, but awkward, and is generally responsible for the criticism Ta'ziyeh has received from the progressive elements of twentieth-century Persian society.

The advancement of film and television in the post-World War II period, together with the decline of religious ritual, has brought about a crisis in the theatre throughout the world. In order to preserve theatre, innovative producers and directors have been trying to break down the barriers which divide the audience from the actors, for film and TV cannot recreate the excitement generated by the close working together of living organisms. The touch, even the odor of the actor's sweat, the blink of his eye, the rhythm and warmth of his breathing create intimacy between actor and spectator for which nothing can be substituted.

Grotowski, who exemplifies this effort as a producer, has developed what he calls the "poor theatre." By "poor" he means stripping the theatre of extraneous outward appearances and achieving a purity of interaction between audience and actor that is based on their common humanity. This is only possible by reinvesting dramatic action with ritual and establishing a common denominator or archetype, such as, in Ta'ziyeh, the redemptive martyrdom of Hussein at Kerbela. Grotowski seems to be striving for what

10

have always been the fundamental principles of Ta'ziyeh. The important difference is that Grotowski regarded the theatre as his laboratory and controls intimacy by limitation of space, number, and distribution of spectators; his is a chamber theatre. Ta'ziyeh, on the other hand, achieves the same goal in enormous spaces and with masses of spectators.

The actor-spectator confrontation in Ta'ziyeh and its archetypal themes induce self-analysis in all who participate and create in them an inner harmony. Ta'ziyeh is such a personal and serious drama that it captures the very essence of thought and emotions embracing life, death, the Supreme Being, and fellow men. To students of the history of theatre and to those who are engaged in experimental theatre, Ta'ziyeh holds the promise of stimulating new theatrical ideas and experiences.

There are still living Ta'ziyeh producers who are a good source of information on this drama form. There are still Ta'ziyeh troupes who perform in the traditional manner. There are still thousands of Ta'ziyeh manuscripts fading in dowry boxes. We have much to learn from them.

NOTES

1. This chapter was written as a preparatory announcement for the International Symposium on Ta'ziyeh. Variations of this chapter appeared in the following publications: *Festival of Arts Series* (Tehran, 1975); *Performing Arts Journal,* II, No. 1 (New York, Spring 1977); *Dialog,* year XXI, No. 6 (242) (Warsaw, 1976), *'Iṭṭilā'at* (Tehran) 28th of Mordad, 2536 (Solar).

2. Abu'l-Rayḥān Muḥammad al-Bīrūnī, *al-Athar al-Bāqiya 'an al-Qurūn al-Khāliya* (The Chronology of Ancient Nations) (London, 1879).

3. Mullā Ḥusain Vā'iẓ Kāshifī, *Rawżat al-Shuhadā'* (Tehran: Kitābfurūshī Islāmiyyah 1341 A.H./A.D. 1962-63).

4. Samuel Greene Wheeler Benjamin, *Persia and the Persians* (London, 1887), pp. 382-88.

2

An Analysis of the Ta'ziyeh of Qasem

SADEQ HUMAYUNI

A summary of the adventure which unfolds in this Ta'ziyeh [1] is as follows: Ali Akbar, youthful son of Imam Hussein, has just been martyred. Qasem, son of Iman Hassan and a handsome youth who is betrothed to Imam Hussein's dauther, decides that he, too, must go to the battlefield. Hussein, as commander-in-chief, considers the boy not eligible to fight. Not only is he the living memory of Hussein's brother, Imam Hassan, but also he is not of legal age to participate in a *Jihad*.

Qasem, restless in his desire to assert his manhood and bear witness to his faith, becomes melancholy. He seeks out his brother Abd Allah for consolation and together they lament his misfortune, believing that Hussein, by refusing him permission to join arms, has slighted them. This thought reminds them of their own orphaned state and their thoughts turn to the murder of their father. Qasem's mother finds him depressed and agitated, and asks him why he is crying. "Although the fields of misfortune are filled with grief and suffering, this is no time for tears," she says. "You must secure Hussein's permission to join in the *Jihad* and make ready for battle." Qasem replies that Hussein has refused him.

His mother comforts him and reminds him of Imam Hussein's benevolence. Qasem, tears welling in his throat, sends her to plead his cause with the Imam. She does so, but again the Imam refuses. "How can I?" he says.

12

"How can I send him? He is the living memory of my brother Hassan, an unwed boy in the flower of his youth who has not yet tasted the pleasures of life."

Finally, moved by her brave and selfless pleadings, Imam Hussein changes his mind. "I will go to console him," he says. "You prepare for his wedding celebration." These last words startle and surprise Qasem's mother.

Hussein summons Zainab his sister. Her heart too is heavy with grief. "Ali Akbar's body is bathed in blood," he says. "There can be no room for joy and mirth." Hussein answers that the marriage was the final wish of Qasem's father. "How can I, at the last moment, ignore this wish and send the son of my brother, unrequited and unfulfilled, to the field of battle? Go, Zainab, and speak with Fatemeh."

Zainab goes to Fatemeh and explains to her her father's wishes. Fatemeh answers that her own brother has just been killed and lies weltering in his own blood. "How can I who am wearing black ready myself for feasting and pleasure?" Zainab responds that circumstances demand it. If the young tree of Islam is to grow and be fruitful the marriage must take place. Fatemeh, when presented with this logic, accepts. She recognizes that her wedding is a responsibility of critical importance.

Suddenly, a riderless horse bursts upon the scene. It is the horse of Ali Akbar. Fatemeh lets out a wail that reaches the heavens.

Zainab goes to Imam Hussein and informs him of Fatemeh's concurrence. The Imam tells Qasem's mother that the wedding must take place. She responds that no one in the world has ever seen a bridegroom with blood instead of henna rubbed into his palms, a bridegroom whose nuptial bed is like the petals of a flower borne away by the cruel winds of villainy and injustice. But Hussein replies that it is a fact of our existence which in all its variety and shapes continues to flow on under the ebony wheel.

Qasem's mother exclaims that since Ali Akbar is dead and Um-e Laila, his mother, is in mourning, wedding festivities should not be arranged. "It is not right," she says. But Hussein orders her to go to Um-e Laila and to use her power of persuasion to convince her that festivities must take place and that Laila herself must prepare for the wedding. She finds Laila sobbing violently, strewing pieces of straw over her head in anguish. She begs her to cease mourning. Laila, while groaning and beating her breast, congratulates Qasem's mother on the wedding.

In accordance with Iranian tradition, Qasem's mother asks Laila to color her palms with henna and to lay aside her black mourning clothes because, as she says, mourning can change nothing. Hussein sends Zainab to Laila to beg her to cease grieving and to accept Qasem's mother's invitation.

Next, Hussein tells Zainab to prepare the nuptial chamber for Qasem's bride. Again, Qasem's mother bursts into tears. Ali Akbar's bridegroom's costume is brought forth and Hussein dresses Qasem in it. He orders Zainab to rub henna into the palms of the hands and the soles of the feet of both young people. The preparations for the wedding celebration are now complete. Zainab bears henna, sweets, rose water, and a robe of honor to Fatemeh. She bids her don the wedding dress and in sorrowful tones expresses her happiness with the wedding. Then, Zainab rubs Fatemeh's hands with henna while Qasem's mother does the same for him. Next, at Hussein's command and in accordance with ancient Persian custom, Zainab tells Fatemeh to mount Ali Akbar's horse, Eagle, that Eagle might bear her to the bridal chamber.

Fatemeh refuses to mount. She tells Zainab to go back to her father with the message that she cannot bear to ride the horse of her martyred young brother. Zainab, with tears streaming down her face, lovingly strokes Ali Akbar's horse, caressing him in Ali Akbar's memory. She tells Hussein what has transpired. Hussein is deeply touched. In anguish over his remembrances of Akbar, of Akbar's voice, of Akbar's hair, of Akbar's eyes and of Akbar's physique, Hussein summons Zainab and agrees that Fatemeh is right. He orders his own horse, Zuljanah, to be brought to Fatemeh. The horse is draped in black. Fatemeh mounts Zuljanah and departs for the bridal chamber regretting all the while that her marital chamber is not a graveyard.

Everyone congratulates one another on Qasem's happiness and all join in the celebration. Imam Hussein even sends sweets in the form of cone-shaped sugar to his enemies Shemr and Umar Sa'd. The bride and groom leave for the bridal chamber. Fatemeh laments that whereas the lyre and the harp are customarily played at weddings, for hers only the drums of war sound.

Brief moments pass. Then Qasem, aware of the bitter fate which awaits him and his bride, takes leave of her. Fatemeh cries out, "Do not be so unfaithful! Do not leave me!" He responds that the consummation of a marriage is impossible under such circumstances and that they must content themselves with this. "See how alone Hussein is as battle nears. Perhaps our marital union shall occur at the Judgment Day."

The discussion turns to the Judgment Day. The bride asks the groom to give her a token so that she may recognize him at the resurrection; Qasem replies that she will recognize him by his rent sleeves, his torn body bleeding from one hundred wounds and his eyes wet with sorrow, marching in the service of her father.

Qasem's mother, bent and stooped by sorrow, feels great anxiety over the imminent departure of her unfulfilled son. She asks him to forgive her for any shortcomings she might have had in raising him. She calls him her brave son and pronounces him worthy of her milk.

Prince Abd Allah, Iman Hassan's other young son, tearfully asks Qasem, "How can I live without you?" Qasem replies, "I entrust you to my aunt." He summons Zainab and places the hands of Prince Abd Allah and those of his mother into hers. He then tells Hussein that he is ready for battle. Hussein wraps a shroud over Qasem's wedding clothes. This is the honorary authorization which Qasem had so desired.

Qasem returns to his bride one last time to bid her farewell. How painful it is for Fatemeh to say goodbye forever! Qasem gives his mother his last will and testament which specifies how his bride should be cared for and then departs for the battlefield. Hussein prays for Qasem and asks his followers to bless his prayers by uttering the word amen. They do so.

Qasem arrives at the battlefield full of vigor. He fights single-handedly and courageously. At last, the fatal moment comes when he falls from his horse, wounded and helpless. Shemr stands over him with his sword drawn. Qasem begs Shemr to allow him to see the face of his sweetheart just one last time. But Shemr rejects his plea, turns to Umar Sa'd and asks for permission to cut off his head. "Give him a brief respite," says Umar Sa'd and begins to converse with Qasem who is now in the agony of death. Qasem's last wishes, to see his wife one more time, to see Hussein, and to quench his thirst are never realized. As Shemr prepared to deliver the death blow, Qasem cries out to Hussein, and Hussein, from the middle of a sea of infidel soldiers, rushes to Qasem's side, cradles his head in his arms, and curses his murderers. Finally, Shemr delivers the final blow. Qasem's last request is that Hussein should not carry him back to the tents in this miserable and broken condition, with a bloody and torn body. He is ashamed to be seen by his wife in this condition. Finally, he dies.

Hussein returns to the tents and announces the death. He asks Zainab to dress Fatemeh in black and to go on his behalf to beg the forgiveness of Qasem's mother.

EVENTS PIVOT AROUND HUSSEIN

In this Ta'ziyeh, as in many, Hussein is the center of all action. Everything pivots around his decisions, his thoughts, his wishes, and his words. Sometimes Hussein, alone in the barren desert, laments his terrible loneliness and cries out to his grandfather, the Prophet, against those of his kinsmen who in their weakness have deserted him. "O illustrious Prophet, so laden with fame, No stranger in foreign lands e'er suffered my pain." [2] He senses how alone he is against the forces of evil. Those who had accompanied him, pledged their friendship, their assistance, and their hospitality, fled when confronted with the awesome wave of catastrophic events. Hussein is so alone that save for the members of his own family who are largely women and children, there is no one he can talk to. Most of his brethren have either defected, broken their covenant, or been martyred. Save for consultation with his women and children, there is little he can do but bemoan his incapacity.

For Hussein, everything is mixed together in this Ta'ziyeh: reason, realism, intelligence, emotion, allegiance to religious and tribal tradition, a sense of responsibility, and most of all, a terrifying and painful tension which casts a shadow over the entire environment of war and violence. The events which have already occurred and the loss of his beloved and devoted friends have distressed him to the depths of his soul. Hussein sometimes appears as the Imam, sometimes as a father who has lost his young son, sometimes as a battlefield commander alone and friendless, sometimes as a great human being, determined and victorious, and sometimes as nothing but an ordinary man who lacks a refuge in which to find shelter.

When Hussein refuses to allow Qasem to go to war, one senses he actually feels the presence of his brother Hassan. Hussein does not consider himself authorized to send his brother's son into battle, since the tragic ending is patently clear.

Hassan had never quarreled with the Umayyads and had himself made the decision that Qasem should be a bridegroom. For these reasons, Hussein is ready to give the boy his own daughter in marriage, hoping that the marriage might forge a new link with Qasem in addition to their already existing bonds of blood, faith, and combat, a new link blessed, yet destined for failure.

The catastrophe peaks when Hussein orders that the bridegroom's clothing of Ali Akbar, his own unfulfilled young son, be worn by Qasem only moments after Ali Akbar has been slain, and orders Fatemeh to mount Ali Akbar's horse. It is as if Hussein, like any broken-hearted father who is still hopeful, determined, and a true Moslem, wishes to experience the presence of his lost child even amidst the sad events which inexorably grind forward. It is as if Hussein either does not—or cannot—accept the fact that his son is dead. Perhaps by these thoughts and actions he wishes to eliminate the distance separating Ali Akbar from Qasem, Fatemeh, and himself, and bridge the distance between the battlefield and death, and the bride and marital union; and hence, via the atmosphere created, to recreate Akbar's voice, Akbar's face, and Akbar's memory in their sweetest and most genuine form. His demand that the wedding take place using Ali Akbar's clothing and his horse Eagle is a manifestation of the humanity of Hussein in his role as a father whose own courageous son has been martyred before he could marry.

Fatemeh's refusal to obey her father's request to mount Ali Akbar's horse is a wonderfully pure, spiritual, and human rebellion, completely Eastern, emotional, and so painful to witness that Hussein, despite his lionheartedness, accepts it and sympathizes with her. He shares her grief. His heart is so overflowing with memories of Ali Akbar that he weeps. Perhaps in no other Ta'ziyeh does Hussein lament and grieve as he does in this one. Is this feeling not aroused by an emotional bond between what is happening, all that has happened, and all that must happen to Qasem and to himself?

Grief dominates this Ta'ziyeh, grief and tears and still more tears. If for a fleeting moment a flash of joy leaps out, it too is rooted in grief and futility, full of high hopes but short-lived, a transitory flash, baseless and without foundation. Joy in this Ta'ziyeh has an aspect of caricature to it. It shows itself with a doleful face as if its inside were empty and its outside were overlaid with sorrow and tragedy. Congratulations and good wishes are spoken against a background of weeping. The moments of joy never achieve enough power to create enthusiasm or delight. A tragedy is unfolding and the transitory, fleeting joy is buried under the weight of catastrophic events. From a distance, death with its despicable face is smiling. Blood is about to flow. Magnanimity has fallen and been trampled by the feet of tyranny. No one can say when, where, or how it will end.

Although the dialogue speaks of conjugal union, the union is not consummated. The dialogue concerns the war and injustice which lie at the end of the road. Is this not the most sorrowful of all love songs? Two young people, eager and full of desire—one facing death in the saddle, the other, defenceless, facing an inexorable fate without a friend. The young lovers' union, occurring as it does amidst a sea of blood, is a farewell pact for eternity.

Despite his youth and inexperience, Qasem realizes that he must die, and he accepts his fate uncomplainingly in the manner of great men. Note his answer to Fatemeh when she inquires how she might recognize him at the Judgment Day:

> With sorrowful eyes and sleeves all tattered,
> Body ripped open and bones all shattered,
> With the other martyrs, Abbas and Akbar,
> With thirsting lips, still serving your father.[3]

Another particularly moving scene comes when Fatemeh watches her father clothe her husband in a shroud and observes the shadow of death fall across his face and body. She cannot bear it and she screams at her father to remove the shroud. Since she considers her spontaneous scream to be blasphemous and rude, she asks Hussein to drape her instead with the shroud. Her emotions are mixed: on the one hand, is fear of death and non-existence coupled with pride and, on the other, a sense of unworthiness in the face of her religion and embarrassment in front of her father, coupled with her hopes for a happily married life.

In the exchange between the two when Fatemeh praises Qasem's father, the meter of the verse shifts its rhythm.

Qasem gives his mother his last will and testament, which pertains to his wife. The will is full of hope in the future, a future in which the questions of when, where, and how are not answered. We sense that although Qasem knows he is leaving forever and has no hope for either life or marriage, he still desires Fatemeh's love, her body, and her soul. He wants his heart to belong to her even unto death's door, hoping that death will not cause her to forget him but will somehow give a permanence to their love. It is as if he plans to go on a journey and even though the journey is death itself he still retains hope for a safe return.

When the time comes to leave for battle, Qasem bids farewell to all that has been part of him, both tangible and intangible. How he loves life! Even though he is facing inexorable fate, he still hopes to live. It is a painful sight to witness Qasem crying in the arms of his friends, bidding them farewell amidst a silence broken only by the soft beat of drums in the background.

When Qasem leaves for the battlefield, Hussein, bearing a prophetic mission on the fields of Kerbela, cries out "Allah Akbar." This cry for help, this warning, embodies the significance of what has already happened and what is in the process of happening—a young lad, inexperienced, full of hope, a fresh bridegroom full of vigor, a believer and a lover headed for the battlefield. It is as if Hussein by these words hopes to comprehend both the present and the future, and grasp the hugeness of the catastrophe which is enveloping him and his kinsmen. He hopes to make fate hearken to the aloneness and the faithfulness of both himself and his followers. This "Allah Akbar" is an extraordinary call to prayer—a wondrous and wonder-creating cry against the tyranny which governed that hapless land. Hussein's prayer is a prayer of blessing to escort those entrusted to him on their journey. It is full of love, loyalty, and selflessness.

The manly boldness which Qasem exhibits on the battlefield against the leaders of the enemy, Shemr and Umar Sa'd, serves as a full-view mirror which reflects the essence of this unfulfilled youth. Here we see him just as he is, in all his worthiness and humanity, full of hope and greatness. Alone he can do nothing. It is impossible for one person to withstand an onslaught by an enemy horde which is greedy for honors and titles, and has banded together in the hopes of achieving material gain. At last, he falls. The inexorable catastrophe reveals its blood-stained visage to Qasem—pitiless, unyielding, and hateful.

The disregard which Shemr shows toward Qasem's request to see Fatemeh one more time and the sympathy which Umar Sa'd displays point up the righteousness in the soul of his honest youth. Qasem's conversation with Umar Sa'd conveys all of his hopes and fears, his joys and his sorrows—all of which lie exposed to futility and fleeting time. Umar Sa'd, despite his expressions of sympathy, feigns ignorance. He cunningly seals his lips when it comes to discussing the facts which caused Qasem to fight. He knows that Qasem is the son of Hassan and Hussein's son-in-law; he knows that Qasem is a new bridegroom. Most important of all, he knows that right is on the side of Qasem and Hussein. But, despite all he knows, he feigns ignorance. Qasem's pure love for Islam and for his wife is fully revealed in his responses to Umar Sa'd. How chastely he responds to his enemy's questions about his wedding celebration:

Umar Sa'd:	To the nuptial chamber with your bride you went.
Qasem:	Upon her face mine eyes feasted to the fullest extent.
Umar Sa'd:	What words were exchanged with your bride, pray tell?
Qasem:	I told her, O my darling, I bid thee farewell.[4]

Perhaps the story of Qasem and Fatemeh is the saddest story of unrequited love ever told in any of the world's greatest tragedies. As the tale unravels, the tension generated by Qasem's fate intensifies. By using every device at their disposal, the actors play upon the already taut emotions of the spectators, moving them to the depths of their souls as with elegance and beauty this Ta'ziyeh is brought to a dramatic conclusion.

The pride and the pain of a defeated human being, alone and sincere, is expressed beautifully. The audience finds itself totally caught up in the action.

The climax of the tragedy and its most moving section occurs when Qasem lies in his death-throes. His face is covered with blood and Hussein rushes to his aid in these last moments of life and cradles him in his arms. He begs Hussein not to carry him to Fatemeh in this pitiable state, defeated and broken, with bloody face and wounded body. This last request best summarizes his thoughts—of love, of defeat, of hope, and of the sorrow of death.

EXTENSIVE USE OF PERSIAN TRADITION

One of the most interesting aspects of this tragedy is the extensive use of Persian traditions. They underlie the action and the dialogue from one scene to the next. The extensive utilization of Persian folklore and customs in many instances dominate the action, adding a delicate yet penetrating tranquility. Selecting the name Eagle for Ali Albar's horse, rubbing henna into the hands, feet, and face of the bride and groom, decorating the nuptial *Akbar* chamber, carrying the bride to the nuptial chamber on horseback, the tribal elders dressing the bridegroom in a robe of honor, preparing a tray of sweets, henna, a cloth for applying it, rose water, giving sweets (a cone of sugar) to everyone including the enemy in order that all might join in the celebration, wearing black in mourning and scattering straw over the head upon the death of loved ones all have roots in ancient Persian tradition. Dressing in brightly colored clothes after the completion of mourning, the manner in which goodbyes are said, and many other details are examples of pure Persian customs. These customs help to bind the Ta'ziyeh deeply into the lives, the consciousness, and the emotions of the people. They create an emotional bond between the people and their clergy. The spectators themselves become participants in the joys and sorrows of the play. In addition, religious traditions such as asking one's loved ones for their forgiveness before taking leave, and the making of a final will and testament are expertly presented.

Another effective device which further captures the audience is the use of the title *Shahzadeh* or prince for the sons of Hassan and Hussein. This title was used exclusively for sons of Persian shahs and never for those of the caliphs. By employing this word, the narrators of the Ta'ziyeh and the clergy created a link between the heroes of Kerbela and the people of Persia. Based on an appreciation of the needs and wishes of the Persian public and an understanding of the popular mentality, the sons of Imam Hassan and Imam Hussein are called Prince Qasem, Prince Akbar, Prince Abd Allah, Prince Asgar even though only one of Hussein's wives was the daughter of Yazdegard, the last ruler of the Sasanian dynasty.

The elegant imagery used extensively in this Ta'ziyeh is rooted in religious exegesis and may be found in other Ta'ziyehs. "Candle of Kerbela," "a leaf in the embrace of the Chosen," "flower of the garden of Muhammad," "Candlelight in the sanctuary of Islam," and beautiful lines such as "moonlike face reddened with blood" and "place him in honor's lap" are but a few examples. Poetic images like "cyprus trees aside the brook," "the ebony sphere," "tangled locks," and "gorgeous eyes" are also frequently used.

The Heroism and Self-Sacrifice of the Women

Another masterful aspect of this Ta'ziyeh is the astonishing portrayal of heroism and self-sacrifice by the women. The female characters put their own needs aside and forget their natural inclinations as mothers, sisters, wives, and blood relations in order to carry out the will of God, promote Islam, and support Hussein who stands out as a symbol of righteousness. The women sublimate their personal desires both great and small because they recognize that an honorable death for their husbands, sons, and brothers is far more to be desired than is weakness and disgrace. With unparalleled passion, Qasem's mother begs Hussein to allow her son to participate in the *Jihad*. Fatemeh, while sobbing over the death of her brother, obeys her father's order. Fatemeh courageously sends her husband to war and Zainab, who should be considered the best example of a true Islamic upbringing, puts aside her personal feelings completely. When Qasem leaves for the battlefield, his mother says:

> O brave lion cub so worthy of my milk
> I'm one thousand times fortunate to have a son of such ilk

And she shouts after him:

> Go my darling with God you consort
> The prayers of the mourners your sustenance and support.[5]

Qasem's farewell to his mother is extremely moving. He raises the question of his wife's fate:

> When I from the saddle fall
> And Hussein my corpse sorrowfully haul
> In grief my body she'll study
> Her hands in my gore she'll bloody
> Let her not mourn and languish
> Nor dishevel her hair in anguish [6]
> My bride, my sunshine, with fate so unjust,
> To thee O mother I lovingly entrust
> And both of you I deposit in the hands of the Lord
> Forgive me my sins when I die by the sword.[7]

She does not feign ignorance of the future when she bids her son farewell. Exemplary feminine characteristics shine against a background of tragedy. The loyal and loving women demonstrate again and again how the sacrifice of personal desires can help attain the higher goals of Hussein.

EMOTIVE FORCES

Another significant point to note is the manner in which the spirit of war and death casts its shadow over the entire play in a nerve-wracking and fear-inspiring manner—a spirit which is constantly present throughout the various scenes of rebellion, joyfulness, decision-making and leave-taking. As the tale moves toward its conclusion, the hero's inexorable fate and the forces of oppression and tyranny rush onward like a flood, smashing, collapsing, destroying, and carrying everything with them. During these frightening moments which seem to last for an eternity, the hearts and souls of the characters are torn by conflicting thoughts and emotions, images which sometimes flash in moments of lightness, sometimes in darkness, sometimes against a flood of rain or in the midst of a wind storm. Sometimes decisions are inevitable from the beginning: sometimes they are made under duress and are contrary to personal desires and wise policy.

The loss of meter in the verse foretells the frightful shadow of death and oblivion which is about to fall. All of mankind's weaknesses are portrayed as undeniable facts of nature, and human needs over a lifetime are discussed and highlighted.

In order to achieve a better sense of inspiration, union, separation and leave-taking—all of which maifest themselves in an atmosphere of fear and anxiety over a painful death and future oblivion—are mingled together and boiled in the same pot. The event which occurred in Kerbela was so dreadful that for Hussein's loyal followers who have accepted an unjust death, it has taken on the hue of eternity.

Does not Hussein's gift of sweets to Shemr and Umar Sa'd from

21

Qasem's and Fatemeh's wedding prove that he was fully aware of his and Qasem's fate, and that he so acknowledged its inevitability that he was even willing to give sweets to the enemy while standing on the battlefield in the very pit of the murder-place? He accepts the relentless unjust tyranny which will bring him and his followers an eternal victory and he anticipates this victory in a most beautiful manner.

One unique aspect of this Ta'ziyeh is the presence of a beautiful new bride who separates from her husband at the very moment of conjugal union. After experiencing honor and happiness, she must face the blackness of death and suffering. Another unique aspect is the close similarity between Akbar and Qasem which keeps Akbar's memory alive in the minds of his friends. Qasem's bloody death is another unique aspect. Together they make this Ta'ziyeh different from all others. The traditions of success and failure, union and separation, marriage and death, hope and hopelessness are closely intermingled, giving a special greatness to this Ta'ziyeh. Many of the events portrayed have become symbols for the self-flagellation by believers throughout Iran on the Ashura Mourning Day. Qasem's nuptial chamber and Hussein's horse, draped in black, which carries Qasem into battle are two good examples.

In this Ta'ziyeh, as in all others, the villains admit to the legitimacy and the greatness of Imam Hussein's cause.

> Accept my challenge, O gem among men
> Accept my challenge, O ruler without a friend
> Accept my challenge, ye from whose locks and face
> One may learn the Surahs of lightness and grace.[8]

Does not Shemr, with these lines, admit to Hussein's legitimacy? And does not Umar Sa'd pay homage to the greatness of Qasem and Ali when he says, "Accept my challenge, O successor to the Lion of God"?[9] Umar Sa'd and Shemr eliminate the distance between themselves and the audience in admitting the fact of Hussein's legitimacy. This action draws the audience deeper into the adventure. The dialogue speaks for reality. The truth must be spoken even if a man is dressed in the clothes of the enemy. And, more important, since the spectators are lost in a world of fantasy, they never imagine that the villains are devoid of religion. Even the enemy claim that they love Hussein and recognize him as one of their own, and shed tears over his fate and that of his followers. When the truth comes from the mouth of the enemy, it has even greater force and validity. One might imagine that the Ta'ziyeh performers while writing and acting out the play wished to acquit the villains of any evil intentions and not allow even a speck of atheistic or blasphemous dust to be seen on their religious visages.

The audience can never anticipate what scene will follow another. Events occur with such speed that the audience can only wonder what will happen next. The events enacted in this Ta'ziyeh can never be fully foreseen, even though fate is predestined, and we must accept the fact that the heroes are prepared to sacrifice their lives. Although they frequently use sarcastic and insulting phrases, the expressions they use have religious overtones and are in fact far removed from their surface mundaneness, requiring a closer examination of the sarcasm, ridicule and insults. Hussein and his followers utter them only because they are in the right and Qasem and the others indulge in no other damning of the enemy. And they never go beyond what the enemy themselves say, uttering only those words which they believe in and have faith in. Examples are "deceitful nation," "cursed," "tyrant," and "shameless."

While the events and scenes which dominate the adventure have imaginary elements and some of the acting and speech has a caricature-like aspect, such as when Hussein laments the death of Akbar by saying that he will kiss the saddle and stirrups of his horse—a section in which the love of a father for a son is honestly portrayed—it should be realized that the Ta'ziyeh narrators, the writers and the players, were not professionals. Rather, they were ordinary people expressing their own faith and devotion within the context of a religious happening. This fact affects all other elements in the play, such as the recitation of verse within the format of various Iranian metrical schemes and the use of drums, musical instruments, and a horse and other symbols to create a greater emotional response from the audience. A passion play has no other purpose than to strengthen the faith of the people by condensing and intensifying religious events in such a manner that the heart-rending juices of the play are extracted and trickled drop by drop onto the palates of the expectant spectators.

NOTES

1. The Ta'ziyeh analyzed in this essay is the *Ta'ziyeh of Qāsim* from *Ta'ziyeh va Ta'ziyeh Khvānī* by Sādiq Humāyūnī (Shiraz: Festival of Arts Series. 1975).

2. *Ibid.*, p. 112.

3. *Ibid.*, p. 124.

4. *Ibid.*, p. 130.

5. *Ibid.*, p. 125.

6. *Ibid.*, p. 126.

7. *Ibid.*, p. 127.

8. *Ibid.*, p. 113.

9. *Ibid.*

3

Cultural Dimensions of Performance Conventions in Iranian Ta'ziyeh

WILLIAM O. BEEMAN

INTRODUCTION [1]

Past research on Ta'ziyeh has emphasized literary and historical aspects of this performance tradition.[2] In these studies the Ta'ziyeh has been the *object* of investigation, and knowledge about literary and historical traditions surrounding it have been used to elucidate it. Another dimension which has been less explored, and which will be treated here concerns investigation of Ta'ziyeh as an aspect of cultural performance in Iran and the wider Shi'a Islamic world.

From literature on the anthropology of performance [3] we understand that the shapes and conventions of performance traditions are not universal, but are inextricably bound up in more complex patterns of cultural symbolism, logic, and presentational conventions. Further, performance traditions are among the most dynamic and powerful components of a given culture. They bear a strong relationship to ritual, as Richard Schechner has pointed out on numerous occasions,[4] in that they consist of symbolic elements made manifest through the offices of specialized practi-

24

tioners whose purpose is to transform the spectators at the performance in some preconceived manner: to make them laugh, persuade them, create in them a sense of heightened reality, elevate their sensibilities, or in the case of Ta'ziyeh, to create a powerful catharsis of emotion.

Performance traditions also bear a resemblance to many aspects of everyday life. As Victor Turner has pointed out, such public events as elections, demonstrations, and public meetings have their performative and ritualistic aspects.[5] These "social dramas" likewise aim to achieve a change in a state of affairs through specific performance. Following this line of reasoning, we see that events like the Ta'ziyeh hold a place somewhere between the sacred and the secular in all cultures. They are "liminal" events in Turner's sense of the word.[6] Thus, through the study of the Ta'ziyeh as performance, rather than strictly as literature or history, we are in a position to turn the tables on the focal concerns of earlier studies [7] and use analysis of the Ta'ziyeh as a tool for investigation of both the sacred and secular worlds within which it is contained.

TA'ZIYEH AS A PERFORMANCE GENRE

Although virtually every commentator on the Ta'ziyeh has identified it as theatre, there is good reason to consider it in other terms. Lassy points out that in Soviet Azerbaijan a strict distinction is made between Ta'ziyeh and other dramatic forms:

> A point to be noticed is that the Tartars themselves expressly deny that the passion play is a drama proper. It is a *Shabih,* that is an "imitation," or a *ta'ziyeh-ye shabih,* a "consoling imitation," nothing more. To a Tartar there exists no sort of tragedy in the form of a drama, comedy being considered by him to be the only form of dramatic art. Therefore when the speeches and songs of the passion play are written, no attempt is made to create impressive *roles* or situations, the sole purpose being to compose more-or-less lengthy monologues in the same fragmentary, crabbed, plaintive and sentimental style as that of the elegies.[8]

It is my contention that it is a great disservice to Ta'ziyeh to consider it a variety of theatre in Western terms. The purpose of Ta'ziyeh performances, the dramatic conventions thus employed, and the unique configuration of techniques of symbolic representation in the Ta'ziyeh serves to identify it as a unique Iranian performance genre which, although it bears superficial resemblance to Western theatre (especially when viewed through Western and Western-trained eyes), should not be robbed of its special status among the unique dramatic traditions of the world.

First, it cannot be emphasized enough (especially to the lay public) that Ta'ziyeh is not *one* drama (i.e., "*the* Persian Passion Play") or even a definitive set of dramas, but is a performance tradition which has an organic existence of own. It is changing, modifiable, and enormously flexible in its realization.

Secondary, although Ta'ziyeh performances are scripted, to identify the written script with the Ta'ziyeh proper is to entertain only a limited view of the tradition as a whole. In point of fact, the tradition allows for extraordinary flexibility in the realization of script material. It is doubtful whether any of the scripts which have been collected were ever conceived as permanent by their authors. In present-day settings, scripts are continually modified, rewritten, amended, lengthened and combined with other scripts both before a given performance, and from the *takiyeh* itself during performance. The series of episodes presented as a cohesive unit can likewise be numerous (Pelly [9] records fifty-two) or few. Furthermore, until recent times, the performance material was being rapidly expanded into a series of nearly secular themes which were not necessarily presented during the month of Muharram at all.[10]

Thirdly, perhaps almost self-evidently, we see the Ta'ziyeh performance consisting almost entirely of verse—most often couplets. This is in sharp contrast to almost all Western theatrical tradition.

Finally, and most importantly, the relationship between audience and performer in Ta'ziyeh is unique among performance traditions of the world. It is this one feature that most completely accounts for the particular representational forms that are embodied within Ta'ziyeh performance. It is therefore to this topic that I turn my attention next.

Representation in Ta'ziyeh

The very special relationship of the Ta'ziyeh audience to the performance has been noted by virtually all commentators writing on the tradition. It stands out particularly against Western theatrical tradition because the spectators are clearly both inside and outside of the drama. They are both on the plains of Kerbela, symbolically representing the forces surrounding Hussein and his followers, *and* simultaneously in the present-day world mourning because of the event.

The actors in the drama express their sorrow and grief through the verbal text of the performance, but it is the people in the audience who provide the explicit, forceful, and sometimes violent expression of grief and mourning which is absent from the performance representation. Thus they complete a portion of the dramatic action which is otherwise lacking.

The explicit expressions of grief produced by the spectators, however, are prompted by their own life experiences, and only triggered by the presentation of the events they witness in the *takiyeh*. Indeed, the audience is exhorted to weep for their own sins, their own troubles, remembering how much greater was the suffering of Hussein and his followers.

As Chelkowski [11] has suggested, this has great import for all who are concerned with the nature and purpose of dramatic expression in the West. The so-called "audience" problem has been one that has been confronted continually in Western theatre. The last twenty years have seen a particularly active experimentation in trying to break down the audience-performer "barrier" and actively engage spectators in the dramatic action. The Living Theatre, the Open Theatre, and Richard Schechner's Performance Group are only a few of the groups who have tried to devise new performance methodologies to deal with this problem.

For the structure of representation within Ta'ziyeh the centrality of the audience-performer tradition becomes crucial. The liminal status of the audience as performer-spectator, existing both within the present and in the past as part of the dramatic action, and being situated both within its own community and on the plains of Kerbela forms the central axis around which principles of representation are ordered.

In order to encompass the situation of the audience within the time frame of the drama at least three modes of temporal representation are necessary. The first is "literal time," e.g., the actual time it takes for a dialogue to take place from beginning to end. "Representational time" is truncated, elongated, or distorted time: most of the battles are represented in this way, taking less time than they might otherwise. Mourning sequences, or the famous "lion" sequence, do not represent literal time. Finally, "non-time" is a kind of dimension which allows the co-occurrence of all sorts of characters and events which could not possibly have existed together at the same time. Even the known dead, such as the body of Qasem after his martyrdom, are able to take part in the stage dialogue. Further, it should be noted that these three time dimensions totally interpenetrate each other with no indication of shift through theatrical devices such as lighting, scene change, etc., as must occur in Western theatre for audiences to understand what is going on. The audience views literal time and representational time in the performance; but it is the dimension of non-time which encompasses the audience along with the action and allows the spectators to be at once in the present and in the past.

A similar practice exists with the representation of space. "Literal space" surrounds most encounters between characters, and events, such as the wedding of Qasem. "Representational space" compresses or elongates actual space. In mobile action such as walking or riding the difference between representational and literal space is marked in that the former involves moving in an arc, and the latter moving in a straight line. Representational space involves also such areas as the battlefield. This area also contains the viewers in their representational roles as the forces surrounding Hussein and his followers. Finally "non-space" creates the co-occurrence of personages far removed from each other spatially as well as temporally, allowing figures such as Yazid, or Za'far, king of the Jinn, to address Hussein as the drama unfolds.

27

The spectators are placed in a liminal position not only in terms of time and space, but in their dramatic role within the performance as well. As participants in the drama they represent not only the mourners of Hussein but also his murderers. Thus the distinction between those who are on the side of Hussein and those who are his enemies becomes crucial in the dramatic representation. There are, to be sure, many ways that one can tell the sympathetic from the unsympathetic characters. In classical tradition the sympathetic characters wear either green or white; the unsympathetic characters, red. Chelkowski notes that the adherents of Yazid might wear sun glasses to mark them as bad characters.[12] Most importantly, however, good characters chant their lines, and bad characters declaim, or shout them. When a bad character converts and becomes a good character he changes his mode of line delivery.

There is very little else in the representation of the drama which needs be fixed. Costumes need adhere to no particular historic period. All sorts of historic characters may be brought into the course of the drama. The production can be upgraded through the use of more realistic props, costumes, or live animals, but these are not necessary components. Neither is the language of the Ta'ziyeh fixed. Performances are given in Turkish, Arabic, mixed Persian-Turkish, Urdu, and most probably other languages as well.

The flexibility of representation in Ta'ziyeh through costumes, props, and language serves to reinforce the connections between the action and the everyday lives of spectators. Nonetheless, the actors must costume themselves in a way that is different from the normal dress of the audience. In a performance I witnessed in Fars this was accomplished by draping the actors in simple red, green, or white tunics which covered their normal dress.

THE MEANING OF REPRESENTATIONAL CONVENTIONS IN TA'ZIYEH

In order to understand something about the meaning of the representational conventions in Ta'ziyeh it will be useful to compare them with some of the conventions that obtain for other dramatic traditions throughout the world.

Indonesian *wayang kulit* is one species of the tradition of leather shadow-puppet drama found throughout most of Asia. This dramatic tradition involves the presentation of stories which are both entertaining and of a sacred nature. The "high" characters in the Balinese form of this drama—royal persons, major demons and gods—speak entirely in an ancient liturgical language which no one in the audience understands at all. The "low" characters—servants for the most part—speak in the vernacular of the spectators, and interpret the action while making broad jokes and humorous remarks.

Indian dance-drama traditions, notably the *Kathakali* tradition of

Kerala, involve a similar set of conventions. The actor-dancers in *Kathakali* do not speak their text, but indicate the plot of the drama through the use of gestures, called *mudras*. The gesture language is somewhat esoteric, and singers in the background narrate the story for the spectators in song simultaneously with the dance presentation.

In Western "naturalistic" theatre actors draw their stage movement and expressions from the stuff of "real life," and are encouraged to research their roles at great length through observing and attempting to create in themselves the feeling and emotions of the real-life prototypes of the characters they are to portray. In their training they are encouraged to draw heavily on their own feelings and self-knowledge for the expression of emotion and action. The audience in Western theatre is supposed to enter into the stage action and be moved by it on the basis of each one's own knowledge of human nature, conventional expression, and probable behavior patterns.

In the two Asian dramatic traditions, the story material portrayed in the dramatic situation is largely known to the audience before it is seen in performance. If anything, the performance is designed to reinforce for the members of the audience in a particularly effective manner the important aspects of their cultural, ideological, and religious tradition. In Western naturalistic theatre the spectators expect to witness story material which is novel, but which is expressed in a manner comprehensible to them on the basis of their own knowledge of life that they bring with them to the theatre. What is repeated in Western theatrical traditions then, is not particular literal stories, but particular human themes played and replayed in infinite variation.

Western drama is successful when it produces a catharsis: when it moves the audience in some way. Making the viewers laugh, cry, feel indignant, ennobled, or angry are all ways that Western theatre touches the emotions. Thus paradoxically, by using the commonplace as a basis for expression in performance, Western theatre aims at removing the spectators from the commonplace and transporting them to an emotional plane achieved only occasionally in everyday life. The Asian traditions mentioned above are not at all naturalistic in their form of expression. The shadow figures in *wayang kulit* are exaggerated representations of humans, they speak in exaggerated vocal contours in either an esoteric language which no one in the audience speaks or understands, or in broad humorous speech which no one in the audience really uses in everyday life. Similarly, in *Kathakali* the stage characters dress in surrealistic costumes and make-up and perform elaborate dance movements which require for their execution special arduous training from childhood on, together with a gesture language which very few spectators can interpret. Asian drama is successful when it is able to create in the audience a sense that there is order in the world, that events are as they should be; that despite adversity and extremes in the vicissitudes of events, proper morality is reasserted.

Given these parameters, it should not be difficult to see that Ta'ziyeh as a performance tradition falls between the two Asian traditions mentioned and Western naturalistic theatre. Ta'ziyeh presents familiar materials to the audience in an unnaturalistic fashion. However, the mode of linguistic expression is not esoteric, and does not require interpretation. Although the mode of performance does not replicate real life, the settings, props and costumes are designed to be comprehensible to the audience without special previous knowledge. Most importantly, however, the Ta'ziyeh performance is designed to reassert moral and religious ideological order for the audience, and to accomplish this by producing cathartic reactions.

Those in the audience in Ta'ziyeh are placed in the position of being both the symbolic murderers of Hussein in Kerbela, *and* being the mourners of Hussein after his death. At the conclusion of the performance they must end up being converted, or renewed, through their profound expression of grief at Hussein's death, and through their demonstrations of loyalty to the ideological order that Hussein represents. There are numerous characters in the drama itself—nonpartisans of Hussein—who undergo the same transformation: Hurr, general of Ibn Ziyad; the foreign ambassador; Za'far, king of the Jinn; and others. The implication presented here is that if even Hussein's enemies, foreigners, and Jinn weep for, and defend Hussein, how can the spectators refrain from demonstrating their emotions in this matter?

Thus Ta'ziyeh performance offers the opportunity for the spectators ritually to renew their commitment to a religious and ideological order of which they are already an integral part. This ideological order does not limit itself strictly to religious dimensions but includes a political and nationalistic dimension as well. The saga of the family of Ali is very much the saga of Great Iran—those areas from Kerbela and Kufa to the Caucasus, Central Asia, Afghanistan, and Northern India—overrun again and again by conquering hordes, but possessing an inner spiritual unity which has sustained the thread of a unique cultural tradition down to the present.

Lassy [13] identifies the complex of practices surrounding the commemoration of the death of Hussein in yet other historical-religious terms. He astutely notes that the Ta'ziyeh and other Muharram practices are similar to rituals marking the death of Christ, Dionesius, Osiris, and many other figures in Indo-European and Semitic tradition. The theme of birth and renewal in ritual practice is virtually universal, carrying with it the message of the renewal of the fertility and productivity of the world's flora and fauna, as well as the beginning of a new cycle in the transit of the heavens. This cosmological interpretation, it seems, cannot be excluded as one of the ritual roots of Ta'ziyeh performance. Thus through participation in the Ta'ziyeh, the audience is also taking part in the modern version of an ancient tradition of cosmic renewal and rebirth.

CONCLUSION

I have attempted to describe Ta'ziyeh in Iran not as a literary or historical product, but as a performance tradition. Ta'ziyeh embodies representational features which make it unique among the performance traditions of the world. The particular representational conventions of Ta'ziyeh arise from the special relationship that obtains between the audience and performers. Further, these modes of representation allow the Ta'ziyeh performance to achieve a particular effect on its audience which is not only emotionally satisfying, but serves also as a reinforcement to the religious, ideological and cosmic order of the Shi'a world.

NOTES

1. I am grateful to Brown University for support during the summer of 1974 which enabled me to carry out preliminary work on Iranian dramatic tradition. I am grateful also to Byron and Mary Jo Good, who have worked extensively on aspects of Ta'ziyeh in Azerbaijan, for much useful discussion leading to the formulation of the ideas in this paper, for which, of which, of course I alone am responsible.

2. I have not provided a full survey of research on Ta'ziyeh by Iranians and Westerners. Peter Chelkowski has provided a most useful bibliography, which contains most of the available sources, in *Ta'ziyeh: Indigenous Avant-Garde Theater of Iran* (Tehran: Festival of Arts Series, 1975); see also his "Dramatic and Literary Aspects of Ta'ziyeh-Khani—Iranian Passion Play," *Review of National Literatures,* 2 (1971); 121-38. The excellent works of Bahrām Baiżā'ī, Namāyish dar Irān (Tehran: Kavyān 1344/1965), and by Ṣadiq Humāyūnī, *Ta'ziyeh va Ta'ziyeh-khvānī* (Tehran: Festival of Arts Series, 1353/1974) are especially useful.

3. See Richard Bauman, "Verbal Art as Performance," *American Anthropologist,* 77 (1975), 290-311.

4. Richard Schechner, *Environmental Theater* (New York: Hawthorne, 1973); and "Selective Inattention: A Traditional Way of Spectating—Now Part of the Avantgarde," *Performing Arts Journal,* 1 (1976), 1-12.

5. Victor Turner, *Dramas, Fields, and Metaphors* (Ithaca: Cornell University Press, 1974).

6. Victor Turner, *The Forest of Symbols: Aspects of Ndembu Ritual* (Ithaca: Cornell University Press, 1967); and *The Ritual Process* (Chicago: Aldine, 1969).

7. With the possible exception of the brilliant early study by Ivar J. Lassy, *The Muharram Mysteries among the Azerbaijan Turks of Caucasia* (Helsingfors: Lilius and Hertzberg, 1916), which deserves much greater attention from scholars than it has received in th past.

8. *Ibid.,* p. 101.

9. Lewis Pelly, *The Miracle Play of Hasan and Husain,* 2 vols. (London: Wm. H. Allen, 1879).

10. cf. Chelkowski, *Ta'ziyeh,* p. 15.

11. *Ibid,* p. 19.

12. *Ibid,* p. 18.

13. *The Muharram Mysteries,* pp. 283-84.

4

Semeiological Aspects of the Ta'ziyeh

ANDRZEJ WIRTH

It becomes increasingly obvious that the application of the Aristotelian dramatic terminology to the confessional folk opera of Iran, Ta'ziyeh, is misleading on both cultural and structural grounds. And yet terms such as prologue, epilogue, climax, action, and above all dialogue, are uncritically used in the discussion on Ta'ziyeh. For Aristotle, dialogue was a device to convey the plot, and in these terms it was considered a timeless form of drama. In Ta'ziyeh, however, what appears on first glance to be colloquial form, does not really promote any plot, and resembles rather a soliloquy, an instance of uttering ones thoughts aloud, without addressing any person in particular.

In the *Hasan and Husain* Ta'ziyeh (Sir Lewis Pelly version) [1] only the manneristically inserted invocations indicate the colloquial structure ("O Han"; "O Muslim"; "O Messenger"; etc.). In the Ta'ziyeh performance the "speechrealm" *(der Sprechraum)* [2] is not identical with the stage, as in the case of the dialogue-based plays of the Western tradition, but also includes the House. Ta'ziyeh librettos which seem to be based on the colloquy, appear in the performance as discourse.

In a discourse a meta-communicative mutual understanding is un-critically reached about what should be considered proved and reasonable.

All the Ta'ziyeh operas are based on discourse in a philosophical sense (Shi'a beliefs), in an aesthetic sense (naïveté as an aesthetic category), and in the theatrical sense (presentational code). An ideal Ta'ziyeh performance has the structure of a discourse which can be analyzed in semeiological terms as a communicative system based on two codes, an *audio-visual* and a *perceptual* code. The first code defines the modality of *acting;* the latter, the modality of *viewing.*[3] In this system the spectator-believer becomes a co-narrator himself. Thus the interplay of the two codes is the most original aspect of the Ta'ziyeh.

The casting is based on the quality of voice; in the perceptual code it signifies, however, a moral value (the high pitched singing voices of the good characters; the low pitched voices of the bad ones). The interplay of acting and viewing has a modality of a discourse, and there is, by definition, no dramatic time in a discourse. Past, present, and future coexist simultaneously in the Ta'ziyeh performance. There is also no specific locality, but all localities are represented simultaneously on its arena stage, which is *die Weltbühne* in a sense similar to the Western morality play tradition. The soliloquial arias convey the plot very poorly as compared with the dialogue; but there is really no need to convey the plot, because it is already known. Any plot in the Ta'ziyeh discourse has only a paradigmatic value. It is communicated through semantic fields of speech, and not through analytical depiction of events. Paradigmatic relations are stressed in an auditory (differentiation of voice qualities) and in a visual way (paradigmatic opposition of red and green).

Any Ta'ziyeh production starts with the establishment of a discourse through the audio-visual code. I do make a distinction here between a dialogue and a discourse. In a dialogue we observe a communicative action of the dialogue partners, while in a discourse as stated above, the mutual understanding has a meta-communicative character and concerns some naïvely accepted prerequisites about what is considered intelligible, substantiated, and reasonable. The naïvely accepted prerequisite of the Ta'ziyeh discourse is a meta-communicative conviction shared by the viewers and the performers about the holiness of the Imam.

In the *Ali Akbar* Ta'ziyeh which serves here as a model for the analysis, the discourse is established through the Karena-players' overture coming from behind the House or from its liminal line (the gate of the *takiyeh);* the initial choral duet of the players who enter through the House is sung on the stage platform to the House. Significantly enough the players in the opening sequence represent only good characters. Their choral duet establishes in the meta-language the elegiac *Grundgestus* of the discourse. However, the self-introduction of the negative characters is kept consistently in the object-language of their roles. Encircling the arena on horseback, they address the House, ignoring the frozen figures of the Hussein party performers. Thus in the perceptual code "on platform" and "off-platform" are not contradictions but an instance of addressing oneself to the House; "on and off-platform" is accepted by the spectator as a specific modality of the production. The established speechrealm embraces the House and the playing area, and makes possible two-directional communication between the performers and the spectators ("Ya Husein"; "Salavat!" exclamations; chest-beating).

As a matter of fact the moments of this two-directional communication are true "climaxes" of Ta'ziyeh in a non-Aristotelian sense. They reveal that the real aim of the Ta'ziyeh is the reinforcement of the feeling of *communitas* between believers on the stage and in the House. This takes the form of a mystical union, and is a ritualistic component in Ta'ziyeh. The true narrator of the story is the spectator-believer who knows the story beforehand; that is to say the complete story exists in the perceptual code only. Ta'ziyeh neither tells the story nor dramatizes it; its performance is therefore neither epic nor dramatic, but confessional. It uses an epic style of acting but is incapable, and also not interested, in presenting alternatives.

Comparisons with the Brecht theatre are superficial and misleading, and are provoked mostly through the manner of acting which presents in the eye of the uninitiated Western observer analogies with the *Verfremdungseffekt*. The Western observer is tempted to confuse style with technique. Brechtian V-Effect expresses a revisionistic and polemical attitude toward reality. This attitude is totally foreign to Ta'ziyeh. Ta'ziyeh is interested in the emotional status quo, namely in the reinforcement of the religious feelings of the spectators and the performers with the redemption effect in mind (the therapeutic element). This is philosophically and artistically not a theatre of alternatives but of confirmation and determination.

The Ta'ziyeh art of acting makes the performer-believer a role carrier *Rollenträger,* not a character.[4] Characters exist only in the perceptual code. Thus, paradoxically, the spectator-believer "plays the character," while the performer plays the role. Or better: the role-carrier is played as a character by the spectator. This again underscores the active role of the perceptual code in a confessional performance.

Rolland Barthes [5] speaks about the carpet of codes. Ta'ziyeh performance creates a real Persian carpet of codes. Through their interplay the discourse is activated and made theatrical. A Ta'ziyeh event is a paradise for an semeiologist. We will limit ourselves only to the most striking examples. The semeiological analysis of Ta'ziyeh is dependent on basic research which is still in an initial stage. Nevertheless, certain features of Ta'ziyeh as a communicative system can be analyzed in semeiological terms.

META-LANGUAGE VERSUS OBJECT-LANGUAGE

(a) The awning of the tent of the *takiyeh* and the representation of a tent on the platform (stage). "A meta-tent" versus an "object-tent": the *takiyeh* awning is a visual "definition" of the space of discourse; the *takiyeh* awning is *"quoted"* as a *pars pro toto* tent in the object-language of the performance; the stage tent is *used* as a requisite. The *takiyeh* tent "makes assertions" about the stage tent in the way a meta-language is used to make assertions about the object-language.

(b) The chest-beating of the director who appears in the playing area and mixes with the performers. This has the character of a stage direction and is therefore a meta-language symbol; the chest-beating of the performers is a symbol in the object-language; the chest-beating of the spectators in relation to the performers' chest-beating is a meta-language symbol, and in relation to the director's, an object-language symbol. Of course this does not undermine the possibility that all the acts are an expression of genuine piety. Semeiologically speaking, stage signification overtakes the House in an act of total semeiosis.

(c) The distribution of cereals among the spectators. Cereals function as a meta-symbol for the left-overs eaten on the Kerbela desert by Hussein's family during the siege.

Symbolic signs are used, such as:

(a) Green versus red used as symbolic representation of Good (Hussein's party) and Evil (Yazid's party).
(b) Throwing straw on one's head signifying sorrow.
(c) A white *kafan* (shroud) symbolizing the approaching death of its wearer.

Stereotyped iconic signs include:

(a) Shemr's finger at his lip signifying amazement, and hitting his thighs signifying anger.
(b) Operatic gestures while singing.
(c) Rhetorical gestures of addressing the House.
(d) The posture of singing and speaking while on horseback.

Stereotyped index signs may be:

(a) A handkerchief for stage crying.
(b) An empty bowl or leather sack for lack of water.
(c) Red spots of stage blood for wounds, etc.

The use of the stereotyped signs in the audio-visual code of the Ta'ziyeh theatre indicates a highly canonized production style. The Iranian popular painting of battle scenes referring to Kerbela preserved the exact documentation of many symbolic signs still alive in today's performing habits. Symbol, index, icon, and other signs enter into complex affiliations of significance. For example, the stage lion (iconic sign), holding in his jaws Hussein's flag (emblem), or pulling out arrows (index sign for wounds) from the bodies of the dead martyrs (iconic sign).

Ta'ziyeh convention also uses syntagmatic blockings[6] (children covered with a blanket); this sign reads that they are hidden and not visible. The props and the requisites are multifunctional, and semeiologically speaking "do read" differently accordingly to the way they are used. Hussein's bed becomes the bed of his General; a chair can, when the situation requires, signify a hill, and then again function as a chair. The representational meaning of the playing area changes constantly as the performers move from platform to platform or through the liminal space around them. The playing area is an abstract referential space in which signification changes with the movement of the performers.

Semeiologically interesting is the operatic aspect of Ta'ziyeh. In the vocal coloratura of the principal performers, language functions on the second articulation level only—we are grasping an attitude but not the particular meaning. This is not unlike the use of verbal material by Robert Wilson and Serban in the New American Theatre. The music in Ta'ziyeh does not usually have any illustrative value and indicates transformations from one sequence to another. This again is not unlike the use of the buzzer by Richard Foreman, to take another example from the New American Theatre.

The semeiological analysis can deal only with certain aspects of the Ta'ziyeh as a communicative system. It is definitely insufficient as a description of the theatre—*Gestalt* Ta'ziyeh. Ta'ziyeh focuses not on producing signs, but on producing signs for *believers*. What is being presented is a horror of signs, not a horror of actions. The "climaxes" of the Ta'ziyeh are purely semeiological, not dramatic. The "climax" is not the physical death of the Imam from the (antidramatic) blows he receives on stage, but the moment when he dresses in a *kafan*. In this moment he becomes a sign carrier of his own martyrdom. The *kafan* is a shirt worn in place of a shroud, and as such, an iconic sign. But it functions also as a sign of death, that is to say as a symbol. This symbolic sign is then used in the fashion of an index, with the red paint spots signifying the wounds. Ta'ziyeh acting is more concerned with the transformation of signs (icon→symbol→index) than with the transformation of "characters."

Ta'ziyeh acting developed its own dramaturgy of signs, distinct from other performing traditions of the world. Maybe the most striking example for the understanding of the Ta'ziyeh's unique performance structure is the symbolic sign of chest-beating. In most performances which I have observed, the "director" gives the performers the signal for chest-beating by hitting his own chest. The director's initial chest-beating is then taken over by the performers, and gradually becomes a stage gestic sign, and paces the movement and the vocal expression of the actors. After being transformed from a stage direction into a stage sign, the chest-beating gradually takes over the House until it becomes a symbolic act unifying all the spectators, and transforming them into participants. At this point, the rhythm of the chest-beating amplified through the House takes over the stage, and as a powerful feedback paces the stage movement, and the "lamentation" of the performers. Now the House is "the director," and on its behalf and under its command the symbolic stage action is performed.

There is a constant attitude of showing, *Gestus des Zeigens* directed toward the audience, and only occasional interaction with other performers. One can speak about "soliloquies as operatic arias" in Ta'ziyeh. The dialogue in terms of two-directional communication occurs between the performer and the spectators and not on stage. They act "to the House," even when they are supposed to address themselves.

There is a powerful performing tradition at work here which takes over all imperfections of craftsmanship. An actor with his eyes fixed on the written text, and his arm gesture addressed to the audience; an actor who virtually plays without eye contact; the stereotyped gestures of singing; the stereotyped, gestured speaking; the symbolic gestures for grief; the iconic stereotyped gestures for anger—all are an expression of very defined performing habits.

Acting on horseback, when the rider and the horse become one *Gestalt;* singing a coloratura which expresses grief; being slow in a "dramatic" situation, and quick in a "non-dramatic" one; the power to sustain the *gestus* of lamentation for an extended period, and to vary it artistically; the chanting; the stage singing; the stage speech of the negative characters as a sign of their negativity; and the high-pitched angelic voices of the good ones as the sign of their nobility; children's choruses, and children's group-acting; the interaction between spectators and actors as members of the *communitas;* "the climax" as a mystical union of believers and a therapeutic relief; the pacing of performers by the gestural signals from the audience (the chest-beating)—all are features of the presentational acting style.

Ta'ziyeh actors are believers carrying their roles on behalf of the other believers gathered in the House. The central notion of the Ta'ziyeh canon—the martyrdom—is visualized symbolically through the *kafan* and its transformations, and not through the transformations of the performer. The performer's ability to carry on a trilling coloratura while receiving deadly wounds is not diminished. There is a whole stage ritual of making the performer a "sign carrier." Long non-dramatic arias by Hussein precede the imposition of the death stigma on his defender, Ali Akbar. The *kafan* is not a costume, but a sign imposed on the costume. Ta'ziyeh convention is not concerned with the anti-suspense effect of symbolic signs, as it is unlikely that the carrier of the death sign can be miraculously saved. Ta'ziyeh convention is obsessed with the stigma of symbolic signs. The Islamic notion of predestination and its fatalistic notion of history are at work here, finding an original theatrical expression.

In Ta'ziyeh the signification comes before the action, and in these terms, it is a non-dramatic theatre event. The signification also precedes narration and after the signs are theatrically established, Ta'ziyeh is no longer interested in a precise rendering of the story. It takes advantage of the fact that the story is known to the audience, and relies on this knowledge. However, this does not make Ta'ziyeh an epic convention.

The paradox of Ta'ziyeh is that being basically a non-epic and non-dramatic event, it produces an epic demonstrative style of acting. The modern Western theatre made its way to epic acting in a polemical strife with the naturalistic tradition of empathy, through the application of the Asiatic techniques, and through the way-breaking mediation of Brecht. Acting in Ta'ziyeh is a part of the great Asiatic tradition. It is focused not on the character, but on the role. The performer appears as a carrier of a predefined character, and concentrates on his role more in relation to the spectators than in relation to himself (empathy) or to the other performers (dramatic interaction). In Western terms acting in Ta'ziyeh is neither Stanislawski nor Brecht. The acting is frontal, expository (to the House which in the *takiyeh* situation is all around), based on stereotyped gestures and masks.

Among Iranologists the story is circulated about a village gendarme playing the role of the Lion in Ta'ziyeh. The fellow suddenly notices his captain in one of the boxes and while on all fours, salutes him with his lion's paw. This delightful story is amazing only for the Western observer who assumes uncritically that all acting is representational. This, however, is not the case with Ta'ziyeh which, being part of the great Asian tradition of presentational acting, does not use either identification or empathetic trance as a necessary condition for performing. Thus the gesture of the Lion-gendarme does not disrupt the integrity of the performance but it is a legitimate aspect of the convention.

A Ta'ziyeh actor cannot "fall out of the role" because he does not identify with it, but carries it in the way the village gendarme carried the skin of the Lion. Therefore the "role carrier" keeps his own identity intact and can react at any time in his capacity as a non-performer. In a Ta'ziyeh performance it is not unusual to see actors on stage drinking tea while waiting their turn.

Ta'ziyeh has to fascinate any theatre critic sensitive to the manifestation of the genuine theatre, and yet being a confessional and therapeutic event, or better, an art form originating from acts of piety, it resists an aesthetic detached analysis from "outside." I suspect that this difficulty exists in the same degree for the Western and the Iranian critic.

A Gothic cathedral or a mosque also originates from acts of piety but it is an object, while theatre is an act of interaction between spectators and performers. In the case of Ta'ziyeh this is a religious and an artistic act which comes into being between believers on the basis of an unwritten contract which is their shared belief. A critic analyzing and appreciating aesthetically a Gothic cathedral or a mosque as a non-believer, does not teel like an intruder. Analyzing Ta'ziyeh as a performance, he has to feel like an intruder. Only participation would give him a status of belonging but it would also prevent him from watching it aesthetically. Obviously this is a vicious circle, a no-exit situation.

For the secular Iranian theatre there is a great opportunity to utilize the conventions of the Ta'ziyeh performing style. Having such a defined tradition of presentational acting is an advantage over the Western theatre. The naturalistic acting style, with its simplistic concept of performer-character-spectator empathy, promoted all over the world through film and television, and still strong in the bourgeois theatre, can be countered in Iran in alliance with its own performing tradition. This could mean not only the secularization of the convention, but paradoxically, also a protection of the religious theatre in its own realm from the invasion of a bastardized naturalism.

I have been describing here the Ta'ziyeh performance as an interaction model of symbolic signification. It is obvious that in such a model the terms "director," "performer," "spectator," "audience" become relative, and we are in need of new terminology. But this is exactly what makes Ta'ziyeh unprecedented among ancient performing conventions still alive. Iran is a unique place where this convention can be studied, learned, and perhaps applied in a secularized version to the reform of the theatre which is in the hearts and minds of the contemporary innovators.

NOTES

1. Sir Lewis Pelly, *The Miracle Play of Hasan and Husain* (London; Wm. Allen, 1879).

2. I am using the term "speechrealm" in the sense similar to what new linguistics calls "communicative situation" (Kommunikationssituation). "Sprecher und Hörer befinden sich in einer gemeinsamen, durch sozial-pragmatische und individuelle Faktoren bestimmten Situation, in der Zeichen gebraucht werden." Th. Lewandowski, *Linguistisches Wörterbuch* (Heidelberg: UTB, 1973). Speechrealm is a symbolic space in which an interactive and communicative process takes place.

3. Compare in this respect M. Wekwerth, *Theater und Wissenschaft* (München: Hanser, 1974). He describes the art of acting and the art of viewing as subsystems of the main system theatre.

4. Compare D. Steinbeck, *Einführung in die Theorie und Systematik der Theaterwissenschaft* (Berlin: de Gruyter, 1970). Steinbeck makes an important distinction between the actor *(der Schauspieler),* the role-carrier *(der Rollenträger),* and the role *(die Rolle).* "Er (der Schauspieler) ist Spieler, insofern er den Rollenträger darstellerisch entfaltet, aber zugleich ein 'Gespielter,' insofern die Rolle auf das Verhalten des Rollenträgers und dieser auf das Spiel in dem er entfaltet wird, Einfluss nimmt." (p. 190)

5. R. Barthes, *S/Z* (New York: Hill and Wang, 1974).

6. Syntagmatic blockings; I call them so as an analogy to the linguistic concept of the syntagma (combination of words into a group).

5

Literary and Musical Developments in the Ta'ziyeh

The purpose of this essay is to provide a brief analysis of the literary developments which have occurred in the Ta'ziyeh over the past two centuries. Since my topic is closely related to the musical and theatrical aspects, I will touch briefly on them as well. With few exceptions, I have relied solely on personal observation and original Ta'ziyeh scripts rather than on the assumptions and opinions of other critics.[1] By employing a comparative and analytical approach, I hope to shed light on changes which have taken place in the Ta'ziyeh.

Contrary to what many critics both past and present believe, the Ta'ziyeh is not a simple or well-defined cultural phenomenon which surfaced at a specific date in history. Rather, it developed gradually over the course of centuries as a result of various social, religious, cultural, artistic and philosophical factors. It assumed its current form sometime during the latter part of the Safavid period.[2] Like the Shi'a religion, the Ta'ziyeh first took root among the common people, both in the villages and in the cities of Iran. Gradually it spread to higher levels of society and finally gained popularity with the elite. This development did not occur everywhere at the same time, and in the majority of villages and small towns in Iran today the

40

Ta'ziyeh has retained its religious format. But in Tehran and in some of the other large cities, it gradually shed its simple, semi-theatrical aspects and evolved from a primitive Passion play into serious drama. The literary and artistic changes in the Ta'ziyeh which came about as a result of social and historical developments reached their peak during and shortly after the reign of Naser al-Din Shah.

Even a festive and entertaining version called *Gusheh* developed which had little or no relation to the real Ta'ziyeh. Ta'ziyeh performers stuck "reams of glue" on the traditional Ta'ziyeh format. In the process of its evolution from a straightforward Passion play into a detailed and complex drama, it acquired considerable embellishment. The theatrical and dramatic aspects increased while the opera-like qualities decreased. These changes resulted in improvements in both quality and content. While historians and critics frequently refer to these changes, they have never been adequately studied. For example, Shadravan Abdullah Mustowfi[3] claims that in the time of Naser al-Din Shah charitable contributions were made to promote the Ta'ziyeh. Mustowfi claims that Ta'ziyeh scripts were revised by people like Mirza Muhammad Taqi and Mu'in al-Buka, and that other writers such as Shahab Isfahani developed and arranged new scripts under the patronage of Mirza Taqi Khan Amir.[4] Unfortunately, Mustowfi's comments are brief and non-specific.

Changes in the fundamental elements of the Ta'ziyeh (the music, the poetry and the theatrics) were not uniform. Whenever one element changed, it naturally affected the others. This interconnection has never been thoroughly analyzed. While separating the music from the literature is not the most profitable way to study the Ta'ziyeh, in the interests of simplicity I have done so here, analyzing first the changes in the music and in some of the theatrical aspects, and second, the changes in the text, but always recognizing the interrelationship between these basic components.

The dimensions of the Ta'ziyeh can be broken into three categories. The Ta'ziyeh story-lines are either historical (like the *Ta'ziyeh of Muslim and Ali*) or pure fable (like *Div-e b'aerelm*) or a combination of the two (like the majority of Ta'ziyeh). The instruments and props can also be divided into three categories. Some are real, such as swords and horses, while others are symbolic, such as wash tubs, nets, and black veils. There are also some that are purely decorative such as nuptial chambers and flags. The characters may also be divided into three groups: the heroes, the villains, and those in-between. I do not intend to address the issue of the reality of these three categories or their historical, philosophical, or sociological roots, but only to draw attention to two fundamental points: (1) In its evolutionary cycle, the Ta'ziyeh took on a greater sense of theatrical realism while straying from its religious and historical roots. (2) The entertaining and pleasing literary aspects of the Ta'ziyeh are a result of extraordinary figures of speech which satisfy both the needs and the expectations of the audience.

41

If this style of composition had disappeared, there would be no Ta'ziyeh today. Efforts have continued to perfect the style and to improve all elements. One should not look at only one aspect of the Ta'ziyeh and try to pass judgment on the whole.

THEATRICAL AND ARTISTIC CHANGES IN THE TA'ZIYEH

The Ta'ziyeh was originally a simple Passion play about the events which occurred at Kerbela and the other tragedies which befell the House of the Prophet. It was an exercise in mourning, a religious custom severely limited in scope. The Ta'ziyeh reciters were coffee-house storytellers limited to straight narration of long-winded, repetitious monologues. Their poetry was simple, loose, and full of colloquial expressions. It was generally written in light verse called *masnavi* (poetry consisting of distiches rhyming between themselves) and sometimes had no rhyme at all. To capture the attention of the spectators and to fire their emotions, the Ta'ziyeh narrator would often mix groans and signs with vulgar, market-place vocabulary. Colloquial expressions such as "Woe is me," "I'm your servant," "Brother-less," etc., were commonplace. The music consisted of a single monotonous beat and was sung in the pitch normally used by mourners. All action centered around the protagonists. The Ta'ziyeh writers were so violently opposed to the Imam's enemies that they de-emphasized the roles of the antagonists. With this simple standard as their guide, subjectively they made every effort to avoid the catastrophic events. "Audience," "reality," and "scene" were not yet issues.

The antagonists were made to appear ridiculous by the frivolous and buffoon-like behavior of the actors playing the parts. For example, an actor playing Shemr might attempt to elicit tears from the audience not by word or gesture but by imitating extremely savage, cruel behavior (such as pretending to behead a corpse and then dragging it across the stage).

There was no room for creativity or initiative. As for musical instruments, only the drum and the trumpet were utilized. But in this evolutionary period, the Ta'ziyeh writers gradually grew more sophisticated and more discerning. They developed a greater awareness of the importance of theatrical and artistic detail even though they were unable or perhaps simply did not wish to observe the logical relationships between the various Ta'ziyeh tales—perhaps because of their own prejudices and the particular place they occupied in the society of the time. Nonetheless, their view of the Ta'ziyeh differed greatly from that of the earlier writers. For example, they increased the number of scenes involving the antagonists. But, while they recognized Shemr and Ibn Sa'd as military leaders, they invariably portrayed them eating, drinking and reveling in the midst of their strategy sessions! The Ta'ziyeh writers were, in effect, killing two birds with one stone. While placing greater emphasis on the dramatic and epic aspects of the Ta'ziyeh, they were also hanging the sin of drinking wine during the mourning period for the Imam around the necks of Shemr and Ibn Sa'd! They realized that the more forcefully they portrayed the roles of the antagonists the more heroic the protagonists would appear. At the time of Naser al-Din Shah, the Ta'ziyeh writer was a strict Shi'ite, a true believer who hated Shemr with such passion that he would overemphasize Shemr's wickedness and lack of mercy. But, contrary to the earlier Ta'ziyeh writer, he did not, perhaps for historical reasons, consider Shemr to be an infidel or polytheist.

Whether intentional or not, phrases like *enshallah* (if God wills it) crept into the lines spoken by the actor playing Shemr. For example, in a free verse version attributed to the city of Kashan, Shemr, while mounting his horse to journey to Kerbela, says:

> It is time I make haste, Enshallah,
> Stirrup the foot of high purpose, Enshallah,
> Visit in Damascus the Great Sultan of the Faithful,
> Bearing wine, I am on my way, Enshallah.

But even though the titles of the antagonists were elevated to their actual historical positions, in practice, the actors performing these roles continued to belittle and ridicule the characters. The ability of the best Ta'ziyeh writers to elevate the position of the antagonists while at the same time maintaining a sense of derision toward them was a real artistic accomplishment of the period.[5] Changes were also made in methods of enacting battle scenes. Some performers developed extraordinary dexterity in swordsmanship and various other combat techniques. Gradually, props and equipment also grew more elaborate. Items such as flagstaffs, butcher's hooks, and even a throne and a court for Yazid were introduced. In order to portray animals, lions for example, actual skins were utilized. In Takiyeh Dowlat (the Government arena-like theatre especially constructed in Tehran for Ta'ziyeh performances) in the Ta'ziyeh *The Lion of Fasseh,* instead of a man dressed up in a lion skin, an actual lion was used.[6]

The musical instruments also became more varied. Kettle-drums, cymbals, horns, clarinets, and various trumpets were introduced. Special songs were written which corresponded to the respective positions and titles of the protagonists. For example Hurr and the Abbass were given tunes with rising epic-like melodies. Ali Akbar and Qasem were given *chahar gah, seh gah* and *Isfahan* modes while the Imam was given dignified serious tunes which, while somber, communicated a sense of peace and hope (such as *nava* mode). During this period, even happy songs with up-beat tempos were written for the protagonists' feasting scenes and for the noncombatant roles of Europeans, Zoroastrians, Jews, etc. An interesting point in this regard is the unique quality of the music. For example, when Gabriel or another angel sang, bells chimed in an attempt to recreate a proper sense of heavenly revelation. The actors playing these parts spoke clearly and rapidly and in time with the music. They became specialists at drawing out the last word of a sentence.[7] Even the voices of the dead were created with a view toward the particular status of the corpse. For example, the dead man whom Imam Reza helps during his first night in the grave recites poetry with a tune similar to the song of angels (Nakir and Munker) and that of the Imam. But the other dead, if they had been relatively good people, were made to groan and wail. They were portrayed in a mixed mode, between that of the villains and the saints. An other unique feature of this period is the use of symmetrical dialogue. For example, in a dialogue between Imam Hussein and Ali Akbar, if the Imam recites in one key, Ali Akbar had to use the same one. The writers utilized similar but different pitches in order to introduce variety and beauty to the verse while at the same time maintaining the principle that each character should recite in a meter suitable to his station in life. They were thus able ever so slightly to vary the quality and mode of the music.

For example, at the beginning of the *Ta'ziyeh of Muslem* (Tehran version, Takiyeh Dowlat and other bits of copy), the Imam recites in *nava* and Muslem in *mahoor*. As we know, the musical figures used in *rak* and *eraq mahoor* are common or similar to those used in *nava*. Obviously this type of artistry is impossible without talented and creative performing artists who have complete mastery of their subjects. Two points should be mentioned in this regard:

(1) In the Ta'ziyeh, the term "combination" singing [8] which is frequently heard should not be confused with "irregular" singing or "mixed" singing commonly found in early Ta'ziyeh. Nor should it be mistaken for the same expression frequently used by musicians performing traditional Iranian music. According to one musical expert, "combination" singing may be defined as follows: "While singing in one key a very quick hint of another key is made. This hint must be made quickly, so delicately and so gently that the ear of the listener is not even slightly jarred and the listener is barely aware that a change in key has even occurred." [9]

(2) Except in a few cases, a Ta'ziyeh performer did not recite to a scale or to a connected musical score. Rather, the actors used whatever notes and melodies they needed for a particular scene.

Master Ta'ziyeh performers occasionally changed mode and tone as the action demanded. They even introduced unique rhymes and rhythms to the traditional dirges. The music, the voice, the face, the physique, and especially the particular role assigned to the performer were of prime importance to the spectators. Some veteran actors developed their own personal styles. These performers made unique contributions to the development of Ta'ziyeh music. For example, some invented special methods of poetry recital. They developed excellent timing, an ability to lay stress on certain words and phrases, and an ability to raise or lower their voices along with many other theatrical gimmicks.[10] Not every Ta'ziyeh performer with a good voice could master the art well enough to be successful.[11] Generally speaking, Ta'ziyeh poetry and its poetic format was selected with a view toward its compatibility with the music or particular theatrical setting. The task of the talented Ta'ziyeh writers (unfortunately not all were talented) was not simply to write poetry or poetic phrases but to concentrate on the dramatic and musical aspects as well. Thus, an analysis of the relationships between the poetry, the music, and the histrionics is essential.

LITERARY CHANGES IN THE TA'ZIYEH

Because of its simple and commonplace nature, the Ta'ziyeh from the standpoint of literature never attracted the attention of men of letters. Those critics who have come to appreciate the Ta'ziyeh as an art form consider its value to lie in its theatrical and cultural aspects. The poetry is viewed as slack, commonplace, and artless—doggerel which some feel has not progressed over the entire course of its history.[12] Critics have not even found fit to praise its simple language.

The descriptive terms "simple" and "popular" are, like everything else, only relative: why then, should we compare Ta'ziyeh poetry with other versified pieces? With which, from what standpoints, and by whose standards? [13] For example, during the reign of Naser al-Din Shah many varieties of mourning poetry were composed. Some were rather lengthy and eloquent, others were simple and geared to the masses. *Farhan Khuda Parasti* by Mirza Muharram might be considered one of the former variety and *Tuhfatulzakareen* by Bidel Mazandarani one of the latter. If we compare the poetry of these two works with Ta'ziyeh poetry, we discover just how rich the latter actually is; and, from the standpoint of literature, we realize that not every vacuous and tasteless poem can be considered popular literature and not every grandiloquent verse a literary work. Those who think this way undoubtedly are looking at the issue from a fixed, general viewpoint without taking into consideration the evolutionary changes in the Ta'ziyeh over the course of nearly two centuries. Generally speaking, from the standpoint of poetic beauty, Ta'ziyeh poetry is loose and written in the vernacular. It is simple but beautiful, flowing, eloquent, and charming.

The Ta'ziyeh as indigenous popular theatre naturally utilizes the ordinary speech of the market place and the street—and the everyday conversational language of common people is not uniform. But ugly, indecent and vulgar slang must not be substituted for simple speech. The contribution which the artistic and creative Ta'ziyeh writer made (not all of them, unfortunately) was to mix the plain language of the people with eloquent, literary expressions and subtle theatrical techniques. They created valuable pieces of literature which should not be simply passed over. Ta'ziyeh scripts have never been carefully analyzed from a textual standpoint. The changes which took place were not simly stylistic: rather, they constituted an all-encompassing evolutionary process which affected all aspects of the Ta'ziyeh.

As has already been pointed out, early Ta'ziyeh poetry was generally loose, simple, and often unversified.[14] Early Ta'ziyeh writers, because of their literary and intellectual limitations, resorted to market-place slang to express their emotions. Examples of this may be found in an old manuscript of the *Martyrdom of Abbas*. The dispute between Shemr and Ibn Sa'd appears more like an argument between two fools rather than a dispute between military commanders.[15]

> You dog, fear not Abbas the General,
> There stands a man, Abbas, the brave,
> If I should meet the son of Sa'd tonight
> I'll tell him, "Wait, you dog, 'till light.[16]

This was the quality of the poetry. Now, if we compare this script with later ones, we shall see a tremendous difference.

Let us turn to another example from the same scene. Shemr enters the stage from behind the backdrop. He is returning from Kufa. He says:

> From Kufa I come with legions numerous,
> To join Ibn Sa'd, the Commander luminous,
> This perfumed land, Ah, tis a sight to embrace
> A barren desert turned into a market place
> As if the antelope's musk spilled onto this plain
> Or King Solomon laid down goods from his train.

And in another text:

> The King of Damascus and the King of Zanzibar. [blasphemy]
> Raising high their standard, throw cruelty into heart of the cruel legions.
> While the moon's radiance shines on the firmament's portico. . . .

Also in a similar fashion note Shemr's debate with Ibn Sa'd:

> What ails thee, black-hearted friend of mine,
> Why such haste to murder the House of the Ali,
> Lay back and sip your wine.

Shemr: Come. cup bearer, fill my cup
                By sipping it then my stature grows. . . .[17]

Early Ta'ziyeh poetry was generally written in a light verse style called
masnavi. One can say that the use of the *masnavi* style is one of the
distinctive characteristics of early scripts. The *chakamah* (elegy), the
mosammat (multiple poem) and the *tarjih* (strophied poem) are among the
various types of quatrains which inventive modern Ta'ziyeh writers contributed to the poetic arts. The addition of a *radif* format was another major
contribution. Examples of this may be seen below in three different texts
from the *Ta'ziyeh of the Elder Fatemeh*. Fatemeh is speaking and the texts
read as follows:

Old Text:

            O Moslems, may hope spring from your loneliness,
            I am alone and my friends mourn their loneliness,
            Where is a comrade to inquire after me,
            O woe is me, woe betide me. . . .[18]

A Later Text:

            Lord, with father's departure my courage has fled,
            Both quiet days and sleepless nights I dread,
            Happy days, there are no more for me,
            Since father has gone away from me.[19]

A Modern Takiyeh Dowlat Text:

            I am not well, a stranger in my homeland, O father, Other
                than Jeddeh, I have no nurse, O father,
            When you went to Kerbela, you failed to remember
            That you left behind a sick daughter, O father.

Obviously, the use of *radif* makes the task of the poet more difficult and
proper word selection all the more onerous. But there are several benefits.
First of all, the poetry reads more easily and sounds better. Secondly, *radif*
greatly affects the music because, in recital, the last sounds can be drawn
out and made more musical. Thirdly, it adds freshness and variety because
the limitations of the format force the poet to invent new rhetorical phrases
to fit the meter. With free verse the average poet tends simply to regurgitate
the thoughts and ideas of his predecessors. And finally, the use of *radif*
increases the number of metaphors and allusions.[20]

    In early Ta'ziyeh, dialogue, whether in the form of question and answer or narrative, was generally arranged in a multi-couplet framework. The number of distiches in each section sometimes ran as high as twenty to twenty seven. But, in recent years, conversation between two characters (question and answer) generally has taken the form of either two couplets or one couplet and a hemistich. The sections were thus reduced and allocated to a special form of chanting, an oratorical form, or to straight descriptive narrative. This change greatly affected the movement and theatrics of the Ta'ziyeh.

Repetitive phrases in the early Ta'ziyeh were frequent. They assumed several forms:

1. *The repetition of certain words or expressions,* such as: "Your slave," "I am a sacrifice," etc. Such phrases are so frequent in early Ta'ziyeh that many critics consider them characteristic of the unique style and literary tradition of the early scripts. Excess verbiage such as the colloquial use of the word *Ke* (that) at the beginning of a sentence is another trait. "That oh Orphan, Hassan should be your sacrifice...." "That at your doorway an army of angels stands in need and...," are but two examples.[21]

2. *Repetition of meter and verse.* This flaw, in addition to making the poetry monotonous, makes the music tedious and boring. For example, in one of the early versions of the *Ta'ziyeh of Qasem* (ascribed to the latter part of the twelfth century, lunar hegiric calendar) only one meter is used from the time Qasem first seeks permission from the Imam to join the *Jihad* (the holy war) through his wedding and leave-taking scenes *(mujtas* meter). "That oh Orphan, Hassan should be your sacrifice...." In more modern versions, however, a variety of verse is utilized.

3. *Repetitive Content:* Repetition was not limited to versification alone. The actual content, too, was repetitive. For example, in the *Ta'ziyeh of Qasem* ascribed to Chodzko, when Qasem begs the Imam's permission to participate in the *Jihad,* the dialogue between the two is composed of five or six versified segments, all of which share more or less the same meaning. But in modern Takiyeh Dowlat and Qazvin versions, each segment, even each couplet, carries a different meaning. If the content sometimes requires repetition, the style shifts. We can cite many examples where innovative Ta'ziyeh writers have breathed new life into the sterile corpus of earlier Ta'ziyeh poetry by creating new metaphors and allusions to replace the long discourses and literary prolixity of the early versions. For example, in the *Ṭa'ziyeh of the Martyrdom of the Imam,* there is a conversation between the Imam and Ibn Sa'd which occupies several segments. A relatively early version reads as follows:

The Imam: O Ibn Sa'd, black oppression's your code,
         O woe unto you, cruel, worthless rogue,
         Of the Almighty Lord, have you no fear?
         For the Creator Himself to us shall appear.

Ibn Sa'd:	I know of your rank and your stature, O Hussein
	Of your power, your purity and of your Fame. . . .[22]

But in a modern Takiyeh Dowlat version, after the Imam delivers his ultimatum to Ibn Sa'd the latter replies:

> Is the leader commanding us with suras and logical thought?
> Your ignorance of the Koran affects us not.
> You yourself comprehend the gist of my meaning,
> For one must not seek wisdom in every Loghman's keening.
> Listen to me and obey the Lord's servant's bid,
> Yazid rules today from Arabia to Iransoxiana,
> And how can the teeth be pained by a knot which the Hands undid?

The Imam:	How can I, O Lord, answer the words of this heathen,
	He invites me to infamous Sham to give up my faith and my reason.
	To Khalilullah he says, come, worship idols,
	To Zabihullah he says, come, share our leaven.
	If the Word for this nation is the Prophet's Koran,
	The Caliphate deems me worthy to open it and learn from its wisdom.

Then, after a moment of silence,

> Seeing me without troops he supposes me powerless,
> If I want blood to cover this field like a sea. . . .[23]

The use of various literary words and expressions combined with military, civil, and court expressions (such as Royal Farman, etc.) broadened the range of dialogue [24] and contributed greatly to the general quality of the poetry.

Borrowing phrases from the classical poets and embellishing Ta'ziyeh poetry with figures of speech merely to allow the poet to demonstrate his own craftsmanship or to amuse himself does not constitute good poetry. As mentioned earlier, borrowing was done primarily for theatrical reasons. Some wonderful poetry was created in the process. The following quotation which is attributed to an unknown poet from Saveh, called Savjeh, is a good example. It is taken from his version of the *Martyrdom of Abbas.*

> I am Shemr who has eulogized you,
> All mortal men I will host for you,
> Now among my legions, now among our tents,
> All this I have planned, all this is my desire for you. . . .[25]

We should also note Shemr's challenge *(mubarezeh Khani)* to Ibn Sa'd in a modern Takiyeh Dowlat version of the *Martyrdom of the Imam.*[26]

> Leader, would you among Kings be a servant?
> Ignite sparks in your heart, come out from your tent,
> Like a giant dragon, mouth gaping in anger
> Trotting and neighing, rolling thunder in springtime
> Brave men surround you, rough rugged riders
> With daggers drawn, curved like the arch of a
> woman's brow.

This is an imitation of the famous elegy by Qaani.[27]

In the excerpt quoted below, which is a conversation between Shemr and Ibn Sa'd, notice how the art of parallel construction is employed. The technique improves the poetry and greatly increases the overall dramatic impact.

Ibn Sa'd: You spread rancor, I will show cruelty,
You execute orders, I will give commands.

Shemr: You give commands, you general the field.
I will sever Hussein's head from his pure body.

Ibn Sa'd: You will sever Hussein's head from his pure body.
I will impale it on a pike.

Shemr: You will impale it on a pike.
I will grind his body into bits with horses' hooves.

Ibn Sa'd: You will grind his body into bits with horses' hooves.
I will cast terror into the hearts of those on the battlefield.

Shemr: You will cast terror into the hearts of those on the
battlefield
I will rope the necks of his weeping children, like gazelles.

Some Ta'ziyeh writers, however, were ignorant of the techniques and subtleties of composing poetry for theatre. They overindulged themselves in imitating the classical poets and in their use of literary rhetoric. For example, in this same conversation between Shemr and Ibn Sa'd, some writers borrowed heavily from classical Persian literature. An example of this overindulgence is cited below. In the example quoted, one of Hafez's lyric poems is stuck into the framework of a *mosammat* poem with unfortunate results.

Abbas: O shameless infidel, how long will you your religion ignore,
            And sail a rudderless ship with no port in store,
            Like me, you should willingly pass through our
                Master's door,
            Even though you be given a Kingdom, this I implore,
            Your wealth amounts to nothing.

Almost all the distiches of this famous Hafez *qazal* have been borrowed in
the form of a *mukhammas* [28] (a poem in which each stanza consists of five
hemistitches), with Abbas reciting the first strophe and Shemr the following. This poetry, while aesthetically pleasing, was little utilized in Ta'ziyeh
performances because the poet wanders far afield from the main subject of
the play.

Another Ta'ziyeh writer, who allegedly lived during the reign of
Muzzafar al-Din Shah, composed a similar elegy for Shemr's *mubarezeh
khani* or call to combat, decorating and embellishing his verse with a
particular form of rhetoric.

> O Sultan astride the palace carpet and the Khan
> Who ruled the world,
> The great Sulaiman and the fair Loghman, wiseman and
>   astronomer,
> All were created through your combat, your will-power
>   and your generosity,
> The world was fresh and loving then,
> Without sorrow or hatred or shame,
> Thanks to the reality of you, the existence of you,
> The presence of you.[29]

The writer seemed unaware that this type of artificial poetry is completely inappropriate for Ta'ziyeh. Moreover, the main reason for having
Shemr and Ibn Sa'd praise the Imam's virtues is to highlight more effectively the meanness of his enemies. The above quotation conveys no such
meaning.

Generally speaking, the literary expressions which entered Ta'ziyeh
poetry can be placed in two categories, the grandiose and the delicate.
Words in the first category are to be found mainly in elegies, *mosammat*
verse, and in combat descriptions and epic-like sections, while those in the
second are used to express or describe grief. This categorization demonstrates well the artistic sensitivities of the Ta'ziyeh writers of this particular
period. In the passage below, attributed to Mirza Huhammad Taqi al-Buka,
the poet masterfully mixes colloquial words and expressions with literary
rhetoric, thus creating a powerful work of art, which represents the very

51

best of Ta'ziyeh poetry. The dialogue takes place when Imam Hussein, astride his horse, Zuljenah, and about to depart for the battlefield is confronted by his little daughter, Rughiyeh. She is standing on a raised area and cries out to her father. With no musical accompaniment and in heart-rending, childish tones, she pleads with her father in broken, blank verse.

Rughiyeh: Father. you're going away. leaving me an orphan.

The Imam: O Heaven. above. what trials have you wrought?

Rughiyeh: Father. after you're gone. Shemr will bind me up.

The Imam: He will bind you and your sisters with one chain.

Rughiyeh: Daddy. my throat is so parched I'm burning.

The Imam: I too am burning with thirst.

Rughiyeh: Father dear. let me tell you something.

The Imam: Tell me. don't cry. Rughiyeh. my little daughter.

Rughiyeh: Get down from your horse. I am so sad.

The Imam: (dismounting and walking toward Rughiyeh)
May the Lord have mercy on the Shi'ites. my little darling.

Rughiyeh: Draw an emblem on your battledress to serve as my
light.

The Imam: (caressing Rughiyeh)
My eyes. O light of my eyes. my little one. my little prisoner.

Rughiyeh: Let me go father. I'll kiss you under your throat.
(She kisses him under his throat).

The Imam: Kiss me. O my soul. I am a sacrifice to all your hopes
and dreams.

The ability to write with specific detail and vividly portray various events and states of mind requires creativity, sensitivity, and a powerful imagination; qualities which the unsophisticated, early Ta'ziyeh writers lacked. They tended to summarize and generalize every event. As a result, they found it necessary to fill up the time allocated for the presentation of the Ta'ziyeh, which was almost three house, with long-winded dialogues. We have already seen examples of this in the *Martyrdom of Abbas* when Shemr meets Ibn Sa'd after returning from Kufa, when he goes in back of the Imam's and Abbas's camp, and when he sends a letter to Abbas pledging safety in return for surrender. The early Ta'ziyeh writers greatly oversimplified these events, describing them in only the most general terms. The modern writers, on the other hand, paid attention to detail. They carefully observed time frames and proper sequence of events. Shemr's monologue conveys a mixture of false bravado and a fear of Abbas. The audience can perceive Abbas as an undefeatable warrior while realizing, at the same time, that his martyrdom is imminent. Ibn Sa'd's quarrel with Shemr, their initial cautious policies, and man's violent yet sometimes frivolous nature are masterfully portrayed. Shemr's letter to Abbas is made to appear to be a deceitful ploy, which in fact it was. Shemr convenes a strategy session with the other division commanders. While drinking wine and carrying on, he screams out his orders, and after a few moments, gets up to head for Abbas's camp. Shemr awakens Abbas from his sleep. The argument which ensues is one of the finest debates in all Ta'ziyeh literature.

It has already been mentioned that early Ta'ziyeh performers excited the emotions of their audiences by imitating vulgar, despicable acts. The modern performers, however, achieved the same results through good theatre—excellent poetry, excellent direction, and excellent acting. The relationship between dialogue and acting is of particular interest. For example, compare versions of the same *Ta'ziyeh of Abbas* in the scene where Shemr and Ibn Sa'd attack Abbas's tents.

The early script reads as follows:

Shemr: O daughter of the Lord's messenger
Come out from the women's quarters
The time for your enslavement has come
And in misery and misfortune be carried off to Sham
[Damascus].

The Imam: How shameless is this misguided horde
By the Family of the Prophet. Allah Akbar! [God is great]
Zainab, fetch Ali's two-edged sword
And bring me my weapons of war.

In the latter version, the excitement of this dramatic confrontation is brought to a fever pitch, proper poetic symmetry is observed, a longer time-span elapses, and additional events take place simultaneously.
The following is an example:

53

Shemr, exuding false courage and bravado, encircles Abbas's camp with Ibn Sa'd and his soldiers.

> O Zainab, sister of the evil-doer's offspring,
> Admit now who is the better King,
> Yazid's brutal and bloodthirsty army is here
> To lay the foundations of his empire.
> Awaken Hussein, tell him who makes this
>   commotion
> That it is Shemr out here yelling at him.

Zainab, startled and anxious, dashes from one side of the stage to the other, saying:

> What tumult threatens the King of Ray, Woe betide us,
> They're killing Zurrah's son, O woe, O injustice.[30]

Ta'ziyeh writers paid special attention to developing to the greatest extent possible a sense of integrity and unity between the music and the action by carefully selecting the verse, the meter, and by alternating the timing between parts. *Rajaz-Khani* and epic poetry are generally in the *mutaqarib* meter. The *monkat,* a verse-form which is average in terms of length, was utilized when there was a need to convey urgency and anxiety. The poetry was written in light verse. *Musammat* and *mustezad* were, as a rule, utilized for descriptive narrative, and *taraneh* for mournful dirges and hymns. For example, when Qasem falls from his horse and Shemr and Ibn Sa'd converse with him, a question-and-answer format is used in which one hemistitch is written in a specific meter, appropriate for recital to the accompaniment of the quick rhythm of the music. Why? Because the denouement is approaching and the Ta'ziyeh writer wants to communicate to the audience a sense of impending crisis. Occasionally, a verse written in a somber meter was changed by the actor in the performance because in his judgment the original meter was not suitable for the character being portrayed. In such instances, the rhythm of the sentences and the syllables is very important. For example, in the Martyrdom of Abbas, when Rughiyeh goes to her uncle and confides in him, telling him her private thoughts, she recites a poem with no rhythm and in childish tones:

> O General without troops
> My gallant Uncle
> Standard bearer of Hussein's army
> Shah of my world
> Do you remember, Uncle, in our homeland how you
>   engaged my cousin
> To marry Ali Khan?

Such a party, such festivities you arranged!
All of Medina was lit up then,
How my heart is filled with rue.[31]

Because the Ta'ziyeh performers' principal goal in changing the poetry of the script was to improve the performance and not simply to show off their own poetic talents, sometimes, instead of composing a totally new poem, they borrowed or adapted old texts. They did this in the following ways:

(1) When they found a poem in another poet's works which seemed suitable, they borrowed it verbatim, or changed a few hemistitches, or added or subtracted some couplets. For example, in the *Ta'ziyeh of the Elder Fatemeh,* a section of the opening poem is taken word for word from *Tufan al-Buka.*[32] Also, in the *Ta'ziyeh of Muslem* (Tehran and Takiyeh Dowlat versions), the conversation in the opening section between the Imam and Muslem is adapted from the same book, the only difference being the rearranging of a few couplets and hemistitches.[33]

(2) Some poems in the old Ta'ziyeh collections were ruined by attempts at improvement and adaptation. At first, we might theorize that the Ta'ziyeh writers had no well thought out purpose in selecting what they appropriated or in making their adaptations—that they only did it to make their own work easier and hence to avoid the agony of original composition: or else they happened by chance to find a suitable piece which they felt could be slipped into their own Ta'ziyeh. But a close examination of many plays proves this theory false. Not only is it more difficult for a poet to fit pieces from other poets into his own work than it is to write a simple original, but also there are other factors which prove that the Ta'ziyeh writers were completely aware of what they were doing. For example:

(a) The opening couplet which Za'far Jena recites in the *Ta'ziyeh of the Imam* (Tehran, Qazvin and perhaps other versions) is as follows:

I am your most insignificant servant, Za'far Jena
Your service has arrived. The army of Jena. . . .

This is taken from *Tufan al-Buka,* cited earlier. But the response which the Imam gives to Za'far is taken from a poem by Bidel.[34]

On this transitory earth, in this fleeting world
No man is ever immortal. . . .

If the writer had simply wanted to find a piece of poetry which contained an answer for the Imam, it would have been much simpler to have lifted a complete section from either *Tufan al-Buka* or *Matemkedeh* because the Imam's response is in both. We note, however, that the writer went to the trouble of selecting one from each. Why? Because he realized that the meter

55

and the quality of the two poems differ and each is suitable for its particular place in the text.

(b) In the *Martyrdom of Imam Hussein,* there is a poem which Hussein addressed to Ibn Sa'd and his legions from Kufa:

> I belong to the honored family of the Lord's worshippers
> Recipient of Gabriel's tidings. . . .

This particular piece is taken from a book written by Mahmud Ibn Kazem Mazandarani. Only three or four couplets are borrowed. Others are taken from Bidel's book. An example is:

> Although I am part Arab,
> Today in my own land, I am a stranger.

The borrowed sections again consist of only a few couplets. If the writers had not recognized and understood the unique qualities of each they could not have made such wide selections.

THE EVOLUTION OF THE TA'ZIYEH PERFORMANCE

Different types of Ta'ziyeh performances evolved gradually. The texts of early versions were simple and overly generalized. Only later on were they embellished. These embellishments, meaning the *Gusheh* format and other amendments which were appended to the original versions, were part of the evolutionary process which changed passion plays into drama. Happy incidents, epic tales, and fables were inserted into the text; for example, Abbas's interception by Hurr, or Abbas by Ali Akbar, the ceremony in the *Martyrdom of Abbas* involving the four generals, and Qasem's fight with the sons of Arzagh do not appear in early versions. It should be recognized, however, that many of these new sections such as the incident depicting the coming of the Lord to help the Imam bring fire, water, and earth to aid him during his martyrdom, etc., were not often performed for various reasons.

Embellishments did not occur only in the old scripts. Another form called *Gusheh* was invented which was built around old stories and tales, some historical, some pure fable. These new Ta'ziyeh were amusing and humorous. While the *Gusheh* began even before the reign of Naser al-Din Shah, only a handful remain in existence today. *Gusheh* content is generally simple and popular such as *'Aghe Valadain, Selling the Shi'a's Son,* etc. These Ta'ziyeh offshoots were performed as introductory pieces prior to the commencement of the actual Ta'ziyeh. Little by little, these *Gusheh* broke away from the original Ta'ziyeh and developed their own independent style. They were performed throughout the country all year round and not just during the mourning month of Muharram. It is said that a play exists

56

for every day of the year. (This writer, unfortunately, has witnessed only about two hundred.) Contrary to what is claimed, the *Gusheh* style is not limited to humorous tales. Love stories and tales of various historical figures and champions (as religious and social conditions permitted) also appeared. For example, the *Binding of the Devil* and the *Wedding of Fatemeh Zahra* are of the first kind.[35] The *Battle of the Gate of Kheybar*, the *Battle of Siffin*, *Abraham*, etc., are of the second variety. There are other stories which are partially love stories and partially religious and historical, such as *Yusef and Zulaikha*. Innumerable stories of this sort were written.

As should be clear from the excerpts from early and recent Ta'ziyeh cited earlier, "similar" poetry, from the standpoint of meter, verse, and rhyme, became fashionable for use in dialogue between two characters and for the question-and-answer format. This was not true in the early plays.

I spoke earlier about the art of improvisation *(badiyeh khani)* in Ta'ziyeh music. Ta'ziyeh performers would occasionally change the lines which they were supposed to recite to more suitable ones or extemporaneously recite their own poetry. These improvisations gradually infiltrated the original texts. In the early days, performers were not allowed to do this.[36] A large number of jokes, witticisms, and social customs which are reflected in the poetry today originated from this spur-of-the-moment improvisation by the performing artist. For example, in the *Martyrdom of Qasem*, the congratulations which Shemr and Ibn Sa'd extend to Qasem on the occasion of his wedding, and the gifts of sweets and cone sugar which Imam Hussein sends them in return are actions quite contrary to what the audience expects and are good examples of improvisation. The quarrel in the family of Hares in the *Ta'ziyeh of Muslem's Children* is similar. The limitations placed on the actors to restrict their improvisations were, of course, the audience itself and the particular character being portrayed. Some overdid it and reduced the dialogue to absurdity. While sometimes improvisation resulted in beautiful poetry, at other times is was mere banality.

Ta'ziyeh in which the Imam or the prophet are present in the opening scene, begin with their *munajat* or prayer (protestations of their innermost secrets and wishes to God, the universe, or the heavens). In the early years, only the Imam or the Prophet (the person playing the leadership role) performed this kind of prologue. Dialogue for the other protagonists was either straight narrative or in the question-and-answer format. In later years, however, a kind of *munajat* was written for the kinsmen of the Imam, which, from the standpoint of verse, meter, rhyme, and rhythm was similar to the poetry written for the Imam. But this *munajat* differed in content from the *munajat* written for the Imam and for the prologues of early Ta'ziyeh. The *pish khani* or prologue took the form of a song or a song-like wail which was presented in choral fashion. The child performers (or one of them) sang a special kind of tune. All the others, antagonists and protagonists together, repeated the first couplet. This took place before the actual

57

performance commenced in order to add a touch of resplendence and luster and to make the in-coming audience aware that the drama was about to begin. It served another function as well. It demonstrated that the men playing the antagonist roles were merely performers doing their job and that they, too, shared in the sorrow and mourning of the people. One of the fundamental conditions of performing the *pish khani* was the participation of all the actors in the cast in the *sarayeh* or choral singing.[37]

In Ta'ziyeh such as the *Martyrdom of the Imam, Abbas, Ali Akbar,* and *Qasem,* prior to the *munajat* by the Imam and his family, Shemr and Ibn Sa'd rush to the battlefield and, in the expression of Ta'ziyeh actors, "issue challenges to combat." These sections are full of violence and threats yet, at the same time, contain high praise for the Imam. Shemr and Ibn Sa'd admit to the greatness of the Imam and confess to their own pettiness and meanness. Sometimes, a description of the battlefield is given, adding greatly to the audience's sense of impending excitement. Because the "challenge to combat" is not an important part of the Ta'ziyeh, performers sometimes added lines to the antagonists' parts. Early Ta'ziyeh did not have such a good standard of *mubarezeh hkani.* Early writers expended their efforts attempting to make everything correspond to the visible action. *Mubarezeh khani* thus usually was only a simple conversation placed after the Imam's *munajat.*

Frequently, the new style of *mubarezeh khani* is mixed with old-style sermonizing. This mingling of styles has unfortunate results, giving the Ta'ziyeh a disjointed, uncoordinated appearance.

DIFFERENT VIEWPOINTS OF TA'ZIYEH WRITERS

At the beginning of this essay, I pointed out how the Ta'ziyeh encountered a variety of new ideas and viewpoints during the course of its development and how each made a contribution to the evolutionary process. Recent developments, however, have destroyed some of the traditional concepts and practices. We previously saw an example in which the Ta'ziyeh writer of one of the *Martyrdom of Hurr* Ta'ziyeh always refers to Yazid in vulgar, insulting tones:

> 'tis a letter from evil Yazid, the fraud,
> Beside the Kufa's governor, Ibn Ziyad.

But in a Takiyeh Dowlat version, Yazid's and Ibn Sa'd's high rank is not repudiated and appropriate descriptive vocabulary is assigned to them even though no real respect is given them.

> An auspicious command from Saturn's great heights,
> By Ibn Sa'd, grandest of leaders and noblest of knights.

The modern Ta'ziyeh writers' love and devotion for the family of Hussein and their hatred for his oppressors is no different from that of the early writers. The difference lies in the handling. Many researchers claim that the martyrdom of the Nation of Believers for their sins is the indisputable, philosophical basis for Ta'ziyeh. Some even think that this concept was influenced by Christianity. The act of "intercession" has a long tradition in Shi'a Islam. In this case, "intercession" and "sin" are mingled with issues concerning fate, predestination, fatalism, and free will, and while each requires a separate treatment of its own, we can conclude here that the Ta'ziyeh writers gleaned different ideas from all of these concepts. In the *Martyrdom of Imam Hussein,* for example, Zainab asks the Imam: "Why did you leave Mecca and Medina and come to Kerbela to place yourself in this danger?" The Imam answers, "Because of the sins of the Nation of Believers." In another version he says, "Fate and the will of God dictated thus." But in another Ta'ziyeh, the *Martyrdom of Ali Akbar,*[38] a wiser and more logical justification for the martyrdom is given, which, to some extent, shows the enlightened thinking of the writer. The example comes from the scene in which the Imam is conversing with Zainab:

Zainab: Brother, you were never like this,
Never so alarmed and concerned as this. . . .

The Imam: Yes, to revolt is better than to endure,
Hatred of this infidel must not destroy our faith,
Even Solomon's Kingdom was transitory,
Although the Fiend works hand in hand with the Devil,
If Allah had not wanted Islam to spread
You and I would have no life.[39]
Those who have not been struck by the Devil
Never ascend to Solomon's throne,
Summon young Ali Akbar, without him I have no life.

This section, aside from its delightful and pleasant-sounding poetry, contains many social and philosophical points which are not completely compatible with pure logic or normal Ta'ziyeh poetry. The gist of the Imam's speech is, "We have arisen to right society's wrongs and we follow this path of our own free will. Our actions are logical and consonant with the Will of God." [40]

Unfortunately, when this new, dramatic form of Ta'ziyeh was gaining acceptance, Iran encountered Western culture and the Iranian Constitutional Movement developed. The Constitutional Movement was blind to Ta'ziyeh quality and it did away with the good as well as the bad. An anti-Ta'ziyeh bloc evolved among the foreign-educated or foreign-influenced intellectuals who joined the ranks of critics in objecting to every national or religious custom. People no longer asked, What is a Ta'ziyeh? Ta'ziyeh offshoots were rarely performed, save by a performing troupe in some remote region of the country.[41] Expanded research into this art form should be initiated before all documentation completely disappears.

NOTES

1. Fortunately, valuable books and articles have been written detailing the historical and social changes in the Ta'ziyeh. The reader may refer to the following: *Namāyish* dar Irān (Theatre in Iran) by Mr. Baizā'ī and to a series of detailed and well-documented articles by our learned friend and researcher, Mr. Māyil Baktāsh, entitled "Tahavvul-i Mawqi'-e Ijtimā'ī va Jihat-i Arzyābī-yi Ta'ziyeh."*(Bāmshād* magazine, numbers 98 through 109, published in 1347.)

2. In addition to travelogs written by Western visitors, various Iranian biographies and literary miscellany confirm this fact. The subject is beyond the scope of this essay and should be handled separately.

3. Shādravān 'Abdullāh Mustawfī, *The Historical and Administrative History of the Qajars* (Tehran, 1334) I, 396-400.

4. Mīrzā Muhammad Taqī was a well-known Ta'ziyeh producer who lived in the middle of the reign of Nāsir al-Dīn Shāh. He gave performances in Tehran and the Takiyeh Dowlat theatre between the years 1275 and 1290 (1859-73). He should not be confused with Muhammad Taqī Nūrī, poet and Ta'ziyeh writer (1201-1263/1785-1847). Mīrzā Tāhir Isfahānī is a pen name associated with a poem in the book *Ganj-i Shāygān* (Treasure of Shaygan). Contrary to popular belief, Shahāb Isfahānī was not a Ta'ziyeh writer. He was only a performer. In my opinion, the various Ta'ziyeh attributed to him were written by others.

5. My point here is, obviously, the genuine Ta'ziyeh masters, not Ta'ziyeh writers in general. Many were nothing but artless frauds who over-indulged in producing worthless rubbish not worthy of the name Ta'ziyeh.

6. The reader must be aware that when I cite constructive changes which enhanced the quality of Ta'ziyeh as theatre I do not mean to imply that set design (decor) as it is known today was as yet a valid concept. The changes in quality were in the details, not in the basic framework.

7. The reason why I have used a verb in the past tense is because the majority of Ta'ziyeh performed in the small towns and villages of Iran today still do not observe this point. This is because most Ta'ziyeh producers are of the opinion that all Ta'ziyeh must be simple. Simplicity, however, must not be confused with artlessness and vulgarity.

8. In traditional Iranian music, the expression "murakkab-Khvānī" or combination singing means movement from one mode to another or a shift from one tune to another. The movement must take place within similar musical scores. In Ta'ziyeh, this method was also used for conversations between two characters.

9. This description is from Ibrāhīm Būzarī, a music master and student of the late Iqbal al-Sultān. Taken from the book, *Irfān va Mūsīqī-yi Irānī,* by Dr. Dāryūsh Saffat.

10. Ta'ziyeh music does not conform exactly with classical Iranian music. It is

thus a futile exercise to compare musical notes. To do so, one must make accurate recordings of Ta'ziyeh performances and if possible break out each individual note.

11. Every loud-mouthed, drunken brawler does not make a good Shimr, Yazīd, or Ibn Sa'd!

12. Refer to "Namāyish Navīsī dar Adabiyyāt" by Hasan Bābak, *Third Iranian Research Congress*, I, 135.

13. If comparisons are to be made, the points in comparison must have common elements. Poems by poets like Muhtisham and Yaqmā cannot and should not be compared with Ta'ziyeh poetry. The two books cited here, however, make for fruitful comparisons (for reasons which space prohibits me to detail). This is probably why the renowned German researcher, Hermann Etteh, cites Ta'ziyeh in his *History of Persian Literature*. He mentions Ta'ziyeh origins in a chapter entitled "The Culture of Believers in God." In two introductions which I wrote for the *Ta'ziyeh of Qāsim* and *Sulaimān and Bilqīs* I pointed out several of his misinterpretations.

14. I say "generally" because some old texts do contain lovely sections. The adjectives "loose" and "simple" nonetheless categorize the vast majority.

15. Quoted from sections of manuscript written by Mīrzā Taqī Nūrī.

16. The phrase "sabr bukun" which is in the printed version of the text is clearly inaccurate. In later years, after the Ta'ziyeh had developed further, this poem appeared as follows. In addition, one or two extra couplets were added:

> If I meet the son of Sa'd tonight,
> I'll tell him the secret from start to finish, tonight.

17. Numerous versions of the *Ta'ziyeh of 'Abbās* exist. The various texts frequently contradict each other and most do not observe poetic principles. These copies require major rewriting. This is true of most copies of the major Ta'ziyeh.

18. Tehran copy accredited to Shaibān 'Alī Baik.

19. Printed version.

20. For further information on the effect of "radīf" on Ta'ziyeh poetry, see *Shi'r uljam-i Shablī-yi Hindī* translated by Fakhr al-Dīn Gīlānī, Vols. 3 and 4. See also *Surat-i Khiyāl dar Shi'r-i Fārsī* by Shafī'ī Kadkanī.

21. This copy is from an old collection. In the modern Ta'ziyeh which are performed throughout Iran's cities and villages many of the original couplets are changed. For example, see the Shiraz versions of the *Ta'ziyeh of Qāsim* collected by Sādiq Humāyūnī.

22. These Ta'ziyeh along with the revisions which I have made are scheduled for publication shortly by the Iranian Anthropological Center, which is affiliated with the Ministry of Arts and Culture.

23. Quoted from a handwritten manuscript of Muhammad Taqī ibn 'Alī Nūrī Māzandarānī (1201-1263/1785-1847).

24. For example:

> Your departure for Saturn elicited an Imperial Farman,
> O Greatest of Leaders, Ibn Ziyad, most honored of nobles.

(narrator's copy, *Ta'ziyeh of Hurr*, Takiyeh Dowlat version)

O leader of Legions, speak frankly
Strike the drum and make ready.

(from the *Ta'ziyeh of Bare'elm*. written and recited by Mīrzā Muhammad Bāqir Mu'īn al-Buka'.)

25. Taken from Sa'dī.

26. The majority of "mubārizih khvānī" poetry (poetry written for one performer to use in laying down a challenge to another) was not specially patterned for each antagonist. Further explanation is given in the section devoted to "mubārizih khvānī."

27. This elegy was sung by Qā'ānī in praise of Mīrzā Taqī Khan Amīr. The opening verse is as follows:

Heaven's zephyr gently blows across the brooks,
The smell of musk blows over the meadows. . . .

See the complete works of Qā'ānī, numerous editions.

28. A "ghazāl" with the following opening lines:

My witchcraft, a mysterious voice emanating from the
tavern of the covetous.
Saying, oh, back on the threshhold again.

29. I noticed this poem in one of the Borghan copies. While it is considered to be by the aforementioned veteran Ta'ziyeh performer, Sulaimān Savchi, the claim is not fully substantiated.

30. This section exists in uneven and defective form in old Tehran versions. The poetry consists of dissonant couplets lacking in symmetry. The opening lines are as follows:

Zainab, O sister of the King's son, with the odor of dust,
Dream and sleep, Ḥussain, son of Religious King.

Later poets apparently considered the rhythm appropriate, so they used it in a different format. What is in the text is from revised Takiyeh Dowlat versions.

31. I have not located this section among the numerous versions of the Martyrdom of 'Abbās which are in my possession. What is quoted above is what I remember from a performance I witnessed several years ago.

32. Mīrzā-Ibrāhīm Sarvi Qazvīnī, elegiac poet, died in Isfahan in 1252/1836.

33. The meaning of this section is:

O Ibn 'Amm, my name is Muslim, the wise,
Walk gracefully to me, in the path of Islam.

34. Bīdil is a pen name for a group of poets. Here we are talking about Bīdil Rūdbārī who died in 1266/1850.

35. For example, the *Ta'ziyeh of "Shīr-Afkan,"* with an introduction by Farrukh

Ghaffārī in the book entitled *Iranian Theatre,* published in the Festival Arts Series, 1350/1972.

36. Unfortunately, this point is not observed in many of the Ta'ziyeh performed today. Players performing the antagonist roles still create their own poems hoping to facilitate their acting. This is wrong and results in inappropriate, tasteless performances.

37. "Sarāyah" is an expression invented by Shādravān Rūh 'Allāh Khāliqī for group or choral singing. Also called "choeur" or choir.

38. From Takiyeh Dowlat copy. Appears in many other versions too.

39. Another copy of the same quality has the line, "Life could not be sacrificed"; but the meaning is exactly the same.

40. This is the same principle that followers of Shi'a Islam believe in.

41. Because *Gusheh* provokes far less agitation and passionate differences of opinion than regular Ta'ziyeh.

6

The Ta'ziyeh and Related Arts

SAMUEL R. PETERSON

Whether in the field of calligraphy, manuscript illumination, architecture or minor arts, the Iranian artist has continually revised conventional norms of Islamic art to enhance and to revive them with a clearly definable Iranian character. Occasionally his innovation is so original that the result is not at all a revision of a general norm but an independent and indigenous creation, one which properly qualifies as an Iranian phenomenon. Certainly a spectacular case in point is the religious theatre of Shi'a Iran, the Ta'ziyeh. Within the Islamic tradition which generally opposes human representation, simply as theatre, the Ta'ziyeh is a unique development for any Islamic nation; that it should evolve in Iran, however, is consistent with the country's history of artistic innovations. Our concern here is not in the institution of the Ta'ziyeh theatre itself but in the curious impact it had on Persian architecture and painting, an impact which is no less amazing than the theatre's own development.

THE TAKIYEH

The term *takiyeh,* as used in Iran to refer to sites used for Shi'a communal mourning ceremonies, is applied to any site used for such purposes, whether it be a simple arena at the crossroads of a town or an elaborate building to accommodate an audience of thousands. However, to survey the history of the *takiyeh* (or *husseiniyeh* as it also is commonly known), it is advantageous to distinguish between the various sites traditionally used for mourning ceremonies in general and the permanent theatres built in the late nineteenth century primarily for housing Ta'ziyeh dramas.

TAKIYEH SITES AND EARLY TAKIYEH THEATRES, CA. 1770-1840

Ibn al-Athir's comment that in the tenth century coarse cloth tents were erected in Baghdad for Muharram ceremonies basically defines what were, until the advent of the Ta'ziyeh dramas, the essential needs for a mourning ceremony site: an open space with shelter for those participating.[1] Even after Ta'ziyeh dramas were introduced and then established as a standard part of the mourning ceremony program, the *maidans,* mosques, private residences, and other sites which customarily had been used for ceremonies were simply adapted to accommodate Ta'ziyeh productions by providing provisional stages. Each had its separate advantages. Royal *maidans* such as that outside the Gulestan Palace in Tehran and the Maidan-e Shah in Isfahan were suitable for the large audiences attracted by ceremonies sponsored by the court, whereas an advantage of smaller sites such as a mosque or a private residence was the *houz* which, customarily a feature of the courtyard, could easily be converted into a stage by covering it with wooden planks. Additional advantages of the private residence were the convenience of a kitchen for the preparation of tea, sherbets, and refreshments for the audience, and the separate sections of the house which were used for differentiated seating: rooms looking onto the court served as loges for honored guests, the court for the general public and, if attendance was large, the roof for women and children (Ill.1). Besides these makeshift adaptations of established architectural settings, occasionally, even during the Safavid period, there were provisional buildings erected specifically for mourning ceremonies. For ceremonies held in 1636 to commemorate the death of Ali, Olearius states that a "maison" was built outside Samankha in the province of Shirvan; subsequently in the early eighteenth century de Bruins reports that eulogies were delivered ". . . upon theatres erected for that purpose." However, Olearius' description and drawing of the building indicate it was a simple structure built to provide seating for local dignitaries, whereas the "theatres" of de Bruins were little more than a scaffolding.[2] Neither can qualify as architecture, or even as a prototype for the later *takiyeh* theatres.

The earliest recorded evidence which at least suggests a permanent building dedicated to the use of mourning ceremonies is an inscription which, according to Henri Massé, is dated 1202/1786 and is in a building in

Astarabad he identifies as "a Darvish monastery *(tekye)*." The inscription as translated in his publication is as follows:

It is the azured castle which speaks of paradise, the day that the Sultan of Kerbela was killed. It is the *tekyeh* which creates a stir even unto the divine throne, because of the plaintive cries of the devotees of Kerbela. The vault of its portal, like unto the sky, is so black because of the smoke of the nightly sighs of the captives of Kerbela. This place all gilded which had become so black, it is by the fire of the accursed Yazid, that dog of an imposter, on a day when, like a cypress, the body of the Knight of the faith (Husayn) fell in the middle of the plain of Kerbela. From that day until now, all the world weeps in the edifice of the *ta'zyeh* hall of the martyrs of Kerbela. This *tekye* also starts the tears of its builder, for he is himself a [humble] atom protected by the Sultan of Kerbela. Oh Lord! The sons of Sadiq the unhappy and of his father, pardon them for the love of the prince of martyrs of Kerbela.

Rowzeh-khani in courtyard of private residence.
From C. J. Wills, *Land of the Lion and the Sun* (London, 1893).

66

Intelligence instructs me to inscribe the date 1201 [1786] for the *tekye* of the Sultan of saints.[3]

Although *takiyeh* is defined by Massé as "a Darvish monastery" (i.e., the abode or quarters of Sufis and dervishes) and the Astarabad building perhaps was used as such, the inscription quoted above clearly identifies the site as a place where mourning ceremonies are held. "The edifice of the *ta'zyeh* hall" in which all the world weeps for the martyrs of Kerbela may have been in reference to only a section of the Sufi *takiyeh* or perhaps referred to the entire *"takyeh"* building. In either case, the significance of the inscription is that a *"ta'zyeh* hall" for mourning ceremonies was identified, according to information recorded by Massé, as early as 1786.

As indicated thus far, the term *takiyeh* defines different types of buildings—a Sufi quarters and a Ta'ziyeh theatre. The two meanings are not contradictory and in fact illuminate certain aspects in the history of the development of *takiyeh* architecture. Throughout the Safavid, Zand, and Qajar periods, the program for mourning ceremonies traditionally was divided into two activities, a distinction emphasized by Chardin and subsequently repeated by others.[4] In summary, the *rowzeh-khani* (i.e., the reading of eulogies) was attended by all the populace but generally was the only devotion participated in by the elite and more orthodox; the more public processions, particularly popular with the lower classes, were performed either separately or after public *rowzeh-khani* gatherings. The processions proceeded through streets, bazaars, and *maidans* of towns, and the route often included a tomb, one which frequently was located on the outskirts of the community. The reason for such a station was, of course, that the procession was to simulate a pilgrimage to Alid tombs, particularly to Imam Hussein's tomb in Kerbela.[5] However, another reason for such stations was that tombs—or else buildings immediately in their vicinity— frequently were the *takiyeh* quarters where Sufis, serving as tomb custodians, resided.[6] Because Sufis played a conspicuous and vital role in the ceremonies and particularly in processions,[7] their *takiyeh* with substitutes for Alid shrines naturally became major stations in the routing of processions.

Because definitive dating for the earliest dramatizations of the histories of the Kerbela martyrs remains somewhat controversial, for purposes of convenience here the beginning of Ta'ziyeh dramas is assigned to the 1770s—that is, to the decade before William Francklin's account of the rather complete staging of several Ta'ziyeh *majles* he witnessed in Shiraz in 1787.[8] Although the Astarabad *takiyeh,* which is dated a year later than Francklin's account, included a *"ta'zyeh* hall," it is identified—by the only source, unfortunately, available here—as a Sufi *takiyeh.* By 1808 Ta'ziyeh dramas had become so popular and successful a part of the program for mourning periods that Tancoigne remarks that "the last five representations" of the Kerbela story were performed "on a theatre erected opposite the king's kiosk in the court of the Gulestan Palace." [9] When James Fraser in 1833 and William Holmes in 1844 separately mention being lodged during their travels in the northern provinces in a *takiyeh* for want of a more suitable hostel, each describes the building as "a shed" yet defines the *takiyeh* as a building used for the "ceremonies" or "solemnities" of Muharram.[10] To none of the other *takiyeh* which the two travelers encounter is ascribed any architectural merit. In describing Muharram celebrations in Astarabad, Holmes reports that the actors' pay is included in the expenses of the *takiyeh* [11] and that "in every mahal of the town, one of more large buildings, called *takiyehs*, had been prepared at the expense of the inhabitants, or by some rich individual, as an act of devotion for the various performances of the season." [12] Notwithstanding, then, the inscription in the Astarabad *takiyeh*, the practice of establishing permanent theatres would seem to date from a somewhat earlier period than these reports—that is, from the 1820s.

If the *takiyeh* which was a Sufi quarters was the namesake of the theatres finally built for housing ceremonies and particularly the Ta'ziyeh dramas, such quarters had little impact on the type of theatre architecture which did evolve. Even before the practice of building theatres was established, the term *takiyeh* had already been adapted to designate any site used for ceremonies, including such primitive locations as crossroads fitted with only a rudimentary stage. Once its general meaning no longer referred so specifically to Sufi quarters or tombs but designated sites for ceremonies as well, the term increasingly was applied to the new theatres which steadily were becoming a conspicuous element of the architecture of Iranian communities. Indeed, the only significant links between the Sufi/tomb *takiyeh* and theatre architecture were first, a theatre occasionally was built adjacent to an extant tomb, in which case the whole became a *takiyeh* complex; and second, the Sufi/tomb *takiyeh* suggested to individual founders the practice of having their remains buried on the premises of their private theatres. In summary, although provisional sites continued to be used throughout the history of the Ta'ziyeh, the earliest examples of theatres erected specifically for housing ceremonies and Ta'ziyeh productions seem to date after the first two decades of the nineteenth century and to occur mainly in the Caspian provinces, an area which traditionally was, of course, a stronghold of Shi'a forces.

Takiyeh Theatres, 1840-1933

A *takiyeh* finally credited with some magnificence and which qualifies among the more grand theatres of the last six decades of the nineteenth century is one that was attended by Lady Sheil in Tehran in 1849. She mentions that the founder of the *takiyeh* was "the Prime Minister" and describes the building as "immense, holding several thousand persons" and having two tiers of boxes surrounding the central arena which were reserved for the Shah, his relatives and wives, and Iranian and foreign ministers. Yet her comment that "the stage ... was formed of a large elevated platform in the middle of the pit ... revealing, to the entire destruction of all exercise of the imagination, mysteries which ought to pass behind the curtain" [13] suggests that neither production techniques nor the traditional arrangements of earlier, provisional sites was greatly altered.

In his elaborate accounts of the Ta'ziyeh made during two extended stays in Iran between 1855 and 1863, Comte de Gobineau mentions that each *mahal* in Tehran maintains a *takiyeh* and that since no state funds are spent on the Ta'ziyeh, several ministers as well as the Shah himself are to be included among patrons of the more prestigious theatres. [14]

When Naser al-Din Shah traveled to England in 1873, he attended a concert at Albert Hall and was so impressed that when he returned to Tehran he required his engineers to build a similar monument beside the Gulestan Palace to serve as a royal *takiyeh* (Ills. 2 and 3). [15] Although one traveler remarks that the Takiyeh Dawlat in fact bore little resemblance to its London prototype, the immense circular brick building which was built was somewhat a marvel of Qajar engineering (e.g., walls were estimated to be approximately 24.4 meters in height and 15.0 meters in thickness at ground level; the hall supposedly could accommodate two to three thousand persons). The central arena, surrounded by three tiers of arched loges entered from a vaulted hall, featured two stages (the *saku* in the center and the *taqnama* at the side) which were used separately or simultaneously during a single performance. The only other architectural provision for performers was a large white marble *minbar* from which *rowzeh-khani* was read. Compensation for the immoderate costs to the crown in erecting such a monumental building was partly realized through annual revenues from subscriptions for loges sold to the rising nobility and elite, a sum which one year amounted to 16,250 *qeran* (488 pounds sterling). [16] After the early 1880s the interior walls, previously neither whitewashed nor plastered, were covered with faïence revetments. To light the hall, besides candles once estimated to number five thousand, four electric lights were added to the large central chandelier suspended from ceiling arches, but by 1890 the project to install electric lighting was abandoned. The decoration of the exterior consisted of occasional faïence tile towers crowning the cornice and a typical Qajar portal of faïence-faced bricks and *'ayineh kari* covering *muqarnas* niches, the effect of which was ornate enough so that it was described as having "the geegaw, pretentious, vulgar and ephemeral style" of an English amusement palace. [17] So colossal was the structure of the building that engineers were unable to erect the dome the Shah considered worthy of his project. In its place a system was devised by which canvas awnings were stretched across a framework of wooden arches reinforced by iron braces, a feature which so annoyed the Shah that members of the foreign community intervened to convince him that the dome he had envisioned was physically impossible with the materials available to the Persian builders. When the Shah died, the royal *takiyeh* was used as the site where his body lay in state; [18] that "chained beasts" were kept in the *takiyeh* implies it was also used temporarily to house part of the royal menagerie. Sometime during the second decade of the twentieth century the Takiyeh Dowlat was considered too unsafe to be used for Muharram ceremonies [19] and in the 1950s it was demolished for new construction on the site.

As early as the seventeenth century mourning ceremonies had attracted single gatherings as large as two thousand persons,[20] yet it was not until almost two centuries later—that is, seven decades after the advent of Ta'ziyeh dramas—that a proper theatre on a significant scale was finally built to accommodate, according to Lady Sheil, such numbers. No matter which vizier it was whom Lady Sheil mentions as its patron,[21] his sig-

Ta'ziyeh production at the Takiyeh Dowlat, Tehran.
From Docteur Feuvrier, *Trois ans à la cour de Perse* (Paris, 1906).

Takiyeh Dowlat and surrounding buildings in foreground, Tehran.
From Docteur Feuvrier, *Trois ans à la cour de Perse* (Paris, 1906).

nificance is that as a representative of the court he established the practice
of erecting monumental theatres for housing Ta'ziyeh dramas. Built about
twenty-five years later, the apogee of *takiyeh* architecture was, of course,
the Takiyeh Dowlat of Naser al-Din Shah. Such official endorsement—in
spite of the criticism leveled by the conservative, orthodox segments of the
community at additional sanctioning of drama itself being put to Shi'a

71

use—only encouraged the practice of erecting and supporting *takiyeh* theatres which were emulated in capital cities and provinces alike. Evidence of
their emergence in the Qajar townscape is an 1860 topographical report of
communities in the Caspian provinces. Of the "numerous takiyeh (holy
buildings) on almost every street in which people gather to listen to the
narrative of the tragic fate of 'Ali's sons," [22] G. Melgunof reports that in
Shahrud there are four *takiyeh*, only one less than the separate number of
mosques, baths, and caravanserais, and in Rasht, thirty-six in contrast to
twenty-two mosques and thirty-four *madraseh*.[23] Indeed, during the last
half of the nineteenth century, the pride of any Iranian community was its
takiyeh, whether it were an unadorned structure belonging to the community at large (Ill. 4)—and its halls perhaps also used for funerary orations for
deceased dignitaries and its open arena for a public *maidan*—or, as in some
instances, the symbol of piety and of status for a wealthy individual who,
somewhat ironically, in memory of the Kerbela martyrs filled his *takiyeh*
with furnishings as lavish as those for which the villain Calif Yazid and his
court were cursed by the Ta'ziyeh audiences (Ill. 5).

With its basic requirements being as simple as an arena and accom-
modation for an audience, the *takiyeh* acquired a variety of forms. Of the
various early and provisional sites, it was the plan of the private residence
which the majority of *takiyeh* resembled most. Because of the varied

Covered arena of Husseiniyeh Kuchak, Zavāreh, c. 1905.

72

Takiyeh hall of Takiyeh Baiglarbaigī, Kermanshah, first quarter of twentieth century.

seasonal weather in which performances were staged throughout the year, both an open and a covered arena frequently were provided. Additional features with which a *takiyeh* might be equipped were a *saqqa khaneh* (i.e., a public fountain) in memory of the martyrs' thirst [24] and, if the founder was a private citizen, a *maqbareh* for his burial.

Regional differences also occur. In the district of Yazd the majority of *takiyeh* repeat a type most impressively represented by the huge, portal structure (38.0 meters in height) which served as seating for distinguished witnesses of ceremonies held in the principal *maidan* of the city, Maidan-e Mir Chakhmaq (Ill. 6). Used as a receptacle for fires burned during ceremonies and revealing the Zoroastrian traditions of the region was the altar-like, usually octagonal *kalak* in the center of the arena. The more conventional *saku* generally was omitted since ceremonies in Yazd traditionally featured *rowzeh-khani* and processions (particularly the carrying of the *naql,* the mock bier of Hussein) and not the Ta'ziyeh dramas themselves. In Nayin several of six *takiyeh,* most of which date from the early twentieth century, repeat a plan traditionally used for the *zur khaneh:* an enclosed building with seating alcoves on a platform surrounding an octagonal arena.

Takiyeh architecture, which began on a monumental scale sometime during the 1840s, came to an end when mourning ceremonies officially were curtailed in 1928 and finally were forbidden in 1935.[25] Thus, its entire history encompasses a single century. When it first did appear out of a need for more appropriate and monumental housing for Ta'ziyeh productions, among the types of architecture which had evolved in Iran over the centuries there was none which properly might serve as a model for theatres. Indicative of the situation was that the grandest *takiyeh* ever built in Iran was inspired by Albert Hall in London. Throughout its brief history, the *takiyeh* was constantly in experimental stages in different regions for various patrons with the result that few final solutions were ever found. In contrast to the Ta'ziyeh drama itself, which evolved out of ancient practices of communal worship, the *takiyeh* was essentially without traditions and evolved into a variety of forms. Accordingly, it is its diversity which is one of its most characteristic features, a feature which is only the more remarkable in a country in which art forms traditionally were more certainly defined and generally codified.

THE TA'ZIYEH AND RELIGIOUS PAINTING

Since the beginning of Islam orthodox opinion has held representation of an animate form to be somewhat a sacrilege. Yet in spite of such censure the walls of some of the earliest preserved palaces in Islam (e.g., Qusayr 'Amra) were decorated with innumerable representations of humans. Sub-

Takiyeh Mīr Chakhmāq, Yazd, late nineteenth century.

74

sequently, when Islamic histories were written and then illuminated by Persian artists in the fourteenth century and later, it was not unusual that they included representations of Muhammad, his family, and his companions. Even so, there is no evidence that representation of the human figure was widely accepted by the general populace who followed the interpretation given their religion by orthodox leaders. Indeed, examples such as those just mentioned were generally confined, in the one case, to palaces limited to the viewing of a privileged few and, in the other, to private manuscripts which as treasures were guarded within private domains.

Because of this background, the impact which the Ta'ziyeh dramas had on the visual arts is one of the most curious developments in the history of Islamic art. After hundreds of years of censure, during the nineteenth century there appear paintings of religious subjects which specifically were intended for the Iranian public at large. Basically a folk art, these representations are included in the popular school generally known as *qahveh khaneh* painting, but since the major theme of those dealing with religious subjects is the martyrdom of Hussein and his followers at Kerbela, a more apt and specific term for the particular genre is Kerbela painting.[26]

After ten centuries of censure, what effected such a dramatic change in the attitudes of the general public was not the religious painting of earlier periods, which did not include illustration of the Kerbela tragedy and was, besides, the prerogative of the elite and was rarely viewed by the populace, but instead was the ubiquitous and popular productions of Ta'ziyeh dramas. Once it had been publicly accepted, to the dismay of the orthodox, that the roles of the martyrs and their adversaries were enacted by devout Muslims, the step toward the public's acceptance of religious paintings depicting the same narratives had already been made. To illustrate how these Kerbela paintings were essentially the translation of the Ta'ziyeh theatre into the visual arts, one need only compare the paintings with Ta'ziyeh productions and texts of the plays.

Of the many examples of such paintings which could be used to illustrate this point, those discussed here are the painted tile panels decorating walls of the Takiyeh Mu'aven al-Mulk in Kermanshah.[27] As decoration considered suitable for a *takiyeh,* the Kermanshah panels demonstrate yet another feature of *takiyeh* architecture: that in spite of the fact that the *takiyeh* was a religious building, the rigid strictures which forbade human representation in a mosque were in some instances completely ignored in order that the Ta'ziyeh to which the *takiyeh* was dedicated might be represented in paintings as well as in dramas.

To introduce a *majles* relating an event in the last days of the Kerbela martyrs, there occasionally were staged, as a prelude, incidents in the life of one of the early prophets of the Koran. As in the case of the *majles* which relates the story of Yusef, the five individual scenes of the large Yusef panel at Kermanshah are taken from the Koranic version of the story.[28] Why the Yusef story should be the subject of a Ta'ziyeh drama and thereby serve as appropriate decoration for a *takiyeh* is its message as repeated throughout the drama: the compassion the woeful tale of Imam Hussein's martyrdom evokes from Yusef and his father Yaqub, a message which the latter sums up at the end of the drama by saying, "O, may a thousand ones like me and my Yusef be a ransom for Hussein! May a thousand Yusefs be the dust of his feet. . . . Come, O Gabriel! show me the plain of Kerbela, for the sake of God." The subject of another prelude is the wedding of King Sulaiman and Belqis. While lamenting in the play the fate of the Kerbela martyrs which his vision of all events past and present enable him to see, Sulaiman interrupts his own marriage to introduce the celebrations for the marriage of Hussein's nephew Qasem to his daughter Fatemeh: but these end with a dirge for the groom when he returns from battle mortally wounded.

The Kermanshah representation of Sulaiman (Ill. 7) depicts the enthroned ruler attended by his counselors, *divs,* and various representatives of the animal kingdom, including the fantastic *simurgh* and Sulaiman's special messengers the *hudhud* (Hoopoe) above and at the sides of his head. Such a legendary audience with its inclusion of such royal animals as the elephant and the lion was not likely to have been inspired by productions staged in provinces such as Kermanshah, but instead was probably suggested to the Tehran tilemakers by the spectacular Sulaiman productions in the capital which featured a parade of magnificent beasts through the royal theatre.[29] Nevertheless, if the subject of the panel in fact was suggested by the Sulaiman drama, its iconography and composition repeat a formula which had been used for centuries by Persian artists to depict Sulaiman enthroned. Such tested formulas also are evident in several of the five scenes represented in the Yusef panel, particularly in the scene in which Yusef is serving Zulaikha in front of her guests distraught by the youth's beauty (Ill. 8).[30] Although such manifestations of earlier painting traditions occasionally appear in the Kermanshah panels, their subjects, like the Ta'ziyeh stories which they represent, are intended to portray persons of all ages mourning the Kerbela tragedy.

More typical of the Kermanshah panels are representations of the Kerbela story itself which not only in subject matter but also in iconography are modeled directly after Ta'ziyeh productions. Certainly a case in point is one of the most standard subjects of the Kerbela genre: Imam Hussein's survivors held as captives in Yazid's court in Damascus (Ill. 9). The veiled and haloed supplicants stand in the foreground facing members of the Syrian army and court. In the upper register Yazid is seated on a throne typical of those which Qajar artists modeled after the famous Peacock Throne. To the left of the ruler are a *farangi* ambassador and his private counselor seated in chairs with which European guests traditionally were provided at Qajar receptions. At the foot of the throne stands the new Imam, Zain al-'Abedin, followed by Hussein's sister Zainab. Among the small figures in the foreground are Hussein's daughters Sukaineh,

76

Sulaiman panel, Takiyeh Muʻāvin al-Mulk, Kermanshah, ca. 1917.

Yusef serving Zulaikha (detail), Yusef panel, Takiyeh Mu'āvin al-Mulk, Kermanshah, ca. 1917.

Zubaidah, and Fatemeh, the latter now the widow of the martyred Qasem. In accordance with the Ta'ziyeh characterization of the caliph Yazid which was intended to instill in the audience violent repudiation of the arch villain, Yazid is dressed in bejeweled clothes and surrounded by such symbols of luxury and vileness as bottles of wine and game boards, all mocking the tragic and miserable condition of Hussein at the time of his death and now the plight of his survivors (Ill. 10).[31] Yazid's daughter, who in the Ta'ziyeh boasts of her father's and her own material well-being, stands beside the caliph. Radiating from a gold plate placed on the throne is a multi-colored flame to represent the halo for the Imam's head which is presented at court as the prize trophy of the Syrian troops. After dabbing wine on the Imam's lips, Yazid with the cane in his hand strikes the mouth of the Imam and knocks out the teeth in a single blow. To this most horrendous deed, Zain al-'Abedin laments, "Dost thou with thy cane, Tyrant, strike the very lips that the Prophet himself did kiss?"

After the humiliation scene of the Alids in Damascus, Yazid repents of his evil, releases the Alids from captivity, and commands his attendant Bashir to conduct the holy family to Medina. In the panel representing the caravan on its approach to the sacred city (Ill. 11), Bashir and a second Syrian guide escort the procession of Zain al-'Abedin and his entourage of women survivors in *takht-e ravan* (litters) which in accordance with Yazid's orders are draped in black cloth.

The influence of the Ta'ziyeh on the four panels discussed here is apparent in that each illustrates a specific Ta'ziyeh play and, more particularly, that certain details of the Damascus and Medina panels are only to be explained as copies of Ta'ziyeh productions. The cane of Yazid, the chairs and clothing of the European envoys (which traditionally were lent by the foreign community), and the veils of the Alid women (which disguised the fact that their roles were enacted by men) are all stage devices which have been reproduced literally by the artists. Even for a detail depicted in the panel representing the deaths of martyrs on the Kerbela plain (Ill. 12), the gesture of Hussein holding his youngest son, Ali Asghar, up to the Syrian troops as a plea for water for the women and children in his camp and which is answered by an arrow to the parched throat of the child is directly borrowed from the theatre.

A more general influence which the Ta'ziyeh had on religious painting is demonstrated by the use of the veil. During the last half of the fifteenth century and until the Qajar period, the veil was an exclusive attribute of holy personages and was not used to cover the faces of women. However, once it became in Ta'ziyeh productions a standard part of the costume of women—as a sign of their modesty but also, as mentioned, as a practical theatrical device to disguise the men enacting female roles—it becomes in Kerbela paintings a standard feature of Alid women. No longer used so consistently as the sacred symbol it formerly had been, in Qajar religious painting the veil is ascribed only somewhat arbitrarily to holy figures; thus the faces of the Shi‘a Imams appear either veiled or unveiled. In contrast to the veil is the halo which, while not a device in Ta‘ziyeh productions, is retained from earlier painting conventions as their sacred symbol.

The relatively recent and brief histories of *takiyeh* architecture and popular religious painting have not attracted the attention of the historian concerned with Iranian subjects having a more ancient and prolonged

Alids as captives at Yazid's court in Damascus, Takiyeh Mu‘āvin al-Mulk, Kermanshah, ca. 1917.

Yazid enthroned, detail of Ill. 9.

Zain al-Abedin and entourage on approach to Medina, by Hasan Tihrānī,
Takiyeh Mu'āvin al-Mulk, Kermanshah, ca. 1917.

Imam Hussein with Ali Asghar (below) and with Hazrat-e Abbas (above), detail of Kerbela plain panel, Takiyeh Mu'āvin al-Mulk, Kermanshah, ca. 1917.

sequence. Yet judging by the number of *takiyeh* throughout Iran and such royal, monumental instances as the Takiyeh Dowlat, the *takiyeh* is one of the most phenomenal architectural developments of Qajar Persia. No less remarkable is the appearance of the innumerable Qajar representations of the Kerbela tragedy with no precedent in painting. It is indeed difficult to imagine either evolving as it did, even existing perhaps, if it had not been for the advent of the Ta'ziyeh in the eighteenth century. Nevertheless, in spite of the fact that the Ta'ziyeh affected popular attitudes toward human representation so profoundly that it was to inspire entirely new developments in Persian art, both the *takiyeh* and Kerbela paintings were natural and innocent evolutions of more ancient forms of Shi'a worship. Thus, what seems to be somewhat revolutionary for the arts is only a sequence in the expression of grief for the martyrs and, ultimately, in the Shi'a community's profession of faith.

NOTES

1. Vladimir Minorsky, *La domination des Daylamites* (Paris, 1932), p. 19.

2. Adam Olearius, *Voyages* (Leide, 1719), pp. 580-81. In the original version of de Bruins' *Reizen* (1714) the relevant passage reads, ". . . daer zekere soort van een toneel was opgericht." In the English edition (1737) translated from the French edition (1718), the original *toneel* is translated as "theatres," but "stages" or "scaffolding" would be more accurate. Cf. Cornelius de Bruins, *Reizen over Muskovie door Persie en Indie* (Amsterdam, 1714), p. 168; Cornelius Le Bruyn, *Travels into Muscovy, Persia and Part of the East-Indies* (London, 1737), I, 215.

3. Henri Massé, "Epigraphy. B. Persian Inscriptions," tr. Phylis Ackermann, *A Survey of Persian Art,* ed. A. U. Pope (Oxford, 1939), II, 1797-98. The only recorded version of the original Persian text evidently is the one in Massé's article quoted in the text here.

4. Jean Chardin, *Voyages* (Paris, 1811), IX, 50-56.

5. In 1665, according to de Thevénot's account of Muharram ceremonies in Shiraz, the "procession having passed by the Governor's Gate, went out of town to consummate the festival at a mosque, where Khatoun, the daughter of Aly, is interred; there they had a sermon. . . ." Monsieur de Thevénot, *Travels* (London, 1687), p. 108. The "mosque" is the tomb in the southeastern section of Shiraz which is known as Khatun-i Quyāmat but more generally as Abish Khatun in reference to the Salghurid queen reputedly buried there; that the monument was identified for de Thevénot as an Alid tomb would define its function for the procession. It is also reported that in 1637 in Ardabil ceremonies were held in the court of the *mazār* of Shaikh Safi (Olearius, 624) and that in the nineteenth century in India *tabuts* of processions were carried to Muslim cemeteries. Lewis Pelly, *The Miracle Plays of Hasan and Husain* (London, 1879), I, xxiii. For discussion of Abish Khatun dated from the fourteenth to the sixteenth century, see 'Alī Naqī Bihrūzī, *Julgih-yi Shīrāz* (Shiraz, 1354 A.H.); Nusratullah Mechkati, *Monuments et sites historique de l'Iran* (Tehran, n.d.), p. 126; 'Alī Samī, *Shīrāz* (Shiraz, 1958), pp. 79-80; Laurence Lockhart, *Persian Cities* (London, 1960), p. 50; William Ouseley, *Travels in the East* (London, 1819), II, 20.

6. For examples of *takiyehs* which were tombs and/or Sufi quarters, see, *inter alia,* Engelbert Kaempfer, *Amoenitatum Exoticarum* (Lemgoviae, 1712), p. 112; Chardin, VII, 473; James Morier, *A Second Journey through Persia* (London, 1818), p. 151; and Ouseley, pp. 19-20.

7. See, *inter alia,* Chardin, IX, 53; Thomas Herbert, *Some Yeares Travels* (London 1677), p. 268; Comte de Sercey, *La Perse en 1839-40* (Paris, 1928), p. 208; Comte de Gobineau, *Religions et philosophies dans l'Asie centrale* (Paris, 1957), p. 352; Arminius Vambery, *Life and Adventures* (London, 1914), p. 68; C. J. Wills, *Persia as it Is* (London, 1887), pp. 205ff.; and, Percy M. Sykes, *The Glory of the Shia World* (London, 1910), p. 197.

8. William Francklin, *Observations Made on a Tour from Bengal to Persia* (London, 1790), pp. 240-51.

9. M. Tancoigne, *A Narrative of a Journey into Persia* (London, 1820), p. 198.

10. James Fraser, *A Winter's Journey* (London, 1838), II, 462; William Richard Holmes, *Sketches of the Shores of the Caspian* (London, 1845), p. 326. E. G. Browne also mentions being "... assigned quarters ... in [a] *takyé* consecrated to the Muharram passion-plays." Browne, *A Year Amongst the Persians* (London, 1959), p. 273. A similar use made of Sufi *takiyehs* was that traditionally they were hostels for Sufi travelers and persons who periodically retired from public life for private devotions.

11. Holmes, p. 302.

12. *Ibid.,* p. 296.

13. Lady Sheil, *Life and Manners in Persia* (London, 1856), pp. 126.27.

14. Gobineau, pp. 339-41. For additional comments on mid-nineteenth century patronage, see Robert Grant Watson, *A History of Persia* (London, 1866), pp. 20-23, and Jean Calmard's article, "Le patronage des Ta'zīyeh ..." published in this collection.

15. Unless otherwise noted, the description of the Takiyeh Dowlat in the text here is drawn from accounts by Carla Serena, *Hommes et choses en Perse* (Paris, 1883), pp. 172-76; Agnate Laessøe, *Fra Persien* (Copenhagen, 1881), pp. 214-21; Browne, pp. 602-3; James Bassett, *Persia the Land of the Imams* (London, 1887), p. 106; S. G. W. Benjamin, *Persia and the Persians* (Boston, 1887), pp. 382-86; Henry Binder, *Au Kurdistan* (Paris, 1887), pp. 406-9; George N. Curzon, *Persia and the Persian Question* (London, 1966), I, 327-28; and Pierre Ponafine, *Life in the Moslem East* (London, 1911), p. 347. For further discussion of the building, see Calmard's article, "Le patronage des Ta'ziyeh."

16. Curzon, II, 481.

17. Arthur Arnold, *Through Persia by Caravan* (London, 1877), I, 206-7.

18. Ella C. Sykes, *Through Persia on a Side-Saddle* (London, 1898), p. 346.

19. Eustache de Lorey and Doublas Saladin, *Queer Things about Persia* (London, 1907), p. 282.

20. In 1667 Chardin estimates that more than 2,000 attend ceremonies held at the Tālār-i Ṭavīlih (i.e., Tālār Ashraf) in Isfahan. Chardin, IX, 57.

21. Lady Sheil, according to her dated entries, only arrived in Tehran shortly before attending the Ta'ziyeh performances she describes. She mentions that "the Prime Minister" built the *takiyeh* and sent invitations to foreign ministers but does not identify him by name. It is doubtful, however, if the founder was the vizier at the time, Mīrzā Ṭāqī Khān Amīr-i Kabīr, since he probably was too preoccupied

during his first year in office with more urgent matters than building the "immense" *takiyeh,* and also was known to view the Ta'ziyeh with disdain. Hamid Algar, *Religion and State in Iran:* 1785-1906 (Berkeley, 1969), p. 135. It is more probable that the founder was his predecessor, Hajjī Mīrzā Agāsī, the vizier of Muhammad Shah, and that the *takiyeh* was built toward the end of his twelve years in office, 1836-48.

22. G. Melgunof, *Das Südliche Ufer des Kaspischen Meeres* (Leipzig, 1868), p. 39.

23. *Ibid.,* pp. 130, 242. About fifty years later H. L. Rabino notes the same number of *takiyehs* in Rasht. Rabino, *Les Provinces caspiennes de la Perse: La Guilan* (Paris, 1917), pp. 72, 86-88.

24. An early precedent for the *takiyeh saqqā khānih* was the public cistern such as one in Astarabad which, according to Massé (1798), bears the Shi'a inscription, "May they drink and curse the miserable Shimr and the impure Yazīd, 1010 (1601)." Massé cites H. L. Rabino, *Mazandaran and Asterabad* (London, 1928), Persian text, p. 40, as his source.

25. Elgin Groseclose, *Introduction to Iran* (New York, 1947), p. 104; Peter Avery, *Modern Iran* (London, 1965), pp. 290-91.

26. Instances of representation of holy figures displayed publicly are noted by J. M. Rogers in his article, "The Genesis of Safawid Painting," *Iran,* VIII (1970): 125-39 (or in the re-published copy, Michael J. Rogers, "The genesis of Safavid painting," *Memorial Volume of the Vth International Congress of Iranian Art and Archaeology* (Tehran, 1972), II, 167-88). To be added to those Rogers cites is a representation of Ali reported on the portal of the state mint in Isfahan in the seventeenth century. Chardin, VII, 359. Representations of the Kerbela tragedy on the walls of the Imāmzadeh Zaid in Isfahan were published in 1937 as contemporary with the date 1097/1685-86 indicated in a restoration inscription for the building. Yedda A. Godard, "L'Imamzāde Zaid d'Isfahān," *Athār-i Irān,* 2/2 (1937; 341-48). Such dating for the paintings also is argued by Rogers who states that they are "the first dated religious wall paintings known to us." See Rogers, pp. 127-28, 138; 169-70, 181. However, the veiled Alid women, the prominence given to Hadrat-i 'Abbās, the representation of a Kerbela shrine in the background, gestures, and most iconographic details are entirely consistent with Qajar Kerbela paintings which were modeled after Ta'ziyeh productions. Accordingly, because the Ta'ziyeh itself did not evolve until the last half of the eighteenth century, the Imamzadeh Zaid paintings are dated here to mid-nineteenth century, about 175 years later than the restoration date for the building. For further discussion of the Imamzadeh Zaid paintings and of Ta'ziyeh influences on Qajar religious painting, see S. R. Peterson, "Painted Tiles at the Takieh Mu'āvin al-Mulk (Kermanshah)," in the *Memorial Volume of the VIIth International Congress of Iranian Art and Archaeology,* in press.

27. The original *takiyeh* on the Kermanshah site was built during the last decades of the nineteenth century, but after being damaged during the Constitutional Revolution by cannon shot and fires, it was restored and enlarged sometime between 1914 and 1925. It was during the period of restoration that the Mu'āvin al-Mulk family commissioned Hasan Ṭihiranī and several assistants to come from Tehran to decorate nearly every wall of the three-building complex with painted tile panels. For additional photographs and discussion of the Takiyeh Mu'āvin al-Mulk, see *ibid.,* and Roloff Beny and Seyyed Hossein Nasr, *Persia: Bridge of Turquoise* (Boston, 1975), Pls. 154, 157, p. 346.

28. For texts of the Yusef story and the Kerbela stories compared to paintings discussed here, see Pelley, vols. I-II.

29. Benjamin, pp. 402-3.

30. A feature usually illustrated in the scene in which Yusef attends Zulaikha but omitted in the Kermanshah example is that the women, so distracted by Yusef's beauty, cut their hands with knives with which they peel fruit. For illustration in manuscript illuminations, see, *inter alia, The Chester Beatty Library Catalogue of Persian Manuscripts and Miniatures,* ed. A. J. Arberry (Dublin, 1960), II, Pl. 43 (b); Ivan Stchoukine, *Les Peintures des Manuscrits Safavis de 1502 a 1587* (Paris, 1959), Pls. LXIII, LXXI, LXXI: Grace Dunham Guest, *Shiraz Painting in the Sixteenth Century* (Washington, D.C., 1949), Pl. 44; and in pictorial carpets, *Southeby's Catalogue of Fine Oriental Carpets and Rugs (Sale of 6 May 1977)* (London), p. 138.

31. In some versions of the Damascus court *majles,* the bottles beside Yazid are for medicine for the ailing caliph who is not revived until he sees the severed head of the Imam.

7

Ta'ziyeh and Pre-Islamic Mourning Rites in Iran

EHSAN YARSHATER

Passion plays constitute an isolated instance of dramatic art in Persian literature. Drama was not a channel of literary expression in pre-modern Iran, and therefore it is all the more intriguing that a unique case of religious drama in verse should have developed durinng or after the Safavid period with no apparent ancestry or progeny. Scholars have generally looked to Mesopotamia, Anatolia, and even Egypt for parallels to, or origins for, some of the mythical features of the Ta'ziyeh. Although no doubt Ta'ziyeh attracted and accommodated some old Near Eastern myths and rites in a new form, it is most probably to Eastern Iran in pre-Islamic times where we should look for the basis of a tradition which provided a ready mold for the development of the Ta'ziyeh.

Before we search for pre-Islamic precedents, however, we must stress the character of the Ta'ziyeh as a "ritual play." In its more developed form, it consists of a system of actions accompanied by words, chanted or recited, reenacting a series of events, of which the core is the martyrdom of Imam Hussein and his family at Kerbela. It is to confirm and reinforce the belief in the passion of the holy family and its message, and to provide an outlet for the release of a complex of emotions of which the most evident are grief

88

and "sympathy" in its literal sense. In such plays the course of events is already known to the audience. The play only "reminds" them of these events in a dramatic form. It revives dormant feelings and rekindles an emotive dormant fire. Dramatic technique or poetic art is to heighten such reanimations. Thus, not only are the outcome of the Imam's battle in Kerbela or the captivity of Zainab in Damascus or the frustrated wedding of Qasem all known in detail to the listeners, but they are often forecast by various characters early in the play. Such anticipations, far from "giving the plot away," lay the groundwork for the mood of mourning appropriate to the occasion.

Two well-known tragedies in Persian tradition offer parallels to many aspects of Passion plays. One is the Memorial of Zarer *(Ayadgar i Zareran),* a Middle Persian work which has survived from Sasanian times and which was based on an older, Parthian original. It must have been sung for centuries by bards and minstrels *(gosan* in Parthian) [1] before it was committed to writing. A religious epic like the passion of the Imam, it is centered on the figure of Zarer, a dedicated and valiant defender of the faith. Vishtasp, the holy king of the Zoroastrian church, is threatened by Arjasb, the king of the Chionites, who objects to Vishtasp's conversion to the religion of Zoroaster and descends on him with a mighty army. Against all odds, Zarer volunteers to go into battle against the enemy. He is slain at the hand of Bidarafsh, Arjasb's wily brother.

Two aspects of this tragedy may be noted. One is that the entire outcome of the event is known to Zarer and his kinsmen. Before the war begins, King Vishtasp summons the sage Jamasp and asks him to reveal the fate of the battle. In a prophecy laden with lament he reveals the extent of the calamaties which await the royal house. In particular, he tells of how the valorous Zarer will be treacherously killed by the ruthless Bidarafsh. He predicts that twenty-three of the king's brothers and sons will be slain.[2] His predictions are not meant merely to be informative; but couched as they are in elegiac terms, they are meant to prepare the mood of the audience and foreshadow the high point of the tragedy. This point is reached when Zarer is pierced by the poisonous lance of Bidarafsh on the battlefield. In the Passion plays, too, we notice that the destiny of the characters is known to the Imam and often is revealed through forebodings, presentiments, laments, or outright descriptions of the future events. For instance, in the Ta'ziyeh of the *Martrydom of Abbas,* Shemr tried to attract Abbas to his side, but Abbas refuses, despite the fact that, as he makes evident in the course of an apocalyptic *khutba* (public homily), he knows what is in store for him. In his vision he sees Fatemeh on the Day of Judgment rising from her grave, holding in one hand a bloodied shirt, and in the other the broken teeth of her father, the Prophet. On her head she wears the empty turban of Hussein, complaining bitterly about his killers. As Abbas' elegiac address continues, he even mentions the fact that his two hands will be cut off and his head severed, and that seventy-two other members of the company will also lose their heads. Again, every time one of the Imam's followers asks permission to go into the battlefield, his imminent doom becomes apparent from the Imam's words.

The second aspect is that Zarer's death is followed by a moving lamentation by his young son Bastur (in Ferdowsi, Nastur) who, despite his tender age, volunteers to fight Bidarafsh and avenge his father. He stands by the bloodied and lifeless body of his father and, in a fashion typical of the passion plays, mourns his wretched state.[3] The threnody has clear poetic qualities and there is little doubt that in religious-minded Zorastrian circles the chanting or singing of the *Memorial of Zarer* served the same devotional and cathartic purpose as did the elegies of the Imams in late Islamic times. There are, of course, differences between the events of Kerbela and those of the Irano-Chionite wars, reflecting different outlooks and contexts. But the basic elements are the same: a devoted warrior, inspired by the fire of his faith, faces a large army and a treacherous adversary. He is killed in battle and he is bitterly lamented. His death, however, fulfills a prophecy.

But the closest parallel to the Ta'ziyeh in pre-Islamic tradition is to be found not in the *Memorial of Zarer,* but in the tragedy of Siyavush. His story is well known. The young and innocent prince finds refuge in Turan in order to escape the rancor of his father, only to be murdered by the order of the perfidious Afrasiyab.

The recording of this tragedy by Islamic historians, notably Dinawari and Tabari, as well as its rendering by Ferdowsi, all in a non-Zoroastrian context, have robbed the episode of its religious and cultic aspects. But these can be gleaned from other sources. Our chief source in this respect is Narshakhi. A careful reading of him indicates that a tradition of a mourning cult, with Siyavush at its center, continued in Transoxiana down to his time (tenth century). Narshakhi in his *History of Bukhara* relates that "the people of Bukhara have wonderful songs *(suruds)* concerning the slaying of Siyavush and the minstrels call these songs *kin-e Siyavush.*[4] His subsequent comments leave no doubt that these were in fact mourning songs: "The people of Bukhara have many a lament *(nuha)* on the slaying of Siyavush, which is known in all regions *(velayat-ha),* and the minstrels have made them into songs which they chant, and the singers *(qawwalan)* call them 'the weeping of the magi' *(geristan-e mughan)."*[5] The last two words are particularly revealing and confirm a mourning cult among the magi at least of Sogdiana. The religious character of Siyavush, although generally obliterated in Islamic sources, has left enough traces to reveal a once powerful religious cult. Tha'alebi records a tradition, according to which cosmic disturbances took place when Siyavush was killed: "a violent wind began to blow, a heavy dust arose and a stagnant darkness spread."[6] Such phenomena could only point to the sanctity of the slain hero. A faint reference to this aspect may perhaps be seen also in Siyavush's going through the ordeal of fire unscathed. But a more positive indication is found in Ibn Balkhi, who recounts that when the news of Siyavush's death reached Iran, his father Kay Kavus lamented profusely, saying, "it was not Afrasiyab who killed him, it was I who killed the holy *(rawhani)* Siyavush."

The fact that Siyavush was the focus of a mourning cult in Transoxiana can be clearly seen from Narshakhi's accounts. He says that Siyavush was buried in Bukhara near the Ghuriyan Gate, and that the Zoroastrians *(mughan)* venerated his grave. "Each year on New Year's day and before sunrise every person would take a cock and would kill it there (in commemoration of Siyavush)." [7] This offering of sacrifice is further confirmed by Kashghari, who says that "every year the Zoroastrians *(majus)* go the Diz Ru'in, near Bukhara, where Siyavush was killed. They weep and offer a sacrifice there and pour the blood of the sacrificed animal on the grave; and this is their custom." [8] Biruni provides further detail about the funerary cult prevailing in Sogdiana: "At the end of the month of Akhshum the people of Soghd weep and lament on account of their dead in former times and hit their faces [lit., cut] and place food and drink for the dead, as do the Persians during the feast of Farvardagan." [9]

Hints as to Siyavush's connection with mourning rites can be found in other sources. For instance Tha'alebi tells us that when the news of the death of Siyavush reached the Persian court, profound grief and universal mourning seized the country and "Rustam and the generals sat to mourning, or rather, stood up bare-footed and bare-headed for seven days." [10] In fact, his description of the intense mourning and of Rustam's dragging the culprit, Sudabeh, by her hair and putting her to death before Kay Kavus sounds as if it were the description of a rite. Tabari relates that, according to Persian authorities, the first man to wear black in mourning was Shadus, son of Gudarz, who did so when Siyavush was killed by Farasiyat (Afrasiyab).[11]

The cult of Siyavush was not confined to Sogdiana. His veneration in Chorasmia is attested to by Biruni. According to him, the people of Chorasmia marked the beginning of their era with the advent of Siyavush: "The people of Khwarazm dated the events by the building of this city, which took place 980 years before Alexander; then they made the entrance of Siyavush, son of Kay Kavus, in it ... their era, and that was 92 years after the building of Khwarazm." [12]

What can be deduced from the literary sources about the mourning rites around the person of Siyavush seems to have found unexpected confirmation in archaeological excavations in Transoxiana. Diggings in the ruins of Panjikent, a Sogdian city sixty-eight kilometers east of Samarkand, brought to light a series of extensive wall paintings, the focal theme of which is the mourning for a young prince. "The mural depicts the funeral bier of a youthful personage, whose death is mourned by both mortals and gods." [13] The prince has been generally identified with Siyavush.[14] The fact that Mithra and the goddess Anahita (locally, Nana) take part in the mourning confirms the divine nature of Siyavush before his myth was transformed into legend. Similar scenes appear on a chest from Tok-Kala in the extreme north of Amu-Darya delta, [15] and on a vase found in Merv.[16]

In Siyavush's myth we seem to be confronted with the sacrifice of a divine being whose death generated life, a myth quite familiar from ancient Mesopotamia and elsewhere. According to legend, from Siyavush's blood there immediately grew an herb called "the Blood of Siyavush *(khun-e Siyavushan)"* [17] even though Afrasiyab had ordered his blood to be shed over a barren rock.[18] Traces of the legend can be found to our day in the folklore of the Fars province.

The passion of Siyavush as reflected in literature exhibits all the major features of our Islamic Passion plays.[19] Like the Imam, Siyavush, too, has forebodings of his fate. In fact, he knows in detail all the sufferings which await him and his pregnant wife. In a conversation with the noble Turanian general, Piran, on the subject of fate and future events *(budani-ha)* Siyavush opens his heart, saying:

> Not before long I shall suffer a lamentable death at the hand of the king. Innocent and afflicted, I shall be killed. Someone else will replace me on the throne. . . . Slander and ill-fortune will bring me low, even though I am guiltless. Then the whole earth will be filled with suffering and the world will seethe with the swords of vengeance. . . .[20]

This is followed by a prophecy of the wars between Persia and Turan and their outcome. More akin to the mixture of prophecy, lament, and farewell in the Ta'ziyeh is a passage in Ferdowsi, where Siyavush, who has had a dream, tells his young wife Farangis [21] of the calamities which would befall him. Except for the difference in diction, it could have come from one of the martyrs of Kerbela:

> ". . . they will strike off this innocent head of mine, and will place my crown in my heart's blood. I shall find neither bier, nor shroud, nor grave. Nor would anyone shed tears for me in the assembly. Like an exile shall I lie in the dust, with my head severed by [a] sword from my body. And you, Farangis, will be carried off by the king's men, humuliated, bare-headed and without cover. . . ." [22]

بخون جگر برنهند افسرم	ببرّند بر بیگنه این سرم
نه برمن بگرید کسی ز انجمن	نه تابوت یابم نه گور و کفن
سرم گشته از بن بشمشیر چاك	بمانم بسان غریبان بخاك
سر و تن برهنه برندت براه	بخواری ترا روزبانان شاه

92

The imagery involved in this passage is practically the same as that found in similar scenes of the Ta'ziyeh, and the feeling of self-pity and grief is identical. From a number of references to the manner in which Siyavush was slain, it appears that, as would befit a martyred saint, he was killed cruelly and in a way that could not but arouse deep anguish and overwhelming pity. After he was wounded, his hands were tied and he was humiliated and driven to the place where he had once excelled in physical prowess. Then he was thrown down "like a lamb" and his throat slit with a sword. It also appears that he was mutilated and his handsome and radiant face cut up and destroyed.[23] (Kay Khusrow does the same to his murderer, a figure who is a close parallel to Shemr in the Ta'ziyeh.)

Many other parallels can be drawn between the passion of Siyavush and that of the Imam, but it is hardly necessary to demonstrate basic similarity between the two.

Of course, this is not to say that the passion of Hussein, as it appears in the Ta'ziyeh, is only a late reincarnation of Siyavush's legend. The origin and development of the Ta'ziyeh could be drawn also from Mesopotamian, Anatolian, and Egyptian myths. The whole legend of Siyavush presents striking similarity to the myth of Tammuz, the youthful Mesopotamian god who died and rose annually with dying and reviving vegetation. This typical myth of death and rebirth occurs in many parts of the world, but the possibility of an early adaptation can by no means be ruled out,[24] particularly in view of the cult of Nana (Anahita) in Transoxiana.

The unmistakable point, however, is that ritual mourning festivals of the Ta'ziyeh-type have clear precedents in pre-Islamic Persia. The passion of Siyavush bears too close a resemblance to the Ta'ziyeh of the Imam in ritual, imagery, and emotive underpinnings to be ignored in an explanation of the emergence of the genre. Whereas Zarer's elegiac epic may be considered Zorastrian in conception, the funerary rites of Siyavush pre-date the Zoroastrian reform and belong, like many other old practices and beliefs, to the pagan traditions of eastern Iran. Later however, they were adopted in the Zorastrianism of the *Yashts*. The martyrdom of Hussein and his kin found a ready ground in Persian tradition in order to develop into an inspiring and elaborate mourning drama. It inherited the major feature of a long-standing practice which had deep roots in the Persian soul.

NOTES

1. For *gōsān* and the transmission of epic and historical tradition by the minstrels, see M. Boyce, "The Parthian *Gōsān* and Iranian Minstrel Tradition," JRAS (1957), pp. 10-14.

2. *Pahlavi Texts,* ed. Jamasp Asana (Bombay, 1897), pp. 5-6.

3. *Ibid.,* p. 12.

4. Narshakhi, *Tārīkh*-i Bukhara, ed. Mudarris Ražavī (Tehran, 1972), p. 24.

5. *Ibid.,* p. 33.

6. Tha'ālibī, *Kitāb al-Ghurar,* ed. Zotenberg (Paris, 1900), p. 213.

7. Narshakhī, pp. 32-33.

8. *Kitāb Dīvān Lughāt al-Turk,* III, 110-11.

9. Al-Bīrūnī, *Athār al-Bāqiya,* ed. Sachau (Leipzig, 1878), p. 235.

10. Tha'ālibī, p. 213.

11. Ṭabarī, I, 604.

12. Bīrūnī, p. 35.

13. G. Azarpay, "Iranian divinities in Sogdian painting," *Acta Iranica: Monumentum H. S. Nyberg,* I (1975), 20.

14. The identification was made first by A. Y. Yakubovskii and A. I. Terenozhkin. See G. Frumkin, *Archaeology in Soviet Central Asia* in the *Hbuch. d. Or.* (Leiden and Köln, 1970), pp. 72, 78, 79) and Azarpay, *loc. cit.,* p. 20.

15. Frumkin, *loc. cit.,* p. 101.

16. *Ibid.,* p. 149.

17. Shāhnāmah, Burūkhīm ed. (Tehran, 1934-35), p. 664, lines 2514-15.

18. *Ibid.,* p. 675, line 2391.

19. Cf. Shāhrukh Miskūb's perceptive *Sūg-i Sīyāvush,* pp. 82, 151.

20. *Shāhnāmah,* p. 622.

21. Gasīfarī in Tha'ālibī, p. 205, passim, and Vaṣāf al-Farīd in Ṭabarī, I, 601-4.

22. *Shāhnāmah,* p. 652.

23. See Ṭabarī, I, p. 600; Bal'amī, pp. 512-13; Tha'ālibī, p. 211; Firdawsī, pp. 663f, 1395f.

24. On this point see Mihrdād Bahār, Asāṭīr-i Irān (Tehran, 1973), pp. 50 *seq.*

8

Ta'ziyeh and its Philosophy

MAYEL BAKTASH

In what way does Ta'ziyeh as a religious and ritual drama show an understanding of man? What interpretation has the life of society found in Ta'ziyeh? In the development of the extant connection between the form of the ritual and its content, what factors and values have been operative? What direction has the enquiry about Ta'ziyeh's progress taken and what understanding of it has society ultimately achieved?

Shabih (dramatization), in the Ashura mourning ceremonies and in connection with the social changes appearing in Persian society, earned an important place in the past which was founded upon traditional values. Today it has a respected place in Iran's national culture: however, wider research is still required for a complete understanding of it.

Ta'ziyeh or *shabih* is the product of experiences which originated in religious thought, and consequently possesses a religious content. During the course of history the support of the community's faith gave it life through the participation of the people and the cooperation of individuals in its production.

Ta'ziyeh is a ritual production, a comprehensive and broad spectacle embracing the entire community. Consequently, Ta'ziyeh enjoys a dimension beyond its form which extends to the depths of myth, belief, and the articles of popular faith.

Because of Ta'ziyeh's comprehensive dramatic capacity, it has absorbed and given theatrical expression to values determined by the popular beliefs of the community. That is, the concept of *shabih* is directly connected with and dependent upon the thought of the community which produced it: through it the community enacts the mourning for its heroes. Understanding the philosophy of Ta'ziyeh is possible only by going back to its conceptual and practical foundations in history and to the environment of its own period. Such understanding will illuminate its creative principles of truth and beauty.

Before turning to historical references, it is necessary to note that the words *ta'ziyeh* or *ta'ziyat* and *Majles-e-ta'ziyeh* were not generally used in the context of early Islamic social traditions to mean mourning or a gathering of mourners at the death of ordinary individuals; they were used in connection with the mourning ceremonies of Ashura which included condolences *(ta'ziyat)* for Hussein. They were first conducted in private and later in public; and finally, with the development of these ceremonies and the appearance of "the dramatization of the tragedy of Kerbela" they assumed their modern meaning and are equivalent to "dramatization."

The mourning ceremonies of Ashura in 352 A.H./A.D. 963, which were conducted at the command of Sultan Mu'izz al-Dawla and are considered to be the first public community mourning ceremonies, were held with a twofold purpose and had many implications. It was a new evaluation of the historical events of 61 A.H./A.D. 680, the tragedy of Kerbela, which in the following years in Iran turned into a "commemoration" with the recital of elegies, the beating of head and face, the bringing out of mourning processions in the streets and markets, the pitching of tents, and weeping in mourning assemblies. They had both internal and external objectives, and these objectives were based upon certain principles.

The popularization of the Ta'ziyeh of Hussein the son of Ali, who was sacrificed to the tyranny of the Umayyads, is connected with a time in which the Persians and the party of Ali had revolted to obtain political power vis à vis the caliph. A year before he instituted the *ta'ziyat* at the common level in 351 A.H./A.D. 962, Mu'izz al-Dawla inaugurated his political opposition to the existing caliphate by affixing manifestos to the façades of Baghdad's mosques condemning Mu'awiyah ibn Abu Sufyan and the oppressors of the Prophet's Family. The mourning ceremonies that were held the following year were allegorical affairs, redolent of revolution and designed to obtain psychological control by means of the parallels they drew to stories of oppression and misfortune.

The mourning ceremonies of the Buyid period had an immediate external objective: opposition to the power and establishment of the Sunnis. In the beginning the mourning ceremonies were involved with real events in reaching this objective; for ten years after that declaration, the mourners were confronted with a reaction on the part of the Baghdad Sunnis, and riots ensued.

On Ashura 363 A.H./A.D. 973 the Sunnis brought out a procession to commemmorate the Battle of the Camel and the defeat of Ali. Preceding it, mounted on camels, was a woman representing A'isha, a man as Zubayr, and another as Talha. They said that they were going to fight the supporters of Ali. When the processions of the two factions met each other, fighting erupted. The famous bloody riots in the Karkh quarter of Baghdad continued until after the Buyid period.

Inherent in the mourning ceremonies was a community of feeling and participation in the tragedy and fate of Hussein. As time passed and conditions changed, the external objectives of the mourners were sublimated and theatrical enactment of the struggles replaced real fighting. The appearance and meaning of the event in the past was transformed outwardly into the rites of Ashura mourning. This occurred in various subjective and objective stages.

Elegy was the first articulation of Ta'ziyeh. In the fourth Islamic (tenth Christian) century the poet commemorated the tragedy of Hussein in the third person and in his poem gave expression to his own feelings while arousing the sympathies of the mourners.

While this tradition kept alive the memory of Hussein, his character attained a mythical entity in the minds of his followers. Hussein became a sacred hero who, after his tragic death, reached the frontier of eternal values. Through the language of the poet his mourners, as we shall see, made him immortal, and the role of the myth began to manifest itself from within the ritual of mourning which itself became a kind of worship.

Sahib ibn Abbad, the famous prime minister and poet of the Buyids who had a special interest in propagating the mourning for Hussein, wrote many odes eulogizing the Imam which were recited during the mourning ceremonies of Ashura in order to induce and encourage the mourners to weep. In one of these elegies he said:

The blood of the friends of the Prophet Muhammad is flowing; Our tears pain plentifully. Let there be infinite curses and blame upon his enemies in the past and the future. Distress yourselves about what befell the children. Now listen to the story of the martyrdom and how they deprived Hussein of water; and when he was fighting on the plain of Kerbela how they behaved meanly and unjustly. They cut off the head of a descendant of the Prophet in that fiery land! But the Imam lives, his foot in the stirrup and mounted upon his horse! He will not be killed! Then the sinners and the merciless attacked the Prophet's Family. Fly to salvation while there is still the chance, hurry! Shemr the bastard of Ibn al-Baghi struck his sword on the ground while laughing. This is a kindness to the Prophet and is pleasing! Then the soldiers of the Banu Hind moved out with the heads of the descendants of the Chosen Prophet fixed to the points of their lances. The angels in heaven bewailed their deaths and have wept so copiously that water is flowing from the leaves of the trees and plants. Then you must weep for a while; for after this tragedy of Taff, laughter is unlawful.[2]

Sahib ibn Abbad has been described by one of the Persian writers and poets of the fourth century, Abu Bakr Khwarazmi, who had friendly relations with him, as one who strove hard in the popularization of Ta'ziyeh and elegy. Abu Bakr, who had written elegies himself, said of his own poetry that he retold the story of Hussein ibn Ali in order to show the foulness of the murderers and to condemn them. In a letter addressed to the Shi'as of Persia, in the course of describing the history and burden of affliction of the Shi'a leaders, he wrote: "Whenever one of the Imams of salvation or an important member of the Prophet's Family dies, the Abbasids do not attend his funeral. But whenever one of their jesters, players, or fools dies, the judges and rulers attend his funeral and the commanders of the army and the governors make themselves ready to mourn him in the mosque."

In this manner he implicitly encouraged the Shi'as to revere the Ta'ziyeh of Hussein. Abu Bakr Khwarazmi, who emphasized the principle of "free will" in his writings was influenced by the philosophical sect called Mutazilite whose impact upon Ta'ziyeh will be described below.

The mourning for Hussein associated with the Buyid period and the rule of the Shi'a Fatimids also spread to Egypt. During the reign of Mu'izz al-Din Allah (360 A.H./A.D. 970) the Egyptian Shi'as observed the period of Ashura as days of sorrow and grief, and they recited dirges in their mourning rites. During the prime ministry of Afzal ibn Badr al-Din, mats were laid down in Cairo's Husseini mosque and Afzal took his place in the heart of the congregation with a judge seated on his right and a missionary on his left. Poets recited elegies which they had written in commemoration of the oppression and martyrdom of Hussein amidst the wailing and keening and chanting of the crowd.

But neither the mourning ceremonies of the Shi'a community of Egypt, nor the Sunni processions of Baghdad, nor the playing of fools and jesters among the courtiers, had a part in the establishment of a dramatic rite or a powerful and eloquent theatrical form in Persia from the social point of view. It can be said that mourning ceremonies of Ashura came into being in response to a profound spiritual and social need. They had a sort of philosophical bent which, though implicitly nurtured in the Shi'a movement with tendencies similar to those of the Mutazilite philosophical sect, was derived from one basic principle. In the culture of which Ta'ziyeh was a part, the principles of life, "free will," and *tashabbuh* (imitation, appearing to be the same as something else), had a definitive role in the development and form of Ta'ziyeh.

The Buyid princes, who in 324 A.H./A.D. 935-36 and thereafter came to power in various parts of Persia, were helped by Mutazilite thinkers in their rise to power and in the establishment of their social ideas while at the same time they propagated the Shi'a sect. From early times the Shi'as and the Mutazilites were in agreement on theological matters.

Sahib ibn Abbad, the prime minister of the Daylamites Muayyad al-Dawla and Fakhr al-Dawla, made great efforts to introduce the ideas of Mutazilite thinkers. He invited the people to recognize and accept the philosophical sect of Abu Hashim Jabbai (d. 321 A.H./A.D. 933) who was one of the great theologians in Islamic history. Another great Mutazilite scholar, Qazi Abdul-Jabbar (d. 4l4 A.H./A.D. 1023-24), who was of Persian origin, came to Ray at the invitation of Sahib ibn Abbad in 360 A.H./A.D. 970-71, founded a Mutazilite school in that city and taught and disseminated his own views.

Abbad, who placed a high value upon mourning for Hussein and wrote elegies commemorating his death, found what he had been seeking in the ideas and practices of the Mutazilites. The Shi'as, too, were in agreement with many of these ideas.

From about the second century of Islamic history a group of scholars and intellectuals engaged in the theoretical discussion of religious beliefs and Islamic theology using logical reasoning and debate. These scholars were active until the sixth Islamic century and were known as *mutakallimin* (scholastic theologians) while their discipline was called *ilm-e kalam* (scholastic theology). They were divided into two differing parties, the Mutazilites and the Asharites. The followers of the Sunni and Shi'a sects were attracted by the thinking of the Asharites and Mutazilites, respectively, and more or less accepted their views as philosophical principles.

Along with theological concepts such as the unity of God, divine justice, and the creation or eternal existence of the Koran, matters connected with the human condition such as actions and man's responsibility for them constituted the pivot of the arguments of both sects of scholastic theologians. They had widely differing opinions in these areas. The problem was this: Is man the creator of and responsible for his deeds, or had his actions been predetermined in the past? The Asharites, who were more often the defenders of the status quo, rejected free will and the freedom of man in his actions. The Sunni establishment, from its position of power, preferred comfortable thinking and was close to the Asharites. The unchangeable principle of predestination and the idea that everything had been determined from the beginning of time by divine providence served the interests of the caliphate. The Mutazilite thinkers, on the other hand, held that the intellect was the standard of judgment and they prepared the ground for the exercise of personal judgment *(ijtihad)* and theoretical discussion in Islam. Their school of philosophy was based upon the principle that man possesses freedom in his actions and is therefore responsible for good and bad behavior, thus deserving reward and punishment. The Asharite belief that the social behavior of man is beyond his will power and is within the compass of God's providence was called *zulm* (injustice), and they thought it to be far from the "justice" of God.

The ritual of mourning for Hussein, which in reality consisted of condemning injustice and emphasizing man's right to oppose oppressors, was considered to be an expression of the meaning of justice and was totally in opposition to the views of the scholars and official thinkers of the caliphate. It was a conditional support of the free will concept as "the matter between the two matters" (the middle way) which sought the free will and liberty of man. We shall see its manifestation in the Ta'ziyeh text below.

While rejecting fatalistic ideas, the Mutazilite thinkers also investigated and rejected the articles of faith of the followers of Dualism like the ideas of the Manicheans, ideas which were still current in Islamic lands (including Persia) in the early centuries of Islam.

Qazi Abdul Jabbar who, as we have said, was busy teaching his ideas in Ray and who also conducted debates with the Asharites and the Manicheans, explained his opinion about the knowledge and evaluation of human behavior in this way:

> According to the Dualists all ills and sorrows of man are bad and all delights and pleasures are good. And according to the fatalists [the Asharites], the good and bad of sorrow is dependent upon the agent while the agent of the act is God. Thus the act is good and agreeable regardless of whether it constitutes injustice or not. [In the opinion of Qazi Abdul Jabbar] the goodness and badness of an act, such as pain, is connected to the nature and essence of the action. If a benefit is concealed in it or it repulses a misfortune which in comparison with the pain is greater, from the point of view of merit, it is a good; if not, it is bad. Painful actions like injustice possess ample badness . . . and injustice has no connection with God. . . .[3]

This opinion, with its rejection of ideas that proceeded from the explanation of the social nature of good and evil, held that the goodness or badness of an act was a matter of reason. In regard to the social experiences of man, it strengthened the ground for mourning on Ashura, which provided a feeling of participation in the afflictions of Hussein and his opposition to the oppressor. The Shi'a emphasis upon weeping appeared as a kind of opposition to contrary traditions of society.

During the Buyid period a section of the community had the material means for recreation and gaiety. Part of these were factors in the preliminary stages of theatrical development. Among them were jesters and clowns who, in the courts of the caliphs and princes and similarly in the courts of the sultans and ministers of the Buyids, entertained the court with their sharp replies, jests and jokes, and laughter-provoking behavior and speech.

Occasionally they were critical, but they had no social influence and the intellectual and emotional content of their remarks was negligible. Tha'alibi has mentioned in his book *Yatima tual-Dahr* a boon companion named Abi Ward who acted the fool in the court of Hassan ibn Muhammad Muhlibi, the prime minister of Mu'izz al-Dawla Daylami. He had such skill in mimicking the gestures and speech mannerisms of various people that all present were moved to laughter.

Abu Bakr Khwarazmi, whom we have mentioned above, in a letter in which he sought forgiveness from Sahib ibn Abbad for the banned clowns of the minister Ibn Amid, requested that each clown be reviewed with respect to his particular talents. However, society, which was in search of high human and social excellence and had great aspirations, succeeded in bestowing meaning to the tragedy of life and death through participation in its sorrow and suffering and in faith in religious purity and holiness; that is with a deep and sincere appreciation of human tragedy when dramatic representation was given to that tragedy. For this society "laughter after the tragedy of Taff," in the words of Sabib ibn Abbad, "is unlawful."

The supporters of the principle of predestination (the Asharites) found expression for their fatalistic views based upon the lack of free will in exhibitions like *khiyal-bazi* (shadow plays), *lu'bat-bazi* (a kind of puppet show), etc. In the context of these exhibitions in the Sunni community of Persia in past centuries, philosophical matters with respect to man's role as a plaything of fate in accordance with Asharite ideas were presented. In any case, puppet shows and the like were, in the beginning, a kind of divine comedy which gradually changed into pure comedy.

The course upon which Ta'ziyeh moved internally was the principle of *tashabbuh* (imitation). This principle was operative in the theatre as well as in the purely social sphere in the context of the culture of past centuries. *Tashabbuh,* in the context of "making a resemblance" (the use of which term was derived from a *hadith* saying that "whoever makes himself resemble a group is in the category of that group"), carried a meaning of quest and aspiration, and expressed the necessity for making one's self resemble the good on the one hand, and for keeping one's distance from evil and the emulation of the enemies of religion on the other. In the sixth Islamic century, the meaning of *tashabbuh* was stressed and used to justify the rituals of Muharram mourning. This new interpretation of *tashabbuh* in mourning with regard to impersonation and emulation was made by one of the major Mutazilite scholars.

Abul-Qasem Mahmud ibn Umar Zamakhshari (467-538 A.H./A.D. 1074-1143) was a Persian and one of the last of the famous theologians. He wrote a book about education entitled *Atwaqudh-Dhahab fil-Muwa'iz wal-Khatb* in which he explained that according to religious traditions anyone who weeps for Hussein is certainly destined to join him in eternity. He added that anyone who weeps for himself and causes others to weep is one of the good, based on the saying, "whoever makes himself resemble *(tashabbuh)* a group is in the category of that group," and the same merit shall accrue to him. That is, he prepared the theoretical ground for "imitation" and gave importance and value to the act of causing weeping through any means. *Maqtal-khani* (recital of martyrdom stories), the descriptive narrative of the tragedy of Kerbela, is one means which was partly inspired by the views of Zamakhshari.

Tashabbuh and in reality the practical philosophy of Ta'ziyeh, grew out of the accumulation of ritualistic experiences. It had a human quality and was an attainment of spiritual knowledge and development through devotion to the pious ones. It was a kind of self-realization in opposition to another type which it resembled, which was conspicuous in the mysticism of that era and was called the "imitation of God" and possessed a theoretical base.

Zamakhshari's precedent about *tashabbuh* in *maqtal* writing and recital or, in other words, *rowzeh-khani*, was followed by others. One of his pupils named Abul-Muayyed Muwaffaq Khwarazmi (died 568 A.H./A.D. 1172-73) collected traditions and religious stories describing the virtues of the Prophet and his Family. He wrote an epic describing the circumstances surrounding the death of Imam Hussein which is known as the "Martyrdom of Hussein by Khwarazmi." In this work, too, a *hadith* from the Prophet emphasizing and strengthening *tashabbuh* is related in another form: "The Prophet of God addressed Ali saying, 'The first people to enter heaven will be four persons: I and thee and Hassan and Hussein then our children and descendants and their wives, and then our partisans [Shi'as] who follow our faith and virtues.' "

During the reign of Sultan Hussein Bayqara in Herat, Mulla Hussein Vaez Kashefi (died 910 A.H./A.D. 1504-5) wrote *Rowzatu'l Shuhada'* (The Garden of Martyrs) which was the first *maqtal* in Persian. In Baghdad Muhammad ibn Sulaiman Fuzuli (died 932 A.H./A.D. 1565-66), following his example, wrote the first *maqtal* in Turkish, called *Hadiqatu's-Su'ada* (The Garden of the Felicitous). Both these writers thus proclaimed their debt to Zamakhshari and made *tashabbuh* (imitation) and *tamaththul* (resembling), with the sense of emulation in seeking superiority, the objective of their story-telling. These "martyrdoms" were essentially the record of the tragedy of the plain of Kerbela and were recited each Muharram in mourning assemblies and gatherings for the purpose of playing upon the emotions of those present and making them weep. This ceremony, called *rowzeh-khani*, became widespread in association with the Safavids' rise to power, because they were Shi'as. It is at this time that the principle of *tashabbuh* made itself evident in society, and was soon to appear also in the theatre. In reality, *tashabbuh* expressed the value of the individual in society.

Shah Ismail Safavi (died 930 A.H./A.D. 1523-24), profiting from the intellectual values of Shi'ism and strengthened by its religious customs, raised its political standard in Azarbaijan. He was an innovator too. He wrote religious poetry extolling the excellence of Ali and Imam Hussein, and he received support from it in mobilising and arousing adherents to the cause of achieving his social and nationalistic objectives. In this regard a poem written by Shah Ismail under the pen name Khatai deserves our attention. In it he makes the heroes of the Shi'as a model for his own career and for his followers:

> That king has been our ruler from eternity;
> Our saint, our guide, and our chief.
> We willingly sacrifice ourselves for him,
> As the word of the king is our faith.
> Our proof, words that have become arrows
> Rain death upon the envious and the hypocritical.
> We have come forward for the king's rights,
> We are Hussein's men, and this is our epoch.
> In devotion we are the slaves of the Imam;
> Our name is "zealot" and our title "martyr."
> Our road is hazardous and dangerous,
> Obedience to the way is our code.
> Khatai is fond of the secret of Ali;
> The rejectors of the king of truth are our enemies.

The state of the mourning ceremonies after the establishment of the Safavid regime indicates that the outward aims of Ta'ziyeh had been transferred inward, to within the Shi'a community. There was no longer any conflict between the rites of the Shi'as and those of their religious opponents or about the Shi'as holding their mourning ceremonies. In place of former conflicts between opposing sects, the Shi'a mourning processions now competed with each other, using various fanatical pretexts for hostility, so that each group appeared to the other as its imagined enemy. Real battles were fought, and people were injured and even killed. They participated in a drama partly real and partly fantasy.

Travelers who had visited Persia during the Safavid period have left us comments about this situation. The Spanish priest Antonio de Gouvea, who came to Persia during the reign of Shah Abbas I, wrote in 1011 A.H./A.D.1602-3 of his observations in Shiraz:

During the ten days of Muharram, processions of people shouting "Shah Hussein Alas Hussein!" roam the lanes and chant dirges. Some of these processions are armed while others are not. A lot of the people carry bludgeons five or six cubits long in their hands and frequently they split into two groups and attack each other. They fight so vigorously that commonly several are killed.

Pietro della Valle, an Italian traveler who was in Isfahan for a few years at about the same time wrote:

During the Muharram period, processions are brought out of everywhere for the mourning ceremonies. Some of the men hold clubs and are always ready to engage in a fight with other processions, not just for right of way, but also out of plain pugnaciousness, so that they can participate, so to speak, in the mourning for Hussein. They believe that if a person is killed on this day in such a fight he will go straight to heaven. In the city square and in the main intersections, a large number of mounted troops of the nobility are prepared to intervene and separate the processions. Despite all this, while watching mounted on a horse, I myself saw that these measures were ineffectual and some of the people rioted in front of the royal palace. There was fighting in other streets with the result that many returned home battered and wounded. In the battle which I observed, I noticed that some of those who were nearest to the house of the king would carry their trays and standards and other paraphernalia inside the palace whenever they were attacked in order to protect them from damage and pilferage, because during the fighting it is the custom to carry off these articles as plunder from the opponents, and their loss would be a matter of great shame and dishonor to the procession. In 1028 A.H. [A.D. 1618] Shah Abbas watched from a porch on the front of Ali Qapu. Since he did not want fighting to occur he ordered that the processions pass in an orderly fashion, one after another.

When this imitative identification in a society is changed into free and independent behavior, the identification with the ritual of mourning is inverted and in reality is reactionary. Ta'ziyeh connects the group of mourners with the original act, i.e., a natural event underlying the social event. This act occurred in the past, in the tragedy of Ashura with the death of Hussein. The recital of elegies and especially the *maqtals* and the *rowzeh-khanis* which are verbal descriptions of the event of Ashura prepared the groundwork for its reenactment in a realistic translation into action. In addition to the recital of *maqtals* and in order to exacerbate weeping among the people *(ibka),* scenes of the incidents after the martyrdom were suggested in processions through biers, riderless horses, and prisoners mounted on camels. These were paraded through the crowds, but they were in the nature of portable tableaux rather than reenactments. Just as in social life the principle of *tashabbuh* had been changed from a concept to reality, and men in specific historical circumstances sought spiritual identification through participating with genuine feeling in the mourning ceremonies and gatherings in Muharram, *tashabbuh* and "impersonation" became the impetus for the appearance of theatrical roles. In reality, based on the experience of observing the memory of the Ta'ziyeh events, the play *(shabih)* of Ta'ziyeh was the natural product of ritual, the harvest of *tashabbuh*.

Information about the beginnings of drama in the Safavid era is obtainable from the notes of foreign travelers. Antonio de Gouvea wrote further about the ceremonies he witnessed in Shiraz:

> In front of the mourning processions camels are seen draped in green cloth upon which women and children are riding. The heads and faces of the women and children are bruised and wounded as though by arrows and they appear to be weeping and wailing. Then a company of armed men passed shooting their guns into the air [this observation demonstrates the mixture of drama and life]. After them, came coffins followed by the governor of the city [Allahverdi Khan] and other notables of the government. All entered the great mosque of Shiraz. There a mulla mounted the pulpit and recited eulogies, and all wept. . . .

Pietro della Valle wrote at some length about the ceremonies he observed in Isfahan in 1027 A.H./A.D. 1618:

> With the arrival of the tenth of Muharram, the day of the martyrdom of Hussein, large processions appear from all directions and people from all sections of Isfahan carrying flags and standards. A variety of weapons and many turbans on the horses accompany the processions. In addition to this there are several camels accompanying them upon which boxes are transported. In each of these there are three or four children representing the captured children of the martyr Hussein. Besides these, every procession carries biers wrapped with black velvet and upon which a single turban, usually green, and a sword are placed. In the same fashion a variety of weapons and other articles is placed upon the numerous trays carried by some of the people on their heads. They jump about to the music of cymbals and flutes, and whirl about. In this way the trays too spin around, creating a marvelous scene. Around the tray-bearers there are men carrying clubs. . . .

And Auliya Chelebi, the Ottoman traveler and writer who came to Tabriz during the reign of Shah Safi in 1050 A.H./A.D. 1640, described the Ashura mourning in his *Travels:*

On the tenth [of Muharram] each year the nobles and notables and all the people of the city, great and little, erect tents and mourn the martyrs of Kerbela on the polo ground of Tabriz. In this period, water is provided to the people in crystal cups, and some of the nobles and important personages hang flasks around their necks and give water to the people for the sake of Imam Hussein. The khan or *beglerbegi* of Tabriz is seated in his embroidered tent with a group of the notables and nobles of Tabriz in attendance, and they read a *maqtal* about Imam Hussein. Many devotees of Hussein are seated, listening attentively with humility and submissiveness. When the reader of the book reaches the part describing the manner in which the accursed Shemr killed the oppressed Imam Hussein, at that very moment, they bring out to the field from the pavilion of the Martyrs of Ashura mock representations of the bodies of the dead children of the Imam. Upon seeing this spectacle shouts and screams and wailings of "Alas Hussein" mount from the people to the heavens and all the spectators weep and wail. Hundreds of Hussein's devotees beat and wound their heads, faces, and bodies with swords and knives. For the love of Imam Hussein they make their blood flow. The green grassy field becomes bloodied and looks like a field of poppies. Then the mock dead are carried from the field and the reading of the *maqtal* of Imam Hussein is completed.

The dramatic portrayal of the tragedy of Ashura developed from the institution of the recital of dirges by mourners with a vivid description of the tragedy, in the first person or ecstatic language, from the first representations in *maqtals*. This occurred from the end of the Safavid period through the Zand period and to the beginning of the Qajar era, when Ta'ziyeh, in the sense of a sad religious play, assumed a prominent position in the mourning ceremonies. Naturally the religious value of Ta'ziyeh was discussed. What relationship does Ta'ziyeh or *shabih* have to Islamic religious law? Was this innovation acceptable or not from the point of view of religious law? Keeping in mind the certainty that Ta'ziyeh sprang from faith and was nurtured in the cradle of religion, the answers seem obvious. However, from the time of the transition of traditional society to its modern counterpart, the intellectual and cultural continuity has been broken, and the community's understanding of Ta'ziyeh has become distorted. The relationship of Ta'ziyeh and religion is sometimes viewed erroneously. Passing over its undeniable religious background, in order to achieve a definitive judgment about Ta'ziyeh or *shabih* and the general meaning of theatre from the point of view of Islam, we must refer first to the opinions of theologians, because misunderstandings have arisen due to a lack of correct information about those opinions. Generally speaking, religious matters in Islam have been investigated in two areas, theology *(ilm-ekalam)* and doctrine *(usul-e fiqh)*. In the debates of the theologians whose work is the theoretical discussion of religious beliefs based upon theological commentary and the Koran, the problem of *tashbih* (anthropomorphization) is one of the main subjects for discussion. From the theological viewpoint this is concerned with knowledge of God, and in the context of the Unity of God with regard to the possibility or impossibility of comparison *(tashbih)* with the essence of God, an idea which has generally been refuted by both Mutazilite and Asharite scholars. However, they have positive opinions about the possibility of the vision of God which is the subject of much speculation on the part of certain mystics. Therefore, this kind of anthropomorphization has no connection with impersonations of humans which Ta'ziyeh has evolved.

For information about the position and view of Islam regarding impersonation of humans or, in other words, play-acting, we are compelled to refer to the opinions of Islamic scholars whose work involved the discussion of the practical rules of religious law. It must be said that Shi'a scholars have answered this question in relation to the appearance of Ta'ziyeh. They delivered a religious decision *(fatwa)* at the time of the popularization of the religious plays: *shabih* or religious drama has been recognized as free and lawful. During the reign of Agha Muhammad Khan Qajar when the tradition of Ta'ziyeh and the dramatization of the events of Ashura were spreading, the first famous judgment about the religious plays was given by Mirza Abul-Qasem ibn Hassan Gilani, also known as Fazel Qummi (died 1231 A.H./A.D. 1815-16), who was one of the most important Shi'a religious authorities, theologians, and scholars of the Qajar period. He influenced the thinking of Agha Muhammad Khan and Fath Ali Shah, and was the object of extraordinary honor by the Shi'a theologians. He unequivocally expressed the opinion that not only were religious plays lawful and not prohibited but that they were among the greatest of religious works.

This famous judgment of Mirza Abul-Qasem Qummi was later published in 1234 A.H./A.D. 1818-19 in his book on religious law entitled *Jami 'al-Shatat,* and has been reprinted many times. Now, 160 years after the first printing of this historic religious document in which the essential freedom of the *shabih* theatre was promulgated, once again we present its text for the information of the enquiring:

Question: Is it lawful on the days of Ashura to play the roles of the Imam or the enemies of the Family of the Prophet in order to induce the people to weep? Is it lawful that men wearing the clothing of the Family of the Prophet or others should play their roles for the same purpose, or is it not?

Answer: ... We say there is no reason to prohibit the representation of the innocent and pure ones and the generality of the excellence

107

of weeping, causing weeping, and pretending to weep for the Lord of Martyrs and his followers proves this. . . . Sometimes it is supposed that this dishonors the sanctity of religious leaders, but this supposition is invalid because it is not genuine identification, rather an imitation of form, appearance, and dress merely to commemorate their misfortunes. If the meaning of "dishonor to the sanctity of these persons" is that the humiliations to which they were subjected should not be brought to the attention of the people, lest they become aware of those humiliations, that too is invalid because numerous traditions from the pure Imams have been recorded mentioning those humiliations and they have commanded us to read them in assemblies. Now we display the picture of those sufferings through someone other than they themselves. Even though we say in the traditions and the languages of tradition that the metaphor of Ali as a lion which is an animal and of Hussein [as] a sheep whose head is cut off, and the good and pious are compared with white-footed horses whom Ali leads, then why would the personification of a Shi'a among Shi'as, of a friend of his friends not be lawful? In the same way, what harm is there in the portrayal of the women on bare-backed camels by other persons since there are many traditions confirming the event and we read them in assemblies?

However, [as to] the representation of the enemies of the Family of the Prophet: There is no proof for the view that it is prohibited as might be imagined. This is something that is in keeping with the famous saying, "he who imitates a people is of them." It is the sense of a tradition which I cannot recall now that this is not called *tashabbuh* because that means that the player wants to identify himself with the role and he puts on his costume in willingness and desire; he wants to be counted among the good. We submit that this is generally the case. Thus we say after the presentation of documentary evidence and inference and submission to the public, it is the connection between this and the generality of weeping. There is doubt that the common desire for causing weeping is the best proof and support for the sanctity of this kind of role. In the same way we reason about sanctity, the sanctity of the abasement by the believer of his soul. Thus we answer . . . there is a time when it is among the greatest of religious works. And this which is merely to please God is a great *jihad* and God is such that if a person humbles himself in His cause He does not exclude him from His blessing. Furthermore, there are many different persons and in connection with some persons it is not an abasement in respect to the despicability of their souls and the greater part of the enemies are portrayed by these persons.

(The second instance was described by Sayyed Ali Yazdi in 1320 A.H./A.D. 1903-4 in this way: "On the supposition of the doctrine of the prohibition from playing [the parts of] the enemies and the submission to that doctrine 'he who imitates a people is of them' we say: the prohibition is not from merely playing in figure and form. Rather it is with regard to actual deeds and behavior. If the person who imitates them places himself in the same class, or if the intention of the representation is sympathy, friendship, embellishment of the way, and approval of their manner . . .")

Regarding the presentation of the women: The answer is also that which we said it would be; that it is forbidden to portray them. With respect to a man impersonating a woman, it is not done just to play a woman; rather he desires, for example, to portray Zainab Khatun by [wearing a] dress that is not unusually or explicitly feminine, and is not harmful, but like an evening veil that is worn over the body. He repeats the words she spoke in order to induce weeping and this cannot be called female impersonation. For this purpose, portrayal is only of that which is peculiar to woman without any other motive. Here, the dress of women is worn to portray a woman. There is a great difference between the concept of portrayal of a specific individual among women in order to show the details of the deeds of that woman and the playing of women as women. Reflect carefully so that you may comprehend.

(This point was explained by Sayyed Ali Yazdi in the following way: What is the intention of men and women in impersonating each other? What is the truth about wearing each other's clothing which is the subject of the condemnation mentioned? It is evident that the purport of the traditions is not merely about imitation in the ordinary aspect of impersonation; rather the intention is in reference to men who copy the femininity of women, and it is of this that Fazel Qummi says: dressing up as women is forbidden if the impersonation is done for a private purpose in order to appear as a woman and of their sex. It is evident that the custom in the plays is not of this kind and it is plain that a man playing Zainab Khatun, for example, is not dressed as a woman simply for the purpose of appearing as a woman; rather his intention is to portray her form and figure in order to induce weeping. To sum up, the motive is to induce weeping and not to display oneself in female garb. Therefore, he is not truly impersonating a woman. The object of the prohibiting tradition is to prevent female impersonation, and does not refer to the person whose intention is to show a woman's predicament and to express and present her form and situation. . . .)

This same Mirza Abul-Qasem Qummi had an important part in the development of Shi'a law and he tried to bring the principle of free will out of the sphere of intellectual power into the domain of real power and to

109

make it conform with social exigencies. In a letter to Agha Muhammad Khan, the founder of the Qajar dynasty, he wrote:

> If a person supposes that kingship and dominion are by Divine predestination and accordingly to whomever the Lord of the World bestowed the sovereignty, then the consequences of this are not a sin for him. Whatever occurs to him will not be a cause for a reprimand. ... This supposition is false. ... In the Koran, Almighty God has repeatedly assigned the responsibility for man's sins to man and He has separated Himself from it. He says, "We did not wrong them but they wronged themselves." [4] ... Thus, if kingship and dominion are merely from Providence, it is necessary that every deed which occurs to him also be predestined and that God approve of it. ... Therefore the cruel caliphs who were enemies of the Family of the Prophet should not be punished for their despicable behavior. ...."

This is the same belief in free will and rejection of predestination that Shi'a scholars also relied upon in their theological disputes.

Along with the "emulation" in Ta'ziyeh, another factor of "antiemulation" concerning the form of the enemies of the Imam came into existence. The first factor consisted of positive emotions which acted to bring the feelings of the spectators close together, while the second factor consisted of negative emotions which stimulated the people against the emulators. The theatrical representation of the Imam and the Family of the Prophet naturally acted to attract the sympathies of the people while the roles of the oppressors and enemies created a feeling of revulsion and rejection of their example. Therefore, the moral judgment of society about itself was reflected and adapted through the speeches of the villains. As an example, in one Ta'ziyeh play when Shemr goes to cut off the head of the Imam, Shemr says to him:

> I am the hard-hearted shameless Shemr,
> I have no fear of God;
> I have no shame before the Prophet,
> I have no embarrassment before the cheek of Ali;
> I have no fear in my heart of Hassan,
> I am not afraid of the lamenting of Fatemeh.
> I shall cut off the head of her son;
> I shall cause her Zainab to have a scratched face
>   [from mourning].

This style excited the spectators into feeling opposition to the oppressors, and, in reality, it transferred their antagonistic feelings to the representations of the villains. In a kind of reaction, this hatred and spiritual separation strengthened the antithetical emotions of the people toward the pious heroes who were engaged in the struggle with their enemies.

For information about traditional society's view of Ta'ziyeh, we quote comments from the book *Vasail Muzaffari* about the merit and virtues of observing Ta'ziyeh by Sayyed Ali Yazdi, a scholar and legal expert during the reign of Muzaffar al-Din Shah. It was written to encourage Ta'ziyeh observances and it emphasized the necessity of weeping, the importance of *tashabbuh,* the value of free will, and the conceptual relations of these factors in the sufferings:

> It is appropriate that the Shi'a not think of reward and compensation in weeping and observing the mourning for that great person [Hussein]. His devotion to Shi'ism, his love for Hussein, make him weep, nothing else. Heartfelt sincerity to that great one makes him lose control of himself and causes his tears to flow, not the thought of reward and benefit and the pleasure of attainment of merit and the flight from punishment. Can a Shi'a at the level of sincerity and purity and devotion and dedication restrain himself and while listening to the recital of and remembering the sufferings of that great one not break down weeping? Is it not sufficient to cause tears that the Imams of the Shi'a faith are related to him, and he recognizes them as his own? . . . Is not the saying of the great one, "I am killed so that they will weep" enough to provoke the Shi'a? Are not the words of Imam Ja'far of the Family of Muhammad sufficient . . . who said, "Brother, do you not want to accompany Fatemeh in weeping for Hussein?" Is not the *tashabbuh* of the perfect ones of God among the prophets and messengers and saints enough to cause weeping? Does it seem right to you that all the creatures of God . . . are weeping and wailing, being touched and suffering, while the Shi'a with his claim to being a Shi'a and his knowledge that Hussein chose all these sufferings for his salvation, restrains himself? . . . Are you content that you not show your agreement and sympathy with the Prophet of God and Ali and Fatemeh and Hassan and the other guiding leaders who are beloved of God, and show that you resemble and follow the Umayyads. . . .?

How was the philosophical principle of free will reflected in Ta'ziyeh? Mulla Hussein Vaez Kashefi in his *maqtal Rowzat'ul Shuhada'* quotes from the *maqtal* of Khwarazmi about the reason Hussein sought a respite from battle on the eve of Ashura and the proposal he made to his companions that night?

111

Thus the day of Tasua passed and the day of Ashura began. Hussein assembled his troops and addressed them eloquently. After praising God, he said to them: "Know that I have relieved you from your oaths of obedience to me and I have requested this respite on your behalf. Now each one of my companions, take the hand of one of my household and scatter throughout the land so that you may find deliverance from suffering and relief from oppression. My thought is this, that when these people see me they will not pursue you.

Mirza Muhammad Taqi. an influential religious authority during the reign of Fath Ali Shah. wrote numerous Ta'ziyeh texts. One of them is about "The Seeking of a Respite by Imam Hussein." We quote a part of it from a manuscript written in 1261 A.H./A.D. 1845:

Hussein
to Abbas:
	O brother address this army a while
	Saying. O hard-hearts. vengeful. disgraced ones.
	The descendant of the Prophet has spoken thus:
	We have yielded our bodies to a deplorable work
	    and we shall expend our lives;
	But tonight grant a respite; tomorrow is the time
	    of battle.
	Refrain from it now and resolve upon a postponement
	So that I may take a last farewell from my God.
	Commune with Him. weep. sigh. and wail.
	I shall sweeten the desire of my soul with the honey
	    of the sight of the Beloved;
	I shall expel sorrow from my heart with the blessing
	    of the word of the Beloved.
	I continually desire to serve Him in secret.
	The taste of these fiery nights and days is on my soul.
	A respite of one night is easy. O hard-hearts!
	I am. after all. of the Family of the Seal of the Prophets.

Abbas to *the army:*	O army of evil deed. O bad-natured troops. Faithless. cruel. adulterous evil-doers! Our sovereign has sought an evening's respite from you So that he may take farewell from our God. Hold back from him tonight. O rascals, So that he may commune with God until tomorrow.
Shemr *to Abbas:*	O youth. there has not been a moment of peace for you these days;

112

There was no respite for you, it is the end.
Now I shall destroy your men,
Now out of rancor I shall plunder your garden,
I shall carry away your foundations with a flood
    of hatred.
I shall cause your cries to reach the heavens by my
    cruelty.

The Army: What mercilessness and injustice is this. O elders?
The seven heavens are astonished at this treachery
    and hatred.
After all. this is the admirable one of the Lord of
    the worlds:
After all. this is the child of the Best of Messengers.
    O men!
After all. this is the illustrious son of the Best of
    Women:
After all. the Lion of God was fortunate to see him.
If an infidel seeks a respite. you grant it quickly.
What has made your hearts like stone against the
    descendant of the Prophet?
The grandson of the Best of the Messengers seeks a
    night's respite:
Why do you refuse him in this way? Be ashamed!

Umar Sa'd: Know, O vengeful army. from the old and young. the
    white and the black.
We have given to Hussein and all his army
Security tonight, O courageous ones!
Refrain from battle this night,
On tomorrow rain disaster upon them.
Sheathe your swords,
Tomorrow is the moment of pleasure for you.
Tell the Imam of the Epoch, O youth,
That we have granted him security tonight.
Do whatever you want to tonight—
For there will be no opportunity after this.

Abbas
addresses   O you for whom the soul of the world would be a
    sacrifice,
Imam   They have given us respite this night after the importuning
Hussein: of these stone-hearted ones.

113

The Holy Ones of heaven are struck with wonder at this test.
The Praisers of God are astounded by this patience.
No one among the ancients or the moderns could endure
    this.
Your place is in the heart of the court of God
    the Soul-creator.

Imam   O my supporters and companions,
Hussein: O my brothers and children,
            O my helpers, old and young,
            O my friends, small and great.
            Quickly gather around me now
            Like moths about a candle.
            I want to reveal the hidden secret
            To him who is suited for this honor.

The   Our souls are in our hands as an offering,
Compan-   O king of religion, O monarch of the world.
ions: What is your order that we may obey it?
            If you want our lives, we commit them willingly.
            We are all slaves and you the king,
            We are the stars and you the sun and the moon.
            We are attentive to your commands,
            We look to your favor.
            Our foreheads are pressed on your threshold.
            All is lighted by the beams of your moon.
            What is the decision? Tell us now, speak:
            Seek our hearts a bit in your mercy.

Imam   I Praise God.
Hussein: For from Him the whole world finds color and scent.
            The God who causes the day and night to appear,
            The God who created good and evil;
            The God who raised this sky,
            Whose lamp is a guide for the world.
            He has given it a golden thread
            He has ground the surface of the sky with rust:
            He has set two gem-studded wings over all the sky,
            With the stars like pearls
            On this turquoise leathern cloth showing jewels.

The eye is dazzled by its brightness.
Enough ambergris has been poured into the censer,
The shining sun is consumed in flames.
He makes it die and revives it again;
He humbles it and caresses it again.
From the old crone of the world all the old ones
Become manifest from it as numberless youths.
All the elegant speech and sweet language,
All the good action of eloquence;
From the waves of air in the space of the mouth,
He makes all speech as though it were in Eden.
Then the jewels come out, strung together;
For them He barters that which was concealed.
The world in its wideness hides them,
Not with pain in the throats of the observers.
By His dignity an atom has a hundred colors
For a moment. How marvelous is His counsel.
His command can create a thousand great worlds
In a moment.
For the pleasure of the eye of man
How turquoise He has made the sky!
What a heavy burden has been suspended in the sky
By the thread of the command of God.
He made the world a veil
Between mankind and the hereafter.
The God who created the Fire and the Light
Has made evident the wretched and the content.
He sent His orders with the messengers,
For the growth of the peoples of earth.
Such coming and going for the sake of salvation,
He manifested to us the Seal of Prophecy.
He honored us with this rank,
My pure grandfather was praised by all.
I praise him, auspicious praise;
I praise in public and at ease,
O God, I praise thee
Who taught us the great revelation.
Thou hast granted us Thy religion,
Thou hast guided us with Thy institutions;
Thou has bestowed upon us all that Thou knowest,
Thou has led us and developed our intellects.
Praise belongs to Thee in good times and bad,
In the open and in secret this is right for me.

Imam	After the praise of the Dispenser of Justice of the
Hussein	Universe, God,
to his	Know, O faithful army,
Compan-	I have not seen in these wretched times
ions:	Any more faithful than my own companions,

Better than my own beloved supporters.
No one has seen his fellow crawl to sleep.
My lord will give you a good reward for my sake.
He will grant you a boon from His mercy.
A revelation came upon me now,
That a thousand disasters lie ahead of us.
Now I have released you from your oaths of obedience,
This is an opportunity for you.
I have no expectation of help from you,
No one is free of sorrow in these times.
Night has come and enveloped the world,
Turn your faces to wherever you want to go.
They will come after me, these infidels,
They seek me, no one else.
[Many leave] . . .

According to the writer of *Majales-e Husseiniyeh* (about whom more will be said below):

He sent away all those who were concerned for their own lives and wealth and who for these reason had followed the Imam. He openly released them from their oaths so that they would not be involuntarily involved in his own actions. Then, all those who did not have this good fortune and were not suited for martyrdom departed.

Muhammad Rafi' Tabatabai (Nezam al-Ulama) was a famous religious scholar of the period of Naser al-Din Shah and Muzaffar al-Din Shah. In 1322 A.H./A.D. 1904-5 when he was 72 years old, he wrote and published a book entitled *Majales-e Husseiniyeh,* describing the philosophy of the sufferings and mourning for Imam Hussein. It sheds light on the real problems of Ta'ziyeh and on its meaning. He expressed his opinions about the sensitive stages of development in traditional society and, similarly, Ta'ziyeh in Persia. From the point of view of Shi'a thought, the question is why was it that God did not relieve Hussein of all those afflictions? Why did He allow Hussein's enemies to do whatever they chose in the way of oppression and torment? What form does the connection of the will and decree of God with all His power and might have with these types of acts which are hateful to Him? Tabatabai replied:

> Omnipotent God in order that He not forcibly be an obstacle to the exercise of free will by individuals and so that everyone may be a source of good and evil according to his own inclinations and desire . . . does not interfere with them, that is He did not take away the power of free will from them so that the good and evil concealed in the self have no hindrance for its expression. . . .

He then added:

> God, in His perfect power, has made His servants free agents and has given them the power and ability to act and to desist, and has explained and made known to responsible adults the right and wrong way through the language of intelligence and the speech of the prophets and messengers. He has considered the benefits of His servants being free agents to be greater than [if they were] under compulsion. It became appropriate in His wisdom that, after the guidance of the messengers and the presentation of the ways, each person travel any path in accordance with his own inclinations and desires. By not taking back the power and strength from man, He has not coerced him or deprived him of free will.
>
> Thus, in this respect, it is possible that His will accidentally takes an interest in something essentially undesirable so that man not lose his fredom of choice. In that case, the connection of the will and desire of God to that thing is merely for the retention of the power of freedom of His servant, so that He not take away from him that blessing of free will which He granted His servants. In this sense it is secondarily and accidentally a good however bad the act of the individual is in itself. Since Divine Wisdom desires the continuation of the power, ability, and freedom of mankind, the relationship of the Divine Will to the preservation of the power and ability of the servant is not the same as its relation to the good and evil of his act . . . and the relationship of the will of God to these kinds of things is not of themselves or in their own right; rather it is accidental and with attention to its benefits and to the Plans, lest the blessing of freedom which He gave man be lost.

In *Majales-e Husseiniyeh,* while describing the rejection of the Asharite belief in predestination and the change and adjustment of the Mutazilite

117

principle of assignment into the form of free will found in Shi'a beliefs, he writes:

> Khajeh Nasir Tusi has written an explanation of a treatise that the will of man is the immediate cause of an act while the will of God is its remote cause. The Asharite turned his attention to the remote cause and believed in predestination; the Mutazilite, concentrating upon the immediate cause, believed in delegation. The truth is that the occurrence of an act is dependent upon the combination of both wills, as the Learned One of the Family of the Prophet has said: "There is neither predestination nor absolute freedom; rather the truth lies between the two extremes. . . ."
>
> The community of Imamite Shi'as, Mutazilites, and scholars believe that the good and bad of a thing is logical, but the belief of the Asharites is that it is spiritual. The meaning of a good act is that its agent is deserving praise and commendation by God and intelligent people, while the meaning of a bad act is that its agent earns reproaches and blame because of it. . . . It is certain that the Asharites were greatly mistaken in this matter as they believed bad emanating from God to be lawful. The falsity and corruption of this sect is evident to the intelligent and there is no necessity to cite evidence; they have not understood God.

Nezam al-Ulama considered the discussion of the tragedy of Kerbela in the Ta'ziyeh ceremony as a means of demonstrating right and wrong ways. Referring to himself, he wrote:

> Among good deeds: resorting to the Imam, the Lord of Martyrs [Hussein], and the discussion of the circumstances and time of that Imam of Salvation are better than other works and make for the strengthening of the pillar of devotion and freedom. . . . The principle, foundation, and essence of religion is devotion and freedom, the reality of which is necessarily strengthened with pity and sympathy for the Imam and attention to the oppression and injustice suffered by the Family of Misfortune.

He ended *Majales-eHusseiniyeh* with the verse from the Koran which is the justification for the mourning ceremonies of Muharram: "Those who do wrong shall surely know by what overturning they will be overturned." [5]

Tabatabai's book, which was published on the eve of the Constitutional Era, indicated a new awareness and view of Ta'ziyeh (as a play) in traditional society which assisted in the understanding of Ta'ziyeh and helped to make a new aesthetic use of it. By quoting a treatise about religious plays in his book by "Dr. Joseph," who was said to be "a famous French historian," he showed that traditional society in its aesthetic evaluation of Ta'ziyeh had reached a new level since the time of Mirza Abul-Qasem Qummi in development and traditional acceptance.

Now, without comment, we shall quote sections from that treatise, which is an important document about the theatrical culture of that period: [6]

> Among the political affairs which the leaders of the Shi'a sect covered with the cloak of religion and which greatly attracted the minds of their own followers as well as of non-Shi'as is the copying of the principles of the theatre called *shabih* and Ta'ziyeh in memory of Hussein.
>
> The wise men of India originally made the "theatre" part of their worship for several reasons which are outside the scope of our discussion. Then the Europeans gave it political coloration and introduced important political matters in the theatres in order to reach the minds of all classes and win them over. Gradually, this practice served to kill two birds with one stone; both as relief for tempers and [as] a means of gaining popular support. The Shi'a sect completely benefited from this in political matters and gave it a religious coloring. . . . In any event Ta'ziyeh and *shabih* had considerable impact on the minds of both the upper and lower classes. It is plain that on one hand, the continual *rowzeh-khani* assemblies and the recital from pulpits and mosques of the sufferings the leaders of their faith had undergone and the cruelties inflicted upon Hussein, together with all the stories which were told about weeping over the sufferings of the Family of the Prophet [had a profound impact: while on the other hand], the theatrical representation which also displayed those sufferings to their view were very influential, more so than might be expected, in strengthening the beliefs of both the upper and lower classes of this sect. . . . This sect [that is, the Shi'as] produced the plays in various ways. Sometimes, in special assemblies and in reserved places [since in these few non-Shi'as attended] a special theatrical state came into being, and they took the play out into the streets and markets and among all the other sects. . . . Gradually this performance gained much attention among all classes and some other Islamic sects, and some of the Hindus, too, imitated the Shi'as in the production of religious plays and cooperated with them. . . . It may be said that the theatrical principles and production of *shabih* in the Shi'a sect were fortified by the policy of the Safavid kings who were the first dynasty to gain power through the power of religion. The Shi'a spiritual leaders, too, gradually confirmed this [practice] and came to consider it lawful.

We must add that this article was also printed in the newspaper *Hablul-Matin;* for the second time as an appendix to another treatise in a book where it was called *Husseini Politics* in 1328 A.H./A.D. 1910 by Fathullah Khan Zafarud-daulah Sardar Moayyed; and for the third time under the same title in 1331 A.H./A.D. 1913 by Mirza Muhammad Khan Ghaffari Kashani Iqbal al-Dawla. This last printing was distributed free of charge to interested persons.

NOTES

1. Ibn al-Athīr. *Al-Kāmil fī al-Tarīkh;* Ibn Kathīr. *Al-Bidāya wa al-Nihāya.*
2. From *Maqtal al-Husain* by Abū-Bakr al-Khwārazmī.
3. Qazi Abdul Jabbor, *An Exposition of the Fine Principles.*
4. Koran, 16:118.
5. Koran, 26:227.
6. The complete text which describes the history of Shi'ism is to be found in the *Majālis-i-Husainiyyih* of Nizām al-'Ulamā (Tabriz: A.H. 1323/A.D. 1905-06) pp. 61-77.

9

Le Patronage des Ta'ziyeh :
Eléments pour une Etude Globale

Comme j'ai pu le signaler, la commémoration du Drame de Kerbéla telle qu'elle fut revivifiée en Iran depuis l'époque safavide (1501-1722) est l'aboutissement d'une longue tradition de rituels de pélerinage aux tombeaux des martyrs de Kerbéla, de processions et de séances de déploration du jour du Achourâ et de la première dizaine du Muharram pratiquées par des musulmans de diverses tendances confessionnelles, ces commémorations et leurs contre-célébrations par certains autres groupes musulmans ayant entrainé des heurts sanglants dans le cadre du factionnalisme particulier à l'Islam médiéval. J'ai pu aussi mettre l'accent sur le caractère ancien de l'utilisation, à des fins politiques, des ressorts émotifs du chiisme populaire et surtout du motif de la vengeance du sang de l'Emâm Hussein— élément qui domine toute la partie ancienne de la commémoration— largement exploité par Châh Esmâ'ïl, fondateur de la dynastie safavide, pour sa propagande personnelle.[1] Mais si, assurément, Châh Esmâ'ïl valorise mieux que personne avant lui le concept du souverain (spirituel et temporel) vengeur du sang de Hussein en le transposant sur le plan soufi, on ne peut dire qu'il innove en matière d'élaboration de la commémoration publique du Drame de Kerbéla. Les cérémonies du Muharram continuent d'ailleurs à se développer tout au long de l'époque safavide en assimilant des éléments folkloriques, dont certains de type "carnavalesque" qui n'ont rien à voir ni avec le soufisme safavide, ni même avec la dévotion chiite. Quelqu'ait pu être l'action du pouvoir pour sa promotion c'est, à mon avis, sur la base de traditions profondément ancrées ches les Iraniens, indépendamment de leurs confessions, que se fit en grande partie l'évolution de la "Fête de Hussein" jusques dans sa forme la plus élaborée de représentation de drames sacrés.

Le mérite d'organiser des séances de déploration à la mémoire de l'Emâm Hussein et des martyrs de Kerbéla trouve sa justification dans le hadith maintes fois cité dans les polémiques et les textes épico-religieux de l'Iran pré-safavide:" Quiconque pleure pour Hussein ou fait pleurer pour Hussein entrera de droit au paradis." Toutefois, si l'on met à part l'action des princes bouyides (IVème/Xème siècle) pour la promotion de commémorations se déroulant dans l'Irak arabe, on peut difficilement parler à cette époque de donations officielles en faveur de la déploration de l'Emâm Hussein. Alors que l'on peut voir certains dirigeants de l'Iran islamique accorder une sollicitude toute particulière aux mausolées de Nadjaf et de Kerbéla, on n'a même pas la certitude qu'ils aient pu protéger des lettrés pour la composition de récits élégiaques ou épico-religieux à la mémoire de l'Emâm Hussein. En effet, depuis les précurseurs de l'époque ghaznavide et seldjoukide tels que Sanâ'i et Qevâmi Râzi, les quelques fragments poétiques dédiés à la mémoire de l'Emâm Hussein et des siens à Kerbéla que l'on peut trouver chez des poètes de tradition classique n'ont jamais eu l'importance d'un ouvrage séparé; de surcroît, les recueils de *manâqeb* utilisés par les "chantres de vertus" (manâqeb-khânân ou *manâqebi),* ou les compositions du genre *maqtalnâme* ("traité de l'occision") dont l'élaboration se fit surtout à partir de l'époque seldjoukide, ne furent apparemment pas le fait d'auteurs de premier plan. Il faut donc attendre le tardif *Rowzatoššohadâ* ("Jardin des Martyrs") de Hussein Vâ'ez-e Kâšefi—terminé en 1502, quelques mois après le *djolus* de Châh Esmâ'il à Tabriz—pour voir paraître en langue persane la somme des traditions élégiaques et épico-religieuses turco-iraniennes sur le Drame de Kerbéla, sa commémoration et sa vengeance. On se trouve donc là, comme d'ailleurs en d'autres domaines, devant une situation paradoxale puisque l'Iran devenu chiite est redevable de la liturgie de la commémoration du Drame de Kerbéla à un soufi d'obédience *naqšbandi*—que les chiites ont évidemment tenté de récupérer au nom de " la discipline de l'arcane" (taqiye ou ketmân)—mais qui n'est probablement qu'un de ces sunnites qui, dans les milieux du *tasavvof* et de la *futuvvat,* vénéraient de plus en plus les Ahl-e beyt et les martyrs de Kerbéla. On peut le considérer, selon la formule du professeur Mahjub, comme un de ces "sunnites laudateurs" (sonniyân-e tafzili) [2].

On comprend donc pourquoi, dans le "vide culturel" de l'Iran safavide, un si grand honneur est accordé aux poètes qui composent des élégies aux Emâms et aux martyrs de Kerbéla. On peut même dire que les Ta'ziyeh-khâni auraient été probablement peu de chose sans l'impulsion donnée par le fameux *haft-band* de Mohtašam Kâšâni si souvent parodié et si important pour toute l'évolution ultérieure de la commémoration. Bien qu'avec Mohtašam on soit déjà dans la seconde moitié du Xème/XVIème siècle, il ne semble pas que son protecteur, Châh Tahmâsp, ait édicté de mesures particulières pour promouvoir les rituels de commémoration du Drame de Kerbéla. Pour cela, il faut encore attendre les effets de la politique d'imposition systématique du chiisme entreprise par Châh Abbâs Ier lorsqu'il sera parvenu à vaincre les dangers intérieurs et extérieurs et à établir fermement la dynastie à Ispahan à la fin du XVIème siècle.

Dans les premières décennies du XVIIème siècle, on voit se développer dans la plupart des centres urbains les rituels des cérémonies du Muharram qui deviendront coutumiers dans l'Iran chiite, avec: —un deuil général qui a tendance à se prolonger au-delà des dix premiers jours du Muharram, jusqu'au 20 et même parfois jusqu'au 28 de Safar; une recrudescence du factionnalisme, cette fois-ci entre groupes chiites, qui influence de nombreux aspects de la commémoration. Parallèlement se développent les *rowzeh-khâni,* ce qui entraîne, à partir du XVIIème siècle, un accroissement des donations pour l'invitation des personnes qui se pressent toujours nombreuses à ces séances. De plus, bien que l'on n'en possède aucune indication chiffrée, le mécénat officiel dut revêtir une certaine importance lorsque, à partir de la seconde moitié du XVIIème siècle, se développent les préparatifs spectaculaires qui président à l'élaboration de la "Fête de Hussein" surtout dans les jeux sur chars. Ces fêtes funèbres constituent dès lors de véritables dramatisations sociales dont le prestige doit rejaillir sur le prince ou sur le gouverneur qui préside à leur organisation et, selon des modalités qui resteront à déterminer, à leur financement. L'invitation des ambassadeurs et des notables étrangers présents à Ispahan et dans les capitales provinciales à ces commémorations officielles données avec munificence indique d'ailleurs, dès l'époque safavide, qu'elles sont pour les mécènes un moyen d'accroître leur influence personnelle.

Après une éclipse durant la période obscure de l'intermède afghan et afcharide, le rituel de commémoration connaît une résurgence intéressante au XVIIIème siècle accompagnée d'innovations en matière d'éléments dramatiques. Cette évolution observée tant au Nord de l'Iran que dans le Fârs suppose un développement des moyens mis en oeuvre pour l'élaboration des jeux sur chars, des processions, des tableaux vivants, etc., donc un mécénat officiel ou privé avec une participation importante des groupements urbains (quartiers, corporations ou associations diverses).

Bien que j'ai pu retracer ce que fut, dans ses grandes lignes, le mécénat des Ta'ziyeh-khâni à l'époque qadjare sous les précurseurs de Nâseroddin Châh,[3] de nombreuses questions restent posées. Ainsi, le seul fait que Fath Ali Châh n'ait apparemment jamais entrepris la construction d'un *takiyeh* fixe pose de manière aigüe le principal problème du mécénat officiel. Compte tenu des moyens mis en oeuvre celui-ci semble être surtout le fait de grands dignitaires et des vizirs et l'on ignore pour le moment jusqu'où alla la générosité du souverain en faveur des Ta'ziyeh-khâni comparativement aux fastes qui, selon de nombreux témoins, régnaient à sa cour. En fait, c'est à partir de son règne que l'on voit se développer la tendance de ceux qui sont les plus proches du pouvoir à augmenter leur prestige en patronnant les Ta'ziyeh-khâni. On trouve alors parmi les mécènes des personnages tels que le *sadr-e a'zam* Mirzâ Safi Mâzanderâni qui invitait l'ambassade britannique dans sa résidence transformée provisoirement en *takiyeh* [4] et l'ex-ambassadeur Mirzâ Abul-Hassan Khân qui donnait dans son *takiyeh* spécialement édifié pour ces commémorations des Ta'ziyeh-khâni très élaborées et des réceptions somptueuses.[5] Cette tendance fut poussée à son plus haut degré par le *sadr-e a'zam* de Muhammad Châh, Hâjji Mirzâ Aqâsi; véritable maître de l'Iran pendant treize ans (1835-1848), il éblouissait la cour et l'ambassade russe par les cérémonies organisées dans son *takiyeh*.[6] Comme j'ai pu le montrer dans une récente étude, l'histoire du Ta'ziyeh-khâni durant les dix premières années du règne de Nâseroddin Châh (1848-1858) est loin d'être éclaircie.[7] Si Amir Kabir extrapole tout d'abord la politique de son prédécesseur Hâjji Mirzâ Aqâsi en invitant au *takiyeh* l'ensemble des diplomates présents à Téhéran, il ne tarde pas à prendre le contre-pied de cette attitude en voulant (poussé par les ulémas ?) faire édicter l'interdiction pure et simple des Ta'ziyeh-khâni. Cette mesure qui, selon Watson, provoqua un tollé général chez les chiites de l'Iran central et septentrional, n'eut d'autre effet que de relancer la commémoration. Son successeur Mirzâ Agâ Khân Nuri tenta de jouer la carte du fanatisme religieux en faisant proclamer l'interdiction d'inviter les diplomates aux Ta'ziyeh-khâni. Intervenant dans la période des tensions diplomatiques allant jusqu'à la rupture et au conflit entre l'Iran et la Grande-Bretagne (1855-57), cette mesure, qui visait avant tout la mission diplomatique anglaise, eut des conséquences durables sur l'attitude des autorités iraniennes envers les Européens qui, à Téhéran, obtiendront difficilement l'accès aux Ta'ziyeh-khâni officiels.

L'action de Nâseroddin Châh en tant que mécène avant la construction du grand Takiyeh Dowlat circulaire dans l'enceinte de la citadelle qadjare de Téhéran est très mal connue et, il semble que, même après l'édification du premier *takiyeh dowlati* (celui de Niyâvarân, inauguré en 1856), des dignitaires se soient distingués davantage que lui dans la promotion des Ta'ziyeh-khâni. Une autre question mal élucidée est celle des circonstances qui ont précédé à l'édification du Takiyeh Dowlat et à sa mise en service au début des années 1870. L'attitude même du Châh est ici paradoxale. En effet, alors qu'il est connu qu'avant la création de ce grand takiyeh d'état, il avait patronné des Ta'ziyeh-khâni à Téhéran et ailleurs au cours de ses déplacements, sa première intention aurait été de consacrer cette nouvelle construction à des représentations dramatiques profanes.[8] Bien que d'authenticité difficilement vérifiable, cette anecdote confirme, au moins dans la conscience collective des Iraniens, l'existence du sentiment qu'ils avaient de l'inconsistance de leur souverain dans ses entreprises. Nâseroddin Châh, nous dit Abdullâh Mustowfi, " pour qui, toute chose était l'occasion de réjouissances, vit dans le Ta'ziyeh-khâni un moyen de faire étalage de luxe et de donner un plus grand éclat à son règne et il fit de ce théâtre religieux une véritable industrie." [9] Quant à l'architecture du Takiyeh Dowlat, elle confirme amplement le besoin d'imiter l'Europe, si ce n'est de rivaliser avec elle et si, comme on l'a raconté, les constructeurs de ce théâtre d'état s'inspirèrent de l'architecture du Royal Albert Hall, on peut dire qu'ils étaient bien informés puisque les bâtiments furent édifiés à peu près en même temps (dans les années 1867-1871 pour l'Albert Hall; 1868-1873 pour le Takiyeh Dowlat). Dans ce théâtre, les cérémonies spectaculaires données sous forme de parades militaires, de défilés, de processions de pénitents, de *rowzeh-khâni* et de Ta'ziyeh-khâni somptueux ont beaucoup impressionné ceux qui en furent témoins. L'organisation de cette véritable "industrie" du spectacle sacré était confiée à des professionnels et, malgré le caractère de plus en plus décadent des rituels et de la dramaturgie, le Takiyeh Dowlat réussit à survivre au moins pour un temps à son fondateur et même à la révolution constitutionnelle de 1906. Parallèlement au développement des Ta'ziyeh-khâni patronnés officiellement, tant dans les provinces qu'à Téhéran, par le gouvernement, les nobles et les dignitaires, se poursuit une évolution dans l'élaboration de ces drames religieux dans les takiyeh dits bourgeois, dans ceux plus populaires des quartiers des grandes agglomérations et ceux des bourgades de moindre importance. C'est en définitive à une promotion beaucoup plus modeste, au niveau des collectivités villageoises, que l'on doit la survie jusqu'à nos jours de Ta'ziyeh-khâni qui, en dépit des faibles moyens dont disposent les groupes qui les animent, ont su conserver, comme nous l'a montré le professeur Chelkowski, un caractère de fraîcheur et d'authenticité qu'ils avaient perdu en milieu urbain.

Si l'on peut assez facilement identifier les personnages et les groupes sociaux qui patronnent la commémoration et les Ta'ziyeh-khâni, de nombreuses questions restent posées tant sur le plan religieux que sur le plan socio-économique. En effet, quelles que soient les ambitions politiques des mécènes, leur entreprise est, aux yeux du consensus chiite, avant tout un acte pieux *(kheyrat)* qui ne peut en principe leur rapporter qu'une récompense spirituelle *(savâb)*. L'impulsion souvent donnée par le mécanisme des voeux *(nazr)* dont la formulation dépend surtout de l'histoire personnelle du donateur. Il faut donc, à mon sens, établir une distinction entre celui qui ne fait que patronner occasionnellement une représentation par action de grâce (pour l'obtention d'une guérison, la conclusion heureuse d'un voyage ou d'un pélerinage, etc.) et celui qui organise systématiquement tous les ans, au moment des deuils religieux, des Ta'ziyeh où il éblouit l'assistance par ses réceptions, l'étalage de ses richesses, la qualité des acteurs et des prédicateurs dont il peut s'assurer les services, etc.

Une des questions les plus difficiles à étudier, en raison de la rareté des sources accessibles, demeure le mode de financement et surtout l'importance des dépenses engagées dans le patronage des Ta'ziyeh-khâni comparativement à celles occasionnées par les autres actes de dévotion envers l'Emâm Hussein et les martyrs de Kerbéla. Ainsi, quel que soit le bilan que l'on pourra dresser des Ta'ziyeh-khâni au Takiyeh Dowlat, il ne fait pas de doute que le culte des martyrs entrainaît des dépenses beaucoup plus considérables au lieu-même de leur martyre *(mašhad)*. Ces mausolées sont depuis l'époque safavide l'objet d'une vénération croissante de la part des musulmans de diverses tendances. Au XIXème siècle, cette dévotion atteint son paroxysme; les pélerins de tout le monde chiite s'y rendent en foule; la retraite et la sépulture à Kerbéla sont très recherchées; de riches donateurs, tels que le prince indien de Oudh et de Lucknow, lèguent des sommes énormes aux *atabât* de Nadjaf et de Kerbéla.[10] C'est aussi en Inde, et plus particulièrement à Lucknow, que s'élèvent de somptueux Emâmbâra qui n'ont rien à envier au Takiyeh Dowlat pour la magnificence de la décoration et de l'architecture, et que l'on commémore, avec de nombreuses variantes locales, le Drame de Kerbéla dans des rituels très élaborés entraînant de gros sacrifices et de grandes dépenses pour la confection des étendards funéraires *(alam)* et des *tâbut* ou Ta'ziyeh, dont la tradition remonterait à l'Emir Teymour, pour l'organisation de processions ayant conservé de nombreux éléments carnavalesques anciens de la "Fête de Hussein," de tableaux vivants, etc.[11]

Parallèlement au système des voeux *(nazr)* qui a été un élément décisif pour la promotion de tous les aspects de la commémoration, le développement du système de donations pieuses constituées en biens de main-morte *(vaqf)* finira par donner aux Ta'ziyeh et aux *takiyeh* un rang de véritables institutions religieuses au même titre que les Emâm-zâdeh ou autres lieux de culte ou d'enseignement chiite. Bien que l'on puisse difficilement en étudier l'évolution, il semble que les *vaqf* aient été établis en faveur des Ta'zieyeh-khâni dès le début de l'époque qadjare, comme en témoigne par exemple le legs d'un *âlem* de Qom d'un tiers de ses biens pour la célébration annuelle de cérémonies de deuil à la mémoire de l'Emâm Hussein *(rowzeh-khâni, šabih-khâni),* apparemment dans la dernière dizaine du mois de Safar.[12] Comme nous l'ont laissé entendre de nombreux témoignages, le mécène des Ta'ziyeh-khâni devait parfois engager des dépenses considérables pour rétribuer tous les gens du Ta'ziyeh (acteurs, musiciens, régisseurs, *rowzeh-khân,* muletiers, chameliers, figurants, etc.), pour payer les nombreux accessoires et les frais de réception d'un public toujours très nombreux et même parfois pour nourrir et loger pendant un certain temps les gens de Ta'ziyeh. Mais le problème financier le plus important était la construction d'un *takiyeh* fixe qui nécessitait l'acquisition d'un vaste terrain et des frais d'entretien sans commune mesure avec l'utilisation restreinte des bâtiments aux seules périodes de deuil. C'est pourquoi, à mon avis, le nombre impressionnant de *takiyeh* donné par certains auteurs pour la seule ville de Téhéran ne peut être considéré qu'avec la plus grande circonspection.[13] Comme j'ai pu le faire remarquer, ces listes ne tiennent pas compte du caractère éphémère de nombreuses constructions téhéranaises; en fait, il semble qu'il ait existé en même temps assez peu de *takiyeh* fixes et beaucoup de demeures princières et bourgeoises aisément transformables en *takiyeh* par l'adjonction de structures mobiles ou agencements provisoires. Il y aurait même lieu de rechercher si la destination de ces demeures à une utilisation épisodique pour ces représentations n'a pas influencé l'architecture de certains types de maisons qadjares ne serait-ce que par leur taille parfois disproportionnée, même si l'on considère l'importance numérique des familles.

Pour faire face à ces dépenses élevées, les mécènes ont utilisé divers systèmes de compensation. Ainsi Valy Khan, "argentier" de Nâseroddin Chah, dota son *takiyeh* de boutiques dont le revenu des locations était employé aux frais de son entretien et à ceux des représentations.[14] Ce système semble s'être étendu aux *takiyeh* de quartiers sur lesquels nous ne possédons que de rares témoignages tardifs qui ne peuvent nous donner qu'une vague idée de la genèse de leur édification et de leur statut juridique. Selon Abdullah Mustowfi, les *takiyeh* qui existaient à Téhéran dans chaque quartier *(mahal)* et dans presque chaque sous-quartier *(quzar)* avaient été construits par de pieux fondateurs qui les avaient parfois dotés de boutiques constituées en *vaqf;* gérées par un *mutavvali,* les revenus de ces biens étaient employés à l'entretien et au fonctionnement du *takiyeh.* Toutefois, la plupart de ces *takiyeh* n'étaient pas (ou n'étaient plus?) dotés de *vaqf.*[15] Certains appartenaient même à la communauté du quartier— probablement au nom de ses notables comme l'atteste d'ailleurs le témoignage de Gobineau qui, comme j'ai pu le faire remarquer, reflète la situation à Téhéran dans les années 1860, alors que la ville s'enrichit de quartiers nouveaux.[16] Mais de nombreux *takiyeh* avaient été construits dans les quartiers des l'époque de Muhammad Châh et l'on ignore leurs statuts respectifs au moment de leur fondation.[17]

Comme on l'a maintes fois observé, l'élaboration des cérémonies du Muharram est avant tout une entreprise collective qui suscite une grande émulation entre les groupes sociaux, et les Ta'ziyeh-khâni doivent beaucoup à la coopération des associations populaires de quartiers telles que les *dâs* de Téhéran. Ce sont le plus souvent ces héritiers de l'ancienne *futuvvat* qui entreprennent la remise en état des *takiyeh* au moment des représentations. Leur tâche ne devait pas être facile car, en dehors des périodes de deuil, ces *takiyeh* étaient la plupart du temps utilisés par les habitants et les marchands du quartier comme remises, entrepôts ou simples dépotoirs. Selon la coutume bien établie depuis l'époque safavide, les gens du quartier contribuaient largement aux dépenses des cérémonies par des dons en argent ou en nature, par des prêts ou des dons d'objets divers pour l'ornement ou l'éclairage du *takiyeh,* la réception des invités, etc.

Les nombreux échanges que l'on peut observer au niveau populaire dans ces cérémonies se retrouvent d'ailleurs chez les Grands dont les motivations sont loin d'être d'essence purement religieuse. Cela est particulièrement évident chez Hâjji Mirzâ Aqâsi; pour le plus grand prestige de ce *sadr-e a'zam* vénal, les provinces (Chirâz, Ispahan, Kâchân) et les corporations de Téhéran rivalisent d'ardeur pour décorer son *takiyeh* et pour y célébrer le Muharram.[18] Il semble aussi que, du moment où Nâseroddin Châh commença à s'intéresser à la promotion des Ta'ziyeh, des personnages riches ou influents aient cherché à accroître leur prestige en lui offrant les riches accessoires qu'ils avaient apportés pour décorer le *takiyeh* royal.[19] Cette tendance sera érigée en système après la création du Takiyeh Dowlat dont la riche décoration était assurée en grande partie par les hauts dignitaires de l'état. En effet, chacune des loges du premier niveau était assignée à un prince, un ministre ou un gouverneur qui avait également à charge de décorer les loges du second et du troisième niveaux situées au-dessus de la loge dont il était titulaire, il ne restait au souverain qu'à décorer le grand hall du *takiyeh.*[20] Point n'est besoin d'insister ici sur l'étalage de mauvais goût en matière d'objects hétéroclites en partie importés d' Europe que suscitait la rivalité entre titulaires de loges. Assez curieusement, on pourrait établir ici un parallèle avec certains fastes de l'Angleterre victorienne appréciés par Nâseroddin Châh durant ses séjours à Londres. On peut même se demander s'il n'avait pas, dans une certaine mesure, profité de son expérience anglaise pour minimiser le coût d'une entreprise aussi ruineuse que celle de la fondation du Takiyeh Dowlat. Comme on le sait, la fondation du Royal Albert Hall, fut une véritable institution coopérative puisque, pour faire face aux énormes dépenses nécessitées par sa construction, on fit appel à des souscripteurs (personnes physiques ou morales) qui pouvaient devenir propriétaires à vie des places des loges et même de l'amphithéatre. Si Nâseroddin Châh n'avait pu faire usage de ce système de financement pour la construction du Takiyeh Dowlat, il devait en avoir eu connaissance lors de son premier voyage à Londres en 1873, au cours duquel il fut précisément invité au Royal Albert Hall et il n'est pas impossible qu'il s'en soit inspiré à postériori. En effet, l'un des soirs de la première dizaine du Muharram, le Châh procédait à la distribution de châles d'honneur aux officiers, jetait à la volée des pièces de monnaie aux prédicateurs et à leurs élèves et recevaient les "cadeaux" des titulaires des loges qui venaient en déduction des dépenses qu'il avait engagées dans ces célébrations.[21] Bien d'autres moyens furent utilisés pour tenter de "rentabiliser" l'institution du Takiyeh Dowlat, notamment par les prestations que donnait la compagnie *dowlati* (acteurs, musiciens) dans les *takiyeh* importants de la ville.[22] Et aussi par l'utilisation que l'on faisait parfois des locaux du *takiyeh* pour des réunions qui n'avaient rien à voir avec les Ta'ziyeh-khâni.

Malgré l'état lacunaire de la documentation et des recherches sur le sujet ici abordé, on peut dors et déjà avancer que, quelle qu'ait pu être la pureté de leurs intentions, les mécènes des Ta'ziyeh-khani ont, à de rares exceptions près, surtout chercher à tirer de leur action bienfaitrice un maximum de prestige tout en s'efforçant de réduire au maximum les frais engagés pour cela.

NOTES

1. Sur les thèmes anciens de la vengeance du sang de Husein dans la littérature épico-religieuse turco-iranienne (gestes de Mukhtâr, d'Abu Muslem, de Muhammad b.al Hanafiya) et sur certains princes qui sont glorifiés pour avoir poursuivi cette vengeance (dont les Timourides et Chah Esmâ'il), voir ma thèse intitulée : *Le Culte de l' Imâm Husayn: Etude sur la commémoration du Drame de Kerbélâ dans l'Iran pre-safavide* (713 pages, Paris 1975). Cet ouvrage étant en cours de publication et mes recherches sur la commémoration à l'époque safavide pas encore terminées, je limiterai ici mes références surtout à mes articles publiés ou sous presse.

2. Voir l'édition du *Futuvvat-nâme-ye sultâni* par H. Mahjub, Téhéran 1350s., introduction, p. 95. L'oeuvre épico-religieuse de Kâšefi est analysée en détail et en partie traduite dans ma thèse (citée note précédente).

3. Voir J.Calmard, *Le mécénat des représentations de Ta'zieyh I, Les précurseurs de Nâseroddin Châh*, dans *Le monde iranien et l'Islam*, Tome II, Paris-Genève 1974, p. 73-126 (cité: *Mécénat,I*).

4. Voir *Mécénat I*, p. 84.

5. Ibid., p. 88, 99-100.

6. Ibid., p. 100-118.

7. Voir J. Calmard, *Mécénat II*, dans *Le monde iranien et l'Islam*, Tome III, sous presse.

8. Y.Aryanpour, *Az Sabâ tâ Nimâ*, Téhéran 1350s., II, p. 323, no. 2.

9. Abdullâh Mustowfi, *Sarh-e Zendegâni-e man*, 3 vol., 2e. éd., Téhéran 1345s., I, p. 288.

10. Sur ce legs, voir H.Algar, *Religion and State in Iran 1785-1906*, University of California Press 1969, p. 237-238.

11. Sur ces questions on peut voir pour le moment J.N. Hollister, *The Shi'a of India*, Londres 1953, p. 164 seq. L'aire de diffusion de la commémoration est très vaste et j'ai déjà attiré l'attention sur le fait que des éléments anciens en ont été conservés dans certains rituels observés en Inde, dans l'Insulinde ou au Caucase (voir ma thèse citée note 1 et aussi, sur les inter-influences, mon article sur *Les Etendards funéraires chiites et leurs désignations turco-mongoles*, dans *Traditions religieuses et para-religieuses des peuples altaïques*, Paris 1972, p. 27-38.)

12. A. Faqihi, *Târikh-e mazhabi-e Qom,* Qom 1350s., p. 241-242.

13. Voir mes remarques sur les listes citées par certains auteurs (pour P. Mamnoun, dans *Mécénat I,* n.135 et *Mécénat II,* n.136; pour Y. Zokâ, dans *Mécénat II,* n.134).

14. Gobineau, *Religions et Philosophies dans l'Asie Centrale,* 10e., ed., Paris 1957, p. 340.

15. Abdullah Mustowfi, *o.c.,* I, p. 300.

16. Sur le témoignage de Gobineau, voir *Mécénat II,* sous presse.

17. Voir *Mécénat I,* p. 121, n.156 et le plan de Téhéran, p. 124-125.

18. *Ibid.,* p. 110.

19. Gobineau, *o.c.,* p. 341.

20. Abdullah Mustowfi, *o.c.,* I, p. 293.

21. *Ibid.,* p. 298-299 (ce témoignage de Abdullah Mustowfi et celui de Dust Ali Mu'ayyerolmamâlek sur ce même sujet ont été mal interprétés par certains auteurs dont A. Bani Sadr et A. Piemontese).

22. *Ibid.,* p. 300, 301.

10

Quelques Considerations Comparatives entre les Rituels du Ta'ziyeh Iranien et les "Spectacles de la Passion" du Moyen-Age Chrétien en Occident

ENRICO FULCHIGNONI

Il est surprenant de remarquer le peu de cas que la première génération de critiques qui ont étudié le Ta'ziyeh a porté aux différentes formes du théâtre chrétien du Moyen Age. La lacune la plus importante me paraît celle du Comte de Gobineau, qui nous a pourtant laissé l'une des plus admirables descriptions du Ta'ziyeh, en tant que texte et également comme spectacle. Mais la plupart des critiques qui l'ont suivi révèlent également une absence surprenante d'information sur ce domaine, et c'est avec plaisir que j'ai enfin pu retrouver dans les rapports de nombreux participants de notre symposium des allusions comparatives entre les deux formes de théâtre religieux de la Chrétienté et de l'Islam chiite. Tant ms.Chelkowski, que ms.Aziza, que ms.Cejpak, pour ne mentionner que quelques-uns d'entre eux, ont fait appel, pour une raison ou pour une autre, à cette forme de théâtre occidental du Moyen Age, avec des observations pertinentes tant sur le plan dramaturgique que sociologique. Je m'efforcerai, pour ma part, d'en développer certaines hypothèses comparatives de la manière la plus acceptable, en me basant sur un ensemble de recherches cohérentes faites en France et en Italie ces dernières années. Quelques mots seulement pour rappeler le drame liturgique et sa naissance.

Du milieu du Xème siècle au milieu du XIIème en Italie et en France, l'instinct dramatique, sous des intentions édifiantes, s'est progressivement élaboré dans les églises et dans les monastères. L'office liturgique, celui de la naissance du Christ, comme celui de son martyre, s'est enrichi et dramatisé. Les faits commémorés par le rituel, au lieu d'être simplement chantés, ont été joués, les personnages évoqués, individualisés, incarnés. En même temps, les principes de la mise en scène simultanée (qui sera le modèle pour une très grande partie du Moyen-Age chrétien) se définissent. Un peu plus tard, le parler national, la langue vulgaire, le français, l'italien, l'allemand se sont imposés avec l'accroissement du nombre des personnages. Non contents de faire se dérouler dans l'église, sous les yeux des fidèles devenus des spectateurs, une succession de scènes, les pieux régisseurs ont matérialisé les lieux où elles se déroulent. Ce fait devient de la plus grande importance dans l'histoire du théâtre d'Occident, puisqu'en même temps ce drame liturgique a été traversé par un esprit nouveau, laïque et, même parfois, politique.

Les prêtres ne suffiront plus à remplir les rôles. Les artisans, les étudiants, les bourgeois et les nobles interviendront, tous soucieux de répandre la parole du Sauveur. Et ces drames serviront alors aussi à la célébration des Saints locaux, à la représentation des prodiges et aventures des pélerins aux lieux saints. Et ils serviront, en même temps parfois, à véhiculer des légendes du patrimoine littéraire et folklorique bien antérieur au christianisme, agissant ainsi comme une sorte de vaste réceptacle dramaturgique qui aura toujours comme fil conducteur le martyre et la passion du Christ.

Cette condition me paraît offrir une première analogie intéressante avec le Ta'ziyeh. D'après les collections du prof. Bausani et de Cerulli et un examen de plusieurs dizaines de textes du Ta'ziyeh, il est facile de vérifier que leurs thèmes vont souvent au-delà de la tragédie de Kerbéla, bien que les évènements du martyre de Hussein et de ses compagnons y jouent un rôle éminent. Mais le fait demeure de savoir comment on est passé de la représentation des faits de Kerbéla aux autres sujets profanes du drame? Ici, la démarche comparative peut nous aider, car on faisait également pour les sujets profanes du Moyen Age, ce que Cerulli définit comme un "raccord pieux", qui consistait en une ou plusieurs allusions faites à la passion du Christ à un moment ou à un autre du drame. Ensuite, on continuait à developper, dans cette charpente du drame sacré, l'histoire profane.

Le Drame de la Passion, comme nous l'avons rappelé, quitte le Temple pour s'installer sous le porche, ou sur la place publique. Mais quel est le cadre précis dans lequel il va insérer ses spectacles dans les étapes successives de son développement? Ceci est d'importance capitale pour saisir les analogies qui le relient au lieu théatral du Ta'ziyeh. Dans ce but, il nous faut revenir un instant en arrière. Nous sommes au moment où le réalisme croissant du répertoire marque un tournant de la dramaturgie chrétienne. Celle-ci abandonne, nous l'avons dit, le fait théologal abstrait et toute son attention se porte sur la vie terrestre et humaine du Sauveur, vie qui s'étale depuis la lointaine enfance jusqu'au martyre et à la mort sur la croix. Son existence charnelle, son poids de présence historique devient d'importance fondamentale. Les miracles évangéliques sont décrits avec minutie et se déroulent dans le crescendo d'un pathétisme douloureux jusqu'à l'issue sanglante de la passion. Quelle est la structure de l'espace qui a été considérée comme optimale par ces pionniers, dans le but de cerner une pareille situation dramaturgique? Que savons-nous aujourd'hui de la véritable structure scénique qui a permis cette forme de spectacle dans l'Europe chrétienne du Moyen—Age?

Les découvertes les plus récentes des historiens du théâtre montrent de manière indiscutable que le dispositif utilisé pour les représentations des grands mystères cycliques de la Passion du Christ, à la fin du Moyen-Age était un lieu scénique central surélevé, entouré par les spectateurs, et se trouvant en retrait sur des bâtiments ou des échafaudages surélevés, avec des places pour les spectateurs de marque. Nous savons maintenant que seul ce dispositif était susceptible d'accueillir les foules nombreuses qui se pressaient aux représentations des Mystères et qui, ainsi, ne perdaient *rien ni du texte ni du spectacle*.

L'analogie avec le *takiyeh* me paraît surprenante. Je me rapporte à la description de Gobineau, mais également à celles des auteurs successifs qui ont décrit la plateforme centrale du Ta'ziyeh, le *sakou* accessible aux deux extrémités par deux rampes, la haute tente centrale et les mâts qui la soutiennent. Nous pouvons retrouver les mêmes dispositions soit dans les nombreuses références sur le lieu dramatique chrétien en France et en Italie, soit par l'analyse systématique des enluminures et des miniatures d'époque, soit à travers le décryptage méticuleux des indications linguistiques pour les maîtres de cérémonie et pour les acteurs.

Mais quelle est en définitive la valeur symbolique de cette forme circulaire qui entoure la passion du Christ comme celle de Hussein ?

La forme d'un lieu géométrique clos, de forme circulaire ou carrée répond certainement à une tendance fondamentale de l'être vivant. On pourrait retracer la longue suite des édifices à plan circulaire, depuis la hutte ronde des primitifs, jusqu'à tous les "templum" circulaires qui jalonnent l'histoire de l'humanité : baptistères, tombeaux, églises rondes d'orient et d'occident. Le Moyen-Age pour sa part a particulièrement cultivé cette forme géometrique. La forme théâtrale en est un exemple à la fois frappant et poignant.

A l'intérieur de la circonférence qu'ils avaient tracée, les spectateurs pouvaient se sentir, le temps de la représentation, solidaires de ce Dieu qui les avait sauvés et qui, devant eux, répétait les gestes ineffables par lesquels s'établissaient à nouveau les normes et les lois de leur existence. Pendant deux siècles, ils contemplèrent et adorèrent ainsi dans les bourgs et les villages, de Bourges à Paris, de Sienne à Padou, de Louvain à Valenciennes, de Lyons à Lucerne, pour ne mentionner que les sièges les plus renommés de spectacles sacrés, le martyre du Christ au centre du Cercle Magique—ceci à l'intérieur d'un cercle où, justement, le temps, comme l'espace, devenait cyclique, c'est-à-dire inépuisable. Le cercle était devenu lieu théâtral privilégié où se répète et se perpétue le rituel de la création du monde et de la fidélité des croyants.

EVOLUTION DU SPECTACLE ET COMPORTEMENT DU SPECTATEUR

L'évolution du drame religieux en Occident chrétien et en Orient chiite paraît présenter également quelques analogies qu'il vaut la peine de souligner. En Europe on commence par des processions de Pâques qui sont des sortes d'immenses tableaux vivants dans lesquels les participants gardent une immobilité figée. Plus tard les figures de ces tableaux s'animent, les compositions statiques s'articulent, et nous vérifions la naissance du mystère mimé qui oblige le spectateur à se déplacer; finalement la troisième phase: l'apparition d'un texte parlé ou improvisé. L'intervention de la parole comporte, comme nous l'avons dit, un bouleversement total du lieu théâtral précédent. La nécessité de saisir la totalité verbale et gestuelle de l'action dramatique comporte la naissance finale du théâtre en rond qui s'installe partout à la fin du Moyen-Age.

De la même sorte sont les processions décrites par le professeur Chelkowski; les processions du Muharram qui, à l'origine, commémorent le martyre de Hussein sont très semblables aux tableaux vivants décrits par les miniaturistes et les chroniqueurs chrétiens du XIIème et XIIIème siècles, avec les mêmes chariots, les mêmes guerriers et argusins.

Cependant, cette forme primitive suit un parcours différent puisque en Europe elle se transforme rapidement en représentation mimique tandis qu'elle subsiste et se maintient beaucoup plus longtemps en Orient.

Mais, soit dans le Ta'ziyeh soit dans les mystères chrétiens, nous vérifions une flexibilité totale en ce qui concerne l'intervention de personnages anachroniques, l'usage d'objets et d'ustensils propres au lieu du spectacle et non pas à celui de la trame, l'apparition d'animaux familiers à la place de ceux requis par l'histoire représentée. Tout cet ensemble de procédures a pour but de renforcer les liens entre le spectacle sacré et la vie quotidienne des spectateurs. Ainsi, en Italie, comme en France, en Flandre et en Espagne, dans les villes comme dans les plus simples villages, le public découvrait un parent ou un ami sous les traits d'un des personnages de l'estrade, et il retrouvait surtout, au milieu de l'aire du jeu dramatique, la représentation des différentes conditions sociales de toutes les réalités de la vie de chaque jour, recréées, condensées, mais non faussées, à travers l'histoire de la Création et de l'humanité chrétienne, garanties par le martyre inéluctable du Sauveur, sans cesse renouvelé sur l'estrade.

Le déroulement du Ta'ziyeh suit une démarche qui me paraît analogue. Nous sommes ici également à la frontière du rituel et du jeu dramatique qui caractérise le drame de la Passion chrétienne. *Ta'ziyeh et spectacle chrétien, tous deux offrent au spectateur la possibilité de renouveler rituellement son adhésion à un ordre idéologique et religieux dont il fait partie intégrale.*

Et enfin, un dernier point concernant certaines réactions physiques des spectateurs du Ta'ziyeh et auxquelles fait allusion le rapport du prof. Beemann. Beemann dit: "Il est important de remarquer que le spectacle du Ta'ziyeh a été conçu tant pour renforcer un ordre idéologique moral et religieux que pour provoquer chez le spectateur une réaction cathartique de rire ou de pleur, d'indignation et d'exaltation."

Or, cette même double démarche, nous la retrouvons dans le théâtre chrétien du Moyen-Age. Et nous pouvons même y rencontrer les mêmes cas-limites comme ceux des flagellations que nous avons vues dans le très intéressant film montré au Symposium.

A différentes époques, la religion chrétienne a connu des vagues de rituels de flagellation lors des spectacles sacrés. En 1260, en 1280, en 1300 toute l'Italie fut parcourue par des centaines et des centaines de flagellants qui suivaient en chantant les symboles de la croix et de la résurrection. Les époques de leur apparition coïncident avec les années les plus dures de crise et d'angoisse, années de détresse. Or, les comportements collectifs, comme celui de la flagellation correspondent à un dénominateur commun que nous voyons se manifester dans toutes les situations analogues : ce sont les *rituels de possession*.

Leurs causes sont complexes et encore mal étudiées mais ont comme base commune la création—grâce à des procédés physiques et psychiques— d'une sorte d'*état second* dans lequel l'homme s'efforce de sortir de soi-même pour atteindre des états de conscience inédits, plus propres aux visions et aux hallucinations.

Il est erroné, à mon avis, de voir dans ces gestes de la flagellation—ou d'autres pratiques analogues—la volonté de reproduire le sacrifice qu'on contemple sur l'estrade.

Tant dans le cas des flagellations du Moyen-Age chrétien, que dans certains rituels du Ta'ziyeh propres aux régions méridionales et côtières du Golfe Persique, il ne s'agit donc pas de "sympathie" de la part du spectateur à l'égard de la trame, mais plutôt de la survivance probable de rituels hallucinatoires très archaïques qui ont en Afrique leur première source. La greffe et la survivance de rituels plus anciens sur des structures d'autre origine et signification est un phénomène fréquent dans l'histoire des religions et mérite donc d'être pris en considération dans le cas qui nous intéresse.

11

The Effect of European Theatre and the Influence of Its Theatrical Methods Upon Ta'ziyeh

MUMAMMAD JA'FAR MAHJUB

At the time of the First Festival of Arts at Shiraz in the summer of 1967, a short discourse by this writer was published about the origins, characteristics, and performance of Ta'ziyeh. In that piece I discussed the obscurity of the historical antecedents of Ta'ziyeh and the need for research on this problem. In the years which have passed since those remarks were made much has been said about Ta'ziyeh by both Iranian and non-Iranian scholars and critics. However, two points remain which deserve further consideration.

In that article it was stated that "Ta'ziyeh ... in its present shape and form probably came into existence toward the end of Safavid period." [1] Drawing upon all the old traditions of *naqqali* (public story-telling), *rowzeh-khani* (declamations in commemoration of the martyrs appealing to the emotions), panegyric, eulogy, and music, a new vigorous form was produced. Experienced directors took it in hand, and it prospered.[2]

A great deal may be said about Ta'ziyeh, its evolution and its present decline, and the extent and quality of its stories and players

... : the number of the principal Ta'ziyehs which is slightly more than a hundred; the quality of the Ta'ziyeh text, usually in verse or at least poetic in style, that is, composed in the long meter *(bahr-e tavil)* and verse; the mode in which each one of the reciters is to chant his lines; the tune of the adversaries possessing epic grandeur; the functions of each role in the Ta'ziyeh and its name (Shemr, Zainab, or in general, the adversaries, or the villains and the heroes, or the oppressed ...); the emotional condition of the players all of whom, whether in the roles of the oppressed or the adversaries, believe that the Imam (Hussein) was in the right and who look upon the opponents through the eyes of convinced believers ... ; the popular aspect of Ta'ziyeh and the characteristics which arise from that; the manner of costuming the parts in Ta'ziyeh, as in the red dress of the enemies and the green or white dress of the oppressed ones; the theatrical conventions such as circling the stage several times to indicate long trips; not moving on a straight and direct line between two points in order to suggest the distance lying between them; the use of visible and invisible theatrical devices, symbols and objects which represent a particular setting, such as the presence of a tub of water and a few stalks of greenery to indicate a river and a grove of palms; special musical instruments and devices in Ta'ziyeh and the method of their employment; Ta'ziyeh in permanent buildings as against touring, Ta'ziyeh performed by itinerant players; and many other matters.... Careful research must be undertaken about each point, and the name and identity of people who have applied themselves to and worked in this field should be rescued from oblivion.[3]

Now a decade later, I have doubts and reservations about whether the Ta'ziyeh originated in its present form at the end of the Safavid period. Was that really the case? And a closely related question, not included in the above quotation, arises. Obviously I was speaking about the performance of Ta'ziyeh in Iran: but what are the geographical limits of this "Iran"? To answer these questions it must first be established when Ta'ziyeh—that is, the theatrical act of representing the events of the tragedy at Kerbela and having people play the roles of the heroes of that event—was first performed. Only then it is possible to say how extensive the geographical frontiers of the country—then called Persia—were at that time, and, as a result, to study Ta'ziyeh and its performance within (or outside) those limits.

In my previous article I said that Ta'ziyeh probably appeared at the end of the Safavid period. Yet, even though I have never ceased in this research during these past years, I have not been able to discover the slightest trace of Ta'ziyeh or its texts belonging to that period, nor have I even heard of any. We have the works of the poets of the Safavid period;

even popular stories have come down to us from it. Yet there is no trace of Ta'ziyeh material. The first and oldest poetry we possess written in a style similar to the verses of the Ta'ziyeh texts is recorded in the *Divan* of Sabahi Bidguli (died 1218 A.H./A.D. 1802).

> Alas, that oppressing fortune has again drawn the Sword of
>   Tyranny from the scabbard of injustice against the
>   people of the world;
> The army of sorrow has so attacked the hearts of young
>   and old that pleasure has chosen retirement—
> The hand of tyranny has been so extended in every
>   direction that no creature rejoices.
> I am astonished that deceiving heaven wants to perpetrate
>   another deception;
> It has drawn the bloodthirsty sword against the world,
>   it has stolen serenity from the heart and soul of the
>   earth's inhabitants.
> If I am not mistaken, this crescent moon of mourning which
>   appears like the scimitar of cruelty in my sight. . . .[4]

This poem contains 113 couplets and is an elegy of Ali Asghar. It is so far removed, however, from the developed style of Sabahi that the editor of his *Divan* has said that possibly the poet wrote this long *masnavi* "at the beginning of his poetic career, or perhaps as a child."

On the other hand, among the oral and perhaps untrustworthy traditions I have heard, one relates that there were several Ta'ziyeh texts from the time of Karim Khan Zand (1163-93 A.H./A.D. 1750-79) in Fars. Since their paper had rotted, their texts were copied out and the old manuscripts were washed with water because the name of God and the Holy Ones of the Faith were written upon them and it was a sin for such writings to be treated disrespectfully. However, we have no documentary evidence to prove that Ta'ziyeh existed in the Safavid period; instead, we have strong reasons to reject the idea of its existence. One of the foreigners who lived long years in Iran during the height of the Safavid period was the famous Chevalier Jean Chardin, who was a very intelligent and keen observer. He left us the results of his observations in his *Voyages* (Travels), a multi-volume work which has also been translated into Persian. Fortunately this book sheds light upon many matters that were ordinary and commonplace for the people of the period and were afterwards forgotten and lost, and through it we are able to acquire much information about the social and political life of the Persians, as well as their habits and character during the Safavid period.

At times Chardin describes details with such sharp perception that one would say he was a trained investigator of much experience. Those who have read his book know that he was not the kind of man to have left Ta'ziyeh assemblies and Persian plays (with all their details) out of his book, especially since he has described the mourning ceremonies of Muharram with his usual precision. I quote his description of a procession of mourners *(sineh-zan,* breast-beaters) which he saw in Isfahan in A.D. 1667:

In front of each of the processions went twenty standards, banners, crescents, metal hands with occult engravings of Muhammad and Ali raised upon pikes. These were holy symbols for the Muslims from their earliest battles, carried by their soldiers in the same way that the Romans carried the likenesses of eagles with them. Even today they carry these standards although they no longer have the faith in them that they had in those earlier times. When these standards are brought out with the processions they are covered with a very fine light blue cloth. This is so that they may say that there is no threat of war or fighting at present. After these, some beautiful trained horses follow equipped with very expensive armor and harnesses and all sorts of weapons other than firearms suspended from their saddles and harnesses. These weapons which are made of steel, as well as the shields and other equipage, are worked with gold and set with precious stones. Following them are the musicians and after them are men throwing stones, some of whom have blackened their faces and some of whom are smeared with blood. Then there are those who are covered with blood from head to foot, appearing as though they had been struck with many arrows, and after them come the wagons and equipages prepared as though for a very elaborate funeral. The Arks of Good Fortune are drawn before them. These Arks are clothed in blue material and decorated with pieces of gold brocade hung with thousands of ornaments according to the whim and taste of those who prepared them. And then the coffins are carried, and they too are covered with velvet or colored or black brocade with turbans placed on their tops and a variety of weapons attached to their sides and atop them. Those who transport these items (as a kind of buffoonery) lightly and easily dart through the processions or circle around in them. Afterwards a large throne representing Imam Hussein and borne on the shoulders of eight men approaches. Some of these thrones are like luxurious, decorated daises on which two children representing Imam Hassan and Imam Hussein are seated. Others resemble armories, covered inside and out with a variety of weapons like bows and arrows, swords, shields, and daggers, and in which a child sits completely armed for battle. All of this equipment shines resplendently due to the gold and silver employed in its ornamentation as it is prepared at the expense of, and under the watchful supervision of all the people. Among the other paraphernalia there are representations of the sepulchres and we also see a man garbed in bloodied clothes in which

140

arrows are fixed, with his face and head streaked with blood, laid out representing the fate of the Imam and the martyrs of Kerbela. Surrounding all these objects there are people carrying branches in order to shade those in them from the heat of the sun. After these have passed there come the men who are also drenched in blood seated upon dusty and ash-covered horses. They also represent the warriors and fighters of Kerbela. A crowd follows them, unorganized or in processions numbering two or three hundred, from whom the awesome cry *Ya Hussein* is heard. These too are always armed; however most of their weapons are merely thick staves, and instead of walking they run. From time to time they stop in order to give the ceremonial objects and wagons opportunity to catch up, then they jump up from their places and circling around like frenzied ecstatics, they move off. Because of the constant shouting of the names with all their strength, they are giddy and lose control of themselves.[5]

Lest it be thought that Chardin saw something and left it unrecorded, we may note that he witnessed a women's entertainment (mainly of dancing and singing) six years later in 1673, and has mentioned that also in his *Voyages*.[6] We shall return to the observations of Chardin and analyze them later.

A separate discussion about the traditional mourning ceremonies in Muharram and its customs and forms in the Indo-Pakistani subcontinent is presented in this volume by an Indian scholar;[7] therefore I do not intend to discuss this matter in any detail. However, I must note two points here: first, the mourning ceremonies with their processions of breast-beaters, flagellants, and similar groups, like Shi'ism itself, probably spread from Persia to the subcontinent. Among the supporting evidence is the fact that a group still calling itself "Qezelbash," a remnant of the power of the Zezelbashis of the Safavid period, and whose mother tongue is still court Persian, are all Shi'ites. They still have an appropriate role in the formation and direction of mourning processions (at least in Pakistan). There is also another group of Iranians who settled in the subcontinent who also keep the customs of mourning and commemorative assemblies in the traditional style.

As we know, the Safavid period was the greatest era of cultural contact and interchange of ideas between Persia and the subcontinent, and also of Persian artistic and cultural influence in India and Pakistan. It is true that after the Safavids, Nader Shah went to India and fought victoriously as far as Delhi, but Nader never had the relations with the people of India and its rulers that the Safavids had. From then on a variety of increasing troubles for the Persians and their government, plus the colonial activities of the East India Company and later, of the British government, cut off the flow of customs and cultural trends from Persia to the subcontinent.

As a result, many of the Persian customs, traditions, and ceremonies which had been adopted, especially by the Muslim inhabitants—retained the forms used at the time of their adoption, whether they reached India and Pakistan either before or after the Safavids, or during the period of their ascendancy. A cursory investigation shows that the Persian language now current in Pakistan and the manner of its pronunciation among the people there is that of six or seven centuries ago. These people declare that certain linguistic peculiarities, such as the distinction between the stressed and unstressed W and Y, have been retained in India and Pakistan. Also, the religious halls *(takiyeh)*, the houses of retreat, and almshouses, the manners and habits of the Sufis, their sacred dance, the celebration of the anniversaries of the saints of mysticism the dancing by the disciples—all are reminiscent of the period of Abu Said, Abu al-Khair and Mawlana Jalal al-Din Rumi. Even now, if one visits remote villages and has even slight familiarity with the old social life of the Persians and Muslims of these regions, one feels that the environment of five or six centuries ago has remained untouched by the customs and manners of modern civilization.

The term *ta'ziyeh* is not an unfamiliar one in India and Pakistan, but it has a meaning completely different from that which we give to it. *Ta'ziyeh* there means a replica of a tomb or pavilion constructed in each city according to its own artistic traditions and customs, and is smaller or larger or cheaper or more expensive in relation to the care and the means of its builders. Every processional group is accompanied by a *ta'ziyeh* and after the ceremonies are over it is buried. A more complete description will be found in the chapter "Muharram Ceremonies in India." What supports my thesis is this: Ta'ziyeh and the Ta'ziyeh ceremonies in Persia must have been of the same kind during the period of the spread of these customs to India, during the middle of the Safavid period when the Qezelbashis and other Shi'ites emigrated to the subcontinent and settled there. The statement of Chardin about those objects which accompanied the processions of breast-beaters supports this assumption. After that period, the ceremonies and customs of mourning underwent change and continual evolution in Persia while in the subcontinent they retained their older forms. Of course, it is obvious that some of the details may possibly have changed in accordance with the circumstances and character of that region; but basically they are the same as those which came in from Persia centuries ago.

To sum up: on the one hand we see that until the seventeenth Christian century, Ta'ziyeh, that is the dramatic representation of the events at Kerbela, did not exist in Persia while on the other hand—according to available documents—it is known that a European witnessed dramatic scenes about the tragedy of Kerbela during the 1780s.[8] Therefore this great change in which the mourning assemblies and processions of breast-beaters were converted into a theatrical presentation must have occurred during the eighteenth century, and the drama was brought to perfection about the beginning of the nineteenth century. Let us now examine the causes which ultimately brought about this extraordinarily interesting transformation.

Through long centuries Persians have shown that they are an open-minded and open-hearted people and they never approve of undue strictness and zeal in religious matters. This fact can be attested from Persia's ancient history (Cyrus' treatment of the Jews at Babylon) down to the present day. This people would utilize any manifestation of progress and novelty consonant with their own thought, spirit, and taste. It is not inappropriate to quote from the book, *Le theatre et le danse en Iran,* as an example of this:

> [Iranians] do not reject anything [for use in Ta'ziyeh] because of its European origin. No one is astonished by the fact that chairs in the Viennese style are employed in the Ta'ziyeh. . . .
> . . . In one of the scenes there is a particular place in which the severed head of the Imam recites verses from the Holy Koran.
> In Ardebil, in order to enact this scene, a head was made of cardboard and mounted upon a box in which a phonograph was concealed with a record of Koranic verses placed upon it. The phonograph was started and it appeared to the spectators as though the severed head were reciting the Koran.[9]

Were I to cite more of this kind of testimony or other examples of Iranian tolerance for other faiths and their religious leaders from stories and various historical, social, and mystical sources, this discussion would be unduly prolonged. It is stated several times in Aflaki's book, *The Virtues of the Mystics,* written about the life and words of Mawlana Jalal al-Din, that Christians visited the Mawlana's retreat and he in turn visited their shrines. Occasionally he retired to a Christian monastery for forty days. In keeping with their custom, a monk would come to him daily and prostrate himself thirty-three times. Each time Mawlana would respectfully do likewise to him in return.[10] Therefore tolerance in religious matters and recognition of the dependence of a man's deeds upon his intention occasioned the adoption by Iranians of any pleasing custom they found in other people.

During the passage of the centuries from the most ancient times down to the present not only have there been travelers from the West to the East, but there have also been those from the East to the West. The Westerners, in addition to their diligence in writing journals of their travels, have an advantage in that their documents were preserved through the centuries in archives and various libraries. Scholars have examined them and have published interesting material from them. If there were any documents left by the Easterners, most have perished in turmoils, invasions, and massacres, and those which have survived these events have not been studied. As a result, today we know of many Westerners who visited there and their writings are available to us, but all the travelers from the East to the West remain unknown.

Nevertheless, it is undoubtedly true that after the Crusades Persians traveled to all parts of the civilized, or rather known, world. Traces of them remain in the Far East, even as far as China, Malaysia, and Indonesia. There are still people of good social standing living in Egypt and as far away as Zanzibar and Madagascar who bear the names Shirazi and Isfahani. Despite the passage of eleven centuries, the Parsis of India and Pakistan still consider themselves to be Persians. In view of this, is it possible that no one went to the West? [11]

The Persians who lived close to the former Ottoman and Russian Empires were able to reach Europe quickly and easily. Through their activities, Persian language and customs penetrated to the Balkan Peninsula; to Romania, Hungary, and Yugoslavia. In recent centuries too, liberal ideas were carried to Persia from European by these same peoples. Without doubt while traveling to Christian lands these persons saw that pious and believing Christians, with sincerity and faith and in order to reinforce the belief of the masses, dramatized the adventures of the sacred figures of their religion and produced religious plays (called "miracle plays" or "mysteries"). In reality the modern European theatre is based on those plays, enriched later by the study of the theatrical traditions of Greece and Rome. Is it possible that these developments, these plays, which were accompanied by the weeping and lamenting of the believing Christians, would remain unobserved by the descendants of those whose spiritual guide had repeatedly bowed to Christians while drunken Christians obtained entrance to the ceremony of their mystic dance without any hindrance? [12]

It was in Europe in the Middle Ages that artists first tried to depict various scenes illustrating the miraculous deeds of the sacred personages of the religion of Christ and the wonders of his disciples. In Persia and in the entire Islamic world, portraiture and sculpture of both animals and men were prohibited and unlawful. Nevertheless there are still persons in most present day Iranian towns and villages who possess canvases on which are painted scenes from religious stories depicting the self-sacrifice of the martyrs at Kerbela or the revenge wrought upon the murderers of Imam Hussein by Mukhtar. Each day they display a part of the painting to the people. With rousing speeches, eloquence, and the tricks that have been evolved over the centuries of assembling crowds, they are able to hold their audiences. They retell those events with all the artifice of speech at their command and earn a living more or less commensurate with their ability and eloquence.

I suppose that this is one of those phenomena which spread to Persia as a result of the viewing of the paintings of Raphael and Michelangelo. Because of the spread of the Herat school of painting, and later on the easy-going attitude of the Safavids in these matters, painting no longer met with any obstacle and so it began to develop. Even now in India and Pakistan, and indeed throughout the entire Islamic world, except in Iran, drawing imaginary pictures of the great Islamic personalities is considered to be impiety, heresy, and deviation. It is met with the strongest opposition: riots, immolations, and destruction. They have forgotten the facilities created for art in Sunni areas during the Timurid period and the era of Shah Rukh and Abu Said and Baysunqur, and one can see many illustrated manuscripts in which the owner or one of his ancestors, motivated by prejudice, has obliterated the human faces by washing them with water. It is said that the traditions and rules of the Herat school spread to Persia during and after the Safavid period while in other areas they have passed into oblivion.

In any case, during the period we are considering (the seventeenth and eighteenth Christian centuries), in the years before the French Revolution it would seem that the tradition of staging and giving life to the events at Kerbela came to Persia from Europe. Apparently the people of northern Persia—who were less strict believers—first put on these plays in obscure places. The results were excellent. The people accepted them warmly and the faithful shed many tears. Gradually the plays moved from very simple to larger, more complicated and splendid stages. But Ta'ziyeh had not yet achieved the splendor it deserved. Since, according to the old proverb, "the people have the faith of their kings," it was to be perfected only when it had attracted the attention of the government which then provided greater facilities for its production.

A brief reference has been made above to this point: What was the "Iran" of which we are speaking in which the Ta'ziyeh plays were current? Up to the middle of the reign of Fath Ali Shah Qajar (1243 A.H./A.D. 1827-28) Caucasia was part of Persia, and though its people were quite close to the territory of Russia they were Muslims of the Shi'a sect. Just as many liberal ideas spread from that region to Persia with writers like Akhundof and Jalil Muhammad Qulizadeh (the author of the famous newspaper *Mulla Nasr al-Din* who left a deep impression upon the minds of their fellow-countrymen, so it is possible that in earlier times Ta'ziyeh entered the country.

We cannot suppose that Ta'ziyeh came in by way of the Ottoman Empire, for there mourning ceremonies, breast-beating, and other such customs were always considered impious and heretical. Even if Persians resident in those dominions had such ideas they would not have been able to carry them out in Ottoman territories, but would have had no alternative save to come home to execute their plans, whilst in Caucasia there was no such obstacle or hindrance.

In *Le theatre et le danse en Iran* there are numerous references to the fact that Ta'ziyeh presentations have been recorded in Transcaucasia and even in other Muslim republics of the Soviet Union (Tajikistan, Uzbekistan, etc.). Let us not forget that at the time of the rise of the Ta'ziyeh, those lands were either part of Persia or only recently separated from it. The similarity in traditions, customs, and manners has not yet disappeared.

When it is said that the Ta'ziyeh is derived from the religious plays of the Western world in the Middle Ages it does not mean that our Ta'ziyeh is a blind imitation of Western religious theatre; no, Ta'ziyeh is a kind of rebirth. Its sources and elements originated thousands of years earlier. One should never think in terms of blind imitation in respect to popular arts, because when a people are to adopt something and diffuse it among themselves, they must first comprehend it and then find it agreeable and harmonious with their own needs, aspirations, and traditions.

It must not be supposed that the Ta'ziyeh plays in their length and elaborateness, detail, and with the rich development of "dramatization" appeared full-blown immediately upon the diffusion of Ta'ziyeh. It is from books about the details of the martyrdoms, or histories of the lives of the Imams and saints (such as *Nasikh al-Tawarikh* whose writer felt himself obligated to record sources, origins, and all that he thought to be authentic) that particulars of the tragedy at Kerbela found their way into the Ta'ziyeh texts.

Of course the oldest sources are very brief; but with every passing year and century, additions were made, more and more being related about the events. What prompted the masses to embrace all this, the factor which more than any other really had the greatest effect in the spread of Ta'ziyeh and its acceptance by the people, was popular faith in, zealous love of, and undying devotion to, the Imams and the members of the Prophet's Family, and especially the martyrs of Kerbela. In truth the people were awaiting a spark that would explode the powder-magazine of their feelings and emotions. They ignored the question of the appropriateness of actors playing the parts of Imam Hussein, Ibn Ziyad, Shemr, Ibn Sa'd, Hurr, Hazrat-e Abbas, and Hazrat-e Ali Akbar; the people did not see that which saw, but rather that which they desired and believed in the mirror of the action of the Ta'ziyeh. In this connection there is a charming anecdote which deserves to be related here:

Even though they thought that participating in a Ta'ziyeh was meritorious, still there were fewer volunteers to play the parts of the villains. A pleasant story is told about this:

In Darband [Caucasia] no one wanted to appear in the role of Shemr. After a great deal of searching, the producers of the Ta'ziyeh finally found a Russian laborer who knew a few words of Persian and was ready, for a sum, to play the role of the killer of Imam Hussein.

The Ta'ziyeh directors, considering the Russian laborer's circumstances, shortened Shemr's part as far as was possible. In reality he was only to wear Shemr's costume and stand beside a wooden tub repre-

146

senting the Euphrates River, not allowing anyone to approach it. As the time for his performance approached, the laborer put on Shemr's costume and, taking a whip in hand, stood by the tub. The children and companions of Imam Hussein one by one tried to approach the water while the laborer assiduously kept them away. Unfortunately the person playing the role of Imam Hussein was an old and respected elder. When he neared the water, the Ta'ziyeh director saw, to his astonishment, that the laborer never even tried to prevent him from reaching the water according to the demands of his role; instead he called out to him to drink without any fear or anxiety. The Ta'ziyeh director shouted at the Russian not to let the old man get near the water, but the laborer humbly replied, "Let him drink; he's an old man!"

This incident was not the occasion for consternation or astonishment among the audience and it did not cause laughter; on the contrary it was a strong stimulus to even greater and warmer weeping and tears. The sobbing spectators said, "See! How mean and evil Shemr was! He showed mercy neither to the children nor to Imam Hussein who was the grandson of the Prophet. He killed them, but when the Russian fellow who was outside the faith saw the old actor with a white beard he showed him mercy and permitted him to quench his thirst." [13]

It was this stock of faith which converted every deficiency in the Ta'ziyeh into a virtue and let the viewers accept whatever happened as a pretext for the display of their affection for the Family of the Prophet while at the same time satisfying their psychological and inner inclinations.[14] Ta'ziyeh spread to the remotest villages of Persia.

It is remarkable that until now not one Iranian or non-Iranian scholar has unequivocally commented upon the influence of the European theatre on Ta'ziyeh or has followed up the similarities between the two. The earliest European writers came under the influence of the spell of Ta'ziyeh, and its miraculous effect upon the people seduced and fascinated them. Religious plays had long since vanished in Europe and industrial civilization left no room for such simple faith; as a result they busied themselves with praise of Ta'ziyeh and paid little attention to its origin and sources. All the statements of Count de Gobineau, Sir Lewis Pelly, and others are rhetorical and laudatory; this praise, too, originates in the deep and broad effect of Ta'ziyeh. Other Westerners, including William Francklin who was the earliest among them, disliking Ta'ziyeh due to their unfamiliarity with the customs and manners of Persian society and ignorance of its language, and comparing its performance with developed Western theatre, generally dismissed Ta'ziyeh as ridiculous and clumsy.

The only great Iranologist who, because of his profound knowledge of

Iranian society and repeated observations of Ta'ziyeh, had noted this similarity was Edward Browne; but he too did not dare to express his opinion plainly and openly. And he was right, for during his time all the documents and evidence had not been assembled and no one had done any research on this subject. Browne expressed the belief that "the only indigenous form of drama is that connected with the Muharram mourning, the so-called "Passion Plays" . . . , and even in their case it is not certain they owe nothing to European influence." [15] In another place he marks the similarity in belief between the Shi'ites of Iran and the Christians:

> Certain episodes of the Hussein-Legend would almost seem to indicate an unconscious sense of solidarity with Christians on the part of the Shi'a Persians arising from their participation in the doctrine of the Atonement. . . . To the Persian Shi'a, therefore, Hussein occupies the same position that Jesus Christ does to the devout Christian. . . . The best-known example of this is the conversion and martyrdom of the "Farangi" ambassador at the court of Yazid, a very favorite scene in the ta'ziyahs. . . . .[16]

After Ta'ziyeh presentation became regular and accepted, apparently during the reigns of Fath Ali Shah and Muhammad Shah, every one of the nobility participated in its development according to his understanding and sophistication. According to the story in *Tazkereh-e Ganj-e Shayegan,* Amir Kabir commissioned Mirza Nasr Allah of Isfahan, a master-poet of his era, to write twelve Ta'zieh plays. The reason for this commission is explained thus:

> At the beginning of this government . . . when the prime ministry of the kingdom and the command of the army was bestowed upon the late Mirza Taqi Khan, Amir-e Nezam [Amir Kabir], who was one of the capable men of the epoch and one of the prodigies of the period. . . . Since most of the poetry that was spoken by those playing the members of the Holy Family in the Ta'ziyeh performances and the assemblies depicting the mourning and calamity of the Fifth Person of the Family of the Robe [Imam Hussein] is poor, inappropriate, nonsensical, and erroneous, Mirza Taqi Khan commissioned him, saying, "Elegantly prepare twelve texts about those events in a style both pleasing to the aristocracy and comprehensible to the commons. . . ." He wrote the firebrand of verses so movingly . . . that if the heart of the auditor was as hard as the stone of Moses, listening to them would have had the effect upon it of the rod of Moses. . . .[17]

This is perhaps the first amendatory step taken in way of elevating the level of the Ta'ziyeh texts. Since, according to Mirza Taher She'ri in *Ganj-e*

Shayegan, Amir Kabir ordered the implementation of these reforms when he was prime minister and they must have taken place in the years between 1264 and 1268 A.H./A.D. 1847-52.

After the return of Nasar al-Din Shah from his first trip to Europe (1290 A.H./A.D. 1873-74) the government theater was built in the architectural style of London's Royal Albert Hall. The writer of *From Saba to Nima* states that he built this in order to propagate European theatre, but because of the opposition of the religious leaders to plays and the theatre, the hall was converted into a place for the performance of Ta'ziyeh.[18] However he does not offer any authority for his statement. Regardless of whether this edifice was built as a theatre and then converted into a religious hall, or was from the first day used for Ta'ziyehs, the influence of European architectural style and theatrical construction in it cannot be denied. When the Shah brought the design of so grandiose a building back from his European travels, one may be sure that he had plans about its use after it was finished, and that occasionally they were also implemented.

In the same book we also find without documentation: "It would seem that the observations of European theatre by the Shah in his travels were not without effect in the progress of the performance of Ta'ziyeh and religious plays." [19] His opinions about Ta'ziyeh's employment of Western theatrical methods are all in the same indefinite style, lacking clarity.

What has been said thus far has been only theory and deduction. But these views are also confirmed by positive evidence. A treatise written in Turkish in 1311 A.H./A.D. 1893-94 by Colonel Ahmad Amin, the military attaché and supervisor of the Ottoman Embassy at Tehran is now preserved in the Central Library of Istanbul University, containing information which officials gathered for the edification of their own government and sent to Turkey.[20] Although some matters are discussed from a prejudiced point of view, yet it should be the object of critical study, since there is much useful material in it. Amin has written about Ta'ziyeh, mourning assemblies, and breast-beating. The document is replete with interesting information about the social conditions in the Persia of eighty-odd years ago; but of primary interest to us are Amin's remarks about Ta'ziyeh:

> Ta'ziyeh is also called *shabih* (representation). *Shabih* in imitation of the theatre was created by one of the officials who had gone to Europe on a special mission, and two-story buildings called *takiyehs* usually built in the form of a theatre can be seen in every city and town of Persia, even in the smallest villages.[21] At times other than the mourning days, the upper story serves as storerooms while the lower story is given over to shops and usually resembles a bazaar; but on the mourning days of Muharram each row of shops is decorated by one individual. Hangings and flowers are put in place. For ten consecutive days the tragedy of Kerbela is enacted and the rest performed [*sic*]. For

example on one day the martyrdom of Imam Hussein is given and on another the part about Yazid and the humiliations he inflicted upon the members of the family of Imam Hussein. At this time Hazrat-e Ali appears, Gabrial comes, and music is played, and anyway a series of plays incompatible with Islamic traditions [*sic*] is given.

The Shi'ites think that the more they weep and mourn for Imam Hussein the more merit and virtue they acquire. In order to bring about the people's weeping, these extraordinarily exaggerated dramas are performed.[22]

There are some points in this material requiring explanation: The first is that during 1311 A.H./A.D. 1893-94, the last part of the reign of Naser al-Din Shah, every city and town and even the smallest village possessed a hall for Ta'ziyeh. Even though the government had provided a fine model, nevertheless the inhabitants of the rural areas were influenced by their environment and local building materials. Undoubtedly the halls constructed in mountain valleys and plains, in cold and hot regions differed from one another. They were not uniform then, nor are they today.

The second point is that neither the name nor the building of the *takiyeh* was originally connected with dramatic representations. Centuries before the rise of Ta'ziyeh *takiyeh* existed, and they still are to be found in countries (like Pakistan) which consider Ta'ziyeh blasphemous and heretical. The *takiyeh* in non-Shi'a lands were Sufi assembly halls, which is still the case in the Indo-Pakistani subcontinent. At present, usually most of those dervishes who repair to *takiyeh* are mendicants and call themselves mystics in order to avoid the trouble of useful work. In any case, it is not our intention to discuss the meaning of *takiyeh* and its uses in various countries, but merely to note that *takiyeh* existed before Ta'ziyeh.

Third, Amin, in giving information about the year 1311 A.H. states that Ta'ziyeh productions were common in all the villages of Iran. Accordingly, years must have passed after their introduction: it takes a long time for such customs to spread to remote villages (especially in view of the conditions of that period), and this usually occurs after they have won general acceptance among the masses.

On the other hand, we see that during Amir Kabir's incumbency Ta'ziyeh presentations were common in the cities at least, though he disliked their execution and ordered a famous poet to effect reforms. Therefore the statement of the author of the treatise about the sending of "one of the officials who had gone to Europe on a special mission" must refer to an earlier time. Clearly this "special mission" was the study for the initial preparations and production of Ta'ziyeh. Undoubtedly before this "mission" there were also individuals who had freely but more imperfectly brought Ta'ziyeh to Persia. One can surmise that the mission was the result

150

of the interest of the Shah or the Crown Prince in this type of mourning ceremony, and was the occasion for strengthening its foundations, rather than that Ta'ziyeh first came to Persia through the mission of an official. This latter supposition is illogical, and those who have studied social trends know very well that such a thing is not possible.

Fourth, the opinion of the writer that these exhibitions are incompatible with Islamic traditions, though it is not without prejudice, is the general and prevailing view among the followers of other Islamic sects. Even the Shi'ites living as minorities in non-Shi'a countries view these performances with astonishment. When an experienced Pakistani director and actor, who had worked for years in large and reputable theatres in England, witnessed the Ta'ziyeh at the Shiraz Festival of Arts, he remarked upon returning to his homeland, "I was struck by seeing this performance! It is really very remarkable that the people of Iran are so open-minded that they permit someone to play the roles of the Imams and sacred figures of the faith. It is this open-mindedness which has caused such progress in the theatre in Iran."

Let it not be denied that breast-beating and other ceremonies connected with mourning (including Ta'ziyeh) are rejected not only by the spiritual leaders of other sects, but by Shi'a scholars as well. However, since the latter recognize that these enhance the faith and interest of the people in the saints, and heighten their feelings toward the family of the Prophet, they enjoin a patient forbearance and indulgence in this regard and are not unduly strict. In the past, too, the interest of the governors, kings, and upper classes in Ta'ziyeh was an important factor in the tolerance shown it by religious circles.

The last point we wish to add to the discussion of the document cited is a quotation which confirms our hypothesis about the coming of Ta'ziyeh to Persia by way of Azarbaijan and Caucasia: "Breast-beating: some persons collected around a decorated banner beat their breasts hard while chanting 'O martyr of Kerbela, peace be upon you,' and march around the bazaar. The Azarbaijanis in comparison with other Persians are more zealous and fanatical, and sometimes they injure themselves in these ceremonies...." [23]

One of the most famous religious scholars of Darband in Caucasia was Mulla Aqa, the author of *Sa'adat al-Naseriyyeh,* who opined that the day of Ashura, not counting the night, was seventy-two hours long! It is recorded that he beat himself with a knife *(qameh-zani)* on Ashura. Apparently he was the first, and perhaps the only, religious scholar of note who encouraged this act.[24] If such an act, not consistent with religious standards, was deemed permissible by an important religious scholar and popular leader merely to demonstrate devotion to the martyrs of Kerbela and the family of the Prophet, there could be no further obstacle to less serious acts, including the performance of Ta'ziyeh.[25]

151

1. The word "end" came before "Safavid period" in my manuscript. Due to an error it was omitted from the printed text. I have included in here.

2. *Ancient Iranian Theatre and Story-Telling* (Tehran: Festival of Arts Series, 1346), p. 9.

3. *Ibid.*, p. 11.

4. *Dīvān-i Ṣabāhī Bīdgulī,* edited and introduction by E. Partaw Baiżā'ī, through the efforts of 'Abbās Kaimānish *Mushfiq-i Kāshānī* (Tehran: Tehran Musavvar, Azar 1338), p. 153.

5. Medjid Rezvani, *Le Theatre et la danse en Iran,* quoting Jean Chardin, *Voyages en Perse* (Paris, 1917), T.X. 55, p. 94.

6. For this, refer to the above book, p. 110.

7. See Syed Husain 'Alī Jaffri, "Muharran Ceremonies in India."

8. William Francklin, Observations made on a Tour from Bengal to Persia (London, 1970.)

9. Medjid Rezvani, *Le theatre et la danse en Iran,* p. 84.

10. Shams al-Dīn 'Aḥmad Aflākī, Manāqibal-'Arifīn, edited with notes and appendices by Taḥsīn Yasīkhī (Ankara: Anjuman-i Turk Press, 1959), I, 360-61. There are many references in this book to the intercourse of Mawlānā with monks, priests, and leaders of other religions, like the forty-day retirement of Mawlānā with a monk in the Monastery of Plato (I, 549-50). Followers of all religions loved him (I, 519), and he prevented his companions from chastising a drunken Christian who had entered the meeting of the mystic dance and, not knowing what he was doing, struck Mawlānā (I, 136). Jews, Christians, and monks participated in his funeral according to their own customs with complete sincerity and faith (II, 591-92). All these stories speak of the excellent behavior of the mystics with all mankind, their sympathy with God's creatures, and their broad-mindedness.

11. The late 'Abd Allāh Mustawfī has related the story of an Isfahani named Mashhadi Hassan in his book *My Life, or the Social and Administrative History of the Qajar Period,* 2nd ed. (Tehran: Tehran Musavvar, undated), 11, 233. He had brought some engraved metal work from Isfahan to St. Petersburg and though he knew no Russian, he published an advertisement in a local newspaper. Gradually his trade prospered and he traveled to Paris, making that city the center of his commercial activities, where he continued his business with great success. In the *Manāqib* of Aflākī, too (I, 97), there is a story of a merchant who in the time of Mawlānā would go to Europe for trade and usually suffer loss. Mawlānā said to him that he had looked upon a mendicant in Europe contemptuously . . . etc. This kind of story is good testimony to the continual and unceasing intercourse that has always existed between Iran and European countries.

12. "So great was his perfection of nobility and abundance of forbearance and good temper (i.e., Mawlānā Jalāl al-Dīn) that one day while he was absorbed with the sacred dance and overwhelmed with the perception of the Friend he had entered a state of ecstasy. Suddenly a drunkard appeared at the assembly shouting and, not knowing what he was doing, threw himself upon the person of Mawlānā. His companions chastised him. He said, 'he has drunk wine and is very drunk, what are you doing?' They replied, 'He is a Christian *(Tarsā).*' He said, 'He is a Christian. Why are you not fearful *(tarsā)?*' Bowing they sought forgiveness." (Aflākī, I, 356).

Mawlānā's meaning in the second *tarsā* is as in <u>Kh</u>udā-*tars* (God-fearing) and the like (from the word *tars*, "fear." with an *alef* of agent, *tarsā*).

13. Medjid Rezvani, *Le theatre et la danse en Iran*, pp. 86-89.

14. Refer to my article entitled *Ancient Iranian Theatre*.

15. Edward Browne, *Literary History of Persian*, Vol. IV, trans. into Persian by Rashīd Yāsimī, pp. 161 and 327, quoted from Ṣādiq Humāyūnī. in *Ta'ziyeh va Ta'ziyeh-<u>Kh</u>vānī* (Festival of Arts Series Tehran, 1353), p. 31.

16. In order to see the original story of this Christian and the various narratives that have been related about him (he was thought to be the messenger of Constantine the emperor of Rome, or Rasūl Jālūt, a Jewish scholar, or the Christian patriarch) and also his murder, refer to Amīr Kabīr, *Nāsi<u>kh</u> al-Tawārī<u>kh</u>* (Hikmat-i Qumm Press, n.d.) VI, 343ff.

17. Tazkirih-yi Ganj-i <u>Sh</u>āygān, lithographed at Tehran, 1273 A.H., written by Mīrzā Ṭāhir, *Dībā<u>ch</u>ih-nigār,* with the pen name Shi'rī, pp. 246ff (in the context of the translation of the biography of <u>Sh</u>ihāb of Isfahān). The original book has no pagination.

18. Yaha Aryanpur, *Az Sabā tā Nīmā,* (Tehran, 1351) I, 343, note.

19. *Ibid.*

20. Translated into Persian by Muhammad <u>Gh</u>aravī, *Barrasīhā-yi Tārī<u>kh</u>ī* (Ninth year, No. 4, Mehr-Aban, 1353 Solar/October-November A.D. 1974).

21. In his valuable book (I, 288ff) 'Abd 'Allāh Mustawfī has given us precise and detailed information about various aspects of Ta'ziyeh production and performance. Among these are many descriptions of the *takiyehs* that existed in various localities of Tehran and their appearance during the mourning periods and at other times (I, 300-301). However the field is still open for research with regard to *takiyehs* in rural areas and other cities.

22. *Barrasīhā-yi Tārī<u>kh</u>ī,* Ninth year, No. 4, p. 91.

23. *Ibid.,* p. 92.

24. For more information about the life and works of Mullā 'Aqā of Darband, refer to Qisaṣ al-'Ulamā, by the late Mīrzā Muḥammad Tankābunī (Tehran: 'Ilmiyyih Islāmiyyih Haydari Press, n.d.), pp. 107ff. 'Abd 'Allāh Mustawfī has also recorded some interesting anecdotes about this famous and immoderate sage (I, 276-77).

25. From the sociological point of view, Aḥmad Amīn's treatise is very important and its text should be studied carefully and compared anew with the Persian translation so that any error in its rendering can be corrected, thereby giving us an accurate and valuable document about the years that immediately preceded the Constitution and the assassination of Naser al-Din Shah, a period in which the actual groundwork for the Constitutional Revolution was laid.

12

Ta'ziyeh from the Viewpoint of the Western Theatre

PARVIZ MAMNOUN

In order to recognize the dramatic values and integrity of Ta'ziyeh, there is no need to apply the criteria of the Western Theatre. Such criteria have never been used by Indian or Japanese students of the drama in evaluating *Kathakali* or *Nō*. Nevertheless, there is good reason to examine Ta'ziyeh using the standards and canons of the Western Theatre. The spread of Western civilization to India and Japan in the early part of the twentieth century did not destroy the integrity of their theatrical traditions. We in Iran are also greatly affected by that civilization and culture, and are influenced by the theatre imported from the West; but we have forgotten Ta'ziyeh or think of it as worthless. Since we have attacked it from the citadel of the Western theatre in the past, it is forgivable if today we convene to revise our evaluation, looking at Ta'ziyeh from that same base.

At the turn of the twentieth century, that is at the very time when Ta'ziyeh had been consigned to oblivion in Iran as a rude and primitive exhibition, a style arose in the Western theatre in reaction to the realism and naturalism which had pervaded every scene, that in one comprehensive term can be called "theatricalism." This first appeared in Russia where the realistic theatre had reached its apogee under the auspices of Chekhov and

154

Stanislavski. In its vanguard were the same persons, like Myerhold and Vakhtangov, who had begun their theatrical work in the realistic school.

This "theatricalism" was inherited a little later by Bertold Brecht. Following in the steps of the earlier champions of realism, in the twenties and thirties, he made famous his own theatrical style in opposition to it. This style which is known as "narrative" (and has become incorrectly known in Iran as "epic" theatre), is the same well-known narrative theatre that has attracted our attention more than any other kind of Western drama from the time of the translation of *Galilee* and the publication of the famous introduction by Abdal-Rahim Ahmadi. It is from this point of view that we wish to reexamine Ta'ziyeh today.

What were the principles of the narrative theater of Brecht? From the time when the idea of the play first occurred to man, Western theater, especially after the Middle Ages, has sought to imitate life. Today we divide its history into various periods and styles: romantic, realistic, naturalistic, etc. Of course we give them these names in reference to the mores of our everyday life, that is, according to a standard corresponding to extant reality. We call the writers who are farthest from this standard romantic; those nearer to it, realistic; and those closest to it, naturalistic. But at the same time we know that however much we may consider Hugo and Delavinier as belonging to the romantic school, the object of these writers was to depict real man and real life. The motive for their rebellion against the classical writers was that in the characters of Corneille and Racine, for example, they did not see real people in real situations. We know that Dumas and Ugarte in turn had the same objective in raising the flag of realism in opposition to the romantics. Zola and Hauptmann, too, were the standard-bearers of naturalism, and opposed the realistic theatre. They called it the "cardboard theatre" and described its representations as non-human, false, and remote.

Every dramatic school that came into existence charged its predecessor with being unrealistic, and claimed that the characters they themselves created and the life they showed upon the stage were real. At the end of this chain of controversy they invented the name "naturalism," a name which, according to Brecht, contradicted the essence of art and whose use was the "greatest crime."

On the stage itself an effort to obtain the most realistic acting could also be observed. From the pompous oratory and declamation of the classical theatre, actors' speech gradually assumed a more popular form. An actor would even turn his back upon his fellow performers. In 1838 the first book about the aesthetics of vulgarity was published, and gradually spitting on the stage and similar actions, which the earlier theatre had decried, became permissible and commonplace. The insistence upon natural acting and natural production reached a point where Zola, in his essay "Naturalism in the Theatre," counseled students to go to the markets, public places, and especially to the coffee houses as well as to dramatic school and, having carefully observed the behavior, speech, and manner of the people, to represent it faithfully on the stage. When his friend and director Antoine needed his stage set as a butcher shop, he ordered the carcass of a skinned cow brought from the slaughterhouse a few moments before the performance began, then hung from a meathook on the stage, still dripping blood.

The climax of this naturalistic and realistic production is the style which is called by the name of Stanislavski. It was he who, with a series of experiments at the turn of the century along the lines that Zola had been seeking, gave the method a scientific framework and popularized it throughout the world; we call this the sensitive theatre, or in more popular language, portraying the role by natural acting.

Though it affected dramatic art throughout the world and is still the most widespread style in the West and the East, the work of the theatre of naturalism soon reached a dead end. Strindberg, who had started with it early in his career, shattered the constraints of this style and entered the open spaces of expressionism. Hauptmann, the greatest exponent of the naturalist movement, after writing dozens of plays which were even composed in dialect, finally turned to Greek mythological subjects written in literary German. The most outstanding students of Stanislavski, like Meyerhold and Vakhtangov, rebelled against the methods of their preceptor.

In such circumstances, after Meyerhold had first broken down the wall of the realistic theatre, Bertold Brecht took to the field and fought against it. His view, insofar as it related to the repudiation of the realistic method, was logical, correct, and clear. He would say that we are not realistic; rather that we have defrauded reality. If we are realistic, the reality is that the stage upon which we act is the stage of a theatre; that the set is nothing more than boards, burlap, and paint. He would say that the only reality in the theatre is that the theatre is not real. In his first step along this line in *Drums In the Night,* he ordered placards hung in the theatre with this statement addressed to the audience: "Don't be surprised that this is such a romantic theatre!"

Brecht sought a style which testified to the truth that the artist was only an actor and the performance only acting. Taking into consideration that it was not easy for an actor to forget his own identity, he recommended emphasis upon the separation of the actor from his role, both for the sake of the actor himself and for that of the audience. It should always be evident that the man who is striding across the stage was not really the Venetian commander Othello, but an actor doing his job in playing the part. For Brecht this method not only seemed more truthful, but also enabled the actor to exercise his own judgment.

In any event this approach at least theoretically destroyed the basis of the work of the earlier realistic acting of the West. New canons took its place which sought not the merging of the actor with the role he was to interpret, but his maintaining a distance from it. In the theory of the Brechtian narrative theatre two words stand out more than any others: *Zeigen,* which means to point out, to show, and *Verfremden,* which means to be strange to, to keep at a distance, to keep away.

Now from the point of view of the Brechtian narrative theatre, Ta'ziyeh is theatre; a theatre whose form, one might say, Brecht strove unsuccessfully to attain. This was not because Brecht's knowledge of the theatre was inferior to that of the Ta'ziyeh producers; rather his failure was due to a misunderstanding, a contradiction which Brecht was unable to perceive as he wanted to invest the realistic content of Western theatre with the form of narrative theatre (which is Eastern in origin) that is peculiar to ritual and religious plays and cannot be used for plays about the predicament of ordinary man and his worldly and social needs and problems. It was also this contradiction which drew the narrative theatre of Brecht toward the invention of complicated formulas, perplexing theories, and obscure ratiocinations; and it was the reason that until now his theory of narrative theatre has remained only a theory.

The proof of this assertion is that even in Germany today directors, like Schweikart who worked closely with Brecht in the production of his works, now resort to the same old method of realism. The current production of *Mr. Puntila* in the state theatre of Munich under the direction of Schweikart is a clear example of this type of realistic performance. Even a few years ago, when the controversy about the Brechtian style was still heated, if one carefully examined the acting of a performer in this style, one did not actually find any separation between the actor and the role. And even if such a separation was apparent, it was the same separation that the realistic theatre, with all its "natural acting" and "entering into the part," was unable to bridge or eliminate. The reason for this situation is the contradiction between content and form which does not permit the separation: in performing Brecht as in every other realistic performance, a total separation between the actor and the role does not exist. It is with regard to this contradiction that we said that Ta'ziyeh is the theatrical goal which Brecht sought to achieve—it is the most developed theatre in the narrative theatrical form.

The proposition is this: From its inception Ta'ziyeh did not seek to be realistic or to achieve realism: the tragedy of Kerbela was so important to the Ta'ziyeh performer, so exceptional and extraordinary that it would have been impossible to show it realistically within the means and possibilities of performance, which are at best only a vehicle by which it is possible to show this tragedy but not to reproduce it. When looked at from the point of view of acting, it is nothing more than this. Contrary to the theatre of Brecht, the role played by an actor in Ta'ziyeh is not the role of an ordinary human like himself. The characters are prophets and imams, superhuman personalities possessing superhuman virtues. Between them and the Ta'ziyeh player, there is a vast, manifest distance, both for the spectator and for the actor himself. No actor, even the most skilled artist of the realistic theatre, could eliminate this distance which is a concomitant of the conception of Hazrat-e Hussein held by the audience of the Ta'ziyeh. Hussein, who on the noon of Ashura flew from Kerbela to distant forests so that he might save Sultan Qais from the attack of a lion, is not regarded as an ordinary man: therefore another ordinary man, an actor, could not realistically portray him.

Nor can the Ta'ziyeh player, who is also a believing Shi'ite, ever permit himself to become one with the Imam, an act which would in his opinion be blasphemy. This situation also pertains in the playing of the villains. The distance between the actor and the person of the villain is clear and unavoidable, first because the inherent loathing and repulsion which the Shi'ite actor feels for Yazid and Shemr is so strong that any artistic desire to identify with the character is nullified. Secondly, the behavior of Yazid and Shemr toward the Imam is inhuman and unbelievable, and they have been converted into such monsters, that it would be impossible for any man to portray them realistically. Therefore the only thing a Shi'ite Ta'ziyeh player desires, and in principle is able to do, is visibly to impersonate Hazrat-e Hussein and Ali, and Shemr (may he be cursed), to allude to their personalities, to recall their existence, and nothing more. This distance between the actor and the role in Ta'ziyeh is so obvious that if (as recently happened in several Ta'ziyehs) a player refers directly to this separation, his action must be considered inappropriate and seen as the influence of new theatrical ideas. In Natanz, for example, one Mr. Sulaimani, playing Abbas, recited an ode that he himself had composed. In the middle of it he emphasized the separation between himself and the character he was playing:

> I am not Abbas; neither is this Kerbela.
> I am Sulaimani, the slave of the king of heavenly power.

Ta'ziyeh has no need for this kind of allusion. The obvious needs no elaboration.

At any rate, now that we are looking at Ta'ziyeh from the viewpoint of the narrative theatre, we must reconsider our judgment. We should not criticize the poverty of Ta'ziyeh, because the poverty of Ta'ziyeh is the nobility of its method. We should not ascribe the indifference to historical reality in the costuming of Ta'ziyeh to the ignorance of the performers. That very cord slipper and the ordinary broad, black trousers which can be seen under the Arabian cloak of the villager playing the part of the Imam in Humayunshahr in Isfahan, or the gendarme uniform worn by the man playing Ibn Sa'd in Maimeh, is the most elegant of costumes. For in Ta'ziyeh just as the players of the Imam and Ibn Sa'd must only allude to those roles, so the costumes in their turn should only suggest the clothing of the Imam and Ibn Sa'd. They should not be replicas of their dress.

We must not ascribe the Ta'ziyeh player's reading from his script while acting to slovenliness in his work; this is itself a direct reference to the "representation," to the actor being a "reader." And finally, we must not think the intrusion of the directors and other non-acting persons in the performance, the traffic of people taking a short-cut across the stage, the drinking of tea and water by the actors even while acting out a play in which the heroes are all panting from thirst, the playing of the role of Zainab by a powerfully built, rough-voiced man, the weeping of the actor playing the part of the Imam for the predicament of the Imam, the weeping of Shemr for the Imam and his praying for the sponsor of the assembly in the name of the King of the Thirsty (this Shemr who is just about to separate the Imam's head from his body), and other examples of this sort, to be proof of the weakness of Ta'ziyeh or of its rudeness. For all these actions and motions are the most beautiful and perfected effect of keeping distance from the characters, which at times remarkably enhances the power and effectiveness of the performance. When the spectator sees that even Shemr has tears in his eyes for the oppressed Imam he is twice as upset and gives way to even greater weeping under the influence of the performance. And finally we must not mock the exaggerated gestures and the "affectedness" of Ta'ziyeh players, for these gestures are the very ones which Brecht recommended to the artists of the narrative theatre under the name *Allgemeine Gestus.*

We must not forget that on the day when the Ta'ziyeh costumes are brand new and historically accurate; that day on which, God forbid, imaginative sets are used; that day on which realistic artists under the Ta'ziyeh and natural acting replaces the present "artificial" gestures; that day on which the performance is removed from the platforms of the *takiyeh,* from the bare fields of the villages, from the asphalt pavements of small towns, and is transferred to the boxlike stages of the modern theatre where a velvet curtain will be hung that will open at the beginning of the performance to the accompaniment of the usual mysterious dramatic music; that day, the day when Ta'ziyeh becomes realistic, will witness its death.

But the dramatic art of Ta'ziyeh is another issue which should be considered here, especially since up to now we have observed that Ta'ziyeh has been repeatedly attacked and belittled from this point of view. Since the standards of this judgment are once again the principles and canons of Western dramaturgy, it is incumbent upon us, if possible, to rely upon those very principles and canons of the West in defense of Ta'ziyeh and for the recognition of its dramatic values. We must, however, limit our discussion to one special problem: The criticism which is made about characterization in Ta'ziyeh is that, first, there are only two groups, the good and the bad; in the vocabulary of Ta'ziyeh, the saints and the villains. Second, that it pays no attention to logic and human psychology and their effects, the first principles of characterization in Western realistic drama.

The roles of Ta'ziyeh, contrary to the claims made, are neither absolutely bad and absolutely good, nor absolutely white and absolutely black. Passing over the character of Hurr who is black in the beginning and white at the end—he goes from one extreme to the other—sometimes there are parts in the Ta'ziyeh in which the characterization is not as simplistic as has been stated. Among the villains, for example, while Shemr is the shameless offspring of adultery who opposes the Imam, another of the commanders of the army of Ibn Sa'd, Senan, who had volunteered to kill Imam Hussein before Shemr had come forward to do it, has some understanding of shame and decency. When he draws his dagger and moves toward the Imam he looks in the Imam's eyes, and he is ashamed of what he is about to do. Casting the dagger aside, he turns back, for he has seen the image of Hussein's mother, Zahra the daughter of the Prophet, in Hussein's eye. The personality of Ibn Sa'd himself, one of the most important of the negative characters, in a few Ta'ziyehs sometimes oscillates between white and black. For example in the long exchange between Ibn Sa'd and Shemr contained in the Ta'ziyeh *The Seeking of Respite by His Excellency the Lord of Martyrs* (No. 8 in Litten's collection), Ibn Sa'd tries until the last moment to dissuade Shemr from his inhuman deed. Though in most of the Ta'ziyehs Ibn Sa'd is seen as totally bad, in *The Martyrdom of His Excellency the Lord of Martyrs* (in the Cerulli collection) he strongly opposes fighting the Imam.

We do not wish to count these instances which are exceptional among the points of strength of Ta'ziyeh; on the contrary, we wish to acknowledge them as points of weakness, and admit that ultimately Ta'ziyeh is concerned only with absolute good and absolute evil, that is, the very quality for which it was being criticized. We may well ask here whether this criticism of Ta'ziyeh is warranted.

First let us examine the reasons for which this criticism is made. One of the most important rules in the art of Western playwriting is that the playwright must be neutral in the creation of roles, whether they be sympathetic or unsympathetic. In other words the writer has a responsibility in his choice of actions and words for a character to look at the situation from the character's point of view, and to record causes and motivation. Schiller considered this neutrality the paramount rule in the craft of the writer. From the beginning of his career as a playwright, with *The Highwaymen*, he endeavored to employ this precept in his own work. Even though in that play Franz Moore is an unsympathetic character, Schiller enlightens us as to the causes and motives for Franz's actions. Among them, he is ugly, hideous, as nature has been unjust to him in regard to face and form.

Shakespeare, too, enumerates motives for the actions of one of his most famous villains, Iago: First, he believed that his wife had been unfaithful to him with Othello. More importantly, in the previous Venetian war he had distinguished himself in courage and bravery above any of

Othello's other officers, so he felt that he deserved to be appointed Othello's second-in-command; however Othello bestowed this honor upon another officer.

There are many more examples of this kind. Nevertheless although the neutrality of the author continued, from the beginning of the naturalistic period the characters become complex in Western theatre. More recently, Martin Walser has entered the arena, calling all previous Western theatre false on the grounds that it shows man, while doing something good or bad, exhibiting only one of many different dimensions.

Now, from the point of view of Schiller's precept—not to mention the realism of Walser—it is obvious that our Ta'ziyeh poets are not distinguished playwrights, because the fact that they are believing Shi'ites is of paramount importance. They are not neutral; they are partisans of the saints. When they first put pen to paper at the top of the script for the Imam, they write, "The script of the Imam upon whom be the mercy of God," while at the top of the script for Shemr they write, "The script of Shemr, may he be cursed." Due to this inherent partisanship, development of the characters according to the rules of logic and reason and the principles of psychological realism does not take place. But we must stress one point: what Schiller sought from the playwright and Walser perfected is only valid for realistic plays which deal with ordinary men and their problems. Now the background of Ta'ziyeh is neither an ordinary event nor are its characters ordinary men. They are not men, in that traits of human weakness and strength cannot be found in them. They are symbols, manifestations, tokens.

In the same way, the tragedy of Kerbela was not an ordinary event. The Ta'ziyeh narrative is ultimately not the story of the dispute of a man named Hussein ibn Ali with a man named Yazid ibn Mu'awiyyah, who in the month of Muharram, 61 A.H., fought over the caliphate. The Ta'ziyeh narrative is the eternal story of the oppressed and the oppressor, the brave and the coward, the ascetic and the corrupt, the future life and the material world, heaven and hell: the story of good and evil.

In Ta'ziyeh we do not encounter characters whom we wish to consider carefully from the psychological point of view. That is one matter, but another is that in reality even in Western playwriting the precept of Schiller is not followed—for instance, in the *commedia dell'arte,* in some of the works of Molière like *The Miser,* and even in Shakespeare. Let's take a look at *Much Ado About Nothing* as an example. Can we give any reason for the churlish behavior of Don Juan, who gives us pleasure but nonetheless always plays the part of a troublemaker for others, other than to say that he is naturally and instinctively malicious? When we come to Brecht it is a totally different matter. We see him, on the basis of his own political view of the world, divide all roles into two groups, the bad and the good, just as in Ta'ziyeh; the "plunderer" and the "plundered." Look at *The Rule and the Exception, St. Joan of the Stockyards, The Good Person of Szechwan,*

Mr. Puntila, and the Caucasian Chalk Circle. It is remarkable that many of us who reject the black and white characterization of Ta'ziyeh forget that it was Brecht, the writer whom we honor more than most of his contemporary playwrights, who in the last period of his writing and at the peak of his creativity turned to the style of "naïve theatre," *Das Naïve Theater,* in which, just as in Ta'ziyeh, the parts of the good and the bad are distinguished. We forget that Brecht, in his last period of activity, went so far in this direction that in the production *The Caucasian Chalk Circle,* he left the faces of good characters alone but used masks for all the bad characters, thus plainly distinguishing between the good and the bad.

Therefore if our standards are not simply the principles of the classical dramaturgy of Western realistic plays, and we look at the characterizations of Ta'ziyeh from the point of view of the narrative or naïve theatre of Brecht, then we do not object to Ta'ziyeh because of its black and white characters. We recognize that it is the most perfect theatre in its own category; of course, the most perfect in the sense of being the most naïve, not with the meaning of primitive or trivial, but simple, without artifice; a theatre whose characters play with all their cards showing.

Perhaps this name, the theatre without artifice, without deceit, without device, is the most expressive name that can be given to Ta'ziyeh in order to distinguish it from the theatre of realism of the West. This is just the opposite, full of artifice, full of decit, full of device, or in the respectable phrase of theatre people themselves, the theatre full of intrigue, whose dramatic art is that of method and device, whose excitement is dependent upon the fact that its unsympathetic characters possess a complex appearance and character, such as Yaner and Franz Moore have. Of course this theatre without artifice is not realistic; it does not reproduce with exactness. In real life men do not behave as do Shemr or Iago. They have a kind appearance with an evil nature; they speak of humanity and compassion with a heart full of misanthropy. In real life one cannot see such an evil disposition as that of Shemr of the Ta'ziyeh of *Alam-e Zar* (Tehran manuscript in a private collection) who confesses that he is a tyrant:

> O men, Shemr of the Coat of Mail
> Is my name. It is my deed
> To stamp my boot upon his chest.
> It is I who take his sister prisoner.
> I do not fear the Great Creator
> That I would be ashamed before the Prophet!
> I do not desire that Hussein, who is my mediator,
> Appear before my Creator (on my behalf).

This confession does not correspond to real life. Accordingly, neither can the character of Shemr be realistic. Nonetheless the character of Shemr is real, and the characterization of Shemr has the logic of actuality because Shemr is in fact (like Iago) malicious, corrupt, evil. Seen from this perspective, we may even say that when it is farthest from realism, the symbolic theatre of Ta'ziyeh approaches the border of reality.

It would be erroneous to suppose that the attainment of this perfection and simplicity in Ta'ziyeh was possible without careful attention to and expertise in the details of the craft. Just as the Western playwright needs technique in his own realistic characterizations, so also the Ta'ziyeh writer, in order to make the despised characters as black and the heroes as admirable as possible, needs techniques. The only difference is that these techniques are not complicated, but simple; not concealed, but obvious. They are techniques whose beauty lies in their being opposed to technique. At first glance, one who is familiar only with the Western realistic and artful theatre regards Ta'ziyeh as primitive and trivial, ignoring the fact that it is made artless through these very techniques and is the ultimate development of the naïve theatre which a section of the modern theatre in the West is striving to attain.

Permit me to give examples of some types of these "anti-technical" techniques. The first type may be seen in the dialogue between the saints and the villains, in which the villain admits that truth and right are on the side of the Imam, and that he has risen to do battle with him only out of worldliness, ambition, and greed. One can see an example of this technique in the verse dialogue of Imam Hussein and Ibn Sa'd in *The Martyrdom of Imam Hussein* (Rasht manuscript, No. 53 in the Cerulli collection):

Hussein: Ask that the base Ibn Sa'd come to me for a moment.

Ibn Sa'd: What balm do you place, O king, upon my wounded heart?

Hussein: Tell me, do you know who I am or do you not know?

Ibn Sa'd: You are the descendant of Ahmad, the son of Haidar the select.

Hussein: Do you acknowledge the truth that my mother was the Best of women?

Ibn Sa'd: Your mother was Zahra, and your brother Hassan.

Hussein: If you do, then why are you my enemy?

Ibn Sa'd: Lo! Then Yazid, O King, will be grateful for my action.

Hussein: Why would Yazid be grateful to you, O bad-omened hard-heart?

Ibn Saʿd:	If I cut off your head, I shall obtain my claims.
Hussein:	If you cut off my head, what reward will you get from him?
Ibn Saʿd:	In return for your pure head, I shall become the governor of Rayy.

The Taʿziyeh writer uses another device to establish the despicability and unworthiness of the villains. He has the friend of the individual villain call him despicable and unworthy and let loose a torrent of abuse at him. Not only does the villain himself not object to the words and tone of his friend, but instead he addresses him with great deference, in this way confirming his own meanness and unworthiness.

An excerpt from the dialogue of Hazrat-e Abbas with Shemr in the Taʿziyeh *Hazrat-e Abbas* (Qazvin manuscript?) from the archives of the Theatrical Association of Tehran University:

| *Shemr to Abbas:* | O standard-bearer of Hussein! O son of the king of Badr and Hunain! Sit beside me in the way of friendship so that I may humbly offer some words which have become incumbent upon me at the feet of your noble excellency. Otherwise I have no design upon your person, and I have no quarrel. A moment, O my chief, my leader. . . . |
| *Abbas to Shemr:* | O scion of an adulter, offspring of the shameless and indecent, possessor of the coat of mail, rejected, tyrant! What, do you make exaggerated boasts and display to me at every moment your army lying in wait? By right of the Great Creator, by the grave of the Prophet, by the injured side of Zahra the Pure. . . . |

Another device the Taʿziyeh writer uses to unveil the evil nature of the villains is to make them dispute among themselves so that under the pretext of criticizing one another, they make public their own mean objectives. An excerpt from the conversation between Shemr and Ibn Saʿd from *Hazrat-e Abbas:*

Shemr:	The old wise man guides the young.
Ibn Saʿd:	O love for the world! You do not know what you are doing with us.
Shemr:	The love for the world causes the loss of faith and heart.

164

Ibn Sa'd:	I don't know what must be done on the Day of Punishment.
Shemr:	Then why have you come to Kerbela with a vast army?
Ibn Sa'd:	Why have you come with spear, sword, and dagger?
Shemr:	You have signed the decree to slay the family of Haidar.
Ibn Sa'd:	You have made manifest the flame of violence and wrath.
Shemr:	You have heard his fame; you said that you have attained your objective.
Ibn Sa'd:	Why did you accept the cloak of honor of Ibn Ziad?

But the Ta'ziyeh writer was able to achieve this not only through mutual repreaches, but also by the support given to one another by the villains, thus, so to speak, raising the curtain on their oppression and tyranny.

An excerpt from the debate of Shemr and Ibn Sa'd from *The Martyrdom of Imam Hussein* (No. 28 in the Cerulli collection):

Shemr:	They have commanded that it is for you to stand on the battlefield. I'll take care of cutting off Hussein's head with a dagger.
Ibn Sa'd:	You'll take care of cutting off Hussein's head from his pure body. I'll take care of placing it on the point of a staff in the way of enmity.
Shemr:	You'll take care of inserting the lance into the back of his head. I'll take care of slapping the faces of the orphaned ones.
Ibn Sa'd:	You'll take care of slapping the faces of the orphaned ones. I'll take care of bringing Zainab out of her tent lamenting.
Shemr:	You'll take care of prohibiting Zainab from weeping. I'll take care of making the orphans weep.
Ibn Sa'd:	You'll take care of chaining the necks of the little prisoners. I'll take care of jabbing at their backs with my spear.

165

Another device: one of the most authentic scenes of Taʻziyeh is that of the declaimed challenge *(rajaz khani)* between the saints and the villains. The Taʻziyeh writers have taken this kind of scene from Iranian epic literature, especially the *Shahnameh.* The declaimed challenge occurs before the beginning of man-to-man combat between two champions. In it each of the parties harangues the other with a description of his own formidable deeds, greatness, and heroism, as well as those of his fathers and ancestors. In Taʻziyeh too, both the hero and the villain recall their own honors, but with one difference—during the challenge of the hero his proud tone is suitable to his generous deeds and appropriate to his character, while the challenge of the villainous person, like Shemr, though he too refers to his deeds and qualities in the same proud voice, in fact they are marks of his meanness, vileness, and baseness.

An excerpt from the challenge of Shemr in *Hazrat-e Abbas:*

Shemr: I who am the slave at your banquet and your liege in your palace.

Standing submissively, I am the obedient servant of this sovereign

At times I am ill-omened, at times bitter, at times a lie, at times water;

At times I am dust, at times I am as sweet as rock sugar, at times I am like the venom of the serpent.

I am the calamity of Kerbela, the offspring of menstruation and adultery.

Look upon me; I have seven nipples upon my chest like a dog.

13

The Literary Sources of the Ta'ziyeh

L. P. ELWELL-SUTTON

One of the problems much discussed by students of the Ta'ziyeh is the source of these plays, not so much the origins of the practice as the authorship and antiquity of the traditional scripts themselves. I do not propose to offer an answer to this question, which requires far wider and deeper research than has been possible in the present instance. My intention is rather to initiate a study of the texts themselves, and to suggest the general lines it should take. If carried out on a sufficiently broad scale, it might be that we would find pointers to the way in which these texts were compiled and the poetic sources upon which their doubtless numerous authors drew.

The immediate problem that faces any enquirer into the structure, language, prosody, and so on, of the Ta'ziyeh texts is the lack of published source material and the scarcity and even inaccessibility of manuscript material. This deficiency has led to confident statements being made from time to time on various aspects, statements that are found to be at variance with the facts as these become better known. For instance, one respected scholar has stated that "*Mujtas* is the basic meter of the Persian passion plays," [1] whereas the truth, as evident from even a limited study of the prosody of the Ta'ziyeh texts, is considerably more complex than that. It is

167

most important therefore that oral and manuscript text should not only be recorded, collected and preserved, but should also be printed and made available to scholars as rapidly as possible. The survey that follows covers no more than seventeen plays, ten printed in popular "chapbook" form in Iran,[2] five by Iranian scholars,[3] and two by European researchers.[4] On such a limited foundation it is impossible to make any dogmatic statements; nevertheless certain trends can be observed. It should be understood that any general statements which follow must be taken as qualified by the foregoing considerations.

METER

The immediate point that strikes any student of the Ta'ziyeh meters is the fact that almost without exception they are the standard 'aruzi meters. The prosody, in other words, is in literary form, and has no relationship with the metrical system of popular poetry. The second feature is that, contrary to the normal practice of literary poems, short or long, in which the same meter is maintained from beginning to end, the Ta'ziyeh changes its meter frequently and employs a number of different ones throughout its length. The following statistics will serve to illustrate these points.

In the collection of seventeen Ta'ziyeh studied here, totaling some 6300 *baits* or distiches (in a few cases there is more than one text with minor variations) thirty-eight different meters are to be found. In classifying these I have taken the liberty of abandoning the traditional nomenclature in favor of the classification promulgated in my recently published work, *The Persian Metres*.[5] By reference to that work the meters here identified can easily be converted to the 'aruzi terminology. I believe my new classification to be more relevant to the meters of Persian poetry than the system devised centuries ago by Khalil b. Ahmad for the categorization of Arabic meters.

The commonest meter, as indicated earlier, is 4.1.15 *(mujtatt mutamman maxbūn mahdūf,* etc.), which accounts for 2062 baits, 32.6 percent of the whole. The next ten meters are 2.1.11 (16.8 percent), 2.4.11 (8.9 percent), 2.1.16 (5.3 percent), 4.5.11 (5.1 percent), 4.7.14 (4.8 percent), 2.4.15 (4.7 percent), 3.1.11 (4.5 percent), 5.1.10 (3.5 percent), 1.1.11 (3.5 percent), and 3.1.15 (2.8 percent). It is worth noting that nine of these eleven, accounting for 92.4 percent of the total, are also to be found among the first eleven meters according to their placement in Persian poetry as a whole,[6] though the order and percentages are somewhat different. For example, 4.1.15 is twice as frequent in the Ta'ziyeh, though it still accounts for only one-third of the *baits* in the texts studied, this being partially explained by heavy use in one or two of them. As noted below, it has the highest frequency in only nine out of the seventeen plays. Nine of the Ta'ziyeh meters are not listed in the *Persian Metres* survey, though only six of these are not attested elsewhere in classical literature. These rare ones are all in the standard patterns: only thirteen *baits,* or 0.2 percent of the total. are found in irregular non-classifiable meters.

Another deviation from classical practice is rather greater preference for the "short" meters (under thirteen basic syllables). Whereas the classical poets use them in 37.3 percent of their output,[7] the Taʻziyeh show a figure of 44.5 percent. Nevertheless, allowing for statistical margin of error, it is possible to say that the popularity of individual meters is much the same for the Taʻziyeh as for Persian poetry in general.

Of course all thirty-eight meters are not to be found in any one Taʻziyeh. The largest number used is twenty (in a Taʻziyeh of 480 *baits,*) and the smallest number, twelve (in one of 224 *baits)* apart from an incomplete text of 209 *baits,* which has only nine different meters. Two plays are in fact longer—one of 627 *baits* (with thirteen meters), and one of 501 *baits* (with sixteen meters). Three meters only are used in all seventeen texts—4.1.15, which comes first in nine of them, 2.1.11, which comes first in two, and 2.4.15. The other six "winners" are 1.1.11 (used in ten texts), 2.1.16 (used in fifteen texts and first in two), 2.4.11 (used in fifteen), 3.1.11 (used in seven), and 5.1.10 (used in fourteen texts).

The practice of frequent changes in the meter used is so marked that it is evidently felt to be a desirable and necessary feature. The longest continuous passage in one meter (in the texts studied) consists of 68 *baits* in meter 3.1.11, but this is an isolated example, and though there are other individual instances as we work down the scale (57 in 4.1.15, 49 in 2.4.11, 48 in 4.1.15, and so on), it is only when we come to passages of 17 *baits* or less that the number of examples begins to exceed two figures. These are, of course, not necessarily delivered by the same speaker, though the shorter the continuous passage the more likely this is. More than a quarter of such passages number only two *baits;* one-seventh, three *baits;* and one-tenth, four *baits.* The average for individual texts ranges from ten to four, the overall average being six.

Although there is some reason for thinking that certain meters are regarded as more appropriate for certain types of subject—for instance, short meters for lamentation, 1.1.11 for *rajaz xandan*—[8] yet the figures above make it clear that change of subject alone is not enough to account for the high frequency of alternation. It is worth bearing in mind that the texts of these plays normally exist in the shape of separate scripts for each actor. This is not necessarily to imply that parts for each actor were composed separately, and certainly there is no evidence of distinctive meters being used by particular characters, whether beneficent or malign; in fact the larger a role the more meters it is likely to use. The longest single part of the collection studied consists of 273 *baits* and uses nine different meters.[9] The largest number of different meters, fourteen, is used in a role totaling 92 *baits.*[10] The longest part using only one meter amounts to 21 *baits;* using two meters, 30 *baits;* using three, 59 *baits;* using four, 72 *baits;*

and using five, 107 *baits*. Seven roles of only one *bait* each naturally use only one meter each, but there are also cases of two-, three- and four-*bait* roles in two meters, five- and six-*bait* roles in three meters, and so on. Between these extremes there is considerable variety, but the overall average of *baits* in the same meter spoken by the same character is 6.4. By way of example, the following table has been compiled by adding together the roles of the characters named from all of the plays in which they occur.

Character	No. of Plays	No. of Baits	No. of Meters
Imam Hussein	11	864	22
Zainab	11	469	22
Shahrbanu	7	235	17
Fatemeh Zahra	9	189	17
Shemr	9	182	13
Ibn Sa'd	8	164	10

Of the above, six meters (2.1.11, 2.1.16, 2.4.11, 3.1.15, 4.1.15, and 4.7.14) are found in all six roles, four in five out of six, three in four, six in three, five in two, and seven in one out of six. Only eight meters, out of the total thirty-eight in the texts studied, are not used by any of these major characters. Similar results would doubtless be obtained for other characters.

Short speeches—in whatever meter—are the norm. The longest speech noted consists of thirty *baits*,[11] seven *baits* in 2.1.16 and twenty-three in 2.4.11. Of all the speeches, 92.5 percent are of 5 *baits* or less, and well over half, of not more than two *baits*. Included in this calculation, though not sufficiently numerous to affect the percentages, are a number of speeches divided by alternate hemistichs between two speakers. Such speeches, generally of the *su'āl u javāb* (question-and-answer) form, are a noteworthy feature of the Ta'ziyeh.

رقیه   زینب

عمه دارم سؤال چند امشب   کن سؤالت ز عمهات زینب

پدرم کو که در نظر باشد   پدرت عمه در سفر باشد

از سفر او مگر نمیآید   خواهد آمد غم تو بزداید

خواهد آمد کی از سفر آیا   از سفر خواهد آمد او فردا

چیست عمه بزیر طشت طلا   هست منظورت عمه در اینجا

[12] من طعام از کسی نخواستهام   عمه زین حرف سینه کاستهام

الخ ،

They can vary quite considerably in length, from two to twenty-three *baits* in the sample studied, but the largest number are between six and twelve with the average figure working out at nine.

No. of *baits*	2	3	4	5	6	7	8	9	10	11
No. of examples	3	5	2	4	13	8	9	4	6	6
No. of *baits*	12	13	14	15	16	17	21	22	23	
No. of examples	5	1	1	1	4	1	1	1	1	

Total 76

There is one case of an eleven-*bait* speech divided between three speakers.[13]

The meters used for these alternating speeches are fairly widespread, with a preference for the shorter ones. Out of the seventy-six examples noted, thirty-one are in 2.1.11 (including the three longest), fifteen in 2.4.11, ten in 4.1.15, and the rest fairly evenly distributed between nine other meters—1.1.11, 2.1.16, 2.4.15, 3.1.11, 3.1.15, 3.4.11, 4.5.11, 4.7.14, and 4.7.07 (2). Fifty-four are in short meters and twenty-two in long.

RHYME

Another feature that adds to the appearance of piecemeal composition is the variety of rhyme-schemes. There are, of course, only two widely used rhyme-schemes in classical Persian verse, the *masnavi* (rhymed couplets), and the monorhyme, the latter being further distinguished by the rhyming of both hemistichs *(miṣrāʿ)* of the first *bait* of a passage. The bulk of the texts studied are in the *masnavi* form (82.7 percent), leaving only 17.3 percent of the monorhyme form. A negligible number of verses do not lend themselves to classification by rhyme. As regards choice of meter, both forms use virtually the entire range found in the sample; the *masnavi* uses thirty-two meters and the monorhyme thirty. Certain meters, however, show a marked leaning in one direction or the other; as against the overall ratio of approximately 4:1 in favor of the *masnavi*, 2.1.11 shows a 34:1 preference for it; 1.1.11, 19:1; and 2.4.11 as much as 42:1. On the other hand 2.1.16, 2.4.15, 3.1.15, and 4.7.14 show a modest majority in favor of the monorhyme, equivalent to a 5:1 swing from the norm. It will be observed that in two respects these figures show a departure from classical practice; in the latter the use of the *masnavi* is much more limited in respect to both numerical use and choice of meter. It is perhaps worth noting that no *masnavi* were found in seven meters—2.1.15, 2.4.05 (2), 3.1.16, 4.8.08 (2), 5.1.08 (2), 5.2.08 (2), and 5.5.07 (2).

It is quite common for two or more speeches in the same meter to maintain the monorhyme system. In such cases the opening verse of each speech is generally *muqaffā* (both hemistichs rhyming, though this is not invariably the case.

حورعين با زلف مشكين خاكروب در بود	(شوذب) ايكه اندر درگهت روح‌الامين چاكر بود
در كنار حوض كوثر ساق كوثر بود	اذن ميدانم بده تا جان خود قربان كنم
ز آنكه‌اصحاب‌مرا تاج‌شرف برسر بود	(امام) شكرلله مرخدايت ناصر و ياور بود
جسم‌زارت اندرين‌صحرا زكين‌بيسر بود	[14] ياتو نورسيده‌ميهبانى كى رواست

171

Sometimes the rhyme may change in the middle of the speech, and the new rhyme be continued by the following speaker.

در زمین کربلا در کار خود حیران شده   (قاصد) سرورخیل ملایک زار و سرگردان شده

از یزید بیحیا برقتل او فرمان شده   کرده آهنگ عراق از کوفه فرزند رسول

چونقر دورشگرفته لشکر چندینشمار   ششطرف دورشاحاطهکردهلشکربیشمار

در رکابش جانفشان و جمله کف برجان نثار   [15](عبداله) منشنیدمبوده از اصحاباو چندین سوار

الخ

In other cases all the lines in the speech are *muqaffā*.

هر زمانی برتو باد از من فراوان احترام   (عبداله) ایغلام نیک طلعت هم علیك از من سلام

بازگو از شوکت و اجلال آن والامقام   [16] بازگو سلطان ما شه چیست احوال ایغلام

Sometimes a separate rhyme-scheme is maintained by each speaker.

وی بیکسوبیاقربا مادرشود قربانتو   (فاطمه) ای کشته تیغ جفا مادر شود قربان تو

ای بیکس و بییار من یکدم بیا حالم ببین   (امام) ای مادر افکار من وی در بلاغمخوار من

منبیکسویار توام مادر شود قربان تو   (فاطمه) منمادر زارتوام مندیدهخونبارتوام

قربانتو با چشم تر یکدم بیا حالم ببین   [17] ایمادر خونینجگر وی گشتهزار و نوحهگر

The internal rhyme is a common feature of the "doubled" meters.[18]

(علیاکبر) آه قلب من خون است زخم از حد افزون است

دیدهام چو جیحون است درد من مداوا کن

(املیلا) نور دیدهام اکبر، غم رسیدهام اکبر

از فراقت ای اکبر، مادرت تسلّ کن

[19] (علیاکبر) عنبر و گلاب آور، عود و مشک ناب آور

قطرهای تو آب آور، خاطرم تسلّ کن

الخ

An unusual example occurs in which the rhyme is lost owing to the substitution of an onomatopoeic phrase at the end of each *bait*.

ای کودك صغیرم، لای لای لای لای   (شهربانو) ای اصغر صغیرم، طفل نخورده شیرم

ای ماه بیقرینه، لای لای لای لای   [20] همبازی سکینه، آواره از مدینه

Occasionally a complete *murabba'* is found, for instance the following in meter 1.3.10, extending to 14 *baits*.

کنج ویران غریب و فکارم   ای پدر جان بین خوار و زارم

ای پدرجان امان از یتیمی   هجر تو برده از دل قرارم

شور و هنگامه شام دیدم   ای پدر جور ایام دیدم

ای پدر جان امان از یتیمی   [21] سیلی شهر بدنام دیدم

الخ

An even more interesting point is raised by the use of the *rubāʿī* meter (3.3.13/5.1.13). In classical literature this is scarcely ever used except for the two-*bait rubāʿī* itself; the exceptions are so rare as to underline the rule. In the Taʿziyeh, use in other forms is not uncommon. Out of 40 *baits* in this meter in the texts studied, 18 form nine normal *rubāʿīs*, and six form two *sadāsis* (three-*bait* verses).

عرضی است مرا بخاکپایت گفتن   جانم بفدات ای شهنشاه زمن

روزیکه برون شدیم از شهر و وطن   از بهر خدا و طفل برداشتهام

جانا تو بیا و دل ما را مشکن   قربانی کوچک ارچه نبود مقبول   [22]

On the other hand, seven are in the form of single rhymed couplets, and there is one case of two forming a pair of rhymed couplets with different rhymes, and one case of as many as four *baits* with different rhymes.

ای کشته زار بینصیب مادر   ای شاه شهید ای غریب مادر

جا داده سرت ز کینه در یخدانی   از کینه کدام ظالم نادانی

از زمره قاتلانت ای شاه شهید   دادم بستاند از کرم رب مجید

بر قائمه عرش زنم من فردا   دستم بدهد خدا که در روز جزا   [23]

There is also what appears to be a hybrid (though a few words are missing from the text in Virolleaud's edition), where a rhymed couplet in the same meter but a different rhyme appears to have been inserted into the middle of a normal *rubāʿī*.

در دست ستم نگر اسیرم بابا   (سکینه) بایاد فراق تو بیرم بابا

تاب غم تو ندارد ای جان پدر   ای قطره خون که دل شدش نام دگر

بابا ز فراق تو بیرم بابا   کن رحـم و مرو.........   [24]

A strange mixture of meters and rhymes occurs in the following passage, where the first speaker begins in 4.1.15, then switches to 4.7.14, and ends with a rhymed verse in 3.3.13 (the *rubāʿī* meter). This meter is picked up by the next speaker, who utters a normal *rubāʿī* and is answered by the first speaker in a single rhymed *bait* in 5.1.13 (the other *rubāʿī* meter).

شود چو صبح شوم کشتهٔ گروه دغا   (امام) شبست جمله بخوابید یاوران زوفا

هر کس که میرود برود بیخجالتی   خود پرده حجاب کشیدم بحالتی

از سستی این قوم گرفتار شدم   فریاد که بیمونس و بییار شدم

یارب ز کجا صوت حسین میآید   (زینب) ایوای فغان و آه و شین میآید

در کرب و بلا غریب و بییار شدم   (امام) خواهر بنگر که بیمددکار شدم   [25]

Complex rhyme schemes involving three or more rhymes include the following: *Rhyme scheme*—ab cb ab ab cb.

(سکینه) کردم فدات ای پدر مهربان من   خواهی روی بجنگ مرو کی گذارمت

تا جان مراست برتن ایاباب مهربان   باور مکن که دست ز دامن بدارمت

(امام) ای طفل پرور شیرین زبان من   جان منی و بیش ز جان دوست دارمت

ای مرغ پرشکسته گلزار جان من   چون کشته میشوم بخدا میسپارمت

26 ای نور جان من تو مکن ناله و فغان   برشوی دوست میروم و میگذارمت

Rhyme scheme—ba cb ca db, the ā rhyme having been established in the preceding monorhyme speech.

(ابن‌سعد) هل من مبارز ای خلف شیر کردگار   هل من مبارز ای شه بیخویش و اقربا

هل من مبارزای که زروی و ز موی تو   ارکان ممکنات وجود است پایدار

هل من مبارز ای که نمانده ز بهر تو   یك تن دیگر ز یار و زانصار و اقربا

27 هل من مبارز ای که دراین دشت پرفغان   امروز نوبت تو بود شیر کردگار

A form of *mustazād* is sometimes found.

برادر جان بیا با هم بنالیم   وای که ما هر دو یتیمیم

28 یتیم و بیکس و افسرده حالیم   وای که ما هر دو یتیمیم

الخ

عیش داماد حسین است مبارك باشد   همه گویید مبارك

29 قاسم آن نور دو عین است مبارك باشد   همه گویید مبارك

A further possible indication of a literary origin for or at least literary influence on, the Ta'ziyeh texts is the comparative rarity of incorrect rhymes.

30 حریم سینه بطحا وداع آخرین است این   جواب چون تو شیطانی نه جزتنها جوابستی

     وداع آخرین است و فراق واپسین استی   چنانیکه بشیطان‌طعن و لعن‌شیخ و شابستی

31 حسین کو ذوالجناحش مانده تنها   یقین باشد حسین او بهمراه

32 میروم تا فدا کنم جانم   همـرهت سر برهنه میآیم

33 من خلیل‌آسا فدا آورده‌ام   منهم از بهرت فدا آورده‌ام

34 (ابن‌زید)تو در مردانگی و پردلی مشهور آفاق   تو میگوئی ز راه حق شوم من یاغی و طاغی

LANGUAGE

On the strength of meter and rhyme alone we must conclude either that the compilers of the Ta'ziyeh were skilled practitioners of the art of writing *'aruzi* verse, or that they drew their material directly from existing literary sources. In fact the evidence for the latter belief is by no means as scanty as might be thought, even in the small sample studied. First, there is the question of language. It is commonly supposed that the language of the Ta'ziyeh is strictly popular and even colloquial. Gobineau wrote in 1865:

> Les drames, en effet, qui font les frais des tazyèhs, sont écrits en dialecte populaire. On n'y voit guère figurer de ces mots arabes si recherchés pour les autres compositions, mais que l'homme du bazar, le soldat, les femmes ne comprendraient pas, et, au contraire, on y peut relever en foule les façons de parler les plus familières, les abbréviations de mots les plus courantes, tout ce qui constitue, en un mot, la façon de parler commune et journalière.[35]

More recently Dr. Mehdi Forough wrote:

> The language of the Persian passion plays, in contrast to the highly stylized Persian poetry in general, is very simple and direct. No attempt is made to include the artificial rhetorical devices and literary graces so abundant in most Persian poetry.[36]

This statement is contradicted by his own observation elsewhere in the same work:

> It must be pointed out that a general knowledge of the Persian language and of the literary conventions of Persian literature would be necessary to understand all the allusions and fully appreciate the poetry of these plays. A considerable amount of technical knowledge would be required as well—not only of prosody and grammar, but also of the various branches of rhetoric and euphuism—to recognize all the tropes, similes, metaphors, innuendoes, hyperboles, antitheses, quotations, aetiologies, amphibologies, homonymies, anagrams and the like which abound in Persian literature.[37]

In fact the truth is much nearer to this last statement than it is to either his first remark or to Gobineau's belief (and this is not to deny the possibility that a greater or lesser degree of colloquialization may take place in the course of actual performance). As a few examples will serve to show, though the language is on the whole simple, it is, like the versification, predominently literary.

[38] (امام)   ای صبا از دیدهٔ قاسم تو مشک تر بریز   کن نثار مرقد پاک پر انوار حسن

[39] (زینب)   شربت جام شهادت میچشی آهسته رو   میرسی آخر به زهرا زینبی هم داشتی

175

فغان و ناله والای ایزدی برخاست   (فطمه) صدای بلبل باغ محمدی برخاست

کەما دوعاشق‌زاریم‌وکار ما زاریست   40 بنال بلبل‌اگر ناله‌است ز بی‌یاریست

بن حکایت شرح فراق میگوئی   41 (اسمعیل) حدیث درد و غم اشتیاق میگوئی

Such language is not so very different from that used by the classical poets like Sa'dī, Hāfez, Mawlavī, and so on. All the same, it may be noted that, quite apart from any colloquialism that may be introduced in performance, a certain number of popular words and expressions do appear in the written texts, for instance, **Bāb** = "father."

42 و علیك ای پیك ای خلاق جهان

باری گذشت شام و پریشان شدم حواس

43 زین میرود مرو دلم افتاده در هراس

Geographical neologisms are found.

دهید راه روم سوی زنگبار و فرنگ   44 اگر ز آمدنم خاطر کسی شده تنگ

A Turkish character uses a mixture of Turkish and Persian—though his language becomes more purely Persian as his commitment to the cause of the Imam Hussein becomes more firm.

میان لشکر کفار زار و درمانده   قالوب غریب عزیزان حسین بومیدانده

فدا اولوم باشینه از این دیار بلد   گیدوم بوخدمتینه بلکه اذن آلوم ز وفا

نظاره کن ز وفا سوی این غلام فکار   سلام من سنه ای سبط احمد مختار

سنون رکابینه بولاشوم قزلقانه   45 مرخصی ایله منی تا گیدوم بومیدانه

Nor is there sound reason for claiming that the Ta'ziyeh verse is free from the figures of speech so prevalent in literary Persian poetry. On the contrary, as Forough says, one can find examples of many of them, of which the following are only a tiny sample.

بی‌کس و بی‌معین و بی‌یاور   46 ای شه بی‌سپاه و بی‌لشکر

ناله تو ربوده هوش از سر   آه تو آتشی به جانم زد

وی جسته ره کوی ترا هر که بآهی   47 ای درگه لطف تو بهر خسته پناهی

با آتش مهر تو چه کوهی و چه کاهی   با شربت مهر تو چه نوشی و چه نیشی

گر بنشیند کند نشسته قیامت   48 چون بره آید قیامتی است بقامت

Even on the question of the use of Arabic vocabulary Gobineau is far from accurate. A rough sample check shows an average of three Arabic words to a *bait,* or roughly 30 percent—exactly the same as the average for literary poetry of the classical period. While many of these words are in common use, there is also a fair sprinkling of more obscure "literary" terms; for instance, the following contains three Arabic words, miṣrā', none of which would be used in normal colloquial speech.

كه اذن حرب مخالف بتو نخواهم داد ⁴⁹

Further light may be thrown on this problem of sources by comparing the language and style of the various Taʻziyeh texts from different origins, as well as comparing them with verses from other literary compositions. One is immediately struck by the fact that, while plays on the same subject may differ widely in construction and even plot from one source or area to another, nevertheless the same kind of phraseology is to be found in all of them. Speeches are often introduced by such expressions as:

خطاب من بتو ای فلان....
شوم فدای تو ای فلان....
سلام من به تو ای فلان....

Particular characters are given stock epithets. For instance, the Imam Hussein is called:

نور دیده ثقلین، فرزند شاه دین، شه بی‌خیل و لشکر، پادشاه تشنه‌لبان، عزیز هر دو سرا

He receives such titles even when he is addressed or spoken of by his arch-enemy, the villainous Shemr. Similarly Shemr, Ibn Saʻd, and Ibn Ziyad are invariably described as

لعین، نامعقول، رانده درگاه حضرت باری

and so on, even when they are addressed by each other or their own followers. Appropriate stock epithets are similarly applied to the other principal characters. The rendering of the name Kerbela as كرب و بلا , as in the verse

هر کرا آرزوی کرب و بلاست   همره آید به کربلای حسین ⁵⁰

certainly goes back as far as the *Rowzatu'l Shuhada*

گر نام این زمین بیقین کربلا بود   اینجا نصیب ما همه کرب و بلا بود ⁵¹

There is other evidence that the *Rowzatu'l Shuhada* is, as might be expected, a source for the Taʻziyeh material. For instance, one of the texts collected by Chodzko during the nineteenth century contains the following farewell lament:

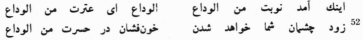

الوداع ای عترت من الوداع   اینک آمد نوبت من الوداع
خونفشان در حسرت من الوداع   زود چشمان شما خواهد شدن ⁵²

177

The same verses with only minor variants appear in the *Rowzatu'l Shuhada* though in a different context.

الوداع ای عترت من الوداع   اینك آمد نوبت من الوداع

سوزناك از فرقت من الوداع   زود دلهای شما خواهدشدن

گریه کرد از حسرت من الوداع   دمبدم خواهید چون ابر بهار [53]

Research would certainly reveal similar parallels in such works as the *Riyazulhuseini,* the *Chavushnameh, Makhzan al-Ash'ar,* and so on. It is also worth noting that several versions of the same play, though in most respects differing widely, often contain identical or closely similar passages. For instance, two versions of the *Shahadat-e Hazrat-e Imam Hussein,* one in the Chodzko collection of the mid-nineteenth century and one in the Tehran "chapbook" printing of nearly a century later, provide such parallels.

CHODZKO

حور بود و باغ بود و قصرها نگذاشتی   خواب دیدم مرغزاری با صفا نگذاشتی (امام)

یك طرف باهم علی مرتضی نگذاشتی   جد من خیرالبشر از یك طرف ایستاده بود

TEHRAN

داشتم با جد و بابم گفتگو نگذاشتی   خواب میدیدم ریاض مشكبو نگذاشتی (امام) [54]

CHODZKO

بکن وداع حریم خودت به شیون و شین   مرخصی تو ایا نور دیده ثقلین

TEHRAN

بکن وداع حریت به دیده گریان   مرخصی تو ایا پادشاه تشنه‌لبان [55]

The original text of the *Ta'ziyeh-e Qasem,* as translated and printed by Gobineau in his *Religions et Philosophies dans l'Asie Centrale,* is unfortunately lost; nevertheless it is possible to discern, from a comparison of the French translation with the much later Tehran "chapbook" edition, some fifty or sixty *baits* (about one-sixth of the total) that must have been virtually identical in the otherwise very different texts.[56]

A final curiosity: a number of speeches are introduced by the conjunction *ke,* suggesting that they originally formed part of a longer poem in which the preceding *bait,* here omitted, identified the speaker with some such expression as و خطاب کرد و گفت: etc.

رضا بکشته شدن ای عزیز هردو سرا   ایا ای حسین تو چرا میشوی درین صحرا (باقر) [57]

178

58 (ابراهیم) ایا ای ز کنه کمال تو عقل بیخبری   ز قدرت تو ملایک تمام مشت پری

59 (امام حسین)ایا ای عزیز برادر مگو خدا نکند   ترا ز اهل حرم یکدمی جدا نکند

60 (شمر)   ایا ای خیل جنوب و فرقه شامی و اختر   دلیران صف هیجا شجاعان غضنفرفر

61 (مأمون) ایا ابنعم به چه سان لحظهای از این سامان   روی به کشور روم ای امام عالیشان

On the basis of the analysis here presented, we must conclude that the material from which the Ta'ziyeh are composed is largely literary in origin. The compilers, most of whom are anonymous though a few are named, must have drawn on this stock, strung it together in various combinations, composed standard linking matter, added other non-literary embellishments, but in general contributed nothing original to the material on which they worked. What they can be credited with as original is the molding of the material into dramatic form, but the discussion of that falls outside the scope of this chapter. The most that can be suggested from the material studied here is that the literary sources of the Ta'ziyeh could be at least as old as the Safavid period, and in some instances a good deal older. A more thorough examination and comparison of the Ta'ziyeh texts with their possible sources might enable us to reach more definite conclusions as to their age.

NOTES

For Persian meters in the Ta'ziyeh, consult the author's book, *Persian Metres* (1976).

1. Mehdī Forough: *A Comparative Study of Abraham's Sacrifice in Persian Passion Plays and Western Mystery Plays* (Tehran, n.d.), p. 80.

2. *Chapbooks*

Imām: *Ta'ziyeh-yi Shahādat-i Sayyid al-Shuhadā* (Tehran, 1330/1951).

Hurr: *Ta'ziyeh-yi Hurr ibn-i Yazīd Riyāhī* (Tehran, n.d.).

Ruqaia: *Kitāb-i Ta'ziyeh-yi Vafāt-i Janāb-i Ruqaia Khātūn* (Tehran, n.d.).

Zahrā: *Vafāt-i Shafī'-yi Rūz-i Jazā Fatimah-yi Zahrā* (Tehran, n.d.).

Shahrbānū: Kitāb-i Ta'ziyeh-yi Hazrat-i Shahrbānū (Tehran, n.d.).

Sughrā: *Ta'ziyeh-yi 'Alīli-yi Bimār Janāb-i Fātimah-i Sughrā* (Tehran, 1330-1951).

'Abbās: *Ta'ziyeh-yi Shahādat-i Qamar-i Banī Hāshim Hazrat-i Bāb al-Havā'ij 'Abbās* (Tehran, n.d.).

'Alī Akbar: *Ta'ziyeh-yi Shahādat-i Shāhzādih Hazrat-i 'Alī Akbar* (Tehran, 1330/1951).

Qāsim: *Ta'ziyeh-yi Shahādat-i Shāhzādih Qāsim ibn-i al-Hasan* (Tehran, n.d.).

Muslim: *Ta'ziyeh-yi Shahādat-i Hazrat-i Muslim* (Tehran, 1330/1951).

3. Sādiq Humāyūnī, *Ta'ziyeh va Ta'ziyeh-Khvānī* (Shiraz, n.d. [1354/1975]), containing texts of "Ta'ziyeh-yi Qāsim," "Ta'ziyeh-yi 'Abbās-i Imām," "Ta'ziyeh-yi Imām Rizā," and "Ta'ziyeh-yi Hazrat-i Ma'sūmah."

4. Bausani, "Drammi popolari inediti persiani sulla leggenda di Salomone e della regina di Saba," *Atti del Convegno Internazionale di Studi Etiopici* (Rome, 1960), pp. 167-209; and Virolleaud, *La Passion de l'Imam Hosseyn,* drame persan publié et traduit par Ch. Virolleaud (Paris/Beirut, 1927).

5. L. P. Elwell-Sutton, *The Persian Metres* (Cambridge, 1976).

6. *Ibid.*

7. *Ibid.*

8. Hurr, pp. 18-20.

9. The Imam Hussein in Virolleaud.

10. Ali Akbar in Ali Akbar.

11. Fatemeh-ye Zahra in Sughra, pp. 27-29.

12. Ruqaiya, pp. 26-27.

13. Humayuni, pp. 173-74.

14. Imam, p. 20.

15. Shahrbanu, pp. 3-4.

16. *Ibid.,* p. 3.

17. Virolleaud, pp. 56-57.

18. Elwell-Sutton.

19. Ali Akbar, p. 21.

20. Shahrbanu, p. 6.

21. *Vafāt-i 'Ulyā-Mukhaddarah Ruqaiya Khātūn* (Mashhad, n.d.), pp. 23-24.

22. Ali Akbar, p. 22.

23. Ruqaiya, p. 11.

24. Virolleaud, p. 26.

25. Hurr, p. 24.

26. Virolleaud, p. 25.

27. Humayuni, p. 113.

28. *Ibid.,* p. 114.

29. *Ibid.,* p. 123.

30. Imam, p. 8.

31. Shahrbanu, p. 10.

32. Ali Akbar, p. 16.

33. Hurr, p. 14.

34. *Ibid.,* p. 7.

35. Comte de Gobineau, *Les Religions et les Philosophies dans l'Asie Centrale,* 6th ed. (Paris, 1932), p. 351.

36. Forough, p. 80.

37. *Ibid.,* p. 2.

38. Qasem, p. 9.

39. Virolleaud, p. 39.

40. Zahra, p. 7.

41. Forough, p. 97.

42. Bausani, p. 175.

43. Hurr, p. 6.

44. Virolleaud, p. 46.

45. Ali Akbar, p. 26.

46. Virolleaud, p. 21.

47. Bausani, p. 175.

48. *Ibid.,* p. 176.

49. Humayuni, p. 114.

50. Imam, p. 2.

51. Mullā Husain Vā'iz-i Kāshifī, *Rawżat al-Shuhadā',* ed. Hājī Muhammad Ramażānī (Tehran, 1334/1955), p. 206.

52. Virolleaud, p. 35.

53. Kashifi, p. 274.

54. Virolleaud, p. 6; Imam, p. 10.

55. Virolleaud, p. 17; Imam, p. 11.

56. Gobineau, pp. 360, 362-65, 367, 371-79; Qasem, pp. 8-10, 12, 15-19.

57. Virolleaud, p. 16.

58. Forough, p. 86.

59. Humayuni, p. 114.

60. *Ibid.,* p. 140.

61. *Ibid.,* p. 174.

1.1.6	mutaqārib murabba' sālim
1.1.10	mutaqārib mutamman abtar
1.1.11	mutaqārib mutamman maḥdūf
1.1.12	mutaqārib mutamman sālim
1.2.05(2)	mutaqārib mutamman atlam
1.3.10	mutadārik mutamman aḥadd
2.1.11	hazaj musaddas maḥdūf
2.1.15	hazaj mutamman maḥdūf
2.1.16, 2.1.08(2)	hazaj mutamman sālim
2.3.08(2)	rajaz mutamman sālim
2.4.05(2)	
2.4.05(3), with 4.8.05(3)	
2.4.11	ramal musaddas maḥdūf
2.4.15	ramal mutamman maḥdūf
3.1.11	ramal musaddas maxbūn maḥdūf
3.1.12	ramal musaddas maxbūn
3.1.15	ramal mutamman maxbūn maḥdūf
3.1.16	ramal mutamman maxbūn
3.3.13, with 5.1.13	hazaj mutamman axrab maqbūḍ makfūf majbūb
3.3.14	hazaj mutamman axrab makfūf maḥdūf
3.4.11	sarī' musaddas maṭwī maksūf
4.1.05(2)	mutaqārib mutamman maqbūḍ atlam
4.1.15	mujtatt mutamman maxbūn maḥdūf
4.1.16	mujtatt mutamman maxbūn
4.4.9	munsariḥ musaddas maṭwī maxbūn
4.4.13	munsariḥ mutamman maṭwī maxbūn
4.5.11	xafīf musaddas maxbūn maḥdūf
4.7.14	muḍāri' mutamman axrab makfūf maḥdūf
4.7.07(2)	muḍāri' mutamman axrab al-ṣadrayn
4.7.15	
4.8.05(2)	
4.8.05(3)	
5.1.10	hazaj musaddas axrab maqbūḍ maḥdūf
5.1.13	hazaj mutamman axrab maqbūḍ maḥdūf majbūb
5.1.08(2)	
5.2.08(2)	rajaz musaddas maṭwī maxbūn
5.3.08(3)	
5.5.07(2)	hazaj mutamman aštar al-ṣadr

14

Stereotyped Imagery in the Ta'ziyeh

WILLIAM L. HANAWAY, JR.

The language of the Ta'ziyeh has been studied very little. This lack of basic research is due to a number of reasons, the more important of which are: that most work on the Ta'ziyeh to date has been historical and concerned with the origins and development of the plays; that an insufficient number of texts have been published in Persian; and that the study of Persian poetic language in general has not been sufficiently pursued. Nevertheless a start must be made, and one must work with the materials at hand. It is hoped that as a result of the present symposium, a new perspective on the Ta'ziyeh will develop which will lead to increased efforts toward the collection, critical analysis, and publication of these plays as they are performed. This would allow us to build on the valuable work already done, and to broaden the base of our research into one of the most interesting manifestations of Persian popular culture.

The present discussion will focus on one aspect of the language of the Ta'ziyeh, namely, the stereotyped imagery used in the plays. The function of these stereotyped images as compositional elements of the texts will be considered, as well as their function in the structure of imagery in the Ta'ziyeh as a whole. It is important to examine these stereotyped images in

182

terms of both their metrical function and their function as figurative language. These images cluster around two major concepts, which are manifestations of the deeper meaning and structure of the Ta'ziyeh as a whole. While these conclusions should be considered tentative, it is hoped that they will indicate directions for future research.

Historical research has shown that although the origins of the Ta'ziyeh as we know it today are diverse, two main sources can be discerned. The first consists of the processions, demonstrations, spectacles and rituals commemorating the martyrdom of the Imam Hussein, his family and his supporters at Kerbela. The second is a variety of literary sources concerned with these martyrdoms and related events. The latter sources are such books as the *Rowzatu'l Shuhada* (fifteenth century), the *Haft Band* of Muhtasham of Kashan (sixteenth century), and the work of nineteenth-century poets such as Qa'ani and others.

Commemoration of the central event, the martyrdom of Hussein, was the basis for the dramatic presentations which developed into the Ta'ziyeh as we know it today. As the plays developed, this basis was broadened, in concentric circles so to speak, to include the martyrdom at Kerbela of others connected with Hussein. Then another circle was added of events preceding and resulting from the central tragedy, such as the death of the Prophet Muhammad, the murder of Ali, and the captivity of Hussein's family in Damascus after the massacre. Finally, there is an outer circle of plays on Koranic and Biblical themes, themes from popular Islam, and humorous and satirical themes, all of which are quite peripheral to the central events. In all cases however, the gravitational force which keeps all of these plays in their orbits is the tragedy of the tenth of Muharram.

As a result of this process of development, we now have a large number of plays each telling a separate story.[1] Each of these plays is, with the exception of the most peripheral, an integral part of a larger, extended story. The individual play cannot be understood in all its implications without knowing the larger story. The larger story, on the other hand, cannot be fully understood without an appreciation of its individual component parts. The audience sees each play both as an individual story and as a part of a larger whole or continuum, and knows any single play or piece of action in the larger continuum at any particular time. Given this relation of the parts and the whole, it is reasonable to posit a *Ta'ziyeh as a Whole,* which is equal to or greater than the sum of its parts, i.e., the individual plays. This larger, hypothetical Ta'ziyeh is focused on the tragedy at Kerbela, its antecedents and results, and includes all but the most distant and peripheral plays of the outer circle. From this point of view, each play can be seen in its relation to other plays, and also to the larger Ta'ziyeh of which it forms a part. Such a perspective can, among other things, help us to understand the function and meaning of the stereotyped imagery in the individual plays.

For the present purposes, three printed Ta'ziyehs were examined in detail. These plays were chosen for two reasons: first, they represent texts from different sources, i.e., one collected from Fars in recent years by Sadeq Humayuni, one collected in the nineteenth century by Chodzko, and one collected by Litten in the early twentieth century. Second, all three plays are part of the central core of the *Ta'ziyeh as a Whole,* in that they are all concerned with individuals martyred at Kerbela. While it can be argued that three texts is an insufficient number from which to generalize, the results obtained here confirm general impressions gained from reading the Persian texts of a much larger number of these plays.

Extensive reading of Ta'ziyeh tells one that certain images occur frequently, and in similar lexical and metrical contexts. The most frequent of these images in the core plays of the Ta'ziyeh are "sacrifice," "light," and a cluster of garden and flower images not discussed here. For the present discussion fifty-seven examples of these images were isolated from the three plays, and analyzed according to their metrical pattern and their place in the whole line of verse. A small number of other stereotyped expressions were also included. It should be noted that there are other frequently recurring expressions and images which could also have been chosen, and that there are other occurrences of the key words studied here which were not isolated for analysis because their contexts or the words bound to them were not of the stereotyped pattern of the others.

Any discussion of the stereotyped expressions and imagery raises the problem of oral-formulaic composition. This has been discussed at length with regard to Classical Greek, South Slavic, and Old English poetry, and recently for Classical Arabic. The theoretical arguments will not be reviewed here, because until now the presence of formulas in texts has been used in an attempt to demonstrate the oral nature of their composition. I have avoided the term "formula" in this study so as not to raise the question of the orality of the Ta'ziyehs. The problem of formulaic or stereotyped expressions in written (i.e., non-orally composed) texts has been very little investigated, and here only the surface will be scratched.

Milman Parry's definition of a formula in an orally composed text is "a group of words which is regularly employed under the same metrical conditions to express a given essential idea." [2] In many respects the stereotyped images listed in the Appendix fulfill these requirements, as would other sets of expressions from these plays. Since, however, in functional terms the formula as defined by Parry is an aid to the poet in the process of oral composition, this term can not be used for the expressions analyzed here because the Ta'ziyeh is *basically* a written text, although as we shall see, it can have an oral component too. What then is the function of the stereotyped images in the Ta'ziyeh? After examining the images and their contexts in more detail, a tentative answer will be suggested.

184

Persian verse is divided into half-lines or hemistichs of equal metrical length, and the position of the stereotyped images in the line is interesting to observe. Of the sample analyzed (147 occurrences of 57 stereotyped images), 75.5 percent of all occurrences were in the first hemistich, and 24.5 percent were in the second hemistich. Of the first hemistich occurrences, 73.9 percent were at the beginning of the line, and of the second hemistich occurrences, 61.1 percent were at the beginning of the hemistich. Thus the first hemistich in general, and the beginning of this hemistich in particular are the favored positions for the majority of the stereotyped images. What are the metrical implications of this?

An essential aspect of the "formula" in the context of traditional oral-formulaic composition is its metrical structure. It can be seen, from the Appendix, that the stereotyped images of the Ta'ziyeh also have a metrical structure. The Appendix shows these images, categorized by the meter of the verse in which they appear. The meter *mujtass* predominates in the plays examined here, accounting for 77.5 percent of the occurrences. The second most frequent meter is *hazaj,* in 16.3 percent of the occurrences. The remainder of the occurrences are distributed more or less evenly among *mutaqārib, xafīf,* and *ramal.* A larger sample would change the relative percentages, but Professor Elwell-Sutton's research indicates that *mujtass* would still predominate.

If we examine the "sacrifice" imagery, we see that the two words are *fidā* and *qurbān* (both meaning "sacrifice"), whose metrical shapes are -u and -- respectively (read the scansion right to left). The meter *mujtas* has the general form:

$$--uu|-u-u|--uu|-u-u$$

and the meter *hazaj* has the general forms:

$$---u|---u|---u|---u$$
$$--|u-u-|uu--$$

Fidā plus a grammatically obligatory syllable linking it to the following nominal form (the resulting metrical phrase being u – u) is an ideal word to begin a verse in *mujtass.* Because of technical problems in the scanning of Persian verse, certain syllables can be counted either long or short as the meter as a whole requires. Thus in a few cases *fidā* could begin a line of *hazaj* or *mutaqārib* (as – – u), but these cases are rare.

The word *qurbān,* having the metrical shape – –, cannot begin a verse in *mujtass,* but must appear in the middle or at the end of lines in this meter. *Qurbān* fits more comfortably in *hazaj,* where it can begin a line (as in numbers 40-42 of the Appendix), or where it can start with the second syllable of the line, following a metrically short preposition (numbers 37-38). Given the clear preference among the authors of these plays for a stereotyped expression and image at the beginning of the line, and the metrical shape of *fidā* and *qurbān,* it is clear that *fidā* would have to be used more frequently than *qurbān.* This is borne out by the number of actual occurrences of the two words, *fidā* occurring 92 times (83 times at the beginning of a line) and *qurbān* occurring 17 times (7 times at the beginning of a line). This frequency is the reverse of the frequency of these two words in colloquial speech, where *qurban* occurs very frequently, to the almost total exclusion of *fidā*.

In the "light of the eye" expressions, the key words are *nūr* and *ziyā* (both meaning "light"), which have the metrical shapes u– and –u, respectively, and *chashm* and *dīdih* ("eye"), both of which scan u –. Since *nūr-i dīdih* ("light of the eye") and its variants are metaphorical epithets, they are usually preceded by a metrically long vocative particle *ay* ("O!"), as in *ay nūr-i dīdih* [*-i man*] ("O light of [my] eye"). This means that such expressions cannot begin a line of *mujtass,* which must begin with a short syllable, but can and often do appear medially or finally in lines of this meter. They can, however, begin a line of *hazaj,* which can begin with two long syllables. (*Ziyā* is quite infrequent.) Again, actual occurrences bear this out, since these expressions appear at the beginning of lines of *hazaj* (numbers 48-51) and medially or finally in other meters.

To understand more fully the implications of these stereotyped images and expressions in their metrical function, the *Ta'ziyeh as it is performed* must be studied closely. Several Iranian scholars of the Ta'ziyeh have mentioned that although the basis of any individual performance is a written text, there is still a certain measure of improvisation in the actual performance. Presumably the performer who diverges from his written text says the lines (which he has just made up) in an appropriate form of verse. If this is the case, and if the orally composing actor were to employ stereotyped images and expressions in a way similar or parallel to how they are used in the written texts, then the entire problem of the stereotyped images would take on a new dimension. In this case, the stereotyped images could be looked upon as oral formulas, and their relation to similar "formulas" in the written text studied. The fact, then, that Ta'ziyeh texts are written texts with an orally composed dimension places them in a special category. Transcripts of actual performances must be compared with their parent written texts and the deviations carefully noted. Research in this area could have profound implications for the theory of oral-formulaic composition in particular, and the language of Persian poetry in general.

From this very brief analysis it can be seen that in the actual dynamics of composition, the choice of meter has a strongly determining effect on the choice of words that a writer can use. It has been observed that while *mujtass* predominates in the Ta'ziyehs, the writers very frequently change meters, often from speech to speech. One reason for this could be the writer's unconsciously felt need for flexibility in word-choice, since the principles at work in the case of the "sacrifice" and "light" images operate for all stereotyped images to be found in these plays. The implications of this are broad for the study not only of the language of the Ta'ziyeh, but of Classical Persian poetry as well. Research in this area could surely throw light on the question of the standardized vocabulary of metaphors and similes in Persian classical poetry, and their relation to the meters of this poetry.

THE IMAGERY

In colloquial speech the word *qurbān* and the expression *nūr-i chashm* appear frequently and have the status of clichés. They have, in colloquial speech, lost their original richness of meaning and have become as commonplace as "the apple of his eye" in English. In the Ta'ziyeh, however, their context is entirely different. Although they have become stereotyped, their sheer frequency of occurrence in the context of these martyr plays gives them a new dimension, or rather returns to them some of their original dimensions. How is this so?

Recent thinking has revealed the Ta'ziyeh to be more than just a religious drama or martyr play in the Iranian popular tradition. When considered in the larger context of ceremony and ritual, the Ta'ziyeh reveals unexpected affinities with both. The formalized and abstract nature of the characters, the relationship of the audience to the players, and the repetitive language of the plays all point to their ritual nature. It is this ritual aspect which revitalizes the popular clichés noted above, and allows them, *as images,* to manifest and support the deeper meanings of the plays.

The images under consideration, "sacrifice" and "light" (plus a large image cluster centered on flowers and gardens not discussed here), are the most prominent and also the central images of the central core of the Ta'ziyeh plays. These images are polar opposites: sacrifice concerns death and darkness, while light (and the flower and garden imagery) is the opposite, representing life. Thus this imagery manifests the central theme of the Ta'ziyeh, which is the significance of the events at Kerbela, their antecedents and results.

The polar opposition of this imagery is revealed on one level in the plays as the opposition of good and evil characters. As suggested above, the characters of the Ta'ziyeh are formalized and abstract. I do not mean by this that they are not human and not able to inspire the deepest emotion in the audience. Their formality and abstraction stem from the fact that the audience is already welll acquainted with the characters before they see the play. In fact the audience knows the story perfectly, and this situation obviates the need for any exposition of character development in the plays. There is no need for the author of the Ta'ziyeh to supply any significant details about the background of the action, the setting, or the personality of the characters. The evil characters know that they are evil and often say so, while the good characters all know in advance the outcome of their actions, and often refer to this. Thus, in the core plays of the Ta'ziyeh, much time

187

can be spent on such emotional scenes as tearful leave-takings and lamentations.

The good and bad characters are puppets, so to speak, of the larger forces of good and evil which motivate the action of the plays. As the members of the family of Hussein go to their inevitable captivity or martyrdom, the forces of evil are seen to overtake those of good. It is the pitiless and inexorable nature of this process that gives these plays their desperate and mournful nature. Evil and good require each other in these martyr plays, as only the presence of the one can account for the poignancy of the other.

But there is also more than this to the meaning of the imagery in question, and this leads us to the deepest level of the Ta'ziyeh. This is the level of Shi'ite belief as it is objectified in these plays. It is expressed clearly in some of the plays and well known in Shi'a doctrine that Hussein went to his martyrdom for the benefit of all other Shi'a believers. Hussein's *sacrifice* of himself is to bring salvation (eternal life, light) to the rest of the Shi'a community until the return of the twelfth Imam at the end of time. Here then is the ultimate significance of the "sacrifice" and "light" imagery so prominent in the Ta'ziyeh. The basic structure of the individual play is generally a model of the structure of the Ta'ziyeh and the individual conflicts of the several plays are representative of the larger conflict involved. The individual sufferings and martyrdoms all drive toward or derive from the martyrdom of Hussein. Evil triumphs in individual plays, but the untimate result of Hussein's sacrifice of himself is the salvation of the community. At that point, evil is defeated. All of these movements and forces lie below the surface of the imagery discussed above.

CONCLUSION

If one were to try to define the Ta'ziyeh generically and locate it in the general spectrum of Persian literature, one would have to say that it has ties with both written and oral literary forms, but that it has non-literary affinities as well. These latter are its ties to ceremony and ritual, which feed the creators of Ta'ziyeh as they write or extemporize just as the classical poets and prose writers feed them. We have seen that these plays are a web of stereotyped images and expressions. Some of these images and expressions have been isolated and examined in terms of their metrical function in the lines of verse, and in terms of the larger implications of the images. Because of the special ontological status of the Ta'ziyeh due to its partly written, partly oral genesis, these stereotyped images are seen not as mere repetitions of clichés but as essential building blocks of the verbal and symbolic structure of these plays.

APPENDIX

TEXTS: SEE NOTES FOR FULL CITATIONS.

AA = 'Alī Akbar
Q = Qāsim
V = Vahab

SACRIFICE IMAGERY I: *(fidā)*

Mujtass

1. Q 116, 117, 121   ...فدای جان تو ای نور دیدۀ
2. Q 120; AA 31, 41, 61; V 144   ...فدای جان تو ای
3. Q 124 (2); V 142; AA 55 (1 medial,
   1 initial), 73, 93, 115 (2)   ...فدای جان تو
4. Q 126   ...فدای جانِ
5. V 134; AA 41   ...فدای جان عزیز تو گردم
6. V 146   ...فدای جان عزیزت شوم
7. V 133; AA 31، 55   ...فدای جان تو گردم
8. AA 105   ...فدای جان پدر
9. V 141 (2); AA 69   ...فدای خاكِ
10. V 142; AA 31, 41 (2)   ...فدای این لب خشك
11. AA 65   ...پدر فدای تو گردم
12. AA 69   ...بگو فدای تو گردم

Hazaj

13. AA 53   فدای چشم گریان تو عمه
14. AA 91   ...فدای جان و زلفِ
15. AA 47   فدای این صدایت ...

Mutaqārib

16. Q 127   ...فدای تو با
17. Q 127   ...فدای دل پرفسونت

Xafīf

18. AA 113   ...بفدای دل پر از
19. AA 113   ...بفدای تو خواهرِ
20. AA 137   ... بفدای تو...

189

Mujtass

21. Q 117; V 145; AA 65, 97   ...شوم فدای تو

22. Q 117 (2), 121 (2), 124 (2), 126; V 133, 137 (2),
    139, 142 (2), 143 (2), 144 (2), 145 (2);
    AA 31, 41, 47, 69, 75, 105, 117, 119, 131 (2)   (خواهر، مادر الخ) ...شوم فدای تو ای

23. AA 69   ...شوم فدای شما ای

24. V 134, 137 (2), 138, 139, 146; AA 43   ...شوم فدات

25. Q 114   فدات شود...

26. V 135, 136   بفدایت شوم...

Hazaj

27. Q122   ...فدایت ای

28. Q 125; AA 79 (initial)   ...فدایت جانِ

29. AA 57 (2)   فدا کنم جان ...

Ramal

30. AA 35   ...من فدایت ای

SACRIFICE IMAGERY II: *(Qurbān)*

Mujtass

31. Q 115   به قربان تو شود مادر ...

32. Q 114, 126   جانِ کنم به قربانت ...

33. Q 114   جانِ عمو کنم قربان ...

34. Q 114   بقربان خاک پات شود ...

Hazaj

35. Q 120   ...به قربان تو گردد زینبِ ...

36. AA 109   به قربان تو گردیم ...

37. Q 120   به قربان دل بیصبر تو گردم...

38. AA 91   به قربان دو زلفِ...

39. AA 63, 109   به قربان تو ای... ...

40. Q 118   قربان تو باد جان زینب

41. AA 107, 139   قربان تو ای... ...

42. AA 137 قربان تن بیسر...
43. Q 122 شود جانم به قربانت
44. AA 91 ...شوم قربان رویت

Light of the Eye Imagery

Mujtass

45. Q 123, 124, 126; V 144, 146;
    AA 75, 77, 105 ... ای نور دیدۀ (زهرا، مادر، امعان الخ)
46. Q 123 ... ایا نور دیدۀ اوتاد
47. Q 121; AA 103 ... نور دیدۀ تر من

Hazaj

48. AA 57 ای نور دو دیدۀ من...
49. AA 107 ای نور دو دیدۀ تر من
50. AA 109 ای نور دو دیدگان مادر
51. AA 107 ای نور دو چشم شاه...

Mujtass

52. Q 114 ... ز نور دو چشم من...
53. V 142 ... نور چشم پیمبر
54. AA 45, 75, 99; V 144 ... نور هر دو دیده (من، تر)

Mutaqārib

55. Q 128[1] ...آن نور چشم حسن

Mujtass

56. V 141 (medial), 146 (initial),
    Q 121 (initial) ... ضیاء دیدۀ...

Ramal

57. Q 130 ... ضیاء هردو عین

191

OTHER STEREOTYPED EXPRESSIONS

Mujtass

58. AA 27, 37, 39; Q128; V 142   (خطاب من به (تو، شما الخ)

59. AA 27, 121   سلام من بتو

60. AA 83, 85, 103; V 136, 138   ...بزرگوار خدایا

NOTES

1. Ṣādiq Humāyūnī, * Taʻziyeh va Taʻziyeh-khvāni* (Shiraz, 1354/1975), lists 99 basic Taʻziyeh plots: see pp. 45-63.

2. Robert Henri de Generet, ed., *Le Martyre d'Ali Akbar* (Paris: Société d'édition Les Belles Lettres, 1946), "Taʻziyeh-i Qāsim," in Humāyūnī, *Taʻziyeh va Taʻziyeh-khvānī*, pp. 113-31; "Majlis ... dar Kaifiyat- Shahādat-i Vahab," in Wilhelm Litten, *Das Drama in Persien* (Berlin: de Gruyter, 1929), pp. 133-47.

15

Elegy in the Qajar Period

ZAHRA EQBAL (NAMDAR)

There are only a few kinds of Persian religious (or sectarian) poetry:

1. *Didactic Poetry:* The purpose of the poet here is to express the principles of his beliefs and to encourage and persuade others to accept his religion or sect. Among the more famous poems of this kind are those of Naser Khusrow, whose entire poetic output was dedicated to this purpose.

2. *Poetry of Maxim and Counsel:* This is designed to encourage people to do good works and to restrain them from molesting others, and from evil and sin. This type is really included in the above category, and most religious poetry is laced with passages of this sort.

3. *Panegyric and Eulogistic Poetry:* This type contains praise of the saints of the religion or sect, the description of their compassionate natures, their elevated status near God, and the recounting of their brave and generous deeds. From ancient times there have been poets who wrote eulogistic poetry, and according to the author of *Al-Naqz,* men called "eulogizers" *(manaqebkhan* or *manaqebi)* used to recite their poems in the streets and markets.

4. *The Religious (or Sectarian) Epic:* Epics relate stories in which the heroes are the great personalities of the religion or sect. The hero is usually the Lord of the Pious, the Commander of the Faithful, Ali the son of Abu

Talib; or Hamzeh, the Prince of Martyrs, the uncle of the Holy Prophet (may God bless him and his family). Epics have also been composed in honor of other important religious figures, such as the descendants of the Imams and the grandchildren of the Holy Prophet.

5. *Poetry of Martyrdom:* This is devoted to the martyrdom of the saints, especially that of Imam Hussein, the Lord of Martyrs, and his chaste companions, and to the description of the events at Kerbela. However, sometimes descriptions of the deaths of the heroes are also found in the religious epics.

6. *Elegy:* Elegies, also, are written about the martyrdom and the sufferings of religious and sectarian figures. The distinction between these and the poetry of martyrdom is that less attention is paid to the details of the historical events; rather, the poet assumes that the reader is already familiar with the circumstances. He therefore emphasizes some of the sadder and more heart-rending aspects of the tragedy and inaugurates lamentations for the martyrs.

The subject of our discussion is the development of the elegiac type covering a little less than a century and a half, from the beginning of the thirteenth century of the Hijrah to the end of the first half of the fourteenth century—about A.D. 1785 to 1930. The situation is not that there is no element of martyrdom in elegy; or that in martyrdom poetry there is nothing elegiac; or that in a didactic poem there is no hint of either eulogy or elegy; or that in eulogy too there are no maxims or references to historical occurrences, etc. In other words, these are general divisions, and if most of a poet's output is devoted to eulogy, elegy, or martyrdom, we refer to him as an eulogist, poet of martyrdom, or an elegist. Some poets occasionally tried their hands at different forms and often produced works in every category. Sometimes their poetry is a collection composed of various kinds of religious and sectarian verse.

The custom of writing elegies in honor of departed loved ones is quite ancient, and it is almost certain that elegies were composed in Persia before the advent of Islam. In addition to narratives about the mourning for Siyavush and the weeping of the Magians, [1] we come across many other situations in the *Shahnameh* of Ferdowsi and the *Goshtaspnameh* of Daqiqi where, after the death of a leader or hero, the bereaved persons, especially those who are to avenge the death, have recited elegies.[2] The elegies which presumably were in the prose original of the *Shahnameh,* have been beautifully rendered into verse in that epic.

In the Islamic period too, in the most ancient poetry that has come down to us, we find examples of elegy. Among the poems of Rudaki there are several verses elegizing Muradi and verses in memory of Shahid Balkhi. In the poetry of Farrukhi there is a very famous and moving ode to the memory of Sultan Mahmud. We see elegies in the collected works of Mas'ud Sa'd for his son Saleh who died while Sa'd was still in prison, and also for the famous poet Sayyid Hassan of Ghaznah. Examples of this type of elegy are found in the works of most poets, even in versified romances by Nezami like *Layli va Majnun, Khusrow va Shirin,* and the *Eskandarnameh.* Elegies may also be found in the poetry of Kisai of Marv, Sayyid Hassan of Ghaznah (in memory of the Seljuq King Mas'ud), Khaqani (many elegies honoring Imam Muhammad ibn Yahya of Nishapur and his son Rashiduddin), Kamaluddin Ismail (on the death of his son), Amir Mu'ezzi (an elegy on Khwajah Nezamul-Mulk), Sa'di (in memory of the Caliph Mustasem and others), and Hafez (on the death of his son). However, the elegies with which we are concerned are only those written in honor of religious figures and martyrs "in the way of God."

If one is able to rely upon the narrative in the famous *Abu Muslem-Nameh,* and there is no reason to reject it except to say that the writer or narrator, according to the dictates of the art of story-telling, has somewhat exaggerated his account, there was an immediate reaction to the events at Kerbela among the Muslims, especially the Shi'as and those among the Sunnis who supported the Family of the Prophet. Parties arose to avenge the martyr. The whole period of the rule of the Umayyads was filled with disturbances and rebellions, and according to the *Abu Muslem-Nameh,* seventy-one leaders rebelled in turn against the Umayyads before the seventy-second, the Khurasani leader Abu Muslem, was finally victorious against them.

Probably every one of the rebels had his own particular political, social or religious objectives, but the cry to avenge the grandson of the Prophet was one which gained the widest support. It was used with much zeal and effect to encourage the people to join in rebellion. Throughout the text Abu Muslem's aim is shown to be revenge for the death of the Lord of Martyrs (Hussein), and in some manuscripts (e.g., Mss. No. 843 Suppl. Pers. in the Bibliothèque National, Paris) it is explained that Abu Muslem himself and some of his companions recited eulogies about Imam Hussein on the battlefield or while stirring up the people to rebel against the Umayyads. In this manuscript, examples in both verse and prose of the kind of propaganda and the style of speech employed by the eulogizers appear in several places.

Our extant documentary evidence shows us that the first eulogizer in Persian verse was Kisai of Marv (b. 341 A.H./A.D. 952-53). In the *Maj ma'ul-Fusaha* Hedayat writes of him:

> His name was Hakim Majduddin Abu Ishaq and the fame of his poetical abilities spread throughout the world; a virtuous man of good faith and a eulogizer of the glorious Family [of the Prophet] ... they say that the origin of his pen name *(takhallus)* is that he wore the cloak *(kiswa)* of asceticism and placed the cap of poverty upon his head, for he was also of the party of the ancients, and like the ancients his poems are lost labor and dust. ...[3]

195

Kisai was a contemporary of Hakim Naser Khusrow who had devoted his poetry to the praise of wisdom and moral principles.

A few verses in the *Hadiqah* of Sanai may be considered as the historical antecedent of the elegy. They are included in a chapter eulogizing the Commander of the Faithful, Hussein, the son of Ali, thus:

A Description of the Murder of Hussein the Son of Ali, Upon Whom Be Peace, at the Command of Yazid, May He Be Cursed.

> The enemies plotted against his life
> Intending to destroy him.
> Amr As counseled from evil;
> He impudently kicked aside divine law.
> He swore allegiance to the foul Yazid,
> And to obliterate the Family of the Prophet,
> He cast aside all shame and reverence;
> He appointed a group of enemies over him,
> So that by letter and deceits,
> They could draw him from Medina to that place.
> When [Hussein] made Kerbela a camp and a halting place,
> Suddenly the party of Ziyad fell upon him.
> They cut off access to the water of the Euphrates;
> They afflicted him with care and sorrow.
> Amr As and the ill-starred Yazid
> Surrounded the water source.
> The cursed Shemr and Abdullah Ziyad
> (Both their souls be accursed!)
> Drew their swords shamelessly,
> Neither fearing God nor ashamed before men.
> They cut off his head from his body with a sword,
> And they counted this deed to their profit!
> His body was shredded by the sword of the enemy
> While men looked on.
> In his palace at Damascus the foul Yazid
> Awaited the arrival of the head.
> It was placed before him and he rejoiced;
> He relied upon this world and sought security in it. . . .
> Taking a rod in his ill-omened hand, smiling cheerfully,
> He struck those lips and teeth!
> Shahrbanu and Zainab, weeping,
> With bare heads, seated upon saddled camels,
> Moaning with the sorrow in their hearts in their presence,
> Were struck with amazement at the behavior of those
>   vile people.
> Ali Asghar remained standing
> While those dogs satisfied their tyranny. . . .[4]

Anyone who wishes to read the rest of this passage should consult the *Hadiqah*. There are three other sections in the *Hadiqah* elegizing Hussein, under the following titles: "In Description of Kerebela and the Essence of the Honored Site of the Martyrdom"; "The Representation of Longing for the Exalted Site of the Martyrdom"; and "A Description of the Persistence of the Enemies and the Oppressors, May God Curse Them." Before he had turned to composing the elegies for Hussein, Sanai had already written panegyrics, elegies, and poems commemorating the deaths of the Imams Ali ibn Talib and Hasan ibn Ali.

Another well-known panegyrist among the poets of elegy was Badruddin Qavami of Rayy, who died about the middle of the sixth Islamic century (twelfth century A.D.) and apparently was active a little later than Sanai. The *Divan* of Qavami of Rayy is replete with moral material, maxims, and eulogies on the Family of the Prophet. As one of his pieces shows, he was a reciter of eulogies, and he declaimed his own poems (and the poems of others) in public assemblies and gatherings. His *Divan* was printed in 1334 A.H./A.D. 1955-56 in Tehran. In this collection there is an incomplete ode of fifty-nine couplets elegizing Imam Hussein. The first line is:

> "On the tenth day of the month of Muharram at Kerbela,
> A manifest tyranny struck the descendants of
> Muhammad."

This ode was written in the real spirit of elegy. At the end of the extant portion, the poet addresses the martyred Hussein thus:

> The ignoble shut thee away from the water of the
> Euphrates;
> They mingled thy blood with the dust of Kerbela.
> The enemies of faith lay in ambush for thy life;
> Not a friend or acquaintance was left to thee—
> Neither a kind person to befriend thee,
> Nor a hard heart who would show thee respect.
> Thy breast torn open, throat cut, hands cast down,
> Head sundered from thy body, rolling in the blood and
> dust.
> They rode their horses over thy beloved breast,
> O thou who in the entire world wert like the Prophet in
> distinction.
> How could thy body be trampled by the hooves of horses,
> When the breeze would not dare to cast pollen upon thy
> rosy face?
> Clothes and baggage plundered, wife and children taken
> prisoner;

Thy children and family were stunned with terror,
And the air grew cold from their chilled sighs.

No more can be said about this here. Until the time of the Safavids when Shi'ism became the officially established religion, many poets and prose writers produced works in this category, some of which can be found in the *Book of Naqz* (where it speaks of the mourning ceremonies for Imam Hussein);[6] in *The Assemblies of the Believers* by Qazi Nurullah Shushtari; in *The Epic in Iran* (the section on religious epics, especially panegyrics and eulogies); and in *The Garden of Martyrs* by Mawlana Hussein Va'ez Kashifi of Sabzevar. We are in need of a separate work on this subject for further enquiry.

There is no doubt that with Mawlana Muhtasham of Kashan and his twelve-stanza elegy *(tarkib-band)* the art of elegy reached its highest point up to the Safavid period. In the *Divan* of Muhtasham there is another ode in memory of Imam Hussein and there are some other eulogies; but none is on a par with his elegy. This poem achieved a fame and popularity upon its publication that no other elegy has ever attained to the present day, nor perhaps ever will. It remains one of the masterpieces of Persian literature. Even now in decorating halls for Passion plays and the assemblies of high mourning, its verses are inscribed vertically on hangings attached to the pillars and horizontally under the ceiling, and even on the walls. There is virtually no assembly of significance unadorned by such quotations. Clearly no poem with such influence, fame, and popularity would go unimitated and unappreciated by later poets.

After Muhtasham, every poet of note who tried his hand at elegy attempted to write a work in the same style—in twelve stanzas in honor of the twelve Imams, or in fourteen stanzas in honor of the fourteen Pure Ones, or even longer poems. Just as the imitators of Ferdowsi's *Shahnameh,* or Nezami's *Khamseh,* or Mawlana Jalal al-Din's *Masnavi,* or Sa'di's *Gulestan,* were ever able to achieve the perfection of those masters, similarly not one of the imitators of Muhtasham has been able to reach his level. Nevertheless, if we disregard Muhtasham's masterpiece, some of their efforts are worth attention in their own right, while the works of others passed into oblivion even during their own lifetime.

Since writing poems in the style of Muhtasham's elegy constitutes a separate chapter in elegiac history, and since the earlier poets of the Qajar period imitated him, we must examine the works of some of the more famous ones in this category. The list is not exhaustive; we are presenting examples of only the better works of these poets.

1. Sabahi Bidguli: The first great Qajar poet was Haj Sulaiman Sabahi Bidguli of Kashan, who was the teacher of the "King of Poets," Fathali Khan Saba of Kashan and the intimate friend of the famous poet Sayyid Ahmad Hatef of Isfahan. Sabahi, according to the best information avail-

able, died in 1218 A.H./A.D. 1803-04, and he panegyrized Fathali Shah Qajar who ascended the throne in 1212 A.H./A.D. 1797. From Sabahi we have a *Divan* containing more than 3,500 couplets which was edited by the late Partu Bayzai and published in Tehran in 1338 A.H./A.D. 1959-60. Sabahi was one of the first persons to compose a poem in fourteen stanzas (apparently in honor of the fourteen Pure Ones) in imitation of the twelve-stanza elegy of Muhtasham. Among the elegies of Sabahi there are several others for the martyrs of Kerbela, none of which, however, measure up to his fourteen stanzas; and there is ascribed to him a long poem in distich *(masnavi)* elegizing Hazrat-e Ali Asghar which resembles Ta'ziyeh doggerel in weakness. In a footnote to it the editor has observed that "if . . . this poem be compared with the fourteen-stanza elegy, one will perceive that Sabahi wrote it at the beginning of his career, or perhaps during his childhood." 7

In the introduction to the *Divan* of Sabahi, the following is said about the fourteen-stanza elegy: "This elegy is superior to all the other elegies in stanzas written after and in imitation of Muhtasham." 8 However if one cannot consider the poems of Vesal (in fourteen stanzas) and Saburi of Kashan as superior to that of Sabahi, they are certainly not inferior. In my opinion Saburi's poem is the best of those written in imitation of Muhtasham.

The first stanza of Sabahi's elegy begins with a beautiful allusion to the subject matter, showing that this is the story of martyrdom, fighting, and death:

> At eventide, by the edge of the horizon fell
> The sun like a severed head in an upset bowl;
> Heaven has thrown down the golden helmet [of the sun]
> And dragged the hem of the blue tunic of twilight in
> blood.9

In the works of Sabahi there is another ode elegizing Imam Hussein beginning with these lines:

> This is the day of mourning for the champion of the Faith;
> The heavens join the earth in lamentation.10

The editor has noted at the end of this piece: "In my opinion this work has the form of a dirge *(nawheh)* and was written for mourning processions." If the supposition of the editor be correct, this work may then be considered the earliest poem that has come down to us composed for chanting in the mourning companies.

2. "The Vesal of Shiraz": Mirza Muhammad Shafi' ibn Muhammad Ismail of Shiraz, known as the Little Mirza, with the pen name of Vesal (d.

1262 A.H./A.D. 1845) was a poet, calligrapher, and musician of the Qajar period. Among other works, he has left us an elegiac poem in fourteen stanzas. The first stanza begins with these couplets:

> For whom does the world put on black mourning?
> And for whom has the dawn torn its collar open [in
> sorrow]?
> This stream of tears of blood which is flowing from the
> eyes of the people
> Is for whose misfortune and for whose misadventure? [11]

Vesal has written other elegies some of which were well received and imitated by later poets. His poem has acquired considerable fame.

3. Qa'ani: Mirza Habib Allah of Shiraz (d. 1270 A.H./A.D. 1853 was the most famous poet of the Qajar period whose *Divan* has been printed many times. He has no peer in his command of words and his masterly use of them. Most of his poetry is devoted to eulogy, although he also wrote lyrics and poems in stanzas with a variety of formal rhyming schemes.

Among his works is the famous elegiac ode on Imam Hussein, in which he employed throughout the device of question and answer:

> It rains. What? Blood. Whence? The eyes. In what
> manner?
> Day and night? Why?
> From sadness. What sadness? Sadness for the king of
> Kerbela.
> What was his name? Hussein. From whose family? Ali's.
> Who was his mother? Fatemeh. Who was his grandfather?
> The Prophet.
> How did it happen? He was martyred. Where? On the
> plain of Kerbela.
> When? On the tenth of Muharram. Secretly? No, before a
> multitude.
> Was he killed at night? No, in the day. At what time? At
> noontide.
> Was his head cut off from the front? Nay, Nay; from
> behind.[12]

4. Yaghma: Mirza Abul Hasan of Jandaq (d. 1276 A.H./A.D. 1859), was a famous writer of prose and poetry of the thirteenth Islamic (nineteenth Christian) century. His *Divan,* consisting of facetious verses, satires, dirges, and elegies, was lithographed in Tehran in 1283 A.H./A.D. 1886-87 and that edition was reproduced by offset in 1339 A.H./A.D. 1960-61. It contains eleven books, one of which is in prose, while the remainder are in poetry.

Among the ten books devoted to verse, the eighth contains his elegies and dirges.

Yaghma did not try to imitate Muhtasham and was independent and innovative in his elegies. The section of the *Divan* devoted to elegy has only two types of poetry: one, short odes entitled elegy or dirge; and the other, "pieces in the form of *mustazad* poems which are labeled dirges for breast-beating *(sineh-zani)."* Apparently these are the oldest examples of this type of poetry which we possess (since it is only speculation that the ode by Sabahi mentioned above is a dirge for breast-beating). In this *Divan* the elegies are of sixteen sections and all in the ode form. The dirges for breast-beating also are in sixteen parts. At the beginning of the book of elegies, it is written: "This is the Book of Elegies and its couplets are . . . at the height of perfection in elegance; it is extremely difficult to create the mood for lamentations and weeping while retaining poetical quality. Nevertheless this has been accomplished."

The first couplet of this book is:

> The great king for whom the sphere of the heavens was
> like a ball for his bat;
> His head, like a ball, fell to the battlefield, struck by the
> bat of enmity.

And the first dirge for breast-beating begins in this way:

> My Akbar returns from the Euphrates with parched lips;
> My young Akbar!
> Flow forth, O fountain of my moist eyes; My young Akbar!
> While the turquoise vat [of heaven] has dyed the robe of
> thy life with red blood,
> The world has dyed my veil black with the indigo
> of mourning;
> My young Akbar!

In some of his dirges, Yaghma has been free with the forms of poetry and created something combining both the poem with stanzas and the *mustazad* poem. In an elegy on Qasem he writes:

> O Qasem, the joyous celebration is spoiled;
> The bridal chamber of pleasure is draped in black.
> Do not turn thy horse to the place of sacrifice;
> What can one man do against a plain covered with troops?
> By the arrayed eyes, an oath!
> By the arrowhead searching out thy liver, an oath!
> From the point of the arrow to the feather, a vow!
> From the handle of the sword to its tip, a vow!

The succeeding stanzas continue in this fashion except that after each eight lines two couplets are added, the first ending in "oath" *(qasam)* and the second in "vow" *(sawgand).*

The last two couplets in the third stanza follow the scheme of the first, and the fourth repeats the scheme of the second. This pattern is followed to the end of the poem. As a further example, the second stanza is quoted here:

> Do not array thyself for the battlefield;
> Do not rush in that way toward the Tartars.
> Do not open the bosom of eternity upon thyself;
> Do not make mourning the companion of my happiness.
> By thy quickly wearied heart, an oath!
> By the long-lasting sorrow for thee, an oath!
> By thee and the kiss of the houri of paradise, a vow!
> By myself and the blows of the enemy upon me, a vow!

The assertions at the beginning of the Book of Elegies about Yaghma's poetry have been completely vindicated. With their clarity and elequence, his elegies can also be read as processional dirges; indeed, they are still used for this purpose. The meters, too, are rhythmic and capable of being broken into shorter sections or are in themselves short so that they can easily be adapted to the particular chanting style of the breast-beaters. It is believed that none of the major Persian poets after Yaghma has tried his hand at writing poems for breast-beating.

5. Sorush: Mirza Muhammad Ali Khan, the "Sun of Poets" (d. 1285 A.H./A.D. 1868) is one of the literary masters of the Qajar period. His *Divan* contains eulogies and panegyrics and he also wrote different types of religious poetry. A collection of his eulogies entitled *Shams al-Manaqeb* (The Sun of Eulogies) was lithographed at Tehran in 1300 A.H./A.D. 1882-83. An incomplete religious epic, *Ordibehest,* of 9219 couplets on the life and campaigns of the Holy Prophet, is also extant. In the field of elegy he has left us two independent works: one, an elaborate poem in sixty stanzas in memory of the martyrs at Kerbela known as the *Sixty Stanzas of Sorush.* The first stanza opens with these verses:

> O eye! Shed tears, for this is the month of Muharram;
> The weeping eye is honored by God.
> The king of religion said, "I am killed so that thou mayest
> weep;
> Thy tears are an ointment on the wounds of the king.
> In the memory of the light of the eyes of the Prophet,

> By God, if thou turnest the world into an ocean with thy
> tears,
> It is not enough.[13]

This poem, also in stanzas, was composed in imitation of Muhtasham and his followers, although its length gave Sorush the opportunity to go into greater detail and to describe something of the story of the heroes of this sad event. But with regard to literary value, Sorush has not here risen above other poets: rather, due to its prolixity and elaborateness, in places it descends to the level of doggerel.

Sorush's second elegy, *The Garden of Secrets,* is in rhyming distichs. It, too, is a description of the tragedy of Kerbela and honors the memory of its martyrs. Its 1159 couplets are written in the same meter as that chosen by Mawlavi for his *Masnavi (remal-i musaddas-i mahzuf* or *maqsur)* and the work is known in literary and religious circles as the *Thousand Couplets of Sorush.* According to the information at my disposal it has been printed four times to date.[14] It is most eloquent, lucid, and affecting, and is one of the poet's greatest works. Preachers and reciters at the important assemblies commemorating the martyrdoms know it by heart, and it is also recited from the pulpits. It begins:

> In my hand is a pen dipped in blood
> So that I might write a Book of Tragedy;
> But I fear that my pen will burst into flame,
> And thus my book has remained unwritten.
>
> I fear that my pen will turn to fire,
> Or that the page will burn from the heat of my sighs.
> When God revealed the fate of that faithful king
> To Abraham and Adam,
> Adam forgot his sorrow for his Abel,
> And Abraham forgot his Ishmael.

Describing the martyrdom of Abbas, Sorush writes:

> That Abbas, the prince of the loyal,
> That standardbearer of the army of the beloved, came out.
> He was parched with thirst and from the fervor of loyalty—
> The king of religion wept at his condition. . . .
> He fought enemies on the right and left,
> Like Ali wielding his sword Zul-Feqar . . .
> An evil-natured man suddenly severed from his body
> The hand of the one born of Ali, the Hand of God.
> He said, "O hand, you have fallen; well-fallen!"

203

He took his sword in the other hand and said:
"I have come to die; what is a hand?
A dedicated man who flees at a blow is not dedicated". . . .

However not all the verses of the *Garden of Secrets* are so eloquent. Besides, Sorush was attracted to some weak and untrustworthy stories that were circulating among the common people of his period and he included them in his poem. Despite this, the work has attained a kind of popularity, and some poets imitated him and wrote elegies in the same style and meter.

6. Saburi of Kashan: Haj Mirza Muhammad Kazim, the "King of the Poets of the Shrine of Imam Reza," the father of the "King of Poets," Muhammad Taqi "Bahar," was a major poet of his era (d. 3122 A.H./A.D. 1904). His *Divan* was printed once at Tehran in 1342 A.H./A.D. 1963-64. Saburi has left us two elegies: one of twelve stanzas in honor of Imam Hussein, and the other with nine stanzas of five couplets each, into which nine stanzas of a poem by Vesal have been worked. Saburi's first poem has attained considerable fame in preaching circles (especially in Khorasan). It begins thus:

> The bells of an exceedingly pained and sorrowful caravan
> can be heard,
> Like the burning sigh which comes from the saddened
> heart.
> I think it is a caravan strayed from its homeland,
> For with the sound of camel bells come heart-melting cries.
> If this be the caravan of Hussein, the descendant of the
> Prophet,
> Why does death come out to meet him at every stage?
> Behold, master of the tents, set up the pavillion of honor;
> For the Chaste One of God, Zainab, is approaching from a
> long journey.

Before Saburi, Muhtasham's poem had been so influential that all later poets wrote in the same meter that Muhtasham had used. The first thing which attracts the reader's attention in Saburi's poem is that he has changed the meter and selected one which is more dignified and more appropriate to elegy. In addition, the poem opens with a beautiful allusion to its subject. Reading it, one can appreciate the conscious effort Saburi has made to liberate himself from Muhtasham's domination. Perhaps the secret of the success of his poem is to be found in its frank acknowledgement of the fact that whoever wants a poem in stanzas in the meter and with the content of Muhtasham can find no better poem than the one Muhtasham wrote; however one can see newness and originality in the poetry of Saburi:

Heaven, behave gently with the family of the Best of
Mankind,
Behave gently with the People of God and be ashamed
before Fatemeh.
The road to Syria lies ahead and a thousand afflictions
lie behind;
Have mercy on the Holy Household, O heaven, in the
mountains and the desert.
The night is dark and the conveyance a naked she-camel;
Drive the camel slowly. I do not ask that you prepare a
golden litter for them.
If an infant falls off the camel from behind,
Take it up by the hand gently and pull the thorns
from its feet.

In my opinion, Saburi has been more successful than any poet other
than Muhtasham in writing elegies in stanzas. However his other elegy has
not become so popular, and probably half of its fame is due to Vesal's
poetry which so affected the poet that he included its verses in his own:

If anyone contemplates the day of judgment,
Or the adventures of the family of the Prophet;
It is not suitable that anyone compare them.
If anyone thinks about their calamities
Don't believe Vesal, so that others will believe.

In order to make the difference between this poetry and that of Vesal clear,
a few verses of the elegy of Vesal are quoted here. These couplets follow the
fourth and fifth lines (taken from Vesal) of the stanza of Saburi given
above:

Does one acquit himself of his obligation of mourning
Even if the surface of the whole world is wet with tears?
No one can describe his Kerbela
Unless you call it another judgment day.
On this day does anyone recall his loneliness for his brother,
Or describe the capture of his sister?
Their manifest cries are for the oppressed ones,
Or for the tyranny of the oppressing enemies.

The custom of writing elegies was maintained throughout this period
and has continued to the present day. Many poets have entered this field—
masters of style, second- and third-class poets, and even ordinary individuals who have only natural gifts and no formal education in the

fundamentals and techniques of prosody. Reference to only a few may be added here.

7. Jaihun of Yazd: The "Most Eloquent of Speakers," the late Agha Muhammad Yazdi, whose pen name was Jaihun, died in 1318 A.H./A.D. 1900-1901. He and his brother Saihun were well-known poets during the reign of Shah Nasir. Jaihun's elegies are as famous as his satires. At first he would go to the mosque in Yazd on the mourning days and recite poems he had written elegizing Imam Hussein. Since his verses sprang from his feelings they affected the feelings of others. In due time he appeared in the capital and began to recite his elegies in the mourning assemblies sponsored by the government and in the presence of the king. One of his elegies begins with these couplets:

> Once again, emotion-arousing moon of Muharram, you
>   have appeared,
> And you have struck the spark of Ashura in my heart. . .
> You have returned, and like last year,
> You have been lancing my wounded heart with sorrow
>   again and again
> You are none other than that which rushed from good
>   to evil,
> And then plundered the descendant of the Best of Mankind.
> You are none other than that which instead of a handful of
>   water
> Shot an arrow into the throat of wretched Asghar.

8. Mirza Taqi of Aliabad, Saheb-e Divan: He has left us one elegy in distichs, apparently imitating that of Sorush since he used the same meter. His verses from an elegy on Ali Asghar are quoted below:

> He said, "I have found wholesome milk for you,
> So I have rushed back from the battlefield to you.
> If your palate is parched, deprived of mother's milk,
> When is mother's milk like the milk of God [martyrdom]?
> The milk of God is harsh and bloody,
> When the infant drinks that he survives a year or two;
> When the man drinks this he becomes immortal."
> Clutching the infant to his bosom, he ran toward the field,
> He saw that which had been concealed behind
>   the veil [death].

9. Oman of Saman: Saman is a village in the northwest of Chahar Mahal-e Bakhtiari connected in the west with Isfahan by the Zaiandeh River, and lying to the north of that river. It is said that most of the people

of that village have a poetic gift; among them two individuals, Dehqan of Saman and Oman of Saman, are best known. Oman has also composed an elegy in distichs which appears to be in imitation of Sorush of Isfahan. These couplets from that elegy are very famous:

> His sister, beating her breast and head,
> Went off to seize the reins of her brother's horse.
> The flood of her tears closed the road to the king,
> The heat of her sighs frightened the king.
> He saw that her black hair was that of a woman,
> With one hand on the reins and the other stretched
> toward heaven.
> Don't say "woman"; she is the creator of men in this world.
> Don't say "woman"; rather the daughter of glory and the
> sister of dignity.
> Don't say "woman"; people prostrate themselves at
> her threshold.
> Don't say "woman"; rather the Hand of God in the sleeve.

10. Mirza Yahya Mudarres of Isfahan (Dastgerdi) has also left us an elegy in stanzas on the martyrs of Kerbela. This poem was printed in the *Book of Literary Mournings* (pp. 228ff.) and these verses are taken from it:

> O sufferer of sorrow, the world loves thee;
> Old and young mourn thee with broken hearts.
> The dust of thy threshold is too the place of prayer
> of mankind,
> And Kerbela is the prayer ground of angels.
> The robe of heaven is still red from glow of twilight
> For the death of red-robed Akbar.
> When Hussein saw that newly married Qasem is drowned in
> blood,
> His soul was anguished.

11. Probably the last poet of the Qajar period to write elegies was Iraj Mirza, Jalalul-Mamalik. Iraj did not survive to the Pahlavi era (died toward the end of 1304 A.H./A.D. 1926). He cannot really be counted among the elegists, since it is love poetry and the social criticism of his *Arefnameh* with its simple rhetorical style which has given him considerable fame. Nonetheless, two elegies can be found in his *Divan*. These, like his other poems, are simple, fluent, and possess new and pleasing themes:

> It is the custom that the friends of whoever is bereaved
> of a youth,
> Have compassion upon the plight of that bereaved one.

One friend takes him by the arm in faithfulness,
Another wipes the tears from the bereaved's eyes.
In short, each one, in one fashion or another, out of pity,
Consoles the afflicted one.
Did anyone give consolation to Hussein's thoughts
When he saw the body of Akbar rolling in blood?
After the son, the heart of the father became the target
of arrows;
They fired the nest of the flown bird.

* * * * *

The women wandered amid the burning tents,
Like the reflections of stars on water.
The small children, from around the tents,
Ran in all directions, like fiery sparks from the heart.
Other than their lacerated livers which could not be
reached by the vicious enemy,
Nothing remained to them of their torn possessions.
Fingers were cut off for the sake of rings;
Earlobes were torn for their earrings.
The grandson of that king whose exalted name is called
At morning, noon, and night from the minarets,
Has fallen in the blood and dust, and they trample his body
With their horses' hoofs which strike screams from rocks.

NOTES

1. Concerning the mourning for Siyavush, refer to the *Shāhnāmeh* of Ferdowsi;
the Story of Siyavush; the History of Bukhara; the book of Shahrukh Messkub of
the same name.

2. Some elegies of this kind are recorded in several stories contained in the
Shāhnāmeh, such as the story of Siyavush in the *Gushtaspnāmeh* of Daqiqi (numerous instances), the Story of Forud, and the story of Rustam and Esfandiyar. Refer to
those stories.

3. *Majma' al-Fusahā*, lithographed in Tehran in 1295 A.H./A.D. 1878, pp 481-82.

4. *Hadīqa* by Sanā'ī of Ghaznah (Tehran, 1329 A.H. Solar/A.D. 1950-51). Edited
by Raẓavī: pp. 244-73.

5. The *Dīvān* of S̲h̲arḥ-i Hāl-Shu'arā Badr al-Dīn Qavāmī of Ray, edited by
Mīr Jalal al-Dīn Ḥusainī Urmāvī, known as Muhaddith (Tehran, 1334 A.H. Solar/
A.D. 1955-56), pp 125-28.

6. *Ba'd Ma̲th̲ālib al-Nawāṣib fī Naqz Ba'd Fasāihur-Rawāfiḍ*, more commonly
known as the *Book of Naqz*, compiled by Nāsir al-Dīn Abdul-Jalīl Qazvīnī of Ray,
edited by Sayyid Jalal al-Dīn Muhaddith (Tehran: 1331 A.H. Solar/A.D. 1952-53),
pp. 401ff.

7. The *Dīvān* of Sabāḥī Bīdgulī, edited and with introduction by Ḥusain Partaw Baiẓā'ī (Tehran 1338 A.H. Solar/A.D. 1959-60). Note on page 153.

8. Sabāḥī, Introduction, p. v.

9. To see the poem in stanzas by Sabāḥī, refer to his *Dīvān,* pp. 131ff.

10. *Ibid.,* p. 151.

11. *Dīvān* of Visāl; also in Sūgvārīhā-yi Adabī dar Irān, by Kūḥī Kirmānī (Tehran, 1333 A.H. Solar/A.D. 1954-55), pp. 196ff.

12. The *Dīvān* of Mīrzā Habī Allāh Qā'ānī of Shiraz (Tehran: Amīr Kabīr, 1338 A.H. Solar/A.D. 1959-60); (also several odes in Sūgvārīhā-yi Adabī), p. 207.

13. The *Dīvān* of the Sun of Poets, Surūsh of Isfahān, edited by Muḥammad Ja'far Maḥjūb (Tehran: Amīr Kabīr, 1339 A.H. *Solar/A.D.* 1960-61), II, 732ff.

14. Printed in Tabriz (1286 A.H./A.D. 1869-70), Tehran, Mashhad, and most recently in the *Dīvān* of Surūsh II, 777ff.

15. The *Dīvān* of Haj Mīrzā Muḥammad Kāẓim Sabūrī, the King of the Poets of the Shrine of Imām Riẓā, edited by Muḥammad Malik-zādih (Tehran: Ibn Sīnā, 1342 A.H. Solar/A.D. 1963-64), p. 465.

16. Sūgvārīhā-yi Adabī, p. 209.

17. The *Dīvān* of Iraj, edited by Muḥammad Ja'far Maḥjūb (Tehran: Andīshih, second edition, 1349 A.H. Solar/A.D. 1960-61), pp. 166-67.

16

The *Marsiyeh* in Sindhi Poetry

ANNEMARIE SCHIMMEL

When I traveled in Upper Sind in 1961 I saw a high pole with flags in the small town of Ratodero, and became aware, for the first time, that the Shi'a element in Pakistan, and particularly in the province of Sind, the Lower Indus Valley, is still comparatively strong. The last independent rulers of Sind, the Baluch Talpurs, were of Shi'a persuasion, and some of the leading families who had come from Iran also professed this creed. Besides, an extreme veneration of the sayyeds was always apparent in Sind, whether the populations was officially Shi'a or not. Literary evidence shows that in previous centuries the celebrations in Muharram on the famous burial ground Makli Hill near Thatta were typical features of religious life in Sind, and the stern Naqshbandi theologians of the then capital, Thatta, such as Makhdum Muhammad Hashem (d. 1763) composed treatises against these "unislamic" customs. It is small wonder that the Sindhi language, too, has produced a considerable number of *marsiyeh*. I have not yet come across "ta'ziyeh" in the true sense of the word as "passion play," although further research may produce some examples; in any case Sind cannot compete with the Ta'ziyeh which were so popular in the kingdom of Oudh, in Lucknow, during the early nineteenth century. Lucknow was the scene of the most spectacular performances, in which even the rulers

210

actively participated, and the historians relate with admiration that even King Ghaziuddin Haydar's favorite elephant had been trained to trumpet "Wah Husseinaaah. . . ." Neither can Sind boast of anything similar to the *marsiyeh* in Urdu, which developed first in the Deccan, where King Muhammad Quli Qutb Shah, around 1600, wrote the first simple threnodies on the martyrs of Kerbela, and was then developed by the great eighteenth-century poet Sauda, to reach its apex in the hundreds of *marsiyehs* by the Lucknow poets Anis and Dabir in the nineteenth century.

The first written poems in Sindhi go back to the sixteenth century: they consist of short poems by mystics. Classical literature reached its apex in the eighteenth century with Shah Abdul Latif of Bhit (d. 1752). It is during this century that we find the first poet who devoted himself exclusively to *marsiyeh* writing in his mother tongue. He is, as Ghulam Muhammad Gerami has shown in a fine article, Thabit Ali Shah (1740-1810). He performed the pilgrimage to Kerbela, and wrote in Persian, Urdu, and Sindhi. To be sure, even before him some scattered *marsiyehs* can be found in Sindhi, for instance in the work of Makhdum Abdullah Thattawi, a member of the leading religious family in Thatta, and in the poetry of Sayyed Haydar Shah and Maulwi Ahmad Chinan Faqir; but Thabit Ali concentrated upon this art more than any of his predecessors. He himself claims: "The *marsiyeh* had previously no root in Sindhi, and whatever was there, that was not famous." This poet's greatness in this field was readily acknowledged by his compatriots.

We should, however, not forget that there was also a *marsiyeh* tradition in Persian in the country: the works of 'Allama (1682-1782), of Muhammad Mu'in Tharo of Thatta who had composed a *rubaiyat* commemorating the martyrs of Kerbela, and Muhammad Muhser Thattawi (1709-1750) are worth mentioning. The latter, a devout Shi'a poet, introduced the form of *tarji'band* for the Persian *marsiyeh* in Sind. He was probably the first artist to use the form of *salam* for the martyrs, a form which later became popular with the Sindhi poets. Muhsen, who called himself "the bewildered nightingale of the garden of Hussein," has composed a twelve-*band marsiyeh;* one of his *qasidas* dramatically describes how the boat of Mustafa's family has been drowned in blood, the black cloud of infidelity had waylaid the sun, and the candle of the Prophet was killed by the breeze of the Kufians. All these themes are taken up by Thabit Ali Shah, who used the form of *salam,* but also that of *suwari,* "riding song," which was to become widely used by the Sindhi poets to describe how the beloved offspring of Mustafa and Murtaza went out riding toward his fate.

سواری ٹی حبيب مصطفیٰ جی
سواری ٹی انيس مرتضیٰ جی

Sometimes we find in his poetry dramatic forms, such as the introduction of the complaining *radif: hay hay hasrat wawayla!*

211

ثابت مرثیه خوان مدام

چئی سرور قی صلواة و سلام

شاه جو ماتم ثنی نه تمام

هئی هئی حسرت واویلا

Sindhi *marsiyehs* are usually filled with Persian and Arabic terms and expressions, but Thabit Ali Shah has also produced a pure *thet Sindhi salam,* without any loanwords, in which he addresses the beloved child of al-Batul, who died from thirst:

لادسین پالیئی بتول   ناز نپایئی رسول

توق صلوة و سلام   اچ مری مارئین ملول

He thus set the model for the following poets who used the *marsiyeh* form: there are only a few powerful lines by Sachal Sarmast, the enthusiastic late eighteenth century writer, and by his spiritual successor, Bedil of Rohri (d. 1872). We find the form used by Mir Hasan, Shah Naser, Mirza Baddhal Beg, Khwaja Naser Ali, and particularly Mirza Qalich Beg, the great translator and novelist (d. 1929). Even more famous is the prince from the Talpur family, Abdul Hussein Sangi, a friend of Mirza Qalich Beg. These authors follow the Persian-Urdu tradition rather than the Sindhi one by incorporating Arabo-Persian meters in their poems, while classical Sindhi uses indigenous meters. Sangi's *marsiyehs* follow the established models: *salam* and *suwari* can be found, and his *suwari* achieves a distinguished connection with the fact that Hassan and Hussein once used to ride on their grandfather's, the Prophet's, back; a theme lovingly used by the folk poets of Sind.

Sometimes Sangi indulges in strange images, trying to surpass his models:

> From the arrows' rain the most holy body became
> like a sieve,
> And the blood came out of the body as spring
> rain falls.

تیر باران کان تن اقدس ثیو غربال وار

رت ٹی بتمان تئین و هیو جنین ٹو و سی ابر بهار

But he has also used a motif that leads us into the more mystical interpretation of the martyrdom of the Imam:

> The prince has made his *me'raj* on the ground
> of Kerbela,
> The Shah's horse has gained the rank of Buraq ...

212

كربلا جى سرزمين تى شاهه هو معراج كيو
ذوالجناح شاهه كى براق جو رتبه مليو....

And in another *suwari* he sings:

> Today the Shah of Kerbela has mounted his horse,
> just as though Mustafa were mounting the Buraq
> today.

چؤ هيو گهوڙى تى شاه كربلا اج
چؤ هيو براق تى چى مصطفى اج...

In the same *marsiyeh,* written in the classical form of *musaddas,* he promises his listeners:

> Who weeps here, He will make him laugh there,
> for the sake of the Imam you will become justified.
> When one becomes worthy of the Divine state
> Duality becomes distant, and then one reaches Unity.

روئى جو هِت، هُتي تنهن كى كلائى
امام حق اوهان كى حق ملائى
جذهن لاهوت مه لاتى رسائى
دوئى ڤ دور پوءِ وحدت جى ائى

Here we reach the point where the *marsiyeh* is connected with mystical poetry proper: the experience of martyrdom is the experience of meeting God. Sangi's verses remind the reader somehow of the way in which some Turkish poets in the Bektashi tradition would compare the fate of Hussein ibn Ali in the battlefield of Kerbela with that of Hussein ibn Mansur al-Hallaj, who found the fulfillment of his mystical love on the gallows. Dr. Farhadi has shown how Mansur Hallaj, Shams-e Tabrizi, and Mulla Jalal al-Din are woven into a strange relationship in one of the Persian Ta'ziyeh plays. In both Husseins the secret of Divine love, which means affliction, becomes apparent.

It is in this tradition that we have to place the most touching poem in honor of the martyrs of Kerbela in the Sindhi language: it is *Sur Kedaro* by Shah Abdul Latif, *Kedaro* being the old folk melody used for threnodies and dirges for those who have fallen on the battlefield. Shah Abdul Latif's poetry precedes that of Thabit Ali Shah, and he has set a model for later purely Sindhi *marsiyehs* in his *Kedaro,* as he has set models in other poetical forms for the generations to come. In Shah's *Risalo,* which consists of some thirty chapters, each centering around one topic of traditional tales which are mystically interpreted, and sung in a specific melody, *Kedaro* describes in six chapters the sufferings of the children of the Prophet. Shah Abdul

Latif uses the traditional motifs but combines them with the mystical path which is, to use Rumi's term, a path in blood: thus the tragedy of Kerbela is interpreted as the manifestation of highest Divine love. It seems that a partial translation of the *Sur* will show the character of this poetry best. It should not be forgotten, however, that the poetry of the *Risalo* is meant to be sung, hence, expressions may be found which are due to alliterations, internal rhymes, and other poetical requirements without being necessarily connected with the exact meaning of the sentence.

Shah begins with the descriptions of Muharram:

> The moon of Muharram was seen, anxiety
>   about the princes occurred,
> The One Allah may know what He pleases
>   to do. (I, 1)

ذتو محرَمُ ماه   سنكو شهزادان تيو

جاڻي هيك الله   ڀان و لنديون جوكري

> Muharram has come back, the imams have not come
>   back—
> O Lord, bring me together with the princes of Medina!

This sigh is repeated in the following lines (3, 4), and then the poet gives a colorful description of how the princes of Medina have "gone out from Medina," sending men to fetch all the necessary implements; but what will be the end?

> The Mirs have gone out from Medina—they
>   have not come back
> Dye the clothes in black, brother dyer! (I, 7)

ميرَ مديثيان نكري   آثيانه   موٹي

كارا رگج كپڙا   ادا   نيروٹي ....

From here Shah Latif reaches his central statement when he sings:

> The hardship of martyrdom, hear, is the
>   day of happiness [or: wedding *shadi*],
> Yazid has not got an atom of this love,
> Death is rain [of grace] for the children of Ali. (I, 8)

سختي شهادتَ جي   سن! شادي جو ذيُنِهن

ذرو ناهِ يزيدكي   نسوروٹي   نيُنِهن

مرگ آهي مينهن   عليءَ جي اولاد كي

214

The term "rain," which is used so often in these verses, is the rain of mercy, rain being the sign of Divine grace and mercy, as it was alluded to in the Koran, and as Shah Latif himself has said so often in his grand hymn in honor of the Prophet, in *Sur Sarang*, the "Rain-Song."

> The hardship of martyrdom is all the joyful
>   rainy season,
> Yazid has not got the traces of this love,
> The decision of being killed was with the
>   imams from the very beginning. (I, 9)

ملارُ   مُروئی   سختی شهادتَ جی
ای عشقَ جو آثارُ   ذرو ناه یزید کی
اصل امامن سین   کُسن جو قرار

That means, this martyrdom had already been accepted by them at the covenant of *alast,* just as the other heroines of his mystical poetry, such as the loving and longing Suhni and Sassui, had accepted death in the way of love from the very beginning of creation. Verse 10 repeats this idea in different wording, and then the poet continues:

> The hardship of martyrdom is all coquetry [*naz*]
> The intoxicated ones [*rend*] understand the secret
>   of the case of Kerbela. (I, 11)

نازُ   یسوروئی   سختی شهادتَ جی
قضیی کربلا جو   رند پروژین راز

Here, the terminology of *naz* and *rend* leads the listener immediately into the tradition of Persian mystical poetry.

The closing *wa'y*, a poem with a refrain, complains that everything beautiful has gone due to the departure of the princes:

> Today the princes of the faithful have left
>   Medina and gone,
> They have left Medina and gone, who are gone
>   out of Medina
> Woe, woe, they have gone out of Medina!
> Sun, moon—toward Mustafa they all have gone,
> Woe, woe! Darkness has fallen without them,
>   the stars have gone away!

215

اج مير مومنن جا، مدينو چڈّى هليا
مدينو چڈّى هليا، سي مدينئون لڈى هليا

هّىء هّىء! مدينو چڈّى هليا

سچُ، چنڈ، مصطفى ڌى يكدِل گڈى هليا
هّىء هّىء! اتذارُ ٿيو اُن رِي، تارا لڈى هليا

The second chapter describes once more how the princes have gone
out with drums, falcons, axes, daggers, and other war implements, and how
they have pitched their tents on the plain of Kerbela (II, 4).

> Killing with Egyptian swords do they show their
> heroism, and
> Certainly Bibi [i.e., Fatemeh] has borne such heroic
> darlings. (II, 5)

سپج ك بيبىَ چايا هڑا سورهَ سپرين

The activity of the "lion-like sayyeds" is described in powerful images:

> Having cut with swords, they made heaps of carcasses—
> Heroes become there confused, seeing Mir Hussein's
> attack. (II, 6)

مـارى مصريُن سـين دونو كيائـون ديرَ
دهليا اُت دلَير بسى حملو ميرحسين جو

Seeing this display of heroism,

> The earth trembles, shakes, the skies are in
> uproar.

ڌرق ڌُيى، لـرزى لـوٿليـا آسمان

But then, Shah concludes, this is more than normal fighting:

> This is not a war, this is the manifestation
> of Love. (II, 7)

كره هُئى كـان هو نظاره نيَهن جو

From here he can easily turn to the central theme of his whole poetry, and
of mystical poetry in general:

> The Friend kills the beloved, the lovers are
> slain,
> For the elect friends He prepares difficulties,

216

God, the Eternal without need—what He wants,
He does. (II, 10)

دوست كهائى دادُلا، مـحبَّ مــارائى

خاصن خليلن كى سختيــون سهـــائى

الله الصــمد بى‌نياز جا ساكرى چاهى...

God loves to afflict those whom He loves—just as the *hadith* says, "The most afflicted ones are the prophets. . . ." Mystical poetry in Iran, Turkey, and Muslim India has often dwelt upon this aspect of suffering as the true manifestation of love, remembering Hallaj's daring word, "Happiness is from Him, but suffering is He Himself." Whether it be Hallaj's great commentator Ruzbehan Baqli in his *Sharh-e Shathiyat,* or the Sindhi poet Sachal Sarmast, they know that God comes to test those who love Him by showering afflictions upon them, and one of the most touching expressions of this knowledge is Sachal's poem in which he enumerates all the martyrs of love, from Noah and Abraham to his own near contemporaries in India, such as Sarmad, the "heretic" poet of the Mughal court, and Shah Inayat of Jhok, slain by the representatives of the Delhi government. But all these heroes knew, again, that one *hadith qudsi* promises the martyrs of love: "Who My beauty kills, I am His blood-money." And this conviction gives them strength to endure the most cruel afflictions.

Shah Abdul Latif closes this chapter with a *wa'y* in which he once more sings of the battle field in the plains of Kerbela, an area without water, without rain, but:

From the side of Fate, the black clouds of grief
    have come
Seeing the hardship of Mir Hussein, the prophets
    have cried bitterly,
Angels, skies, earth tremble, from above the
    Throne came sobbing.

جُهر ورائى جهورىَ، جهليا طرف سندى تقدير

پسى سخى ميرحسين جى زنو نبينُ زارون زار

ماك، فلك، ذرق ذبى آئى عَرشَ مثان اوچنگارَ

The following chapter goes into a more detailed description of the final battle, and Prince Hussein is described as the bridegroom:

with flower embroidered dresses, O man, be
    prepared for the wedding! (III, 10)

217

كانذ كلارين كپزين ورا! و ناهيو اأ

And he is admonished to walk forward. Shah uses here an allusion to Sindhi wedding is celebrated. The bridegroom has decorated his horse, and, we may conclude, he rides to his fatal battle proudly, decorated, and embellished, in the company of his faithful friends as if he were a real bridegroom, meeting his bride and experiencing union. The fact that the anniversary of the death of a saint is also called *urs* (wedding) looms large behind this imagery: death is the mystical marriage. And the one who has "given his head in the arena has honored his elders" (III, 14).

The fourth chapter turns first to the treacherous Kufians: The Kufis have written a paper, taking an oath by God:

> We are following you, you are our King,
> Come once here that the throne may be handed
>   over to you. (IV, 6)

كوفين كاغذ لكيو، وچ وجهى الله
اسين تابع تنهنجا، تون اسانجو شاه
هيكر هيذي اأ نه تخت تابيني تنهنجي

But "The Kufis in Kerbela did not give water to drink," and the Prophet is implored for help. The old motif of the bird that came to the Prophet's tomb is elaborated here:

> The morning bird has come in the morning,
>   traveling,
> To the sanctuary of the Prophet it complained:
> "The heroes have been slain, get up, Mir
>   Muhammad Arabi!"
>
> The morning bird has come yesterday from Kerbela:
> "I am sullied by blood, the situation is confused,
> The bridegrooms have been annihilated, the friends
>   of Mir Hussein!" (IV, 9, 10)

پره پکي آليو، صبح سوارو
روضي پاس روسل جي، هنيائين هاکارو
مانجهين کيو مارو، چڑه، ميرمحمد عربي!

پره پکي آئيو، کربلا مان کال
آه آلودو رت مه حيرت گذيو حال
گهوث و تاهيا کال، پيلي ميرحسين جا

218

And the *wa'y* is a sad complaint about the imams who have remained all day in the desert and have sent a little crane to their grandfather to tell him the sad news.

In the following chapter, Shah regrets that Mir Hassan is not with Mir Hussein, otherwise he would come like a moth to be with his brother; then, the poet goes into the story of Hurr, who joined the faithful, coming from the army of Yazid:

> Hurr has come, manly,
> "I am a lover of fire, a butterfly,
>   a moth,
> The messenger of the Lord, the Prophet,
>   your grandfather should be content
>   with me,
> This honorable secret, bridegroom, I ask
>   it from above!" (V, 6)

حرؑ هلي آئيو، مانجهي مردانو:
آهيا عاشق آگ جو، پتنگ، پروانو،
مان راضي ثئي رسول ربؑ جو، نبي تو نانو
هي سُر سمانو، گهوٺَ مٺان ٺي گهوريان.

For "Hurr's right guidance has come from pre-eternity," and the Koranic verse "God does not burden a soul with what it cannot endure" is quoted for him (V, 7). His beard has become red from blood and his turban shines like the moon in the fourteenth night in the place so that his mother on doomsday will smile. "Bravo to the hero who has given his head into pieces!" (V, 9)

تنهن سوره کي شاباس، جو مَئي پڙ پرزا ثئي

The use of the word *pirr*, "place, arena" is certainly important, for it also designates, in Sindhi, the *imam barah,* and thus is the most fitting expression for a Muharram event. In the following lines, the poet connects the shining turban of the hero with the light verse of the Koran, whose manifestation is seen here on earth, and likewise with the Koranic saying "Their signs are in their faces" (Sura 48/29): these words are the pearl strings for the hero whose face is reddened by blood. Ali himself will wipe away the drops of blood, and the Creator will forgive every sin as exchange for the blood thus shed.

The *wa'y* once more takes up these themes, and ends with the note that even:

> Duldul, the Shah's horse, had a red caparison.

دلدل گهوڙو شاه جو، مٺس لال پلاڻي

219

And now the battle is over. Everyone, including the faithful Duldul, is covered with blood, and Shah Latif begins his last chapter by admonishing the vultures not to pluck out the eyes of the martyrs, which are like stars. Once more he remembers that the beloved heroes did not stay in the fort of Kufa, but rather sacrificed their heads, for they "are fighting for God's sake" (Sura 5/59), that is the work they do:

يى هدوون فى سبيلالله كمُ اهوئى كنِ

The houris bind rose chains, flower decorations
for the martyrs. (VI, 10, 11)

حورون هار يذَنِ، سهرا سهيدنِ كى

They have reached the place of mystical union, and the word *sahra* once more points to the wedding ceremony, when the bridegroom wears the colorful cover over his face.

First the brothers, secondly the nephews, thirdly
the dear darling friends . . .

هلك پانى، ييا پائثپبا، ثيان جانى جگر يا

All of them have gone out from Kufa, and reached Paradise.

Paradise is their place, overpowering they
have gone to Paradise,
They have become annihilated in God, with
Him they have become He,
Lord, show the face of those with grace! (VI, 12)

جِنت سندين جوءِ، فائقَ هليا فردوس ذى

فانى ثيا فىالله مه هوءِ سين ثيا هوءِ

ربَ ذيكارِنِين روءِ، أنين جى احسان سين

That means, they have attained the highest mystical state, that of *fana fi Allah,* and have been united with Him, becoming He *(hu).* The ideal of mystical Islam is clearly expressed here.

Once more Shah Abdul Latif takes up the more popular motif of weeping for Shah Hussein:

Three communities have wept for Hassan, for Mir
Hussein:
Men in the house, animals in the wilderness,
angels in the height,
Birds have beaten themselves: The beloved ones
have gone away!
Allah! give victory to the princes, true God! (VI, 14)

حسن، ميرحسين كى، رنو ثن ثولن

گهر ماژهين، جهنگِ مرونين، أپن مو ملكن،

پكين پاك پچاژيو، نه ثريو هوت وجِن

الا، شهزادانِ، سوپون دِنِين، سيحا ذئى

220

And he concludes:

> Those who have no pain of Hassan and Mir Hussein,
> the Creator, the powerful Lord, will not forgive
> them. (V, 15)

حسن، ميرحسين جو، جن نه هنئڙى جار
خالق، ربّ جبّار، كين مرهيندو تن كي

and closes with a *wa'y* that calls for constant weeping, although again he admits that:

> What has happened to the imams: God Himself
> has created it.

جيكي امامن سين ٿيو، سوپان ذلءَ پيدا كيو

It seems to me that Shah Abdul Latif's *Sur Kedaro* shows a most fascinating blending of folk tradition and high mystical experience. On the one hand, Imam Hussein is seen, as in hundreds of poems, as the martyr, fighting in the service of God, a martyr whose fate should be duly mourned by everyone. Those who do not pity him will not be forgiven, and although the sad fate of the Imam was predestined from the day of *alast*, still, animals, men, and angels weep for their sake, and their departure—the departure of the lighted stars—has left the world in darkness. On the other hand, Hussein becomes the model of the loving mystic who follows the pre-eternal call for love and willingly takes upon himself suffering and death in order not only to reach Paradise as the bridegroom reaches the festive wedding place, but rather to become completely annihilated in God. The two trends are closely intertwined in Shah's account of the events of Kerbela, but we may not be wrong to assume that the mystical aspect of this suffering was more important for him than the external one: Shah Hussein becomes, once more, a spiritual brother of the martyr mystic Hallaj, and also a spiritual brother of and model for the heroines of Shah's Sindhi folk tales: it is no accident that the tragic story of the loving Sassui is once told in the melody "Hussein," which was usually sung for Muharram dirges. If I were asked which lines of *Sur Kerdaro* seem most revealing to me, I would choose the remark:

> In their martyrdom was all the coquetry of Love:
> Some intoxicated people may understand
> the mystery of the case of Kerbela.

17

Muharram Ceremonies in India

Syed Husain Ali Jaffri

The cold-blooded massacre at Kerbela on the tenth of Muharram of Imam Hussein, the grandson of the Holy Prophet Muhammad and the son of Ali and Fatemeh, along with his relatives, companions, and friends, is observed all over the world wherever Muslims live. However, the manner of its observance differs from place to place. India, which has a very large population of Muslims, is famous for the great zeal with which the martyrdom of Imam Hussein is observed by Muslims and Hindus alike. This observance, however, is not at all like the Iranian practice, which centers in the ritual theatre, the Ta'ziyeh. In this unique dramatic presentation, performers and spectators alike participate in the reenactment of the tragedy of Kerbela. The word *ta'ziyeh* has a different connotation in India, referring not to the theatre, the drama presented on its stage, but to an actual object, a small reproduction of the tomb of Hussein. This is carried in Muharram processions, accompanied by various symbolic devices which illustrate the Kerbela legends.

The practice of *Ta'ziyeh-dari* (Ta'ziyeh Ceremonies) was first introduced in India by Timur-Lang. The Mughal Emperors firmly established it as a custom, which gradually became popular with the masses. The parade, or procession, became a spectacular event, evoking great interest and religious fervor. Here the *ta'ziyeh,* since it is a replica of the tomb of Imam Hussein situated in Kerbela, commands the utmost respect from Muslims and non-Muslims alike.

The making of the *ta'ziyeh* has developed into a fine art over the centuries. They differ in their overall design and size, each city having its own peculiar version. One can easily distinguish the *ta'ziyeh* of Delhi from those of Lucknow, Hyderabad and Calcutta, etc. Even in the same city no two are likely to be identical. There are many varieties of *ta'ziyeh.* Those which are permanent are kept throughout the year for *ziyarat* (pilgrimage) are called *zareeh.* They are generally made of wood and metal with gold and silver plating. Every historical, or big *imambarah* (shrine) has its own *zareeh.* Usually *ta'ziyeh* are made of bamboo-sticks, ivory, paper, and other beautiful pieces of art work and handicraft. Sizes also vary. Some are small and some are five to six meters high. They are also made of newly grown wheat or barley and other similar plants which give them added beauty. I have seen in hilly areas *ta'ziyeh* made of branches of trees and decorated with leaves and flowers. All such *ta'ziyeh* are buried at the termination of the procession on Ashura day or on *Arba'iyn* (observance forty days after death) which will be described below.

The *Rowzeh-khani* and *Nuhe-khani* (dramatic narration of the life, deeds, suffering, and death of the Shi'ite martyrs and the dirges) came to India from Iran. In earlier days, practically all the *Nuhe-khani* were done in Persian, and even now the compositions in this sweet language form an important part of the recitations. It is also an historical fact that various Ulemas (learned religious leaders), traders, artists, poets, and writers migrated from Iran to India from time to time, and made India their home. The Indians were very impressed and influenced by their culture and system of *Azadari* (mourning for the Martyrs) which took deep roots in all parts of the country. One can still hear the famous Persian *Nuhe* during Muharram:

> Yousef-e gulgoun qaba ah Ali Akbarem
> Gum shudeh dar Kerbela ah Ali Akbarem

The great Sufis who migrated to India also added to the observance of Muharram and *Ta'ziyeh-dari* and laid much stress on *Azadari.* The following quatrain of the revered Sufi saint of Ajmer, Hazrat Khajeh Muinuddin Chishtie Gharib Nawaz, has gained international and everlasting fame.

شاهست حسین پادشاهست حسین

دینست حسین دین پناهست حسین

سر داد نداد دست در دست یزید

حقاً که بنائ لااللهست حسین

In India, Lucknow is the centre of *Ta'ziyeh-dari.* It took deep roots during the rule of Shahan-e Oudh. In addition to small *imambarahs* *(Azakhaneh,* or houses of mourning), three big *imambarahs* were built by the Oudh kings, i.e., Asafuddaula, Husainabad, and Shah Najaf. The Kerbela of Talkatorn, Dargah of Kazamain are also historical *imambarahs*.

During Muharram, *ta'ziyeh* and *zareeh* form the main part of the celebrations. From the first of Muharram, practically all the *azakhanehs* are decorated with *alams,*[1] *ta'ziyeh* and *zareeh. Majales-e Aza* (mourning assemblies) are held in big *imambarahs*. In certain parts of the country non-Muslims also conduct Ta'ziyeh celebrations and hold *Majales-e Aza* during Muharram and *Arba'iyn*. On the seventh of Muharram, there are processions of *mehndi*[2] (a *zareeh* which symbolizes the marriage of Qasem, the son of Imam Hassan, with Fatemeh Kubra, the daughter of Imam Hussein, in Kerbela, followed by *Zuljanah*[3] and *alams.* Though the procession of *mehndi* occurs in practically every part of India, yet in Lucknow, it has its own historical background. This mile-long procession includes *tabarrukkat* (food or drink offered to persons attending different Muharram rituals) which in olden days were brought by the Oudh rulers. It is embellished by rows of elephants,[4] horses carrying black banners, and army bands. The procession passes through the main streets of the city and is attended by thousands of persons. On the ninth of Muharram the entire night is spent in *marsiyeh-khani* (elegiac recitation) and *Nuhe-khani* (dirge singing) in the *imambarahs*. In other words, a *shab-bidari* (night vigil) is observed. On the tenth of Muharram, *ta'ziyeh* are taken out in processions which gradually proceed toward the local Kerbelas with *Zuljanah* and *alams* and with *Matam (sineh-zani* or breast-beaters) and *Nuhe-khani.* The *ta'ziyeh* reach the Kerbelas by the evening and are buried before sunset. After sunset, *Majles-e Sham-e Ghariban* (supper of the displaced persons) is held. *Azadari* (mourning in Lucknow continues till the eighth of Rabiul Awwal. During this period processions of *ta'ziyeh* go out from different *imambarahs* on different dates which have been assigned to each *imambarah* by ancient custom. Again, the observance of *Araba'iyn* is not less important than the observance of Muharram. On this day, as on the tenth of Muharram, the processions of *ta'ziyeh* accompanied by *Zuljanah* and *alams* are taken out on a large scale and proceed to various Kerbelas with *Matam* and *Nuhe-khani.* In the evening, these *ta'ziyeh* are buried with *Fateheh-khani.*

In Lucknow, the eighth of Rabiul Awwal is the most important day. It is the last day of mourning. The traditional *zareeh* is taken out in procession early in the morning. As this holiday is not observed in all the cities, most people from towns and villages come to Lucknow to participate in the procession, and so it becomes the biggest assembly of the year. The formation of the procession is the same as that of the tenth of Muharram or *Araba'iyn.*

Delhi, the capital of India, is not in any way second to Lucknow in the

Muharram celebrations. Here also there is a *ta'ziyeh* procession on the ninth and tenth of Muharram, *Arba'iyn,* and the seventh of Rabiul Awwal. It goes out from the city and reaches the historical Kerbela of Aliganj in New Delhi by evening.

The *Arba'iyn* is also observed at Dargah-e Shah-e Mardan, Aliganj, where a big crowd attends the *Majlis-e Aza* addressed by prominent speakers of various faiths and religions, and renowned Ulemas. After the *Majles-e Aza,* a procession of *ta'ziyeh, Zuljanah* and *alams* starts from this Dargah and ends at the Kerbela Aliganj. Dargah-e Shah-e Mardan is an historical monument, and has what is believed to be the footprint of Imam Ali in one of its shrines.

The Muharram celebrations of Calcutta, Bombay, and Madras are also worth mentioning. There are old historical *imambarahs* where *majales* are held and processions of *ta'ziyeh* are taken out.

Hyderabad again is a city of *imambarahs* and *Azakhanehs* tastefully decorated with *zareeh* and *alams.* "Hazrat Bibi-Ka-Alam" is taken out in a huge procession. The *ta'ziyeh* of Hyderabad is also famous. In Hyderabad and also in Bombay many Iranians have settled down, and have richly added to the success of *Ta'ziyeh-dari.*

Matam is also performed on burning coalfires in Lucknow, Delhi, Madras, Calcutta, and other parts of the country. Our Hanafi brethren and Sufis also celebrate with *ta'ziyeh,* hold *Majales-e Aza* to commemorate the memory of the *Shahedan-e Kerbela* (Martyrs of Kerbela), but do not do *sineh-zani* like Shi'a Muslims.

The Government of India extends all help and patronage to maintain law and order and to make the *ta'ziyeh* procession a great success.

Some former Hindu Maharajas of India also took an active interest in *Ta'ziyeh-dari.* The former Maharaja of Gwalior used to take part in an official *ta'ziyeh* procession, walking with the procession barefooted.

Among the Hindus who observe Muharram in a big way are the Mohyal Brahmins. They have the surnames of Datt and Vaid (decendants of the ancient Indian sage Bharadwaj), Chhibbar (descendants of Bhargava), Bali (descendants of Parashara), Mohan (descendants of Kashyapa), Lau (descendants of Vasishtha), and Bhimwal (descendants of Koshal). Mohyals have a prominent place in the annals of India and in the affairs of Arabia, Central Asia, Afghanistan, Persia and China.

When they were in Arabia, it was commonly sung about the Datts:

Wah Datt Sultan
Hindu ka Dharam
Mussalman ka Iman
Wah Datt Sultan
Adha Hindu, Adha Mussalman

225

Mohyals were never forced to embrace Islam. On the other hand, fraternal bonds evolved between the Datt Chief, Sultan Rahab, and the descendants of the Prophet Muhammad, Hassan and Hussein. According to tradition, Mohyals were allies of Hussein in *Jang-e Kerbela* (battle of Kerbela). Later, Sultan Rahab and the Mohyals avenged the defeat at Kerbela. Consequently, the descendants of the Prophet, i.e., the Sayyeds, continued to show great reverence to Mohyals as dauntless defenders of humanity.

After avenging the defeat of Kerbela and extending their influence to Iran and Afghanistan they reentered India, through the northwest and the Arabian Sea, spreading out in the Indian states of Pubjab, Sind, Kashmir, Uttar Pradesh, Bihar, Bengal and Madhya Pradesh.

On their way home from Arabia, the Mohyals established a Brahmin dynasty in Kabul also where, according to Sir A. Cunningham, they reigned from about A.D. 860 to A.D. 950. Even today Mohyals residing in Kabul are called Diwans (ministers).

Sir T. P. Russell Stracey, a British historian, has acknowledged that the martial instincts of the Mohyals, cherished and confirmed by the noblest traditions, would countenance nothing subversive of discipline. And the annals of the Mughal, Maratha, Sikh, and British governments record no instance of treachery as far as this community is concerned.

For over ten years I have delivered lectures in Jammu on the tragedy of Kerbela during Muharram and *Arba'iyn,* and I always noticed the womenfolk of Datt Brahmin offering *chadars (reeda,* i.e., pieces of muslin cloth), in memory of Zainab and Kulsum. The Husseini Brahmin march in the *ta'ziyeh* procession up to the local Kerbelas and return home after paying their homage to the *Shahedane-Kerbela.*

Hindu and Sikh poets of great repute like Pandit Amar Nath Sahir, Munshi Sheshchander Talib, Malkush-shoara Ufaq Lucknowi, Gopinath Amam Lucknowi, Sardar Darshan Singh Duggal, Professor Javed Vashisht, Rajkavi Inderjeet Singh Tulsi, Pandit Labhoo Ram Josh, Pandit Arsh Malsiani, Kunwar Mohinder Singh Bedi Sehar, Professor Talok Chand Mehroom and many others have given us masterpieces of elegy, and poems on the tragedy of Kerbela, and their work forms an important part of the literature.

I can confidently say that in India *Ta'ziyeh-dari* has gone a long way to advance the gospel of National Integration and Fellow-feelings.

I may also make mention of some historical religious shrines where pilgrims come to pay homage from all over the country, and where *ta'ziyeh* processions are held to celebrate Muharram and *Arba'iyn.* The Tomb of Shahed-e Sales Nurullah Shahed Sustari in Agra, the Tomb of Shahed-e Rabey in Delhi, the Najaf-e Hind Jogipura, Hussein Tekri-Jaora, Taragarh-Ajmer and Ali-Maula-Ka-Pahar (Mountain of Hazrat Ali), Hyderabad, are some of them.

Processions of *tabuts* (representing a bier or coffin) are also held on the twenty-first of Ramazan to mark the martyrdom of the Prince of the Faithful—Hazrat-e Ali. Such *tabuts* also form a part of *ta'ziyeh* processions in Muharram and *Arba'iyn*.

In India, the local culture has added to the success of *Ta'ziyeh-dari*. We have borrowed many new ideas and specimens of arts to make *Ta'ziyeh-dari* more attractive. The non-Muslim speakers and poets have also greatly added to our success, and are an important part of our celebration. Their speeches and poems are published in book form. The Government of India has also published an excellent book, *Moharram in Two Cities—Lucknow and Delhi*,[6] which contains pictures of *ta'ziyeh* processions and important *imambarahs* of the two cities and full details of the Muharram and *Arba'iyn* celebrations.

NOTES

1. An *alam* represents the banner of Imam Hussein's army and is considered to be the most important symbol of mourning. The *alams* are of different colors and sizes with golden or silver tops (Panjeh).

2. A *mehndi* is just like a *ta'ziyeh; mehndi* is a Hindustani word, used by the bride during marriage.

3. A *Zuljanah* is the representation of the faithful horse of Imam Hussein.

4. Elephants, camels, and horses form the front portion of the procession carrying *alams* and black banners, the signs of mourning and grief. These banners are carried in the front section of the procession, as are *ammaries,* which represent the seats with "purdah" in which the harem of Imam Hussein traveled to Kerbela.

5. *Tabuts* represent the biers of coffins of Imam Hassan, Imam Hussein and Hazrat-e Ali Asghar, the six-month-old son of Imam Hussein at the time of his martyrdom. The *tabut* of Hazrat-e Ali is also taken out in procession on the twenty-first of Ramazan. Other features of processions may be the *burraq,* which represents the flying horse of the Prophet Muhammad, the *kafani,* a cloth tied on the heads of the children to receive the blessings of Imam Hussein; drums and *naqqaras,* which in some places are played in mourning tempo in front of the *ta'ziyeh* procession.

6. This book is a collective work and was published in Delhi in 1966. It is a part of *Census of India, 1961,* monograph series.

18

SHI'ISM AND ASHURA IN SOUTH LEBANON

MICHEL M. MAZZAOUI

There are two important Shi'a *(ithna'ashari)* [1] communties in the Arab countries, beside Iraq, that have not received much attention by scholars who deal with the general topic of Shi'ism. These are the closely-knit Shi'a community of Jabal 'Amil in south Lebanon, and the more diversified Shi'a groups of the Qatif region, Bahrain, and al-Hasa on the Arab side of the Persian Gulf.

At a colloquium in Strasbourg in May 1968, the leader of the Lebanese Shi'a community, Imam Musa as-Sadr, participated with a paper in Arabic on the subject of "The Imami communities in Lebanon and Syria of today." It seems that Imam Musa as-Sadr had intended to supply a summary in French of his contribution at the colloquium for purposes of publication. This however did not take place; and the papers that were read at that meeting appeared in 1970 under the title *Le Shi'isme Imamite*[2] without the Imam's paper.

There are a few Arab writers (mainly Lebanese and Syrian) who have dealt in their writings with the Shi'a community of Lebanon. These include such well-known names as Muhammad Jawad Maghniyah, Muhammad Kazim Makki, 'Arif and Ali az-Zayn, Muhammad Mahdi Shams al-Din, and others.[3] The voluminous writer, the late Sayyed Muhsin al-Amin, treated the subject of *ithna'ashari* Shi'ism in a grand style in his *A'yan ash-Shi'ah*.[4] This multi-volume work, almost an encyclopedia of Shi'a knowledge, contains much useful information on Shi'ism in Lebanon and Syria. There is even a specialized journal that deals almost exclusively with the Shi'a movement in Lebanon. This is the well-known and long-lived *al-'Irfan* which is published in Saida (Sidon), the main city in south Lebanon.[5]

Works by these essentially traditional scholars are quite useful and often contain material that is not to be found elsewhere. Unfortunately, however, much of this writing does not meet the rigorous standards of modern scholarship. A large part of the material presented is polemical in nature and often does not serve any useful purpose. Some of the more recent issues of *al-'Irfan* contain articles that leave much to be desired.

Much less is known about the other Shi'a community referred to above, namely, the Qatif-Sahrayn-Hasa group.[6] The Shi'a adherants in this geographical area live under the Saudi-Hanbali-Wahhabi rule in Qatif and al-Hasa, or under the Al-Khalifah regime in Bahrayn, and research on them and their history has not yet been forthcoming.[7]

Older, more classical, works on Shi'ism contain a wealth of information on these two Shi'a communities (of Lebanon and the Gulf), on the great scholars who lived in these areas, and on their contributions to Shi'a ideas and to general Muslim thought. It is sufficient to mention in this context the comprehensive *Majalis al-Mu'minin* by Qadi Nurallah Shushtari (in Persian), the great *Rawdat al-jannat* by Khwansari (in Arabic), and the specialized *Amal al-amil* by al-Hurr al-'Amili.[8] The undigested material in these and other works has not yet been fully utilized in secondary works.

The fact that very little scholarly work has been undertaken on these two Shi'a communities of south Lebanon (Jabal 'Amil) and northeast Arabia (Qatif-Hasa-Bahrayn) is to be strongly deplored. No modern scholar can do any serious research on *imami (ithna'ashari)* Shi'ism without coming across 'Amilis, Qatifis, Ahsa'is, and Bahraynis (or Bahranis) who have dealt with various aspects of Shi'a *ithna'ashari* thought during several centuries of Islamic history. The first and second *shahids* (martyrs), Ahmad ibn Makki and Zayn ad-Din al-'Amili, are luminaries in *imami* theology and *fiqh*.[9] The *Lum'ah ad-Dimashqiyah* of the former, and the *Sharh al-Lum'ah* of the latter are milestones in their genre. The activities of Shaykh Ali ibn 'Abd al-'Ali al-Karaki and of Shaykh-e Baha'i, both of the Jabal 'Amil area, made possible to a considerable degree the spread of *ithna'ashari* Shi'ism in Iran under the Safavid Shahs Isma'il, Tahmasb, and Abbas.[10] In fact, the chapter on the establishment of Shi'ism in Iran after the rise of the Safavid dynasty in the early sixteenth century cannot be written without direct reference to the role played by 'Amili scholars from south Lebanon who flocked into the country as soon as the new regime gained military and political control. And finally, Shaykh Ahmad-i Ahsa'i was the founder in the late eighteenth century of the famous "Shaykhi School." [11]

In short, the so-called "Three early Muhammads" (Kulayni, Ibn Babavayh, and Tusi "Shaykh at-Ta'ifah") who flourished before and partly during the great era of the Buyid dynasty, may have been responsible for the early efflorescence of Shi'a *imami* thought during the classical Islamic period, but the "Three later Muhammads" (al-Hurr al-'Amili, Mulla Muhsin-i Fayz, and the great Muhammad Baqir Majlisi) who flourished during the high Safavid period are not possible to understand and explain without reference to the 'Amilis, Qatifis, Bahraynis, and Ahsa'is who in many ways laid the foundations for what may be referred to as "Iranian Safavid Shi'ism." [12] The influence of these latter-day Shi'a scholars on the *ishraqi* philosophy of Mulla Sadra and Mir Damad—not to mention Mulla Hadi Sabzavari—has yet to be fully investigated.[13]

This is the high-Islam Shi'a orthodox picture as it has been preserved by the great Shi'a *'ulama* throughout many centuries: scribal, argumentative, elaborate, dogmatic, but balanced. It was made to start with Hazrat-e-Ali, through Muhammad, from the beginning of time, and concealed the Twelfth Imam, the Mahdi, till the end of time in inexorable religious-eschatological continuity.

On the other hand, the great Shi'a dimension of the Islamic tradition has with time developed a more human, folk-Islamic, popular aspect preserved in the Hussein-Kerbela-Ashura-Ta'ziyeh complex. Away from the formalism of the scholars, this aspect of Shi'a Islam has survived over the centuries and has kept Shi'ites of all countries united in their search for a more meaningful expression of their everyday life. Many Muslim peoples have shared in this tremendously vital experience: but the Shi'a Arabs who brought forth the family that held this tradition around its members (Muhammad, Fatemeh, Ali, Hassan, and Hussein), and the Iranians who established Shi'ism as the official religion in Iran with the advent of the Safavids in 1501—these two Muslim peoples have among themselves kept the popular, folk-Islamic aspect of this tradition alive in their countries for a very long time. There is every reason to believe that this self-expression of the religious image will develop, artistically and otherwise, forever—or at least until such time as religion ceases to be a meaningful dimension to the everyday life of Muslim communities.

However, it appears that there has always been a difference between the Arab and the Iranian approach to the problem. The former is harsher, social, down-to-earth realistic; the latter idealistic, more mythical, more sympathetic.

Take the well-known Arab historian Ibn Kathir (d. A.H. 774), for example. As is generally accepted, he makes the earliest, somewhat de-

230

tailed, references to Muharram festivities (with some of his material based on earlier references by Ibn al-Athir and other historians). Here is a translation of the text in Arabic of one of these references; it is from his *al-Bidayah wa al-Nihayah,* and he is chronicling the events of the year A.H. 352 in Baghdad under Mu'izz ad-Dawlah ibn Buwayh. Ibn Kathir says:

On the tenth of Muharram of this year [A.H. 352], Mu'izz ad-Dawlah Ibn Buwayh, may God disgrace him, ordered that the markets be closed, and that the women should wear coarse woolen hair cloth, and that they should go into the markets with their faces uncovered/unveiled and their hair disheveled, beating their faces and wailing over Hussein ibn Ali ibn Abi Talib. The people of the *Sunna* could not prevent this spectacle because of the *Shi'a's* large numbers and their increasing power *(zuhur),* and because the Sultan was on their side.[14]

Here we have what may perhaps be one of the earliest descriptions of the mournful days of Muharram. It is in fact the tenth of Muharram, the Day of Ashura. The order comes from above, from the Shi'a Buyid ruler of the land (the Sunni Abbasid caliphate is in eclipse).

In the same year, A.H. 352, on the tenth day of the last month, Dhu al-Hijjah, the anniversary of the Day of Ghadir Khumm,[15] Ibn Kathir details a festive and happy Shi'a holiday as follows:

On the tenth of Dhu al-Hijjah of this year [i.e., A.H. 352], Mu'izz ad-Dawlah Ibn Buwayh ordered that Baghdad should be decorated and the markets be opened at night as during the holidays; and that the drums be beaten and the bugles sounded, and fires lit at the entries to the houses of army commanders *(umara')* and the police (sing. *shurtah),* in happy commemoration of the Feast of Ghadir—i.e., Ghadir Khumm. It was a strange and memorable/well-attended *(mashhud)* occasion, and an ugly, flagrant, and reprehensible innovation *(bid'ah).*[16]

Again the order comes from above, from the same Mu'izz ad-Dawlah. In the earlier reference Ibn Kathir had already used a most uncomplimentary term after his name.

Over the next several years, and until the end of the Buyid regime and the coming of the Seljuks to power,[17] Ibn Kathir makes similar entries describing these Muharram-Ashura activities. In this next entry he uses the term *'aza' al-Hussein,* and describes the fighting that took place in the city between the Shi'ites *(ar-Rawafid)* and the Sunnis *(Ahl as-sunnah).* Looting of property also took place.

231

On the tenth of Muharram of this year [A.H. 353], the Shi'a community (ar-rafidah) celebrated the Ta'ziyeh ('aza') of Hussein as they did the year before. The Shi'ites and the Sunnites fought violently among each other on this day, and property was looted.[18]

The near riot conditions that prevailed on that day, including the looting of property, are a sign of the social malaise for which the religious occasion seems to have been a pretext. Ibn Kathir, however, does not follow this line of argument, but goes on to comment on the religious significance of the 'aza'/ta'ziyeh observances themselves. It is a takalluf, he says, for which there is no need in Islam. If it was a worthy act, he continues, the earlier and better centuries of Islam would have observed it. Expressing what may be construed as a touch of national pride he says that the early Muslims are more worthy and better qualified (awla) to make these observances [than the Buyids?]. The original Arabic is couched in more general terms, but the sentiment is clearly discernible:

This [celebration of Ashura] is a hypocritical religiousity/takalluf which is not condoned in Islam. If this occasion had been praiseworthy, the people of earlier centuries and the leaders and best [people] of this community (ummah) would have observed it—surely they are more entitled to it.[19]

Ten years later (under the year A.H. 363), Ibn Kathir makes the longest entry on the subject of Ashura. He describes a big riot (fitnah) between the Shi'ites and Sunnites of Baghdad, and at this point condemns both groups. He then makes reference to what began as a curious "theatrical performance" and ended in bloodshed:

In this year [i.e., A.H. 363] on Ashura, the despicable innovation was celebrated according to the custom of the Shi'a (rawafid). A great riot broke out in Baghdad between the Sunnites and the Shi-'ites (rafidah): both factions being small of mind or are totally mindless, and are far from level-headed. For a group of the Sunnites placed a woman [on a horse/camel?] calling her A'ishah, while one of them took the name of Talhah and another that of az-Zubayr, and set out to fight the followers of Ali. As a result of that large numbers of both factions were killed.[20]

It is not clear, of course, whether this was intended to have been a performance or whether actual fighting was to take place.[21] It is curious, however, that it was the Sunnites who mounted this seemingly "theatrical" act. Later Ta'ziyeh performances concentrated more on Hussein and his small band of followers at Kerbela.

From these few references on the Muharram-Ashura activities made by Ibn Kathir in his *al-Bidayah wa al-Nihayah,* it appears that the Arab historian's approach to the entire issue is rather severe and quite unsympathetic. Aside from remarking only once in passing (with reference to the celebrations on the Day of Ghadir) that they were unusual *('ajib)* and memorable *(mashhud),* which may indicate a personal enjoyment of the spectacle, Ibn Kathir dismisses the entire thing as a reprehensible innovation which Islam does not need. He denounces both groups, Sunnites and Shi'ites, as "small-minded, or with no mind at all." He points out the social evils, the looting and the killing, that resulted from such activities. He is not touched by the human element and the popular folk dimensions of the occasion.

The more famous Ibn Khaldun, writing in the next generation, is even harsher and more stern in his judgement, perhaps because he makes his argument sound scientific (Ibn Kathir was evidently somewhat emotional at times). The North African historian gives his views on this well-known theory of *'asabiyah* which he applies to Hussein and his movement almost as a test-case. He refers to Hussein's *ahliyah* (qualifications) and *shawkah* (abilities or capabilities), justifying his actions in the former and almost condemning him in the latter. The argument is quite elaborate and deserves to be quoted in full:

Hussein believed that to rise against Yazid was incumbent *(muta'ayyin)* upon him because of the latter's sinfulness/dissolute life *(fisq)*—it is especially incumbent upon those who possess the power to do so. He thought that this applied to him because of his qualifications (sing. *ahliyah)* and capability/power *(shawkah).* He was in fact more than qualified; but as for his capability, he was wrong—may God be merciful unto him. For the tribal solidarity *('asabiyah)* of Muzar was in Quraysh, and the *'asabiyah* of Quraysh was in 'Abd Manaf, and the *'asabiyah* of 'Abd Manaf was surely in Banu Umayah—a fact recognized by Quraysh and everybody else. Nobody denied that. However, this situation was forgotten [or rather the people became oblivious to it] in early Islam because the people were amazed by the unusual events which had occurred, by the phenomenon of prophetic inspiration, and by the coming of the angels to help the Muslims. Custom was thus set aside, and the pre-Islamic *'asabiyah* and the disputes arising from it were forgotten. All that remained was the natural *'asabiyah* of protection and defense made use of in establishing the [new] religion and the performance of holy war *(jihad)* against the infidels. In a case like this, religion becomes paramount and custom is set aside. However, when the question of prophecy and the extraordinary events ended, rule *(al-hukm)* reverted somewhat to the [old] customs. *'Asabiyah* thus returned to the way it had been and to whomever it had

233

belonged; and so Muzar became more amenable to Banu Umayah than to any other group on the basis of conditions that had been prevalent before.[22]

On the basis of Ibn Khaldūn's theory of 'asabiyah, therefore, Hussain's movement was a mistake. For the pre-Islamic 'asabiyah of the Arabs, according to Ibn Khaldun's succinctly expressed argument, lies ultimately in the House of Umayah as recognized by all. During the prophetic and miraculous days of Muhammad this traditional 'asabiyah was laid aside (in favor of Banu Hashim), but as soon as the new religion was firmly established the situation reverted to its previous state and the Umayyeds recovered their supremacy. Thus Ibn Khaldūn is sternly correct, and there is no room in his rigorously balanced argument for Hussein or his cause.

This rather harsh position of the Sunni-Arab Muslim attitude toward the Hussein tradition made life very difficult for the Shi'a communities of Jabal 'Amil in south Lebanon (who, incidentally, claim a history that dates back to the Prophet's companion Abu Zarr al-Ghifari who is said to have been banished to that region by the Caliph 'Umar).[23] Their difficulties were further exacerbated during the Mamluk period when Syria (including Lebanon) was controlled from Cairo. This was the period that witnessed the martyrdom of Ibn Makki, "ash-Shahid al-Awwal" (the first martyr). The activities of Ibn Taymiyah in the next generation made things even worse.[24]

As regards Ta'ziyeh proper, the practice in south Lebanon with its center in the hilly town of Nabatiyah is said to have been a recent nineteenth-twentieth century import from Iran. It is difficult to document this, but perhaps it can be explained on the basis of the ostracized position of Jabal 'Amil during the long Ottoman period of three centuries. The 'Amilis, after losing another shahid,[25] naturally looked to Iraq and Iran for guidance. The old Lebanese-Safavid experience is now a reversed Iranian-Lebanese process. To a considerable degree this is still so today.

And aside from the religious fervor which is common to Ta'ziyeh both in Lebanon and in Iran, the situation in Jabal 'Amil has certain peculiarities most of which arise from the different political and geographical milieu. Some of these may be briefly noted as follows, bearing in mind that they are very closely interrelated:

1. The deprived status of the area which has led quite recently to the rise of the socio-political movement of the so-called Mahrumin (i.e., those "deprived" of social justice, etc.).[26]

2. The physical nearness of the region to the newly created state of Israel which borders it immediately to the south, and the presence in the area of a large community of Palestinians. Over the past three decades the assimilation between the 'Amilis and the Palestinians has reached a degree whereby, as a modern Lebanese sociologist puts it (in French, of course!): "Husayn, c'est la Palestine; Yazid n'est qu'une prefiguration du

Zionisme!" [27] It is a total identification of Hussein, the martyr of Kerbela, with the tragic fate of the Palestinians; and of the arch-enemy Yazid with the alien Zionist movement responsible for the tragedy.

3. The struggle, feudal or otherwise, between traditional families in the region (As'ads, Usayrans, Zayns, Khalils, etc.) and the helpless fate of the small farmers and peasants who seem to be totally lost in the middle.[28]

4. The commanding position and stature of the Lebanese-Iraqi-Iranian political-religious leader, Imam Musa al-Sadr. His charisma touches everything that happens in Jabal 'Amil and throughout the whole Shi'a community in all Lebanon. His "gray eminence" and powerful personality are felt in all political, social, and religious circles in the country.[29]

These conditions, peculiar to the Shi'a community in Jabal 'Amil, should be seen within the framework of a highly confused but essentially "free society" in Lebanon, as compared with say, the more centrally stable and somewhat more uniform political and social conditions in Iraq and Iran.

If one is permitted to make a final judgement in this context, one would like to say that in Iran Ta'ziyeh will safely develop (as indeed it has during the past several years) within the relative safety of art forms. This is politically neutral ground.[30] In Lebanon, on the other hand, I would venture to guess that Ta'ziyeh will remain for a long time to come an expression of "opposition, martyrdom, and revolt." [31]

Notes

1. I.e., "Twelve-Imam Shi'ism" as it is more popularly called. Unless otherwise stated, the term Shi'ism in this paper refers to this major group of the Shi'a (and not to the Isma'ilis, Zaydis, or *ghulāt*).

2. Published by Presses Universitaires de France, Paris, 1970. For reference to Imām Mūsā al-Sadr's paper, see note 1, p. 5.

3. For representative works by some of these writers, see for example, Muḥammad Kāẓim Makkī, *al-Haraka al-fikrīya wa al-adabīya fī Jabal 'Amil* (Beirut, 1963), and Muḥammad Mahdī Shams al-Dīn, *Thawrat al-Husain* (Beirut, 196?). Maghnīyah is more of a popularizer; see his *Ma'al-Shī'a al-Imāmīyah*, second edition (Beirut, 1956), and *al-Shī'a fi al-mīzān* (Beirut, 1974). 'Arif and 'Alī al-Zain have been associated with the editorship of the Shi'a journal *al-'Irfān;* see below, note 5.

4. Muhsin ibn 'Abd al-Karīm al-Amīn al-Husainī al-'Amilī, to give him his full name. More than 50 volumes of his *A'yān ash-Shī'a* were published, many of them several times reprinted.

5. The first issue of the Lebanese Shi'a journal *al-'Irfān* appeared in Muharram 1327/5 February 1909. Its founder was Ahmad 'Arif al-Zain.

6. See articles in *E.I.*[2] entitled "al-Bahrayn," by G. Rentz and W. E. Mulligan; "al-Hasā"/al-Ahsā', by F. S. Vidal; and the passing reference made to Jabal 'Amila in the article " 'Amila," by H. Lammens and W. Caskel. The Arabian American Oil

Company, ARAMCO, due to the nature of its work in Saudi Arabia's eastern province, undertook much social research in this area. It is to be hoped that this company will make the information it has collected over the years available to scholars in the field.

7. The University of Riyadh has accepted a paper by the present writer on the contributions of the Shi'a *'ulama* of Qatif-Hasa-Bahrayn, to be presented at a future conference on the history of the Arabian peninsula.

8. Majālis al-Mu'minīn is an early seventeenth-century work, while *Rawḍāt al-jannāt* is a nineteenth century Qajar compilation based on *Majālis* and other works. *'Amal al-'āmil* is devoted to scholars who hail from Jabal 'Amil.

9. Aḥmad ibn Makkī, "al-Shahīd al-Awwal," was executed in Damascus by Mamluk functionaries in the early fourteenth century; Zain al-Dīn, "al-Shahīd al-Thānī," met his death in Istanbul in the early seventeenth century at the hands of the Ottoman government.

10. On al-Karakī, see Khwānsārī, *Rawḍāt al-jannāt*, pp. 390ff., Khwānd-amīr, *Habīb al-siyar*, IV, 609-10, and al-Hurr al-'Amilī's *Amal al-āmil*, I, pp. 121-22 *passim*. On Shaykh-i Bahā'i (Muḥammad ibn Ḥusain Bahā' al-Dīn al-'Amilī) see a very short anonymous article in *E.I.²*.

11. See article on "Aḥmad-i Aḥsā'ī" in *E.I.²*. Professor Henry Corbin has dealt extensively with Shaykh Aḥmad-i Aḥsā'ī and the Shaykhi school.

12. E. G. Browne, *Literary History of Persia*, IV, 353-411. The chapter entitled "The orthodox Shi'a faith and its exponents, the Mujtahids and Mullas" continues to be a good comprehensive treatment.

13. Seyyed Hossein Nasr and Henry Corbin have dealt with the *ishraqi* School of Isfahan in several books, texts, and articles.

14. Ibn Kathīr, *al-Bidāya wa al-Nihāya* (Cairo: Maṭba'a al-Sa'āda, 1358 A.H.), XI, 243.

15. The Day of Ghadir marks the time when Ali was offered the caliphate while Abu Bakr and Umar were establishing the same.

16. Ibn Kathīr, *op. cit.*, XI, 243.

17. The century or so of Buyid power came to an end circa A.D. 1050 when the staunchly Sunni Seljuk Turks entered Baghdad.

18. Ibn Kathīr, *op. cit.*, XI, 253.

19. *Ibid.*, XI, 254. *Takalluf* in a modern sense means "affectation," while in a more classical context it refers to the concept of requiring someone to do more than he can possibly accomplish or, perhaps, more than is necessary to save his soul.

20. *Ibid.*, XI, 275.

21. The reference no doubt is to the battle of al-Jamal when Ali defeated A'isha and her faction and sent her under guard to Medina. Talhah and al-Zubayr, on the other hand, set up a shadow caliphate in the Hijaz while Ali was trying to consolidate his shaky rule in Kufah.

22. *Tārīkh al-'Allāma Ibn Khaldūn* (Beirut, 1961), Volume I, "al-Muqaddima," pp. 382-83. Cf. Franz Rosenthal's translation, I, 443-44.

23. See short article by J. Robson on "Abū Dharr al-Ghifārī," *E.I.²*

24. The Hanbali Ibn Taimiyah was strongly anti-Shi'a (especially against the extremist groups, e.g., the Nuṣairīs of northern Syria). He also wrote lengthy refutations of some of the leading Shi'a *ithnā'asharī* scholars, e.g., Ibn al-Muṭahhar al-Ḥillī.

25. Zain al-Dīn al-'Amilī, *al-Shahīd al-Thānī;* see above, note 9.

26. See the Beirut daily al-Nahār, 12 January 1974, for excerpts from an address by Imām Mūsā al-Ṣadr outlining some of the demands of the Mahrumin movement.

27. Waddah Chrara, *Transformations d'une manifestation religieuse dans un village du Liban-Sud (Ashoura),* (Beirut; Université Libanaise, Institut des Sciences Sociales, Centre de Recherches, 1968), p. 100.

28. The fact that the Shi'a in Lebanon constitute perhaps the largest single confessional group in the land has yet to be effectively utilized, politically and otherwise, by its utterly disunited leadership.

29. During the bloody civil war in Lebanon, 1975-1976, Imām Mūsā al-Ṣadr almost single-handedly put an end to the fighting (temporarily as it turned out!) by taking *bast* for a week or two in one of the local mosques. For a lengthy statement "explaining" his position regarding certain incidents which involved the Shi'a community toward the end of the war, see the Beirut daily *al-Nahār,* 12 August 1976. The statement was appropriately (!) made on the occasion of the birthday of the Twelfth Imam.

30. As a footnote here, however, I would like to refer to a curious comment made by S. H. Nasr at the Strasbourg colloquium referred to earlier in this paper when the contribution of Enrico Cerulli on *"Le theatre persan"* was being discussed. Professor Nasr is quoted as having remarked, "Dans certains milieux cultives iraniens, une nette tendance se dessine en faveur de l'etude de la *ta'ziye.* Le developpement de cette *ta'ziye* est du en grande partie a ces milieux qui s'apparentent a la gauche iranienne." *Le Shi'isme imamite,* p. 293.

31. To borrow an expression used by V. Minorsky in an article applied to Iran carrying the same title in *Unity and Variety in Muslim Civilization,* ed. G. von Grunebaum (Chicago, 1955).

19

The Muharram Observances in Anatolian Turkey

METIN AND

Ta'ziyeh performances and elaborate Muharram processions are to be found among the Turks, especially among the Azerbaijan Turks of Caucasia,[1] and there are some extant manuscripts of Ta'ziyeh plays in Turkish. For instance, out of 1054 Ta'ziyeh manuscripts in the Vatican Collection,[2] 35 are in Turkish,[3] only 4 are in Arabic, and the rest are in Persian. Yet in Anatolia there is no tradition of Ta'ziyeh performances, since the Sunni element is predominant there. Also in the traditional Anatolian Turkish theatre, tragedy does not exist, comedy being considered the only acceptable form of dramatic art. However, both at the urban and rural levels there is a great variety of dramatic forms. In the larger towns the most usual dramatic performances are *Ortaoyunu,* popular improvised comedies which very much resemble the Ta'ziyeh performances in the style in which they are presented and in their form and staging.[4] In the villages mummery farces and pantomimes are performed by the thousands, most of them survivals of seasonal fertility rites. They also are very much like the Ta'ziyeh performances in dramatic structure. Another dramatic form is story-telling by a *meddah,* or *kissahan,* whose repertoire contains episodes of the Kerbela Passion cycle. Similarly there are also *mersiye, nefes* (elegy)

238

and other literary forms depicting the Kerbela Passion, narrated or recited in the Muharram assemblies in dramatic fashion with the narrator gesticulating, shouting, singing and crying. Here the audience participates by weeping for the martyrs or cursing the slayers of Hussein.

In countries like Iran, where Turks are in the minority, their participation in the Muharram rites differs according to whether they are Shi'ites or Sunnis. For instance, a seventeenth-century Italian traveler who gives a detailed account of the Muharram mysteries he witnessed in Persia in 1694 mentions that "until the very end of the doleful festival, which the Persians call *Asciur* or mourning, no Turk can appear in public without great danger to his life." [5] Another seventeenth-century traveler who gives a detailed account of Persian Muharram mysteries in 1666 mentions that "... After them enter'd three hundred Turks, which were fled from the Borders of Turky. ..." [6] Yet some European writers erroneously associate the Ta'ziyeh tradition with Anatolian Turkey. For instance, an article, entitled "Turkish Theatre," giving short definitions of various dramatic forms, devotes most of its space to explaining Ta'ziyeh, identifying it with Turkey. [7] On the other hand, an Englishman who spent many years in rural Anatolia, in his article on Shi'a Turks, briefly describing Muharram observances in an Alevi village, clearly states that there is no Ta'ziyeh tradition among them. [8]

With these preliminaries in mind, I have divided my paper in the following manner: (1) Muharram mysteries in the Persian colony in Turkey; (2) Muharram observances—rites and beliefs especially among the Bektashi Order and village Alevis consisting of various heterodox tribes in Anatolia, and (3) Semi-dramatic literature of Kerbela in Turkey.

MUHARRAM MYSTERIES IN THE PERSIAN COLONY

Several foreign observers witnessed the processions and other Muharram observances of the Persian colony in Istanbul and gave a vivid and detailed description of them. [9] One such account is as follows:

The Persians resident in Constantinople form a kind of *regnum in regno,* and insist on their privilege of witnessing these religious atrocities every year. We were invited by the Persian Ambassador to be present at this performance, and found our way towards the evening in a large square, a *khan,* surrounded by houses and shops, planted with trees, and crowded with people. When it grew dark the houses were illuminated, and large bonfires were lighted, mostly with petroleum. The mixture of smells—petroleum, escaped gas, sewers, and humanity was terrible even in the open air. After waiting for some time, music could be heard, and the people made room for a large procession that marched in, consisting of more than a thousand men and boys, preceded by children dressed in white, some riding on horseback with grown-up men at their sides, gesticulating, reciting, and crying. Then followed three companies in white shirts, some carrying swords, others carrying heavy iron chains, and all shouting rhythmically, "Vah Hassan! Vah Hussein." The first set struck their bare chests first with their right hand, then with the left. The next company passed by swinging their chains from side to side with a graceful dancing motion. The third and last lot passed along sideways in two long lines facing each other, each man holding his neighbour's girdle with the left hand, whilst they swung their swords in unison with the right. Between these rows marched men reciting the story of Hassan and Hussein. The whole procession passed on thus, slowly around the khan and left by the gate at which they entered.

We wondered why we had been told that only people of strong nerves should attend this celebration. Whilst the procession was visiting another khan we were refreshed with the most delicious tea. After a time we again heard the strains of music, this time louder and wilder, and the people all around us began to show signs of great and increasing excitement and agitation as the procession, lighted by the lurid glare of the petroleum bonfires, re-entered the khan. The children passed by as before, followed by a white horse, on which sat two white doves, emblematic of the souls of Hassan and Hussein. The cries of "Vah! Vah! Hassan! Hussein!" grew louder and louder, many spectators joining in whilst the first company passed beating their bare breasts with such violence and regularity that it sounded like sledge hammers coming down on blocks of granite. The second company passed swinging their chains over their heads, and bringing them down on their now bare backs till the flesh was lacerated and streaming with blood. Then last and worst of all, came the men with the swords, cutting themselves in good earnest, particularly on their heads, so that one had to stand back to avoid the blood which spurted forth in all directions. Soon their white shirts were crimson with blood, their heads looked as if they were covered with a red fez. The pavement was running with blood; and yet these people marched on as if on parade. Very few indeed fell out. One man fell down dead before our eyes. At last a kind of police came forward, holding their sticks over the people so as to prevent their hacking themselves to death in their frenzy. There was little violence and there was no trace of drunkenness. The people, though densely crowded, were perfectly orderly, and we saw old rough men crying and shedding bitter tears, and uttering the names Hassan and Hussein with many sobs. They were all men of the lower and lowest classes as far as one could judge from their outward appearance. If you had asked one of them why they cried so bitterly, they would probably have had nothing to answer but "Oh, Hassan and Hussein!" It is true there were some men who recited the history of

Hassan and Hussein, but no one seemed to listen to them—their voices were completely drowned out by the regular shouts of "Hassan and Hussein!" [10]

Yet another observer gives a more detailed account of it. [11] An English translation of it exists [12] but since I could not obtain it in the Turkish libraries at the present time, I am rendering it in a free translation by paraphrasing the important parts.

The Persian colony in Istanbul at the end of the last century numbered between ten and twelve thousand. They were mainly merchants of carpets, shawls, astrakhan, tea, tobacco for water pipes, arms and finally chiseled metal vases. They occupied three *Hans,* the largest and the best known of all being Valide Han where five to six thousand Persians were domiciled. It had a large courtyard which had two-storied galleries all around. This stone construction was almost like a fortress. Preparatory ceremonies and prayers for nine days preceded the evening of the tenth of Muharram. The courtyard was adorned with black banners. Ten thousand candles lit in crystal lamps of colored glass, decorated with the Shah's portrait or with the armed lion emblem of Persia, brilliantly illuminated the courtyard. Divans and various kinds of chairs were provided for the distinguished guests, among whom were Europeans and diplomats from various embassies. All together there were twenty thousand spectators. The upper gallery was occupied by veiled Persian and Turkish women. The ceremony started with the noise of clashing cymbals. Then the procession approached with funeral music in 2/4 rhythm played on seven or eight wind instruments accentuated by the clash of cymbals. While the Persian spectators were weeping, an inspired man ascended a chair and proceeded to relate the traditional and historical facts in an emotional tone. The procession entered the square in the following order: at its head was a man balancing a long pole from which a variety of beautiful shawls were suspended, followed by another man carrying the standard of the Prophet which was black and white and embroidered with inscriptions and the symbol of the hand. Horses covered with shawls and carpets represented the seventy-two martyrs, the companions of Hussein; on an empty saddle were placed two filigreed shields and two crossed naked swords; another horse carried a sort of palanquin with halfdrawn blue and black curtains through which could be seen a woman and children representing the family of Hussein. Next to this were men on horseback throwing chaff. The last horse had a white cover sprinkled with red paint, representing the family of Hussein. Next to this were two white pigeons (probably attached by their legs) besmirched with red paint, and two long golden

241

arrows, representing the souls of the martyrs. This was followed by a tight line of Persians who beat their breasts vigorously in cadence, shouting "Hussein! Hassan!" They were followed by some devotees wearing black tights embroidered with white inscriptions and holding long iron chains with which they beat their bare backs in time with the clash of cymbals. Then two or three hundred men wearing white shirts descending to their feet and with clean-shaven heads proceeded in two rows; they held one another by the girdle with the left hand, swinging their daggers and swords with the right. They struck their heads in real earnest with their daggers and swords, making the blood stream very copiously down their faces, staining their white shirts. Behind each of these there was a man holding a wooden stick. During the slashing each would put his stick between the head and dagger in order to prevent the blow from slashing the scalp too seriously. Among these self-mutilators there was a boy of eleven, giving his head direct violent blows.[13]

The procession after making three rounds of the arena, would proceed to another *Han,* and possibly to a third one. Just before departing, when they passed in front of the Persian ambassador, they pointed their swords toward him, asking for the release of prisoners, a favor which was never denied. Other processions followed until the whole ceremony terminated toward 9 or 10 o'clock.

The author witnessed this in 1886, saying that out of two thousand participants more than six hundred were seriously injured. The whole ceremony had been arranged by the corporation of *Nezir.* Though their wounds seemed fatal, the author was satisfied that there were not many deaths. The heads of the wounded were bound up with kerchiefs. They kept their white clothes spattered with blood, and subsequently they buried them in a consecrated place.

The next day, just as a funeral procession follows the departed one to the grave, they visited the Persian cemetery in Usküdar on the Asiatic shore of the Bosphorus called Şeyh-Ali Deresi. When the procession reached the cemetery, they threw water on everybody present and then they offered tea, dates, bread and cheese. At the cemetery they prayed for the dead and in the afternoon they sang elegies in groups to music, beating the left side of their chests. Some wore black, carrying the inscription "Ya Muzlum Hussein!" Some Shi'a scourged their bare backs with metal whips.[14]

That does not mean that the Shi'a colony and its Muharram practices can be found only in Istanbul. While preparing this paper, I wrote to a friend and colleague at the Atatürk University in Erzurum, Professor

Fahrettin Kirzioğlu, who is an authority on the folklore and history of the far eastern part of Turkey, asking him for some particulars of Muharram observances in that region. In his reply of March 5, 1976, he stated that observances and traditions still persist, but secretly now since by the law of the secularization of the state in 1928, people cannot practice these rites openly. On the tenth of Muharram the Shi'a population of Kars would march in procession to the mosque of Yusufpaşa Camii reciting Fuzuli's famous elegy *Hadikat-üs-Süeda* (The Garden of the Blessed) with cries of "Şah'se, Bah'se." Cursing Yazid, young boys and men would strike their clean-shaven heads with daggers *(kame)*. During the Russian occupation of Kars in 1886 this mosque was given to the Shi'a colony by the Russians who also provided a military band to play funeral tunes with the intention of helping the Shi'a population in their mourning. These practices were widely disseminated in the fifteen villages (among them, Akuzum, Kinegi, Pirveli, Bayraktar and others) of the Arpaçay district, also in the villages of the districts Iğdir, Tuzluca, and Aralık. Since there was a large population of Shi'ites in this region, they were permitted to emigrate to Iran and Iraq in 1950. In 1934 when the Shah of Persia visited Turkey, the Shi'a population laid down carpets in his honor and hung on their walls the picture of the Shah together with that of Atatürk. Even today one can observe traces of *Kame-zed* on the foreheads of school boys. Professor Kirzioğlu did not answer my question concerning Ta'ziyeh performances. In one of our conversations several years ago, he mentioned that plays were enacted in some border villages, but refused to provide particulars and photos of them, since those performances were jealously guarded secrets. It is interesting to note that a popular novel called *Ali and Nino* by an author from Baku, writing under the pseudonym of Kurban Sait, contains descriptions of Muharram observances in this area.[15]

MUHARRAM OBSERVANCES IN ANATOLIA

All over Anatolia, especially among the adherents of the Bektashi order, and the village Alevis—who are mostly heterodox tribes, semi-nomadic, having summer pasturage as well as a fixed winter domiciles under various names—such as Tahtacı (woodcutter), Yörük, Turkomen, Qizilbash (Red Head) and others—various rites and beliefs are practiced. In their mourning there is no excess. For instance, the Bektashi mourn only with tears, never with dirges and wailing. The most widespread acts of mourning are fasting and other forms of abstinence. All food and drink are avoided between dawn and sunset. The Bektashis mourn the Passion of Kerbela with fasting during the first ten days of the month. Fasting has come to be regarded by many as the most important act. In some other tribes twelve days' fast is observed, one day for each of the twelve Imams, the first being for Ali, the tenth for Hussein, and the last for Mehdi, since the history of the Imams comprises a continuous martyrdom. The last is a short one of three hours since Mehdi is believed to be alive in a cave hidden from his enemies and friends, from which he will return one day. Therefore, among some Alevi Muharram is an occasion for rejoicing, not mourning, since it is the month when Mehdi the ultimate restorer will reappear. This belief in the eschatological Mehdi is expressed in a multitude of traditions. Two versions of it are widespread. According to one, Imam Mehdi will come from the rock cave where he is concealed, and will return to extirpate the old evil and restore order. That is why on the twelfth day fasting ends in the forenoon, and people dress in their best clothes to welcome him. It is believed that he said from his cave, "I am not coming out in the year 1300 but I will not remain concealed after the year 1400." The second reason for rejoicing on the twelfth day of Muharram is that while they are mourning for Hussein on that day, news reaches them to the effect that Imam Zain al-Abedin is alive. Among some other Alevis, fasting extends to fifteen days; twelve days for the twelve Imams proper, and an additional period of three days for the sons of Muslim. There is another kind of Muharram fast called *oğundurma orucu,* lasting two days without a break. This is performed in accordance with a vow especially by people who are incurably ill. Only in the evening do they allow themselves to drink three spoonfuls of soup. Breaking the fast starts with having salt, and the meal consists of soup containing pieces of unleavened bread, rice, dry and fresh fruit, tea, coffee, macaroni, various sweetmeats, and similar things. Customarily the first breaking of a fast is done in one's own home, the second in one's parents' home, the third and fourth among close relatives, and the others can be in anyone's house. On the tenth day the fast again should be broken in one's parents' house, on the eleventh in one's own house, and on the twelfth day in a house where there is a gathering for the occasion. While observing the fast, no bad word must be said nor any harm done to anyone, nor any living thing killed. Therefore, one must abstain from fish, meat, eggs and fowl. No plant may be cut since a plant is a living thing too. During the fasting period when people confront one another, as a salutation they say, *Yuh Münkire!* (Boo, or shame on disbelievers!), and the other will reply, *Lânet Yezide!* (Cursed be Yazid!). Some break their fast in a cemetery, and dedicate their fast to a deceased relative.

There are other abstinences which are acts of mourning (I shall discuss abstinence from water later). They do not wash or change their underclothing; they do not use soap; they do not shave; they do not look in the mirror because doing so would be considered making up one's face—but another reason is that a mirror has an important part in the cults of the dead which are very prevalent in many societies. They also abstain from smelling anything; they do not sing, play a musical instrument, dance, laugh or amuse themselves. They do not drink alcoholic beverages, do not kill bugs such as lice and fleas, do not have sexual intercourse, and abstain from inhaling tobacco. They also cautiously abstain from all other indulgences. Only on the eleventh day is underclothing washed or changed, and in the evening they drink three draughts of water while cursing Yazid.

As a meritorious act some people do not drink a drop of water even after the fasting period. For most people who keep the fast for ten or twelve days, abstention from water is practiced only from the evening of the ninth till the afternoon of the tenth. However, abstention from water is carried on at times other than for the Kerbela Passion; to practice it only once a year would be separating the Muharram fast completely form whatever connection with natural phenomena its origins may have had. The agony of the thirst of the Martyrs is almost the only feature not imitated by the Azerbaijan Turks.[16] Their ceremonies afford manifold occasions to show and to make ceremonial use of the blessing of water. Yet in Anatolia they do recall the Kerbela calamity with a ceremonial thirst. Some who are not so rigid during the fast do drink water, but this must not be pure water. As a substitute they drink tea, coffee, fruit syrup, buttermilk, or a drink made from yogurt and water called *ayran*. From the evening of the ninth day until the afternoon of the tenth the Bektashis especially commemorate Hussein's suffering by drinking no water. Then they sometimes break their fast by drinking water mixed with dust. To make this drink, which is also used for its prophylactic effects, they scrape dust from tablets of dried earth brought by pilgrims from near Hussein's tomb at Kerbela and Najaf,[17] and called *Secde Tası* by the Bektashi, who keep these relics of the Martyrs to press against their foreheads when at prayers, or to use as charms and amulets.

Another important element in the Muharram observances is a special dish called *aşure,* prepared on the tenth of Muharram, Ashura, in rememberance of the hunger of the Martyrs. In different parts of Anatolia it has different names such as *hedik, hadik, hatik, hedek, hedik aşi,* and others, all meaning cooked, unground wheat. In Azerbaijan also this dish is called *hedik.*[18] The chief ingredient is unground wheat with which other grain, beans, chick peas, nuts, almonds, and raisins are cooked, together with sugar. The significance is very important. Since the tenth of Muharram is believed to be the day on which several great events happened, such as the first meeting of Adam and Eve, and Noah's release from the Ark, it is held sacred for many reasons. There is a legend about Noah, that on the last day (Ashura) when Noah and his family went out from the Ark, they cooked porridge with the remaining cereals in the ship, mixing them all together, and this was how *aşure* was first prepared.[19]

There is also another facet of the belief: since the *aşure* dish is also a commemorative object, it appears to indicate the coincidence of the battle of Kerbela with the end of the harvest season, thus supporting the belief that the martyrdom took place at the beginning of August. In Anatolia there are other rites using cereals. Although in fact the first of Muharram in the year 61 of the Muslim era fell upon the first of October, tradition holds that it fell four and a half months after the vernal equinox, that is, at the beginning of August. There is another practice in connection with the Kerbela passion which evinces this belief. Since, according to the lunar calendar, Muharram falls on different seasons in different years, village Alevis in Anatolia have another occasion which they observe called *Yaz Kurbanı*, which means "Summer Sacrifice," when they sacrifice an animal to the honor and love of Hussein. During this period no water is drunk. Instead, it is customary to drink *dolu*, the sacred name given to an alcoholic beverage called *rakı* or *arrack*. Poetry is recited and the sacred dance of the Alevis called *Samah* or *Sema* is performed at this time. Also a special soup is prepared from the meat of the sacrificial animal and other ingredients called *Dovuga çorbası.*

The *aşure* dish and the animal sacrifices are two important elements of Muharram. The Bektashi especially give much importance to the ceremony called *Aşure Merasimi.* The inhabitants of the *tekke* (order) spend several days with preparations, gathering the wheat, hazel-nuts, raisins, almonds and dates needed for the making of the *aşure.*

On the evening itself members gather, and while dirges in memory of Hussein are being sung, the food is cooked in the great *kazan* [cauldron] the Baba in authority, first stirring with a great spoon, and then in order of rank, all present taking their turn. Toward morning the *kazan* is ceremoniously lowered from the fire. All gather around it, while one with a good voice sings a hymn in memory of Hussein. The Baba recites a prayer and then distributes the food to all present. In groups they sit about and eat it.[20]

At Hajji Bektash Tekke near Kirşehir, headquarters and tomb of Hajji Bektash, the founder of the Order, there was an extremely large cauldron which was used only for *aşure.* It is now exhibited in the Ethnographical Museum in Ankara.

Among some Alevis *aşure* is cooked on the eleventh evening, the next day (the twelfth) the fast is broken by eating it. It is meritorious act to distribute it to as many people as possible. Then an animal is sacrificed, usually a rooster. This is called *lokma,* the meat of which is eaten on the evening of the twelfth day. In some places they continue to cook every day until the last day of Muharram, symbolically using eleven or twelve kilos of wheat for all the Muharram *aşure.*

In more recent times the customs during the ten or twelve days of mourning have degenerated, whereby games, gambling and similar amusements are indulged in, which to some extent alleviate the tension of the fasting period.

Other observances connected with Muharram mysteries are pilgrimages. For instance, Qizilbash do not make a pilgrimage to Mecca, but

246

to the Shi'a sanctuaries, Baghdad, Kufa and Kerbala. Another kind of *ziyaret* (pilgrimage) is paid to certain Anatolian holy places, the most important being Hajji Bektash near Kirşehir. Another place is in Sıvas, a *tekke* founded by a certain Halil Paşa, later governor of Beirut. It is reputed to be the tomb of Hassan.[21] The graves of two infants who were identified with Ali Eftar, son of the fifth Imam Muhammad Bekr, and Ali, son of the seventh Imam Musa Kasem, were discovered by revelation.[22] These infants are regarded as martyrs, and the *tekke* is called *Ma'sum Pak* (pure infants or holy children). The infant son of Halil Paşa, the founder of the *tekke*, is also buried there.

In Istanbul a mosque called Hacı Mustafa Camii has been believed, since Sultan Mahmud's time, to hold the apocryphal graves of Fatemeh and Zainab, the daughters of Hussein. Tradition holds that these daughters, having been captured by the Greeks and brought to Istanbul, killed themselves in prison rather than marry unbelievers.[23] Another popular belief was that St. Andrew of Crete, the miracle-working Christian Saint, was buried there also.[24]

There are many popular beliefs like that connected with the Kerbela Passion. For instance, one of the explanations as to why the hare is taboo is that the soul of Yazid passed into that animal.[25] In Qizilbash mythology there are several variations concerning the fate of Hussein's head. The best established version runs as follows: After Hussein had been decapitated, the head was stolen by an Armenian priest, Ak Murtaza Keşiş, who substituted for it the head of his eldest son. When the Turks discovered the fraud, the priest cut off the heads of all his seven sons and offered each in turn as the head of Hussein. He received a divine warning to smear the head of his youngest son with Hussein's blood, and thus deceived the Turks. He then kept for himself the holy relic which he placed in a special apartment, adorning it with gold and silver and silk. His only daughter, on entering that apartment did not see the head of Hussein but instead, a plate of gold filled with honey. She tasted the honey and became with child. One day the girl complained of a cold and when she sneezed her father suddenly saw issue from her nose a bright flame, which changed at the same instant into the form of a child. Thus did Imam Bekir, son of Hussein, come into the world. That a descendant of Ali had been born immediately became known to the Turks, who thereupon sent people to search for the child and slay it. They came to the priest's house while the young mother was washing the household linen. On being told the reason for their visit she hastily put the child into a copper cauldron which was on the fire and covered him with linen. By magic the Turks knew that the child was in a house of copper, but as they were unable to find any such house in the proximity of the priest's dwelling, they were baffled, and the child's life was saved. Because of this incident the child received the name of Bekir, which in Turkish means copper.[26]

As was stated at the beginning of this chapter, Anatolian Turks do not have Ta'ziyeh plays to be enacted, but instead a great number of literary texts, both *mersiye* (elegies) to be recited and *maktels* to be narrated dramatically in the Muharram assemblies. A great many of them are written by established poets and some are collective, anonymous folk poetry transmitted either by written texts or by oral tradition. The following well-known authors have written *mersiyes* on the tragic events of Kerbela: Bağdatlı Rûhi (d. 1605); Kami-i Amidi (d. 1766); Izzet Molla (d. 1829); Seyh Müştak Mustafa (d. 1831); Osman Nevres (d. 1836); Lebib Mehmet (d. 1867) who has written nine—his work entitled *Mersiye;* Ziya Paşa (d. 1880); Yenişehirli Avni (d. 1883); Kâzim Paşa (d. 1883), two of whose *mersiyes* are called *Rivaz-ı Asfiya* and *Makallid-i Aşk;* Osman Semsi (d. 1893) whose printed *mersiye* is entitled *Mersiye-i Seyyidü's-Süheda;* Usküdarlı Hakkı (d. 1894); Mustafa Asım (d. 1904) whose printed *mersiye* is entitled *Nale-i Uşşak;* Ali Ferruh (d. 1904) whose printed *mersiye* is entitled *Kerbela;)* Muallim Feyzi (d. 1910) whose printed *mersiye* is entitled *Matem-name,* and two noted poets of the nineteenth century, Moralizade Leyla Hanım(d. 1847) and Seref Hanım (d. 1809-10, the date of her death being unrecorded). The *divan* of Seref Hanım includes a series of *mersiyes* on Hussein and the Martyrs of Kerbela which are the finest things she wrote.

Important *maktels,* some in verse and some in prose, are listed below:

Destân-ı Adn der Hikâyet-i Hasan ve Hüseyin, by Nakiboğlu
Maktal-i Imam-i Hüseyin, by Yahya b. Bahşi (d. 1436)
Vak'a-i Kerbelâ, by Mure'd-din
Sâadet-name, a translation of Mulla Hussein Va'iz Kāshifī's *Rowzatu'l Shuhada* by, Cami Hacı Hasan-zade Muddin Mehmed (d. 1505)
Maktel-i Hüseyin, by Lamii Celebi (d. 1531)
Hadikat-üs-Süeda, a translation of Mulla Hussein Va'ez Kāshifī's *Rowzatu'l Shuhada,* by Fûzûli (d. 1561)
Kerbelâ-name, by Safi, written in 1747
Maktel-i Hüseyin, by ibn-i Ysuf Mehmet
Maktel-i Hüseyin, by Kastamonulu Şâdi

Some of the extant copies of these contain miniatures depicting various scenes of the Kerbela Passion. Each title listed below is accompanied by the name of the museum where it is to be found and the number of miniatures it contains:

Fûzûli's *Hadikat-üs-Süeda:* Istanbul, Süleymaniye Library Fatih 4321 (7 miniatures); Istanbul, Turkish and Islamic Arts Museum no. 1967 (11 miniatures); Konya, Mevlâna Museum no. 4 (4 miniatures) and Hemdem

Celebi vakfi 101 (2 miniatures); British Museum no. Or. 12009 (15 miniatures) and no. Or. 7301; Paris, Bibliothèque Nationale suppl. turc 10988 (13 miniatures); New York, Brooklyn Museum no. 70-143 (9 miniatures); New York, Collection of Edwin Binney no. 4 (4 miniatures).

Lamii Celebi's *Maktel-i Hüseyin:* British Museum no. Or. 7238 (7 miniatures).

Hussein Va'iz Kāshifī's *Rowzatu'l Shuhada* having an illustrated manuscript by a Turkish artist: Berlin, Staatsbibliothek Stiftung Preussischer Kulturbesitz and Deutsche Staatsbibliothek, Ms. Diez. A fol 5 (I.I. H. 84) (12 miniatures).

Maktels are composed of relatively independent episodes from the Passion history called *meclis* (sitting), usually ten, each episode to be narrated successively on the first ten days of Muharram. People meet to hear or to take part in these *maktels* that concern the fate of the Martyrs, and which create dramatic tension amongst the listeners. Giff, the well-known scholar and the author of a history of Ottoman poetry in six volumes, reports the following incident concerning Lamii's *mesnevi*, the *Maktel-i Hazret-i Hüseyin*, which shows the tradition of narration of *maktels* and the reaction of orthodox circles to it:

> Concerning this work we are told that Mulla Arab, a preacher evidently of some importance in Bursa of those days, having heard of Lamii's production declared from the pulpit that it was blasphemy to recite poems on so sacred a subject at public gatherings and meetings, whereupon the poet invited all the notables of the city, including the said preacher, to assemble in the great mosque, and let him read to them some passages from his work, whereat all were moved to tears and doubtless were convinced that Mulla had been a little too precipitate in his judgment.[27]

From the foregoing it is clear that not only collective anonymous texts are recited but also texts by established poets. For instance, Bektashis during the first ten days of Muharram devote time to the reading of Fūzūli's *Hadikat-üs-Süeda*. It is believed that these *maktels* are also narrated by public, professional story-tellers called *meddah* (literally praise-giver, panegyrist) who are clever impersonators, narrating with appropriate dramatic gestures and sometimes voice modulation to suggest more than one participant. In many Islamic countries we find various kinds of story-tellers. In Turkey these public storytellers, called *kissahan,* have a long-established tradition both at the urban and the rural levels. Their repertoire has been very much expanded to include popular romances, realistic stories (some having only the loosest connection with Islam) and some famous tales and epics known throughout the Islamic world, such as *Shahnameh,* the cycle Amir Hamza (called *Hamzaname* in Turkey), and others. Of course Ali's and Abu Muslim's deeds and episodes from the Kerbela Passion history had a prominent place in their repertoire. It is interesting to note that Şadi, the author of one of the earliest Anatolian *maktel* which we shall deal with below, had a pseudonyme *Meddah* (in some copies of his work, *Meddahi*) so he may have been a professional story-teller.

This *Maktel* of Şadi has been commented on by Irene Melikoff, who is known for her extensive research on Pre-Ottoman and early Ottoman epic literature. First she published a text by the narrator Şadi on Abu Muslim's deeds.[28] Abu Muslim for centuries was greatly beloved by the Anatolian Turks as is shown by the numerous romances written about his life. The Turkish romances total nine in the Bibliothèque Nationale and the nineteen in Turkish libraries, not counting the printed versions.[29] The Turkish novel of Abu Muslim, of which there is also a rhymed adaptation by Hafiz Ferdi, can be considered as a continuation episode of Kerbela cycle, and Abu Muslim as an avenger of Kerbela and the adversaries of the Abbasides. Following this fourteenth-century text, Melikoff made a study of a *maktel* of the same Şadi, which is semi-dramatic, and divided into ten episodes *(meclis)*. Melikoff based her study on two manuscripts, one in Bologna *(Kitâb-ı destan-ı maktel-i Hüseyin ibn Ali,* collection Marsigli, No. 3325, 126 folios) and the other in Ankara University, Faculty of Letters *(Dil ve Tarih-Coğrafya Fakültesi,* Üsküdar-Kemankeş No. 528, 102 folios).[30] There are other copies in Turkish libraries where the author used the pseudonym Meddahi, dated 1361;[31] and there is possibly another manuscript at the British Museum. I would like to comment on this possibility before proceeding further. While preparing this paper, in my notes I found an entry on British Museum oriental manuscripts taken from the handwritten catalogue: "Or.11128. Maktel-i Hüseyin, a passion play in 10 scenes on the death of Hüseyin, by Miknaf, rendered into Turkish by Maddah [?] Copied in Egypt A.H. 1030." As the British Museum manuscript is not accessible to me at this time, I am unable to say whether this is the same work, but three points in the foregoing entry make me think so: (1) This is also divided into ten *meclis* like the other manuscripts. (2) The manuscript is a Turkish translation of Abu Miknaf's work. In the Ankara manuscript the narrator Meddah Şadi points out that he is translating to Turkish Ibn-i Munhip Lutoğlu (he is Abu Miknaf Lut B. Yahya'l-Asdi, d. 774), who has two copies extant on the martyrdom of Hussein. Probably Şadi has never seen Miknaf's work, and had indirectly heard of it through oral recitation. But both the British Museum manuscript as well as the other two mention Miknaf's name as the original source. (3) More important, the British Museum entry mentions that the author's name is the pseudonym of Şadi, "Meddah."

Şadi's *Destân-ı Maktel-ı Hüseyin* is narrated with much detail and elaboration of the loose sequence of ten episodes, frequently presented in the guise of dialogues in the first person. Melikoff makes two significant observations. One is a criticism of its dramatic structure. Introducing the martyrdom of Muslim ibn Akil and his two sons in the second episode, which is an incident of equal value to the culminating scene of Hussein's death, easily switches the minds of the audience to a different story, and thus the writer fails to realize the dramatic intensity of the main catastrophe.

The second valuable observation by Melikoff is that Şadi's *Maktel* is very much in the manner of a Persian Passion play, with one big difference; its mode and the stress it creates amongst the listeners. The motivating force of the Persian cycle is the idea of salvation through the sufferings and the sacrificial death of Hussein; Şadi's *Maktel,* on the contrary, in the last three episodes, which occur after the death of Hussein, excites animosity against the slayers, instead of affecting his audience by the tragic passion of the events. In the last three scenes several incidents are grouped together laying stress on avenging the Kerbela martyrs.

The synopsis of the ten episodes follows:

First *Meclis:* After the usual invocations, and a digression on Fate, the author relates the historical facts: Hussein, following the suggestions of his seventy-two companions who were gathered in the house of Hani ibn Urva in Kufa, entrusted the message to Muslim ibn Akil, his cousin, ordering him to go to Kufa accompanied by his two young sons Muhammad and Ibrahim. Here a sub-story is introduced, as a sort of foreshadowing: Gabriel, bringing a handful of earth to the Prophet, announces, "This is the earth of Heaven, put it in a phial, when it turns the color of blood, you will know Hussein will meet his destiny." The Prophet entrusted this phial to Hatiçe (Khadija), bidding her to give it to Hussein when he asks for it. Hatiçe does this and Hussein, when he sees that the earth has changed to blood, starts crying.

Second *Meclis:* On the same day that Hussein departed on his tragic journey Muslim was decapitated along with his two sons.

Third *Meclis:* The journey of Hussein from Mecca to Kerbela and how the message of Muslim and Hani Ibn Urva reached him is described. When he approached Kufa he was stopped by a troop of twelve thousand men commanded by Hurr ibn Yazid who later repented and fought beside Hussein. When he reached the plain of Kerbela, he took up a handful of earth and realized that this would be the place where he would meet his fate. The general commanding an army of thirty thousand soldiers, Omer Sad Vakkas, (Umar Sa'd), had been promised the rich province of Ray as his reward for Hussein's head. Hussein had only seventy-two men against thousands. The enemy was guarding the river Fırat (the Euphrates) to prevent the besieged from obtaining water.

Fourth *Meclis:* Hussein orders his followers to dig a trench. The fight starts, the first martyr being Abdullah, son of Muslim ibn Akil, who wanted to avenge the death of his father and two brothers. The next martyrs are Zubair, and Hurr who is now on Hussein's side.

251

The Fifth and Sixth *Maclises,* describe the fight and the death of young Qasem, Hassan's son, married to Hussein's daughter. After Qasem falls, his young brother Talib dies of thirst. Then the son of Hassan, Abdullah, and three brothers of Hussein are slain. Hussein pledges to his enemies that he will go to China, Turkestan, or India if only his small children may be allowed to drink water.

Seventh *Meclis:* Tells of the death of Hussein's sons Ali Akbar and Ali Asghar, Hussein, now the only remaining combatant, brandishes the sword Zulfagar, mounts his horse Zuljanah, and holding the shield of Hamza, charges his enemies. When his horse returns riderless, the women immediately recognize the significance of this. Miraculous occurrences follow: the day becomes dark, there are earth tremors, a deep gloom spreads over the quaking earth and floods occur.

The Eighth, Ninth and Tenth *Meclises* depict several incidents after the martyrdom of Hussein. For instance, Christians and Jews affected by the sight of Hussein's head renounce their faiths and profess Islam. Exasperated by the death of Hussein, Muhtar, Yazid's prisoner and his brother-in-law, a Jew Imran, and Hussein's son Zain al-Abedin, all express their determination to avenge his death.

NOTES

1. There is an excellent scholarly book on the subject. See Ivar Lassy, *The Muharram Mysteries among the Azerbeijan Turks of Caucasia* (Helsingfors, 1916).

2. See Ettore Rossi-Alessio Bombaci, *Elenco di Drammi Religiosi Persiani Fonde Mss Vaticani Cerulli* (Citta del Vaticano, 1961).

3. The Turkish manuscripts are in the following code numbers: 48, 49, 334, 412, 542, 709, 711/II, 945, 1028, 1030, 1031, 1032/I, 1033, 1034, 1035/I, 1036/I, 1037-38, 1039/I-II-III, 1040, 1042, 1043, 1044, 1045, 1046, 1047, 1048, 1049, 1050, 1051, 1052, 1054.

4. For *Ortaoyunu* and other dramatic forms in Turkish traditional theater, see Metin And, *A History of Theatre and Popular Entertainment in Turkey* (Ankara, 1963-54).

5. Dr. John Francis Gemelli-Careri, *A Voyage Round the World,* an English translation of G. G. Gemelli Careri, *Ciro del Mondo* (Napoli, 1699-1700), p. 146.

6. J. B., Tavernier *Collections of Travels through Turkey into Persia, etc.* (London, 1677-78), I, 161 seq.

7. See Jacques Ballieu, "Le Theatre Turc," *Revue d'Art Dramatique,* XIII (Janvier-Fevrier, 1889), 344-50.

8. See G. E. White, "On the Shia Turks," *Journal of the Transactions of the Victoria Institute,* XL (1908) 234.

9. See for instance: V.A. Gordlevski, "Dni Mokharema v Konstantinople" (The Days of Muharram in Istanbul), *Sbornik Museya Antropologii i Etnografii,* VII (1928), 167-72; *La Revue Orientale,* IX (1885), 374-75; *Kafkaskii Viestnik,* VII (1902), 163-64; Henry Carnoy-Jean Nicoliedes, *Folklore de Constantinople* (Paris, 1894), pp. 189-201; Paul Horn, *Geschichte des persichen Literature* (Leipzig, 1901),

pp. 209-11. The last mentioned article, though a short one, is very accurate and scholarly. The author witnessed the Muharram mysteries in the month of May in the year 1899.

10. Max Muller, *Letters from Constantinople* (London, 1877), pp. 164-73.

11. Kesnin Bey, *Le Mal d'Orient* (Paris, 1887), pp. 143-52.

12. Kesnin Bey, *The Evil of the East: or Truths about Turkey* (London, 1883, 1888), pp. 144-51.

13. Some counterparts of these self-mutilators among the Ottomans are the processional displays of *delis* (scouts—Arabic *dalil*, a guide) and *gönüllü* (volunteers). These cavalry of the frontier fortresses, to demonstrate their bravery would march in processions with long daggers, swords, and horseshoes stuck into the skin of their chests and foreheads. There are several miniatures depicting them and many accounts both in Turkish and foreign languages. In one they are described in the following manner: ".... a troupe of other naked men exposed themselves to the view of the world all covered with wounds, their bodies being yet larded with the same arms which had inflicted them, some with arrows, others with knives and swords. But before these men had gone thrice about the place, two of the troupe fell down dead, which showed that their wounds were rather marks of their folly than enchantments." See Baudier, *The History of the Serrail and of the Court* .... Translated by Edward Grimeston (London, 1635), p. 89.

14. See Carnoy-Nicolaides, pp. 198-99; the other descriptions in this account are similar to the ones already quoted above.

15. There are English and German editions of this, but I have been able to read only the Turkish translation. See Kurban Said, *Ali ile Nino* (Istanbul, 1971), pp. 129, 290, 293-95, 298, 300-06.

16. See Lassy, pp. 157-58.

17. See Pietro della Valle, *Viaggi* (Roma, 1658), III, 461; V. Cuinet, *Turquie d'Asie* (Paris, 1890-94), III, 202, 209; Carsten Niebuhr, *Voyage en Arabie et en d'autres Pays, Circonvoisins* (Amsterdam, 1776-80), II, 223; John Kingsley Birge, *The Bektashi Order of Dervishes* (London, 1937), p. 169.

18. Lassy, pp. 127-28.

19. See *Encyclopaedia of Islam.*

20. See Birge, pp. 169-70; also see Mouradgea D'Ohsson, *Tableau General de l'Empire Ottoman* (Paris, 1788-1824), IV, 665.

21. See F. W. Hasluck, *Christianity and Islam Under the Sultans* (Oxford, 1929), pp. 150, 511-12.

22. This probably was the pilgrimage of the Qizilbash at Sivas mentioned by Molyneux-Seel as the tomb of Hassan. See L. Molyneux-Seel, "A Journey in Dersim," *Geographical Journal,* XIV (1914), 66.

23. Hasluck, p. 17.

24. See Carnoy-Nicolaides, p. 114.

25. See H. N. Brailsford, *Macedonia* (London, 1906), p. 246.

26. See Hasluck, pp. 146-47; Molyneux-Seel, pp. 64-65; on the variations of the same legend see G. E. White, "The Alevi Turks of Asia Minor," *Contemporary Review* (November, 1913), p. 698.

27. E. J. W. Gibb, *A History of Ottoman Poetry* (London, 1904), III, 23.

28. Irene Melikoff, *Abu Muslim, le "Porte-Hache" du Khorassan, dans la tradition epique turco-iranienne* (Paris, 1962).

29. Melikoff, p. 25.

30. Irene Melikoff, "Le Drame de Kerbelâ dans la Litterature Epique Turque," *Revue des Etudes Islamiques,* XXXIV (1966), 133-48.

31. Millet Library (Istanbul), Emiri No. 1313-14; Turkish Language Association Library (Ankara), No. B/28, ff. 164-213.

20

Bibliographical Spectrum

PETER J. CHELKOWSKI

Ta'ziyeh is a complex subject involving many disciplines such as religion, history, literature, anthropology, psychology, sociology, music, and fine arts as well as drama and theatre. To the present day, emphasis in the study of Ta'ziyeh has been on its historical development, religious meaning, literary style, musical components, and dramatic and theatrical significance. The essays in this volume, all written by scholars in the field, probe the various facets of this complex and unique Persian phenomenon, each from an individual point of view. The literature on the whole subject is diverse and fascinating. In addition to general works on Islamic civilization, which will be listed for ready reference at the end of this chapter, let us examine in some detail those which deal either entirely or in part with Ta'ziyeh.

THE SAFAVID AND POST-SAFAVID PERIOD: 1500-1786

The Safavid dynasty brought Iran back onto the political map of the world and made Iran one of the super-powers of the area. The Shi'ite order of Islam was established by the Safavids as the state religion. This has had a significant and lasting effect until the present day, not only upon religious life but on political, cultural, and social life as well. It was a turning point in

Persian history, and a new phase in the history of Islam. This is discussed by Hossein Nasr, in "Religion in Safavid Persia," and by Hamid Algar in "Some Observations on Religion in Safavid Persia" in *Studies on Isfahan, Iranian Studies,* vol. VII (Winter-Spring, 1974), and by Michel Mazzaoui, *The Origins of the Safavids: Shi'ism, Sufism and the Ghulat* (Wiesbaden, 1972).

The transformation of the country into a predominently Shi'a state had a tremendous impact on the further development of the Muharram mourning ritual, while the popular Shi'ite Islam annual Muharram pageantry helped greatly in spreading Shi'ite doctrine across the Iranian plateau.

The first year of Shi'ite Safavid rule coincides with the writing of the most important book on the sufferings and death of Hussein, written in A.D. 1501 by Ḥusain Vā'iẓ Kāshifī under the title *Rawẓat al-Shuhadā* or *The Garden of the Martyrs.* This is a moving literary description of the martyrdom of the Imam Hussein at Kerbela, and the suffering of the other Shi'ite martyrs. The completion of this book gave impetus to the development of the Muharram observances in that the work gave birth to a new type of activity, namely *Rawẓih-Khvānī (Rowzeh-khani),* or the recitation from *Rawẓat al-Shuhadā.* Two and a half centuries later it served as the warp through which the lyrics and the texts of the Ta'ziyeh dramatic plays were woven.

The elevation of the Shi'a persuasion to the state religion also had a great impact on classical Persian literature. Whereas previously poetry had been court-oriented, it then became centered upon the Shi'ite martyrs and saints. The best representative of this literary genre is Muhtasham Kashānī with his elegies *Davāzdah Band (Divan* Tehran, 1337).

With the new prominence of Safavid Iran, many Westerners, in a variety of capacities, such as ambassadors, tradesmen, military advisors, religious emissaries, missionaries, or simply travelers, visited and sometimes made long sojourns in Iran. Their accounts of, and stories about Iran, including the Muharram celebrations, published in various languages, serve as very important sources for the study of the development of the cult of Hussein. The second half of the Safavid rule, the seventeenth century especially, is very rich in descriptions of the commemoration of Hussein's death, as described by foreigners.

The most searching and detailed accounts are those of Raphaël Du Mans, *Estat de la Perse en 1660* (Paris, 1890; Farnborough, Hants, 1969). Seven years after Du Mans, Jean-Batiste Tavernier saw these rituals; *Les Six Voyages de Jean-Batiste Tavernier* (2 volumes, Paris, 1692). Sir John Chardin gives us a very interesting description of Muharram in the year 1674, *Journal du Voyage du Chevalier Chardin en Perse, aux Indes Orientales par la Mer Noire et par la Colchide* (London, 1686; 10 volumes, Paris, 1811).

The chronological use of accounts written by Westerners in Safavid and post-Safavid times shows an almost year-by-year growth of the pageantry of the Muharram celebration. The processions become larger and more colorful each year. There was an increasing number of costumed characters representing various martyrs of Kerbela marching or riding on horses or camels, and there were more and more visual scenes, depicting either the events leading up to the Kerbela slaughter or the tragedy itself. Most of these presentations were in the form of living tableaux, staged on moving platforms. Some writers described the make-believe battles representing the small group with Hussein fighting gallantly, while outnumbered by the much larger army of their opponents. The development of *Rawżih-Khvānī* *(Rowzeh-khani)* can also be seen to turn into a "one man show" through these descriptions. All of these accounts demonstrate the progression of dramatic and theatrical qualities of the Muharram observances which were bound eventually to give birth to the Taʿziyeh drama.

The following books written by Western observers are also important: Etienne Kakasch, *Inter Persicum, ou description du voyage en Perse entrepris en 1602 par Etienne Kakasch de Zaloukemeny* (Paris, 1877); Pietro della Valle, *Fameux voyages de Pietro della Valle gentilhomme romain* (4 volumes, Paris, 1664); Fedot Afanasievich Kotov, "O prazdnikah Busormanskih v Perskoy Ziemli" in *Izviestia Otdielenia Ruskovo Yazika* (Ros. Ak. Nauk, 1907, vol. 12, book 1, pp. 102-11); Nicolaus Hemmius, *Persia, sue regni Persici status, etc.* (Lugduni Batavorum ex officina Elzeviriana, 1633); Thomas Herbert, *Voyage de Perse et des Indes* (Paris, 1663); Adam Olearius, *Relation du voyage* ... (Schleswig, 1656; Paris, 1676); Sieur de Thevénot, *Suite du voyages* ... (Amsterdam, 1727); Figueroa, *Son Ambassade en Perse,* translated by Wicqfort (Paris, 1667); Gabriel de Chinon, *Relations nouvelles du Levant ou traites de la religion, du gouvernement et des coutumes des Perses* (Lyon, 1671); Struys, *Voyages* (3 volumes, Amsterdam, 1720); Petrus Bedik, *Cehil Sutun, Seu Expicatio Utriusque celeberrimi, Ac Pretiosissimi Theatri Quadraginta Columnarum in Perside Orientis, Cum Adjecta Fusiori Narratione De Religione, Moribusq Persarum* ... (Vienna, 1678); and Engelbert Kaempfer, *Am Hofe des persischen Grosskönigs 1684-1685* (Leipzig, 1940).

The last important account of the Muharram celebration in Safavid times comes from the pen of a Dutchman, Corneille le Brun, in the year 1704, and attests to the further growth of pageantry. Le Brun told of an increased number of participants who, via mimicry and pantomime, showed a variety of tragic scenes of the suffering of Hussein and his family during the siege and battle of Kerbela, as well as scenes depicting the captivity of Hussein's women and children after his death. The tableaux, staged on moving and stationary platforms, were well organized and presented in chronological sequence. It is clear from Le Brun's description that the participants took great pains in arranging appropriate costumes, while some of them painted their bodies in red and black to simulate wounds and bruises.

These demonstrations, however, did not yet constitute a drama: the

257

components of text and lyrics were still missing from Le Brun's account, *Voyages par la Moscovie, en Perse et aux Indes Orientales* (2 volumes, Amsterdam, 1718).

The next important description of the Muharram rituals was written in post-Safavid times by Salamons and Van Goch, and appears in their book, *Die Heutige Historie und Geographie, oder der Gegenwäertige Staat von Köenigreich Persien* (Flensburg, Altona, 1739). These writers were in Persia during the reign of Nader Shah. Parviz Mamnoun, in his "Ta'zija Schi'itisch-Persisches Passionsspiel" (Dissertationen der Universität Wien, 1967), toys with the idea that Salamons and Van Goch were actually the first foreigners to record the Ta'ziyeh-Khvani, that is, the dramatic performance. However, it seems that Salamons and Van Goch saw what can be called the last stage of the lengthy development of the ritual before it became verbal and vocal in the dramatic form.

Samuel Hmelin, who visited northern Persia in 1770-72, was the next important observer of the Muharram pageant. In his book, *Reise durch Russland ... Reise durch das nordische Persien in den Jahren 1770, 1771 bis in April 1772* (St. Petersburg, 1774), he speaks about the protoype of *takiyeh* in the city of Rasht. Each borough of the town had its own special quarters where the Muharram procession would end and where the living tableaux would be staged.

The break-through in the Muharram ceremonies, where ritual observance became ritual drama, was recorded by William Francklin, *Observations made on a Tour from Bengal to Persia in the Years 1786-1787* (London, 1790). In the chapter entitled "Pageants and Ceremonies during Mohurrum" *(sic)*, p. 246, he writes:

> All the various events are represented by the Persians during the first days of Mohurrum. .... Each day some particular action of the story is represented by people selected for the purpose of performing those concerned in it.

On pages 248-50, Francklin continues,

> Among the most affecting representations is the marriage of young Casim [*sic*], the son of Hussun [*sic*], and nephew of Hossein, with his daughter; but this was never consumated, as Casim was killed in a skirmish on the banks of the Euphrates, on the 7th of Mohurrum. On this occasion, a boy represents the bride, decorated in her wedding garment, and attended by the females of the family chanting a mourning elegy, in which is related the circumstance of her betrothed husband being cut off by infidels (for that is the term by which Sheias [*sic*] speak of the Sunnies [*sic*]). The parting between her and her husband is also represented. when on his going to the field she takes an affectionate leave of him: and on his quitting her presents him with a burial vest. which she puts round his neck.

The first edition of Francklin's book was published in 1788 in Calcutta, almost immediately upon his return. The London edition of 1790 was followed by a Paris edition in 1797 under the title, *Voyage de Bengal à Chyraz*. William Francklin has to his credit several other books on Indian history and religion which lend credibility to his accounts.

THE QAJAR PERIOD TO WORLD WAR II

Until now we have been mainly concerned with the growth of the Muharram ritual of processions of mourners, *Rowzeh-Khani,* and the living tableaux. After Francklin's time, our focus will be on the growth of the dramatic execution of theatrical plays and the places of their performance. The burgeoning of the Ta'zieyh drama from a mourning ritual into full-scale theatre in the Qajar period is spectacular. Within a very short time, under royal tutelage, this drama outshone many European operas, according to some Western observers. This does not mean that, with the birth of Ta'ziyeh passion plays, the other forms of the Muharram observances ceased to exist. However, the new theatre and drama captured the attention and imagination of most visitors and researchers and overshadowed other rituals. Some twenty-five years after Francklin, James Morier saw a full dramatic representation of "Hussein's Martyrdome" in Tehran, which he describes in *A Journey Through Persia, Armenia and Asia Minor to Constantinople in the Years 1808 and 1809* (London, 1812).

Three contemporaries of Morier also witnessed the Ta'ziyeh drama and wrote their impressions: André Dupré, *Voyage en Perse, fait dans les années 1807, 1808 et 1809* (Paris, 1819); J. M. Tancoigne, *Lettres sur la Perse et la Turquie d'Asie* (Paris, 1819); and Gaspard Drouville, *Voyage en Perse pendant les Années 1812 et 1813* (Paris, 1825).

Alexander Chodzko, a scholar and diplomat, and the author of books on popular Persian poetry, Persian grammar and customs, was greatly impressed with Ta'ziyeh during his stay in Persia in the 1830s. He bought a manuscript consisting of thirty-three plays from the director of the court theatre. This manuscript is the best document we possess to demonstrate the rapid literary development of the Ta'ziyeh plays. The manuscript was later deposited by Chodzko in the Bibliothèque Nationale in Paris (Blochet, 1928, *Catalogue des manuscriptes persans).* Chodzko edited two of the plays, "The Messenger of God" and "The Death of the Prophet" and published them, in Persian, in 1852 under the title, *Djungi Chehâdet.*

The early nineteenth-century plays of the Chodzko collection are now being published under the title *Jong-i Shahâdat, An Anthology of Martyrdom,* by the Soroush Press in Tehran. The edition was commissioned by the Institute for Traditional Performance and Ritual in Tehran under the editorship of Zahra Eqbal Namdar. The first volume appeared in 1977 and includes six plays. The second volume is presently in press, and the third and fourth volumes will be published in 1979. Toward the end of his academic career, Chodzko published another book based on his collection, *Théâtre persan, Choix de téazies ou drames* (Paris, 1878). In addition to a French translation of five Ta'ziyeh plays, Chodzko included a long introduction in this work.

There are two short descriptions of the Ta'ziyeh plays recorded, one by Charles Texier, *Description de l'Arménie et la Perse et la Mésopotamie* (2 volumes, Paris, 1852), and the other by E. Flaudin, *Voyage en Perse* (Paris, 1841). The importance of these two accounts is that they describe Ta'ziyeh performances in small towns in rural areas.

Chronologically, the next most valuable description of Ta'ziyeh was written by Ilya Nikolaevich Berezin, *Puteshestwie po sieviernoy Persi* (Kazan, 1852). Berezin gives more than a descriptive account. Like Chodzko, Berezin had an academic background in Near Eastern Studies. He had published several books on the Arabic language, Persian grammar, and historical Persian texts. His account of Ta'ziyeh can be regarded as one of the first scholarly renderings of the subject. Berezin's description of *Takiyeh Khaji* is most interesting in that he includes a detailed account of what goes on in a *takiyeh* before the performance begins. Berezin attended Ta'ziyeh from the third day of Muharram, January 1843, until the day of Ashura, and he gives a résumé of each play which was assigned to that particular day. Finally, he wrote a commentary on the language and text of Ta'ziyeh, as well as its staging and acting.

Several works dating from the middle of the nineteenth century record valuable references to Ta'ziyeh: Lady Sheil, *Glimpses of Life and Manners in Persia 1848-1853* (London, 1856); J. E. Polak, *Persien, das Land und seine Bewohner* (2 volumes, Leipzig, 1865); Heinrich Brugsch, *Reise der K. Preussischen Gesandtschaft nach Persien 1860-1861* (2 volumes, Leipzig, 1862); Edward B. Eastwick, *Journal of a Diplomat's Three Years in Persia* (2 volumes, London, 1864); and Carla Serena, *Hommes et choses en Perse* (Paris, 1883).

The Counte de Gobineau spent some time in Iran and considered Ta'ziyeh as one of the greatest events in Persia. Although his description of Persian drama is somewhat exaggerated and is not always precise, his book, *Les religions et les philosophies dans l'Asie Centrale* (Paris, 1865, 1957), had a great impact on scholars and literati in Europe such as Ernest Renan, *Les téazies de la Perse* (Paris, 1884); Matthew Arnold, "A Persian Passion Play" in *Essays in Criticism* (volume 2, London, 1871); and Edouard Montet, "La religion et le théâtre en Perse" in *Revue de l'histoire des Religions,* vol. XIV (Paris, 1886), and *Le Théâtre en Perse* (Geneva, 1888). In Gobineau's book, in addition to his commentary on Persian drama and theatre, a translation of a play, "The Marriage of Qasim" appears, but without a designation to the specific text on which it is based.

Colonel Sir Lewis Pelly spent eleven years in southern Iran from 1862 onward. Pelly was so impressed with the Muharram drama that he wrote a two-volume work, *The Miracle Play of Hasan and Husain* (London, 1879, recently republished). The work consists of thirty-seven plays which he translated from the Persian oral tradition into ornate Victorian English. A comparison of the titles in the Chodzko collection of some forty years earlier, and the Pelly collection, indicates the topical growth of the drama. Whereas thirty-three plays in the Chodzko collection deal primarily with the Kerbela tragedy, the Pelly collection spans the whole cycle from the time when Hussein is destined for martyrdom to the resurrection of mankind when Hussein intercedes on behalf of all those who mourned for him.

The first essay on the Persian theatre written by an American is that of Samuel Green Wheeler Benjamin, the American envoy to Iran. His detailed description of the royal theatre, *Takiyeh Dowlat,* which appears in his book *Persia and the Persians* (London, 1886), is of great importance to the study of Ta'ziyeh. Benjamin was not only a diplomat but also the author of several books on contemporary art in Europe and America. Thanks to his training in art and art criticism, his descriptions of the royal theatre reveal added insightful dimensions.

Contemporary with Benjamin in Iran was C. J. Wills who included Ta'ziyeh in his book *Persia As It Is* (London, 1886). Wills was especially interested in the aspect of Biblical stories incorporated into the Persian repertory. Other Westerners who visited Iran toward the end of the nineteenth or the beginning of the twentieth century who mention Ta'ziyeh are: Leonid Bogdanov, *Persia v geografitcheskom, religiosno-targovopromishlenom i administrativnom otnosheni* (St. Petersburg, 1908); E. G. Browne, *A Year Amongst the Persians* (London, 1959); Auguste Bricteux, *Au pays du lion et du soleil, 1903-1904* (Brussels, 1908); H. R. D'Allemagne, *Du Khorassan au pays de Bakhtiari* (Paris, 1911); C. Lomnitzki, *Persia i Persy* (St. Petersburg, 1902); Eustache de Lorey and Douglas Sladen, *Queer Things About Persia* (London, 1907); N. Mamontov, *Ocherk Sovremiennoy Persii* (St. Petersburg, 1909); K. Smirnov, *Persy: Ocherk Religii Persii* (Tiflis, 1916); and S. G. Wilson, *Persian Life and Customs* (London, 1896). *The Muharram mysteries among the Azerbaijan Turks of Caucasia* (Helsingfors, 1916), written by Ivan J. Lassy, is of great importance as a very precise and meticulous piece of research. B. D. Eerdmans wrote earlier about the same subject: see his "Der Ursprung der Ceremonien des Hosein-Festes," *Zeitschrift für Assyriologie* (IX/1894, pp. 280-307).

Thorough academic research on Ta'ziyeh began with a Russian scholar, E. Bertels, who wrote a monograph on the Persian theatre in a Russian series devoted to Eastern Theatre, *Persidskiy Teatr* in the series *Vostochniy Teatr* (Rosiyskiy Institut Istorii Iskustv, vol. IV, Leningrad 1924). Although it is not a very revealing work, the monograph demonstrates sound scholarship and serves as a good introduction to Ta'ziyeh, particularly for those in the field of drama and the theatre. Bertels' work was followed by a study written by an Ukrainian scholar, Agatangel Krymski: his *Perskij Teatr* (Kiev, 1925) is an important analysis of the origin of Ta'ziyeh drama. It is fortunate that Krymski's work, written in Ukrainian, has been translated into English and is presently in press under the aegis of the Institute for Traditional Performance and Ritual in Tehran.

Following the tradition of scholar-diplomats such as Chodzko, Berezin, and Pelly, Wilhelm Litten collected fifteen plays and published them in facsimile under the title, *Das Drama in Persien* (Berlin, Leipzig, 1929). J. Rypka, in his review of Litten's book, "Besprechung von W. Litten, Das Drama in Persien" in *Arch. Orientalni,* volume II (1930), underlines the importance of this book, since it consists of fourteen plays that date back to 1831-34 and includes only one twentieth-century drama. Litten's book has recently been republished.

In 1929 Charles Virolleaud published *La passion de l'Imam Hosseyn* in Paris based on play number 24 in the Chodzko manuscript. Unfortunately, the book is without a commentary. In 1934 an Austrian Orientalist, Herbert Duda, translated into German play number 1 in the Litten collection, "Abraham Sacrificing Ismael": "Das persische Passionsspiel" in *Zeitschrift für Missionskunde und Religionswissenschaft,* vol. 49 (1934). In 1935 Jean Hytier wrote "Vie et Mort de la Tragédie Religieux Persane" in *Les Cahiers du Sud, l'Islam et l'Occident* (Marseilles, August-September 1935, pp. 127-34).

FROM WORLD WAR II TO THE PRESENT

In the post-World War II period there has been a great deal of interest in studies of the cult of Imam Hussein and Ta'ziyeh. The first of many works to be mentioned is by Abbé R. H. de Generet, *Le Martyre d'Ali Akbar, Drame persan* (Liège, Paris, 1946). This is a French translation and critical discussion of play number 18 from the Chodzko collection which is well annotated. In 1950 Charles Virolleaud published his second book, *Le Théâtre Persan ou Le Drame de Kerbéla* (Paris). In the same year the famous French Orientalist, H. Massé, introduced a partial translation of the "Martyrdom of Qasim," of unknown origin, into his Persian anthology.

During 1950-55 the Italian ambassador to Iran, Enrico Cerulli, collected an incredible number—1,055—of Ta'ziyeh manuscripts from various localities in Iran. These he donated to the Vatican Library. This has become the most important collection of Ta'ziyeh manuscripts to date and forms the basis for current and future critical studies. A descriptive catalogue, begun by Ettore Rossi and completed after his death by Alessio Bombaci, *Elenco di drammi religiosi persiani* (Vatican) was published in 1961. From this Cerulli Vatican collection the unusual mystical Ta'ziyeh play about the death of Mansur al-Hallaj, "Le Majlis de Manṣûr-e Ḥallâj, de Shams-e

Tabrêzi et du mollâ de Roum," was translated by the well-known French scholar, L. Massignon, and published in the *Revue des Etudes Islamiques* (1955). The same play was reworked by Mehdy Soraya and Peter Chelkowski. It was successfully staged at the City Theatre in Tehran in the spring of 1978. This production was sponsored by the Institute for Traditional Performance and Ritual and was well received by the audience.

Other Italian Iranologists have made valuable contributions to the study of Ta'ziyeh, especially Alessandro Bausani who discussed Ta'ziyeh at some length in his *Persia Religiosa* (Milan, 1959). Bausani has also translated and edited several plays from the Cerulli collection, "Drammi popolari inediti persiani sulla leggenda di Salomone e della Regina di Saba" in *Atti del Convegno Internzionale di Studi Etiopici* (Rome, 1960, pp. 167-209).

Ta'ziyeh has been the subject of several Ph.D. dissertations and M.A. theses. In 1952 Mehdi Forough submitted *A Comparative Study of Abraham's Sacrifice in Persian Passion Plays and Western Mystery Plays* as a Master's thesis at Columbia University which was later published by the Ministry of Culture and Arts in Tehran. In 1959, M. Bani Sadr Abbas presented his doctoral dissertation under the title "La Ta'ziye" to the Faculty of Letters at the University of Paris. In 1966 Hildegard Müller submitted her excellent doctoral dissertation *Studien zum Persischen Passionsspiel* to Albert Ludwigs University in Freiburg im Breisgau (published 1966). Two Iranians submitted their doctoral dissertations concerning Ta'ziyeh in 1967: Parviz Mamnoun to the University of Vienna on the subject of "Ta'zija Schi'itisch-Persisches Passionsspiel," and Davoud Monchi-Zadeh on "Ta'ziya des Persischen Passionsspiel" to the University of Upsala. Both were published in the same year. Mamnoun's work concerns the historical development of Ta'ziyeh and its stage technique and acting. Monchi-Zadeh's research included the Maharram procession as well as abbreviated German translations and commentaries of texts from the Litten collection. Also in 1967, Peter Chelkowski submitted his doctoral dissertation on Ta'ziyeh at Tehran University, entitled "Persian Popular Literature and Ta'ziyeh."

In 1975 Jean Calmard received his Ph.D. from the University of Paris with his excellent dissertation on the cult of Imam Hussein in pre-Safavid Iran, "Le Culte de L'Imām Husayn" (Etude sur la commémoration du Drame de Karbalā dans l'Iran pré-safavide). The Institute for Traditional Performance and Ritual is presently considering Calmard's research for publication. In 1976 (or 1977) Abdollah Haidari submitted a dissertation on Ta'ziyeh at the Free University of Berlin in the Department of Ethnology. [The author has had no opportunity to examine this manuscript.]

There are also a number of monographs dealing with Ta'ziyeh of more recent date: Jean Calmard, "Le Mecenat des Representations de Ta'ziye" in *Le Monde Iranian et l'Islam,* vol. 2 (Geneva, 1974); Enrico Cerulli, "Le

Théâtre persan et ses origines" in *La Nouvelle Clio,* vols. VII-IX (Brussels, 1955-57); Peter Chelkowski, "Dramatic and Literary Aspects of Ta'ziyeh-Khani Iranian Passion Play" in *Review of National Literatures,* vol. II, no. 1 (New York: St. John's University, Spring 1971); Jiri Cejpek, "Dramatic Folk Literature in Iran" in Jan Rypka, *History of Iranian Literature* (Dordrecht, 1968); Angelo Piemontese, "La rappresentazione della ta'ziye durante il regno di Nasero'd-Din-Sah (1848-1896) secondo lo scrittore persiano 'Abdullah Mostoufi" in *Annuali dell' Istituto Universitario Orientale de Napoli,* new series, vol. 13 (Rome, 1963); and Ehsan Yarshater, "Development of Persian Drama, in the Context of Cultural Confrontation in Iran" in *Iran: Continuity and Variety,* Peter Chelkowski, ed. (New York: New York University, 1970-71).

LITERARY INTEREST IN TA'ZIYEH

In Iran it is only in the last fifteen years or so that Ta'ziyeh has received attention from the literary world. Several major factors contributed to this interest. The first was the appearance of a growing number of memoirs dating from the second half of the nineteenth century and the beginning of the twentieth, in which the authors not only praised Ta'ziyeh but also gave vivid descriptions of Ta'ziyeh theatrical performances. Ta'ziyeh was shown to be a very important element in the Persian way of life. One of the most outstanding memoirs is that of 'Abdallāh Mustawfī, *Sharh-i Zindigānī-yi Man* (Tehran, 1334/1955-56). Secondly, the Festival of Arts in Iran started to incorporate Ta'ziyeh into its repertory. Thirdly, there were more and more Western theatre directors who arrived in Iran in search of Oriental theatrical modalities. Fourthly, the establishment of departments of dramatic arts at some of the Iranian universities provided a vehicle for students and scholars to realize the importance of Ta'ziyeh in the history of the theatre and to recognize its unique qualities.

The list of Iranian literary scholars and their works concerning Ta'ziyeh should begin with the pioneering book by Bahrām Baiżā'ī: *Nimāyish dar Iran* (Tehran, 1344/1965-66). Baiżā'ī is a playwright, film director and art critic, and it is therefore understandable that the dramatic aspect of Ta'ziyeh is his main concern. The publication of a revised edition has been announced.

The second comprehensive book is that of Ṣādiq Humāyūnī: *Ta'ziyeh va Ta'ziyeh-khvani* (Festival of Arts Series, Tehran, 1354/1975-76). Humāyūnī is a very prolific writer and he has three other monographs to his credit: "Taḥavulāt va Sair-i Takāmul Ta'ziyeh dar Irān" *(Kāvih Periodical,* German ed. #45/46, 1953), "Ta'ziyeh Majmū'ih Dilpazīr. . . ." *(Firdawsi Periodical* #1090, Tehran 1351/1972-73), and a chapter in his book *Farhang-i Mardum-i Sarvistān.* (The text of two Ta'ziyeh plays, "Ali Akbar" and "Imam Hasan," appear also in this book: Ministry of Information, 1349/1970-71).

Historical studies are interesting and varied. Parvīz Mamnūn, who was mentioned earlier, wrote "Nu<u>kh</u>ustīn Ta'ziyehhā dar Irān" *(Rūdakī Periodical #3*, Tehran, 1341/1962-63). In this article he attempts to move Ta'ziyeh performances back before the time of Francklin's account in 1786. Muhammad J'afar Ma<u>h</u>jūb, in the monograph *Nimāyi<u>sh</u>-i Kuhan-i Irānī va Naqqālī* (Festival of Arts Series, Tehran, 1346/1967-68), probed the historical development of Ta'ziyeh within the framework of other traditional performances and ritual. New evidence on the history of the construction of the Royal Takiyeh in Tehran is given by Ya<u>h</u>yā Zukā, in his book entitled *Tārikh<u>ch</u>ih-yi Sā<u>kh</u>timên-i Ark-i Sal<u>t</u>anatī* (Tehran, 1349/1970-71). *Bunyād-i Namāyi<u>sh</u> dar Irān* (Tehran, 1955) by A. Jannatī 'A<u>t</u>ā'ī is somewhat outdated, but is still a useful book.

There have been quite a number of attempts to publish critical editions of Ta'ziyeh texts. The most important has already been mentioned—the publication of the "Chodzko Collection" by the Soroush Press under the aegis of the Institute for Traditional Performance and Ritual. The Center for Anthropological Research of the Ministry of Culture and Arts, Iran, published a very interesting collection of the Ta'ziyeh plays under the title, *Ta'ziyeh dar Khur(#*11, undated). This book deals with the Muharram commemoration in the middle of the Kavir desert in the center of Iran. The editor of this important study is Murti<u>z</u>ā Hunarī.

In 1961-62, Bahrām Bai<u>z</u>ā'i published a "comical" Ta'ziyeh called *Gū<u>sh</u>ih-yi <u>Sh</u>ast Bstin-i Dīv (Ari<u>sh</u> Periodical* #1, Tehran, 1340). In the same periodical a year later (#3), Sīrūs <u>T</u>āhbāz dealt with a Ta'ziyeh which had very nationalistic Iranian overtones, namely "Ta'ziyeh <u>Sh</u>ahrbānū." Three short Ta'ziyeh are contained in a book by Farru<u>kh</u> <u>Gh</u>affārī and Māyil Biktā<u>sh</u>, *Ti'atri-i Irānī* (Festival of Arts Series, Tehran, 1350/1971-72). Parvīz <u>S</u>ayyād, a film-maker and theatre director, published a critical edition of the *Ta'ziyeh <u>H</u>urr* (Festival of Arts Series, Tehran, 1350/1971-72). This is based on the Ta'ziyeh play which <u>S</u>ayyād prepared and staged for the Shiraz Festival of Arts in 1967.

The study of Ta'ziyeh has not been entirely limited to the work of the historian, the observant traveler, the dramatic producer, and the translator. Other art forms have been brought to focus on this important element of Persian culture: we owe much to the film maker, the musicologist, the student of the dance, the researcher in theology and religious rites, and the art critic for adding to our store of knowledge. With each one's input, and as workers in these and other disciplines extend their research, the dimensions of this complex subject are expanded.

The films on Ta'ziyeh which have been produced by Iranian and foreign film-makers and scholars can serve as important documents for the study of Ta'ziyeh. *The Lion of God—Ta'ziyeh in Natanz* was produced by Service de Recherche (Paris, 1975-76) and was directed by Jean Baronet. This is both very informative and singularly beautiful. Two films produced by Rustāi are entitled *Ta'ziyeh in Arak* and *Ta'ziyeh in Shahreza*. Parvīz

Ṣayyād, mentioned above, has produced several films and videotapes. They are: *Taʿziyeh Khurūj-i Mukhtar* and *Taʿziyeh of Abdulla Hafif.* The latter was performed at 25 Shahrivar Theatre in Tehran in 1966 as a part of the "Iranian Collection." It was also shown on Iranian television. Ṣayyād's most important film the *Taʿziyeh of Hurr,* with Khujastih Kīā as co-director, is based upon the Taʿziyeh production for the 1967 Shiraz Festival of Arts. It, too, was shown on Iranian television. Another film on the *Taʿziyeh of Hurr* was produced in 1976 by Askarian. This featured a Taʿziyeh troupe from Qum performing at Takiyeh Niāvarān.

Parvīz Kimiāvī produced seven films on the Taʿziyeh which were performed in 1976 at the Shiraz Festival of Arts, in connection with the International Symposium on Taʿziyeh. In 1977, H. Ṭāhirī Dūst filmed several Taʿziyeh productions in Habib Abād near Isfahan, while Nassir Taqvāī made a very interesting film about the Arbaʿiyn ritual in Būshihr.

Finally, Professor Amin Banani of the University of California, Los Angeles, produced one long and two short films. The long film is about a Taʿziyeh performance by a non-professional troupe in a small village near Hamadan, photographed during the Muharram of 1966 or 1967. The two small films are film "collages."

Many musicologists have praised Taʿziyeh for its role in preserving traditional Persian music. However, so far a definite technical study about Taʿziyeh music is still lacking. There are several books and monographs which touch upon this subject, such as Hasan Mashḥūn's *Mūsīqī-yi Mazhabī-yi Irān* (Festival Arts Series, Tehran, 1350/1971-72); Rūḥ Allāh Khāliqiī's *Sarguzasht-i Mūsīqī-yī-Irān* (Tehran, 1333/1954-55); Abū al-Ḥassan Ṣabā's "Yāddashthā-yi Khūd Rājʿi bih Mūsīqī" *(Majali-yi Mūsīqī,* Tehran, 1336/1957-58) and Yaḥyā Arīn Pūr's *Az Ṣabā tā Nīmā* (Tehran, 1351/1972-73). I am told that M. Taqī Massʿūdiyyih and Josef Kuckertz, the authors of *Mūsīqī-yi Būshihr* (Tehran: The Soroush Press, 2536) are currently engaged in Taʿziyeh musical research and judging from their recently published book, an excellent piece of work is to be expected.

Two interesting books which combine Taʿziyeh and folk dancing are: William Ridgeway, *The Dramas and Dramatic Dances in Non-European Races* (Cambridge, England, 1915; New York, 1964), and M. Rezvani, *Le Théâtre et la Danse en Iran* (Paris, 1962).

In recent years in Iran there has been an increasing interest in collecting "Qahvekhaneh paintings," the bulk of which deal with the Kerbela tragedy. These collections and the research they have engendered lends another dimension to the study of Taʿziyeh. The Taʿziyeh in modified form and with somewhat different emphasis has spread to countries outside the boundaries of Iran. Discussion of the Muharram ceremonies and the Taʿziyeh productions in these areas is to be found in the following publications:

Moharram in Two Cities—Lucknow and Delhi (prepared by the Census of India 1961 and published in the Monograph Series, vol I, part VII B, by the Office of the Registrar General of India, Ministry of Home Affairs, New Delhi, 1966).

Frederic Maatouk, *La Représentation de la Mort de L'Imam Hussein à Nabatieh Liban-Sud* (Beirut, 1974). Both Arabic and French translations of the martyrdom of Imam Hussein are appended to this book.

W. Chrara (Ashura) "Transformations d'une manifestation religieuse dans un village du Liban-Sud," (Publications du centre de Recherches de l'université Libanaise, 1968).

Sources for the death of Imam Hussein on the plain of Kerbela and the development of Muharram mourning ceremonies are contained in this book in the chapter written by Michel Mazzaoui, "Shi'ism and Ashura in South Lebanon." The most thorough work on the development of the Hussein cult is by Jean Calmard, "Le Culte de L'Imam Hasayn" (Paris, March 1975, These pour le Doctorat de 3e cycle, Ecole Pratique des Hautes Etudes, VIe section). Hopefully this will soon appear in print, since it is being considered for publication by the Institute for Traditional Performance and Ritual in Tehran.

At the moment, the most important thing to be done is to edit as many manuscripts as possible. There are several researchers working toward that end: Muhammad-Reza Khaki and Khosrow Shayesteh of the Institute for Traditional Performance and Ritual in Tehran are engaged in the study of two very important collections which have recently been discovered. These are the *Library of the Majlis Collection* consisting of some 260 Ta'ziyeh manuscripts, and the *Ketab Khaneh Malek Collection* of some 82 Ta'ziyeh plays. A. Shahidi is assisting with this project. There are also plans to microfilm the Cerulli Vatican Collection and put it at the disposal of the scholars at the Institute. Also, Peter Chelkowski is in the process of writing a book under the working title, "From the Mourning Ritual to Full-Scale Drama and Theatre—The Case of Ta'ziyeh."

GENERAL REFERENCE WORKS

Since this volume is not intended only for Iranologists or other Near Eastern specialists, but rather for students of the theatre as well as for the general public, an introduction to standard works on Islamic civilization and Persian literature and history will be given here.

F. E. Peters, *Allah's Commonwealth* (New York, 1973), discusses the theological difference between the Shi'ites and the Sunnites. A thorough overall view of these two branches is presented by Marshall G. S. Hodgson in *The Venture of Islam* (3 volumes, Chicago, 1974). Allamah Sayyid Muhammad Tabātabā'ī, *Shi'ite Islam* (translated, edited, introduction and notes by Seyyed Hossein Nasr, Albany, 1975), is of great importance for the understanding of the Shi'a doctrine and also of the popular Shi'a Islam interpretation. The author is the leading living Shi'a scholar. T. Fahd, ed., *Le Shi'ism Imamite* (Paris, 1970), consists of papers delivered at a symposium on the same subject. H. Corbin, *En Islam iranien* (Paris, 1971), also deals with Shi'a Islam as does D. M. Donaldson, *The Shi'ite Religion, A History of Islam in Persia and Irak* (London, 1933). The latter, however, is somewhat out-dated. A more recent title is H. Laoust, *Les schismes dans l'Islam* (Paris, 1963). Alessandro Bausani, *Persia Religiosa* (Milan, 1959); deals with the many religions which were born on the Iranian plateau and places Ta'ziyeh within the framework of Iranian religious life.

The new edition of the *Encyclopaedia of Islam,* as well as the older edition, should be consulted. The following articles are most relevant: L. Gardet and J. Jomier, "Islam" (new ed., vol. IV, pp. 171-77); Ph. Marçais, "Ashūrā" (new ed., vol. I, p. 705); E. Honigmann, "Karbalā" (new ed., vol. IV, pp. 637-39); L. Veccia Vaglieri, "(Al-) Husayn b. 'Alī b. 'Abī Tālib" (new ed., vol. III, pp. 607-15); R. Strothmann, "Ta'ziya" (old ed., vol. IV, pp. 770-72).

Persia is renowned for its poets and writers. Since history and social development can be viewed through the prism of literature, the following works are recommended: E. G. Browne, *A Literary History of Persia* (4 volumes, Cambridge, England, 1959); E. G. Browne, *The Press and Poetry of Modern Persia* (Cambridge, England, 1914); A. J. Arberry, *Classical Persian Literature* (London, 1958); A. Pagliaro and A. Bausani, *Storia della letteratura persiana* (Milan, 1960); Reuben Levy, *An Introduction to Persian Literature* (New York, 1969); and Jan Rypka, *et al., History of Iranian Literature* (Dordrecht, Holland, 1968).

Perhaps the most useful book from which a clear understanding of the Muharram rituals and the Ta'ziyeh drama can be gained is Henri Massé's *Persian Beliefs and Customs* (New Haven, 1954). This is taken from his *Croyance et Coutumes Persans, suivies de Contes et Chansons Populaires,* Paris, 1938). Another interesting work gives a cross-cultural picture: D. Sidersky, *Les Origines des Légendes Musulmanes* (Paris, 1933), discusses how Biblical stories were incorporated into the Ta'ziyeh repertory.

These by no means are exhaustive. They will, however, give a rather comprehensive view of the culture which produced Ta'ziyeh. By using them as background, a deeper understanding of the social and religious significance of this unique dramatic development, and its impact on present Iranian life may be gained.

Index

269

271

273

277

278

nationalistic dimension, 30, 265
nava, 43, 44
nawheh (dirge), 98, 199, 201, 202, 213, 221, 223, 243, 246
Nayin, 73
Newton, John K., xi
Nezami, 195, 198
Nezir, 242
Niyâvarân, 124
Noah, 217
nuha (lament), 90, 110, 177
Nuhe-khani (dirge singing), 223, 224
Nuri, Mirzâ Agâ Khân, 124

oğundurma orucu, 244
Olearius, Adam, 257
Oman of Saman, 206, 207
omphalos, 5
oral-formulaic composition, 184-186, 188
Ordibehesht, 202
Ortaoyuna, 238
Osman, Nevres, 248
Osman, Semsi, 248
Othello, 156, 160, 161
Ottoman, 3, 105, 144, 145, 149, 234, 250
Oudh, 126, 210, 224

pagan traditions, 93
Pahlavi, 207
Pagliaro, A. and A. Bausani, 268
painting, 64, 75, 76, 79, 91, 144
Pakistan, 141, 142, 144, 145, 150, 151, 210
Panjikent, 91
Pâques, 134
Paradise, 220, 221
Parashara, 225
Parry, Milman, 184
Parsis, 144
Parthian, 89
Partu Bayzai, 199
Passion du Christ, 132, 133, 135
passion play, 23, 25, 41, 42, 88-90, 92, 131, 133, 135, 140, 148, 167, 175, 198, 210, 238, 239, 243, 251, 259
week, 3
Peacock Throne, 76
Pelly, Sir Lewis, 32, 147, 260-262

perceptual code, 33
performance traditions, 24-26, 31, 39, 187
Persia, xix, xx, 1, 3, 4, 6, 20, 92, 98, 100, 101, 103, 116, 138, 139, 141-143, 145, 146, 149-151, 194, 225, 239, 241, 243, 258, 259, 260, 268
Persian, xvii, 2, 91, 96, 99, 101, 102, 122, 139, 141, 142, 144-146, 176, 211-213, 223, 225, 229, 230, 238, 239, 241, 242, 251, 255, 256, 258-260, 264, 266
art, 84, 141
artists, 64, 75, 76
culture, 3, 24, 95, 101, 141, 182, 265
customs, 14, 19, 141, 144, 145, 150, 259
drama, 167, 175
dramatic narration, 3, 4
epic, 4
Gulf, 136, 228, 229
literature, 4, 88, 175, 183, 188, 198, 256, 267, 268
music, *see* Iranian music
play, xx, 1, 26, 140
poetry, 48, 168, 169, 171, 175, 176, 182, 183, 186, 187, 193, 194, 199-201, 215, 256, 268
public, *see* Iranian public
society, 95, 147
theatre, 260-262, 264
traditions, 13, 19, 26, 39, 74, 89, 93, 122, 141, 143, 187, 222, 261
verse, 184-186, 194, 198, 200, 201, 206
Persian-Urdu, 212
Persian-Turkish, 28
Peters, F.E., 267
Peterson, Samuel R., ix, xv, 64-87
Piemontese, Angelo, 264
pilgrimage, 8, 125, 126, 246
Piran, 92
pirr (arena, place), 219
Pirveli, 243
pish khani (prologue), 57, 58
Poetry of Maxim and Counsel, 193
Polak, J.E., 260
predestination, 39, 117, 118
processions, 3, 4, 73, 183, 223-227, 238, 240-243, 257, 259, 263

283

286